T0094974

Feminism and
Composition Studies
In Other Words

Modern Language Association of America

Research and Scholarship in Composition

Lil Brannon, Anne Ruggles Gere, Geneva Smitherman-Donaldson, John Trimbur, Art Young, Series Editors

Feminism and Composition Studies

In Other Words

Edited by
*Susan C. Jarratt and
Lynn Worsham*

The Modern Language Association of America
New York   1998

For information about obtaining permission to reprint material from MLA book publications, send your request by mail (see address below), e-mail (permissions@mla.org), or fax (212 533-0680).

Another version of Pamela L. Caughie's essay, "Let It Pass: Changing the Subject, Once Again," appeared in *PMLA* 112 (1997): 26–39. Gail Stygall's essay, "Women and Language in the Collaborative Writing Classroom," contains an invented conversation from Kenneth Bruffee's *Collaborative Learning: Higher Education, Interdependence, and the Authority of Knowledge* (© 1993 The Johns Hopkins University Press, pages 58–59; reprinted by permission of the Johns Hopkins University Press); parts of a transcript of a discussion from Martin Nystrand's *The Structure of Written Communication: Studies in Reciprocity between Writers and Readers* (pp. 192–93 [1986]; reprinted by permission of Academic Press); and a table and parts of a transcript of a discussion from Lester Faigley's *Fragments of Rationality: Postmodernity and the Subject of Composition* (© 1992 by the University of Pittsburgh Press; reprinted by permission of the University of Pittsburgh Press).

Library of Congress Cataloging-in-Publication Data

Feminism and composition studies : in other words / edited by Susan C.
   Jarratt and Lynn Worsham.
      p.   cm. — (Research and scholarship in composition,
   ISSN 1079-2554 ; 6)
      Includes bibliographical references and index.
      ISBN 0-87352-585-X. — ISBN 0-87352-586-8 (pbk.)
      1. English language—Rhetoric—Study and teaching—United States.
   2. Feminism and education—United States.   3. Academic writing—Sex
   differences.   4. Women—Education—United States.   5. Women
   teachers—United States.   I. Jarratt, Susan Carole Funderburgh.
   II. Worsham, Lynn, 1953–   .   III. Series.
   PE1405.U6F465   1998
   808'.042'07073—dc21   97–28149

Printed on recycled paper

Published by The Modern Language Association of America
10 Astor Place, New York, New York 10003-6981

For Eileen Lundy and Bonnie Lyons
and
for Arlene and Betty

Contents

PART II: Specifying Locations

Responses to Part II

PART III: Exploring Discontinuities

Responses to Part III

Preface to the Series

The Research and Scholarship in Composition series, developed with the support of the Modern Language Association's Publications Committee, responds to the recent growth of interest in composition and to the remarkable number of publications now devoted to it. We intend the series to provide a carefully coordinated overview of the varied theoretical schools, educational philosophies, institutional groupings, classroom situations, and pedagogical practices that collectively constitute the major areas of inquiry in the field of composition studies.

Each volume combines theory, research, and practice in order to clarify issues, synthesize research and scholarship, and improve the quality of writing instruction. Further, each volume reviews the most significant issues in a particular area of composition research and instruction; reflects on ways research and teaching inform each other; views composition studies in the larger context of literary, literacy, and cultural studies; and draws conclusions from various scholarly perspectives about what has been done and what yet needs to be done in the field.

We hope this series will serve a wide audience of teachers, scholars, and students who are interested in the teaching of writing, research in composition, and the connections among composition, literature, and other areas of study. These volumes should act as a lively orientation to the field for students and nonspecialists and provide experienced teachers and scholars with useful overviews of research on important questions, with insightful reflections about teaching, and with thoughtful analyses about future developments in composition studies. Each book is a spirited conversation in which you are cordially invited to join.

Series Editors

Acknowledgments

We want to thank the editorial board of the Research and Scholarship in Composition series for its commitment to publishing feminist work. We especially thank Lil Brannon for her vision of a feminist project that would place differences among women at its center. That vision has helped sustain us from the spring of 1993, when this collection was begun, through the arduous process that brought it to completion. From the beginning, the volume has taken shape through the agency of the contributors, who have kept our ideas about feminism, rhetorics, writing, and teaching in motion over the years. Martha Evans has been a helpful and supportive editor, as was Joe Gibaldi before her. We appreciate the help of Ann Brady Aschauer and Shannon Wilson in the preparation of the manuscript. Our students likewise deserve thanks, especially the ones whose words appear in these essays. In every case where student language is quoted within the volume, the student granted permission for its use and was given an opportunity to examine the text of the essay. The permission process raises complex questions about language and power, especially within the shared space of the classroom. Although we don't believe that words fix subjects in timeless expressions of their full selfhood, we do believe that people should have the chance to participate in their own representations whenever possible.

Our deepest debts are acknowledged in the dedication.

SCJ and LW

Introduction: As We Were Saying . . .

Susan C. Jarratt

> *[The feminist is] somebody who has placed the moment of yearning for the impossible within a political context of knowing that it has its time and place.*
>
> —Juliet Mitchell

> *Whether feminism can help forge . . . a collective subject hangs heavily on the mode of reading and writing social relations it promotes.*
>
> —Rosemary Hennessey

As my title suggests, the colloquy among feminists interested in composition and rhetoric is well under way. This volume introduces the conjunction of feminism and composition not by starting at its beginnings or at the beginnings of second-wave feminism but, rather, by immersion. These essays lead the reader to places where feminism attends to discourse and pedagogy and where rhetoric and composition regard questions of difference. The aim is to push the boundaries of knowledge in both feminism and composition by exploring the productive intersections and tensions of the two. Each term of "as we were saying" marks a site for discussion, leading inevitably to more and other words.

As

As signals both temporality and similarity, suggestive topoi for thinking about feminism and composition, temporality placing them in history and similarity in relation to each other. If, choosing among many possible histories, we tell a story that begins with the political and social revolutions of the Enlightenment, both the project of popular

literacy instruction (rhetoric and composition) and the political movement to enfranchise women and recognize their personhood (feminism) would seem to have a common heritage.[1] The concept of
citizenship called for a literate and informed people at the same time
that it inevitably opened the question of who would be included in that
group. In the United States, feminism emerged from black and white
women's experiences of writing and speaking on behalf of abolition in
the mid-nineteenth century (see A. Davis), only a few decades before
composition was created in response to the movement of middle-class
men into the elite domain of the universities (see Ohmann). Growing
out of the civil rights and New Left movements of the 1960s, second-
wave feminism as a social movement has extended its reach into the
academy, acting as a major force for change in higher education since
the 1970s. Likewise, the return of scholarly attention in the 1960s to
theories and pedagogies of writing, dovetailing with those progressive
social movements, has created the need to study socially specific forms
of producing and communicating knowledge. In the recent history of
composition, scholars have drawn attention to the social situatedness
of its constituencies—both within and outside institutions. Composition and feminism, then, currently share to some degree an institutional site, an educational mission, and a conflicted relation to both.

During the last twenty years, and particularly in the last ten, various
forms of feminist inquiry have entered almost every discipline in the
humanities and social sciences. Like composition studies, feminism is
not a monolithic enterprise with a unified research agenda. Rather,
feminisms are transdisciplinary projects, challenging all boundary-
marking logics and literacies, calling into question not only gendered
exclusions in the production and dissemination of knowledge but also
the buttressing of racial, class, and other privileges thereby. Feminist
academic projects seek to transform disciplinary knowledge by pointing out its ideological investments, particularly investments that
sustain oppressive social structures and relations of economic exploitation. Some feminists might find a familiar ring to Patricia
Harkin's characterization of the knowledge created by composition as
postdisciplinary lore—a knowledge whose primary function is to
"help us to see ways of construing relations . . . to which our ideology
has made us blind [and to see that] disciplinary inquiries can be strategies of containment" (135). Composition at its best has worked against
the grain of conventional institutional practices. Insisting that writing
is more than a remedial skill and composition classes more than institutional gatekeeping, teachers of writing have explored writing's epistemological potential and used their knowledge of the writing process

to challenge assumptions about knowledge acquisition throughout the academy. Both feminist inquiry and post-current-traditional composition studies, in other words, seek to transform styles of thinking, teaching, and learning rather than to reproduce stultifying traditions. They share a suspicion of authoritarian pedagogy, emphasizing instead collaborative or interactive learning and teaching. They resist purity of approach and the reduction of their scope by moving in and around many contemporary critical theories and disciplines.

These, at least, are the utopian claims of academic feminism and certain kinds of composition studies. Yet academic feminism and composition studies are caught in a bind vis-à-vis the institution: despite the desire to reconfigure disciplinary boundaries, both need to claim disciplinarity to achieve academic legitimacy and obtain resources (faculty members, courses, research support). Debates about the status of women's studies resonate with those about writing programs in and out of English departments. Should women's studies and writing programs have the same institutional organization as departments? Should they hire faculty members and tenure them by the same criteria that other parts of the university use? How do women's studies and writing programs prepare students for study and work in the world as it is while trying to introduce and create something completely different? (See Harriet Malinowitz's essay, this volume.) The academic locations of feminism and composition, then, operate to calcify what should be liquid, mobile, and malleable, what should be constantly reshaped in synchrony with the changing lives of students. Feminism and composition need mobility to respond to systems of power, which, parodoxically, appear immovable yet are constantly adjusting themselves to keep in place a status quo that distributes unequally not only the extravagant excesses of advanced capitalism but even the bare necessities for life within it.

Despite the institutional bind, feminism and composition actually have achieved some of the transformative aims to which they aspire. Feminisms overlap composition studies, developing a growing body of work on discourses and practices of difference, representation, and the social construction of knowledge and its subjects; composition studies speaks to feminist inquiry where it investigates gendered differences in language, teaching, and learning—the very places where subjects take shape in writing, reading, and teaching contexts, both academic and "real world." These, and many more touchpoints between feminisms and composition studies, suggest the rich possibilities located at their intersection. Our aim is to discover the ways each has already informed the other and what interests are served at those points of intersection. We examine new strategies, "other words," for writing, teaching, and learning at the productive spaces where the two fields meet and diverge. And we imagine how feminism and composition may speak to each other in many still unacknowledged ways.

The starting point for the conceptualization of this volume, then, is a strong sense that composition and feminist inquiry have a productive compatibility; even speaking of them as two distinct objects belies the already existing integration between them. Our naming of them, moreover, oversimplifies. Feminism is far more than a product of United States universities; composition takes in many scholars, teachers, and students, past and present, who have agendas far different from the one laid out above. This collection of essays clearly does not intend to construct a happy union between feminism and composition, to reduce the two to some kind of common denominator. Rather than offer a too easy assimilation of one area into the other, this collection proposes to frame a relation "in other words," foregrounding the alliances and discontinuities created by viewing the one within and alongside the other. We seek a different form of relation: not synecdoche, in which one plays part to the whole of the other, but a form of metonymy (see Brady, this volume), a contiguity, a side-by-side association. The sites and terms visited in this introduction will set up some of the preconditions for contemplating, citing, and practicing a conjunction. This exchange between the two which are not two may help chart progressive directions for change.

We

For both feminism and composition, the question of the subject has particular resonance and complexity. *Subject* is currently used by scholars in favor of a word like *individual* to indicate the ways various determining forces—natural, social, and psychological—control persons formerly thought to be their own masters. It also signals discussions of the relation of people as agents to those things upon which they act (i.e., objects). For a fuller discussion, see John Clifford.

The subject of feminism is obviously women, but who are these women? And how is *woman* to be defined? In the first flush of feminism, the discovery of woman as a neglected subject led to consciousness-raising groups; women told their stories and made the personal political (Millett). The abuses suffered within male-dominated households, businesses, universities, and the new social movements themselves were documented (Echols). Literary critics discovered (or rediscovered) the texts of women and began building a parallel canon of women's literature (Showalter). In the 1970s, composition likewise discovered its subject in the students of the writing class and began asking them to tell their stories through methods like protocol analysis (Flower and Hayes) and personal writing (Elbow, *Writing*). The abuses of error marking were exposed (Shaughnessy), and teachers began to shift the focus of reading away from literary essays and toward student texts, thus altering dramatically the canon of the writing class.

My own entry into these two worlds marks a crossing on the site of a single subject: one "I" within and among the "we." In the mid-1970s, I was a high school teacher trying with ever-increasing fervor and frustration to teach traditional grammar to mostly Latino and Latina students in San Antonio, Texas. The less they learned, the more intensive and torturous became my exercises. As a teacher of grammar, I was the quintessential "subject supposed to know." As Clifford has persuasively argued, "Grammar successfully interpellates subjects into clear relations of power and authority. Students submit, teachers dominate" (47). And since I was a straight, white person teaching mostly people of color within a social space of unquestioned heterosexuality (see Rich, "Heterosexuality"), my teaching practice perpetuated other forms of domination as well. My introduction to the writing process and to theories of discourse through a graduate teaching practicum at the University of Texas, San Antonio, radically changed the way I taught, saw my students, and understood the whole enterprise of the teaching of writing. This transformation simultaneously reordered my relations to authority—to the status of subjects, both student and teacher. One kind of feminist analysis might interpret my conversion as a natural movement into a more fully feminine subjectivity, the newer pedagogy allowing for the expression of a supportive and nurturing ethos that my biology and cultural conditioning made familiar and comfortable to me. An alternative reading—one more characteristic of the theoretical orientation of this volume—would seek the multiple discourses shaping me at that moment, the discourses of maternity, femininity, and nurturing being several among others and not biologically, politically, or theoretically privileged as an explanation of my narrative (cf. Phelps and Emig). Indeed, my new-found sense of shared authority in the classroom actually seemed to provide relief from the control I felt the need to maintain as a single parent; thus my pedagogical and maternal selves were more at odds than merged at that time.

My introduction to feminism came at the same time through one of the early Images of Women courses, but my identification with the women's movement was slower, perhaps again owing in part to the relations of authority involved. That I came to feminism in an academic setting meant that a revolutionary or resistant discourse was introduced within an institutional one; it was delivered by a teacher to me, a student.[2] My mixed response of resistance and interest mirrored my own students' responses both to traditional grammar teaching and to the new process method. Within us, each pedagogical option resonated between, on the one hand, the desire for accommodation, survival, and the success promised for playing the game and, on the other, the need to resist or go against the grain, perhaps in the hope of actually finding new ways of configuring our relation to the world. My reflections on this "I" of around 1977 suggest that my subject positions as teacher, student, and feminist did not at that time actively, consciously collide (see Lu, this volume). It is possible, however, that the break in my subject position as authoritarian teacher effected by process writing created an opening through which feminism found a space to enter the consciousness of my student self. But the counter-discourse of feminism was slowed by the resistance of student subject and conventional feminine subject, both of whom may have been eager to find sites for authority (e.g., in single parenting).

The language with which those negotiations are described—both personally and professionally—determines a subject: a figure appearing in hazy outline on a terrain charted by the discourses of feminism and composition. This sketchy account could be thickened by passages from my journals, by narratives of family and friends, by larger cultural analyses, by assignments in the two classes, by contemporary discourses from feminism and composition, which would multiply the "I"s and lend texture, color, and feeling to this story (Eichhorn et al.). Constructing such accounts in self-reflective and dialectical ways (Phelps and Emig; Lu, this volume) puts distancing quotation marks around the pronoun. Feminist composition's interest in narratives of personal experience connects with and departs from the revolutionary introduction of personal writing into college composition (Murray; Elbow, "Closing"; cf. Jarratt, "Feminism"). The difference between self-reflective feminist narratives and expressive paradigms is theoretical, political, and rhetorical: the difference between the collective "we" of my title and the unbracketed first person evoked by some advocates of personal writing in the composition class. The subjective and epistemological basis of much work in both composition and feminism has been autonomous individuals able to give an accurate account of their thoughts, emotions, and pasts (see Caughie, this volume). The protocol analysis created by compositionists who used cognitive psychology operated on this basis, as does the storytelling of consciousness-raising groups. The recognition of formerly invisible and oppressed subjects fired these efforts. But the process of bringing a subject (women, students) to light does not necessarily demand seeing that subject as constructed. A strong vein of liberal individualism, assuming a fixed and stable person, runs through both composition and feminism in the United States (see Faigley).

In the 1980s, alternative views of the subject began to gain ground. In a 1984 speech about women and national identity, Adrienne Rich reflects on a shift in the subject of feminism. She links writing, revision, and self-critique:

> I wrote a sentence just now and x'd it out. In it I said that women have always understood the struggle against free-floating abstraction even when they were intimidated by abstract ideas. I don't want to write that kind of sentence now, the sentence that begins "Women have always. . . ." . . . If we have learned anything in these years of late twentieth-century feminism, it's that that "always" blots out what we really need to know: When, where, and under what conditions has the statement been true?
>
> ("Notes" 214)

Combining her reflections with an attempt to understand the relation between the Marxist New Left and feminism, Rich finds both movements guilty of working from a subject reduced to one feature: "The faceless, sexless, raceless proletariat. The faceless, raceless, classless category of 'all women.' Both creations of white Western self-centeredness" (219). This complication of the feminist subject occurred at the same time that poststructuralist theory was gaining a broader reach, was adding to the social and vocal presence of difference a theoretical challenge to the humanist subject: the self-aware individual whose race, sexuality, and class had gone unmarked.

In composition, a similar reflection on subjects has surfaced recently with the (re)entrance of the social as a defining concept.[3] Key essays by Patricia Bizzell ("Cognition") and James Berlin ("Rhetoric and Ideology") questioned the subject created by cognitive psychology and by expressivist composition theories. Other compositionists began to sketch out an institutional subject of writing courses (Bartholomae; Bizzell, *Discourse*; Clifford; Ede and Lunsford).

Lester Faigley has been a most articulate theorist of the subject in composition recently, pointing out the assumptions that underlie the evaluation process and the possibilities for new subjectivities in electronic technologies. Meanwhile the first attempts to articulate feminism and the teaching of writing began to appear (e.g., Annas; Flynn, "Composing"). In both composition and feminism the movement is from a rhetoric and politics of recognition to debates over issues of representation. The other—student, woman—is brought to light in a flash of recognition. Then the rhetoric and politics of that illumination come under scrutiny, sometimes in the same essay. Elizabeth Flynn virtually opened the conversation about feminism and composition by asking herself not What do women write? but, rather, Are there any differences in the ways women and men compose narratives about their lives in composition classes? Her carefully derived answer—Yes, we can find patterns that seem to be related to gender difference—recognizes women as subjects in composition at the same time that it focuses on their self-representation (see also Peterson; Stygall et al.; Brady, this volume; Clark, this volume). Pamela Annas, likewise, frames a question about the "politics of style" rather than about "women's writing" and ends by suggesting that female students, in shaping their writing style, may represent themselves simultaneously as women and as writers in academic settings. Feminist compositionists have contributed to the movement from recognition to representation, partly because the subjects of feminism are often its theorists and practitioners, while the subjects of composition almost always remain outside the process of theorizing. The discourses of pedagogy speak themselves almost entirely in the absence of students (cf. Anderson et al.)

The movement toward a more radical conception of the subject has involved reinventing an early insight: process. Both woman and writing, it seems, are made, not born (Beauvoir). From at least as early as Mary Wollstonecraft, some feminists have argued that the feminine takes shape through a social process. Under the auspices of poststructuralism and the urgent need to articulate differences among women, contemporary United States feminists keep coming again to the question of a collective subject. Composition, likewise, apparently has not yet fully realized the radicality of writing as a process (S. Miller, "Theory"; Clifford; DeJoy) and the consequent challenge to fixed subjectivity that approach entails. The contributors to this collection speak to the charge made by Rosemary Hennessey at the crossing of subject and process.

Were Saying

The progressive tense of the verb represents a kind of historical analysis that locates an event in both the past and present but neither fixes its subject in a finished past nor locks past and present together in the bond of cause and effect. The verb speaks not only of time but also of rhetoric: How have we spoken and how will we continue to speak of, about, for, and on behalf of feminism? That the first epigraph of this introduction begins with "the feminist" in brackets is appropriate, for everywhere within you will find recognition of the contingency of feminism—an acknowledgment of the thoroughly rhetorical nature of a political movement whose aim is to supersede itself. An inquiry into the ways feminism manifests itself in composition and rhetoric will contribute to a fuller recognition of this rhetorical character. The paradoxical yearning for the impossible of which Juliet Mitchell speaks, placed within the insistent immediacy of a particular time and place, have marked composition, and those marks now appear as a code newly intelligible in the context of the alliance of composition and feminism.

The most exciting recent developments in feminist theory outside composition have been what I would describe as explorations of feminism's rhetoricity. The maxim that everything is rhetoric, a triumphant discovery for some, leaves unspecified what must be addressed by both composition and feminism: the specificity and materiality of difference. The aim in reading current feminist theory as rhetorical is not to appropriate—to presume to have prior claims of ownership or to colonize a foreign territory (of feminism) for a home turf (of composition). It is to point out how feminists have been staging a double session of rhetoric (Spivak, "Subaltern" 276–80), simultaneously naming and reconstructing difference. In other words, rhetoric understood as a dual process of representation—as both a figurative and political act—gives names to language that articulates difference while exposing the power relations at work in acts of naming. To apply this idea to women as a group is to see women not as a natural class but as a group with shifting boundaries, capable of being constituted in any historical moment or context through the symbolic and political acts of those in the group and those outside it. Any choice of a figure configures simultaneously a relation of power and relation of difference. For example, as the metaphor of sisterhood reached the limits of its usefulness as a political gathering place for feminists in the second wave, this figure began to obscure more than it revealed, hiding differences under wraps, suggesting that all women had common experiences, goals, and languages. Postcolonial feminists, queer theorists, and United States feminists of color have been creating other forms of rhetoric to perform the double function of articulation and disarticulation: unlinking differences that had been unacknowledged, covered over in the words *woman* and *we*, and at the same time establishing new links for connecting political projects under the banner of feminism. Such rhetorics incorporate histories of the literal disarticulation (dismemberment) of bodies, whether under patriarchy, compulsory heterosexuality, slavery, or colonization.[4] Hortense Spillers catalogs the heritage of slavery as not only the separation of families but also the loss of language, history, memory. Slavery, she writes, is the theft of the body, "a willful and violent . . . unimaginable . . . severing of the captive body from its motive will, its active desire" ("Baby" 58). When the legal codes of the southern states link "slaves, working beasts, animals of any kind" with "stock, furniture, plates, . . . and books" in unholy articulation, Spillers argues for the introduction of "a new *semantic* field/fold more appropriate to the projects of humanity and human connection under conditions of liberation" (74). Wouldn't *rhetoric* better describe this new project of collective language practice?

At the same time that Western African women and men were displaced from land and kin, other Africans and Indians east and west were driven ever more deeply into the position of "native," the word redefined by imperialist discourse in the terms of color, habit, degree of humanity. Postcolonial theory has heightened attention to the politics of representation, particularly to exercises of domination in the arena of cultural practices. Gayatri Spivak in her now canonical essay "Can the Subaltern Speak?" warns first-world intellectuals about the danger of obscuring their own discursive practices in any facile act of representing the interests of apparently silent subjects of oppression. Discovering the workings of these two interwoven forms of representation—the textual description of otherness and the political identification of or with a group—is the work of teachers and students of language. Rhetoric mobilizes an interaction between representation (political) and re-presentation (cultural), calling attention to where and by whom groups are described and with what effects. Examining rhetorical configurations keeps at bay any universal subject (man or woman), shifting the discursive grounds for authority. In other words, the "we" of my title cannot be known in any way distinct from the "were saying," and no claim of "as"—signifying either resemblance or simultaneity—will stand unchallenged by the continuing generation of other words.

Finally, this verb—with specific reference to the voice—raises the question of the relations among various discursive acts: speaking, writing, reading, listening. Some scholars in rhetoric and composition make the case strongly that rhetoric and composition are about writing and writing only (S. Miller, *Rescuing*). Certainly much of the energy of and institutional support for composition's recent flourishing has come from identifying writing as a distinct and neglected activity in the field of English, particularly writing in contrast to the reading of literary texts. United States feminists have been concerned with writing; it is the principal among those tools of the master that Audre Lorde cautions us to use with care ("Tools"). The question of writing as a gendered act (or racial, class-oriented, sexually oriented act) is raised pointedly in this volume (e.g., by Gil-Gomez; Ede and Lunsford; Morrison, this volume). But for the most part feminists understand composition as a complex set of symbolic practices, textual inscription being one among many. The students speaking out at Oberlin College in Wendy Hesford's essay, the women exploring a new electronic medium in Gail Hawisher and Patricia Sullivan's study, the students Gail Stygall observes in collaborative groups, the women interrupting a mostly-for-men cultural studies program in Nedra Reynolds's argument, the African American teachers Shirley Logan documents: all these subjects require of us the fullest understanding of composition and lead to connections with a wide range of discourse theories and analytical tools. Feminist compositionists will not find any simple binary framework—master-servant tools, masculine-feminine styles, or even men's-women's writing—that explains the complexities of power and difference at play in these situations. In our very writing—as we were saying—we hope to articulate (i.e., pronounce and link) the multiple media in which we variously work.

Feminisms for Composition

Defining feminism has meant in the recent past a division into categories.[5] Indeed, defining can be more a classically philosophical than a rhetorical exercise: imagine Socrates backing his always fumbling interlocutors into corners with his questions about the difference between courage and the good, between the good and the true. Rather than define a single feminism for this collection, we propose to name feminisms, give accounts of their practices, discover and describe the spaces in which they operate, and evaluate their effects. Like the operations of both psychoanalysis and pedagogy, feminism makes an intervention: into a consumately rhetorical situation it brings an enunciative relationship—"I" speaking to "you."[6]

Avoiding labels does not mean reversion to an easy pluralism, however. While the essays that follow engage a variety of feminisms, we have tried to mark out a space between a rigid party line and an incoherent eclecticism. All the authors share three orientations. Each writes from a vantage point informed by poststructuralist language theory and postmodern cultural theory. Each is committed to a feminism that exceeds institutional-academic boundaries, to an intellectual, scholarly endeavor combined with a social movement. And each accepts the necessity of working from a feminism taking shape among other kinds of social difference. A poststructural vantage point creates an awareness that any word—such as *woman*—gains meaning through its place in a system of binary oppositions. This awareness makes possible the recognition of negative associations clustered around the devalued term in any binary pair: in this case, woman, the "second sex." But the devalued term of a pair can work its own epistemic violence by erasing differences within the category (Lorde, "Age"; Tompkins, "Course"). *Woman* alone, without further specification, may evoke dominant cultural images—nurturing mother, (hetero)sexual object—leaving out many other possibilities. Although most feminists speak as women within our culture's gendered map of imagery and discourse, they work to expose the ways this overly simple categorizing of human difference leads to oppression and inequity.[7] Like Judith Butler, we believe that the political necessity in feminism to speak "as and for *women* should not be invoked as describing or delimiting that constituency in advance" ("Foundations" 15). Indeed, there are many different women in this volume. Particularly through the response essays we hope to enact a feminist politics and scholarship that allow for the kind of "rifting" Butler prizes as the "ungrounded ground of feminist theory [seeking] to release the term [woman] into a future of multiple significations . . . and to give it play as a site where unanticipated meanings might come to bear" (16).

Although the essentialism-constructionism debate makes its appearance in this volume (Brady), none of the volume's authors remains in the trap of that binary; each moves past the arguments about categories by asking some version of the question implicit in Hennessey's epigraph above: How is discourse used? Poststructural language theory has carried feminist analysis beyond the limits of liberalism—that is, beyond the unexamined subject "woman"—but feminist activism has kept poststructural theory anchored in a political collectivity (see especially Hesford, this volume). The feminisms you will encounter here are deeply invested in the social and material effects of their words on the lives of women and men in schools and universities, in homes and jobs, in shelters and streets.

An equally central feature of the feminisms driving these essays is the commitment to research as a political project where gender must be understood in relation to other differences. We seek not to add race or class, say, to gender, forming a "string of coequal terms" (de Lauretis 133–34), but to explore and construct through our rhetoric the complex interconnections among multiple differences. We identify gender as one point of entry into the web of differences, not as a bounded terrain, off limits to those without the appropriate papers, or as a fixed and predetermined identity.

The essays in the first part, "Feminisms for Composition," perform the enunciative function described above, charting some basic parameters of the collection. They engage primary interlocutors and key terms in a discussion of feminisms today. Laura Brady speaks to a group of prominent feminist researchers by taking up the essentialism question that has garnered so much attention in recent years. Though she offers a convenient summary of the theoretical argument against essentialism—an assumed subject "woman"—she is more interested in asking how women's stories have been used in three very influential feminist texts: Nancy Chodorow's *Reproduction of Mothering*, Carol Gilligan's *In a Different Voice*, and Mary Field Belenky, Blythe McVicker Clinchy, Nancy Rule Goldberger, and Jill Mattuck Tarule's *Women's Ways of Knowing*. One key term being refigured here is *experience*: never a self-evident report of "how things are" but a located account—one discourse among others necessary for both writing and political transformation. Brady shifts the focus from experience itself to the tropes enacted in reading any discourse of experience. Rather than accept experience as the metaphoric or synecdochic substitution for all women's experience, she invites us to read experiences metonymically. Examining the citational practices of feminists in composition, she proposes metonymy as an operational strategy for repositioning the evidence of personal narrative.

Shirley Logan places the feminisms of our volume directly in the middle of history and difference by inviting us into a conversation with black women educators in the nineteenth century. Through the recounting of episodes from her classroom, she explores the "triply complex convergence" of race, gender, and institutional authority. Her conviction that "we need to engage in democratic conversations about divisive topics like race and gender, and in a variety of public spaces" locates the politics of our project. Nedra Reynolds links feminism with other progressive methodologies by insisting on a place at the table of cultural studies. Not content to accept the histories of cultural studies offered by male compositionists, she demonstrates how the tactic of interruption can operate on a number of levels to involve progressive educators in collective processes of transformation. Reynolds's interruption serves as another word for agency: thinking about interruption as a kairotic act leads Reynolds to speculate about effects of a tactical rhetoric in institutional contexts such as conferences and meetings.

Finally, Eileen Schell insists on the urgency of a feminist analysis of class and economic determinants in our institutional practices in composition. Like Brady, she challenges feminist theory built on culturally inscribed virtues of the feminine; she critically examines the ideology of nurturance valued by many writing teachers (both male and female) and links it with a pattern of "sex-affective production" still common in the capitalist division of labor. Employing a socialist feminist analysis, Schell interviews women instructors in non-tenure-track and part-time writing jobs. She argues for seeing the situation of contingent workers in terms not of "femininism" but of larger systems of social and economic exploitation.

In Other Words

Though we decline to fix feminism with a single definition, we realize that we construct rhetorics for it through our choice of words. The essays in this volume depend on many of the terms that have become the lingua franca of feminism, but the essays introduce other words as well, refining the languages of feminism through composition work and inflecting them with the nuance needed for rhetorical change. As the first set of essays sets out some terms for feminist theories, the second set specifies locations for practices. The locatedness of the composition classroom gives an inescapable materiality to textuality: the constant stream of student writings in all their variety, the experience for the teacher of always being "read" by the students, and all this occurring in institutional, cultural, and historical contexts that cast their own perpetually shifting shadows over the scene. For the essayists in part 2, feminism and composition demand that particular attention be paid to the multiple determinations of gender, race, ethnicity, region, and sexuality. One of the questions they address concerns naming: are these determinations matters of identities, positions, locations, perfor-

mances? The answers form a continuum, from Pamela Caughie's
scrupulous rejection of positionality in favor of "passing" to Gail Hawisher and Patricia Sullivan's assumption that women can identify
themselves and mark out a place in terms of their gendered identity.
For some of us, fixed identities have given way to a sense of location, a
concept used to designate a site or place, expressed through social categories, body, geography, institution but not limited to or fixed by
those names (Rich, "Notes"). Such naming is provisional, contingent;
it addresses the problem of speaking for others (Alcoff, "Problem"). It
seeks not to fix an identity but, rather, to map a site, a position, a
nexus where multiple lines of power intersect (Haraway). Just as feminist historians of composition are now beginning to show us that
composition applies to more than the university classes in which writing has been taught (Rouse; Gere, "Tables"; Hollis, "Voices"), contemporary feminist composition cuts across any universalizing discourse
of students and teachers and speaks instead from particular settings.

Caughie digs into the debate over the subject in feminism, particularly on the issue of race, defining *passing* in a more nuanced way than
simply as the fraudulent assumption of another identity. She sees
passing not as a choice to assume another identity but as the inevitable condition of postmodern subjectivity. It is not a solution to
the problem of the subject but a descriptive theory of the subject's dynamics. Examining student writing in a class about the Harlem Renaissance, she rejects the possibility of defining oneself through the
confessions of a guilty "I," looking instead to writing as the opportunity to work through rather than take up subject positions.

While Caughie chooses debates among feminist literary critics as
the point of her intervention, Wendy Hesford analyzes an incident at
Oberlin College in which academic discourses about the inscriptions
on a racist historical monument, including the administration's First
Amendment defense of academic neutrality, are contested by racially
specific autobiographical discourses from students. Hesford calls on
compositionists to imagine a fluid relation between campus and writing classroom, seeing both as sites of learning and feminist analysis.
She urges academic feminists "to reinterpret their activist roots" in dialogue with students' struggles to examine their own social locations
and conditions. Hesford strives for a pedagogy of critical reflection
and action by placing experience at the intersections of material life,
history, and discourse.

Christy Desmet likewise endorses narratives of lived individuality
but in answer to the question of how to create a classroom climate
of risk and responsibility. In exploring the usefulness of judicial

metaphors for composition pedagogy, Desmet does not evoke the teacher as judge or make the liberal assumption of equality under the law, such equality meaning the homogeneity of the individual. Rather, she argues for a use of feminist jurisprudence that recognizes everyone's responsibility for the violence of pedagogy and that equitably constructs a subject under the law by paying close and sympathetic attention to narrative detail in order to negotiate the gap between legal categories and particular circumstances. Instead of fixing each of us in an identity, this approach denies all prescribed roles. Such a pedagogy would relate students to one another and to the teacher without proclaiming their sameness or exacerbating their differences—recognizing, at the same time, the institutional power that frames all those relations.

Gail Hawisher and Patricia Sullivan report the results of their attempt, both playful and serious, to create an electronic space for women on e-mail. Complicating images of utopia, the women who participate in electronic exchanges open spaces for difference among themselves when they describe the nature of heated disagreements about what is new or interesting material and about the nature of electronic space itself. Without forcing a too easy solution to the differences that emerged in their group, Hawisher and Sullivan conclude that moving from women's space to feminist space will "necessitate a rethinking of public and private space."

The third group of essays explores places where the discourses of feminism and those of composition and rhetoric part company. Contributors in part 3 pause over some well-accepted and arguably feminine practices of our field: the student-centered classroom, collaboration, nonhierarchical and dialogic administrative practices, and writing across the curriculum. The contradictions and exclusions that they find lead to reflection. Joy Ritchie and Kate Ronald struggle with the canonical history of rhetoric in a graduate seminar, asking why and how they should teach it, given the exclusion of women in the Western tradition. But they move beyond metaphors of marginalization and the common phenomenon of "an essentialist celebration of women's rhetoric." With the help of journal entries from their students, they show how bringing together the writing of women students with the historical work of women writers enables feminist compositionists to "avoid oversimplifying the gendered nature of rhetoric or artificially separating women's discourse and feminist agendas from the historical contexts in which they operate." Min-Zhan Lu returns to the problem of experience; she is frustrated with the ways middle-class white students—some of them self-identified feminists—appropriate or ignore differences other than gender in a writing-intensive literature class cross-listed with women's studies. She shows how, by reading essays by bell hooks, Trinh T. Minh-ha, and Gloria Anzaldúa, her students are led to build new critical vocabularies for using their own experiences analytically. Borrowing, for example, Anzaldúa's metaphor of collision for the meeting of differences in a subject and borrowing the metaphor of baggage for a personal inheritance of beliefs and values, Lu's students rewrite their relations to racial and ethnic differences.

In a third classroom scenario, Gail Stygall challenges claims that collaboration makes possible a new gender equality among student writers, and she redefines good collaborative work as she examines three published "conversations" among students. Employing a methodology of feminist-critical linguistics in her reading of these texts, Stygall shows the tenacity of traditional gender roles in mixed-gender collaborative writing groups. The feminist teacher, argues Stygall, must be willing to "act as a counterweight to the disciplining of students by gender and education" by modeling an authoritative discourse in the classroom. The final pair of essays move from the classroom into administration. Amy Goodburn and Carrie Shively Leverenz tell a story of their experiences with a feminist writing program administrator; they discovered that their desires were shaped not only by a utopian image of a feminist alternative to administration but also by long-term, unrecognized personal investments in traditional bureaucratic practices. Attempts to use collaboration in constructing curriculum and to use power sharing in the supervision of TAs led to struggles over power, authority, and leadership that Goodburn and Leverenz read not as "barriers to enacting feminist principles [but rather as] the embodiment of them." Finally, Harriet Malinowitz wants writing across the curriculum (WAC) to take seriously its own discourse of transformation. Asking why WAC hasn't allied itself with other progressive "force fields" in the academy, such as women's studies, she indicts WAC for its "implicit endorsement of existing disciplinary structures" and offers women's studies as an alternative model of cross-disciplinary work in a "resistant mode." Malinowitz takes on the question that has long dominated composition studies: How do teachers attend to the practical instruction students expect while engaging them in critical reflection on the ideologies that that instruction reproduces?

In no way seeking the last word on feminism or composition, Lynn Worsham closes the volume with an afterword that reflects on generational differences among feminists. Indeed, this is a suitable close, for

none of the essayists offers her ideas as definitive. To define is to delimit, to mark the boundary or barrier across which no one else should
pass. We hope that these "other words" are porous rather than imper-
meable and that they give rise to yet more words about the demands
and possibilities of feminism and composition.

NOTES

[1]Histories of composition as writing instruction and rhetorical practices, as
well as histories of women resisting sexism and patriarchy, can of course be
traced much further back than the Enlightenment. See Joy Ritchie and Kate
Ronald, this volume, for an articulation of feminism with the traditional
canon of rhetorical history. Amy Richlin provides an imaginative categorization of feminist historiographies.

[2]I'm deeply grateful to the two extraordinary professors and mentors at the
University of Texas, San Antonio, who introduced me to feminism and composition: Bonnie Lyons, teacher of my first feminist course, and Eileen Lundy,
teacher of my practicum in writing pedagogy.

[3]As Greg Myers and Mara Holt have both made clear, socially oriented approaches to the teaching of writing have appeared at other moments in the
history of United States composition.

[4]These histories spin out simultaneously with the bright Enlightenment
narrative with which this introduction opened, imperialism enabling in part
the economic conditions that led to the democratic revolutions (see Habermas).

[5]In this volume, see Eileen Schell for a summary of categories, Deborah
Kelsh for the introduction of a new category, Harriet Malinowitz on hyphenated feminisms, and both Suzanne Clark and Lynn Worsham for critiques of
generational thinking often implied in category formation.

[6]See Margaret Whitford on the rhetorical nature of the psychoanalytic encounter.

[7]At the outer edge of *woman*, we find the queer theorist Monique Wittig
arguing that lesbians are not women. Though none of the authors in this volume writes from this position, Wittig's work and that of other queer theorists
mark the limits of discourses that speak of and for lesbians and gay men (see
Sedgwick).

PART I

Feminisms for Composition

The Reproduction of Othering

Laura Brady

I chose my title, a play on Nancy Chodorow's *The Reproduction of Mothering*, because I find myself wondering whether such studies of sexual differences don't, finally, reproduce the very sense of otherness that they set out to invert or erase. Pondering this question has made me increasingly aware of how complex the notion of otherness can be. This essay works through that complexity and its implications for feminist composition theory in four movements: an overview of essentialisms (plural) to open up the sign "essence" to multiple resignifications; a reading of three influential feminist texts; a look at how these texts are currently being cited in feminist composition studies; and some new citations and resignifications. I examine the uses of experience as evidence and suggest an alternative way of citing personal narratives.

Overview of Essentialisms

"The category of the Other is as primordial as consciousness itself," asserts Simone de Beauvoir in *The Second Sex*. And she reminds us that "this duality was not originally attached to the division of the sexes" (xxii). Otherness can be defined simply by contrast; but a more general sense of other presumes a certain reciprocity that Beauvoir finds absent from most Western considerations of gender. Instead of defining man by reference to woman and woman by reference to man, we "set up [man] as the sole essential," and woman is then defined "as pure otherness" (xxiv). Beauvoir sees that the unequal positioning of men as the One and women as the Other is the direct result of male-dominated culture. She argues, "One is not born, but rather becomes, a woman" (267). By focusing on the way culture shapes gender roles, Beauvoir presents a constructionist argument: one becomes a woman through various processes of socialization. But because of her generalizing assertions about men and women, she might also be labeled an essentialist. The title of her book, after all, implies a first sex as an irreducible essence directly linked to the social hierarchies.

The terms "essentialist" and "constructionist," in other words, often slide into each other, so they too, like "otherness," deserve attention. I prefer to think of essentialist and constructionist perspectives as correlatives rather than opposites—much like the reciprocal relation between the One and the Other. Such an approach allows for a wider play of possibilities: anytime I talk about gender difference, I may imply biological differences as one factor, but they are only one among many that I must consider.

As I argue that essentialism and constructionism are intertwined concepts, what worries me is how the essentialism-constructionism debate is being used and to what effects. I resist essentialist theories of gender difference, which reproduce the pattern of woman-as-other that Beauvoir described back in 1953.

Diana Fuss argues that "there is no essence to essentialism, that . . . we can only speak of *essentialisms*" and that "constructionism (the position that differences are constructed, not innate) really operates as a more sophisticated form of essentialism" (xii). Having rendered the division between essentialism and constructionism unstable, Fuss poses a new set of questions. Instead of asking whether a text is essentialist, she asks, "Where, how, and why is [the sign 'essence'] invoked? What are its political and textual effects?" (xi).

I am drawn to Fuss's phrase, "the sign 'essence.'" The power of signs lies in making us believe that signs are transparent, free of any determinations save those of the object they designate. Semiotics, the reading and interpretation of signs, challenges that assumption of transparency. Thus, if we read essence as a sign, as a semiotic reference, it becomes "historically contingent and constantly subject to change and to redefinition" (21). Fuss furthers this understanding of contingency by referring to John Locke's concept of nominal essence:

> Nominal essence signifies for Locke a view of essence as merely a linguistic convenience, a classificatory fiction we need to categorize and label. . . . When feminists today argue for maintaining the notion of a *class* of women, usually for political purposes, they do so . . . on the basis of Locke's nominal essence. It is Locke's distinction between nominal and real essence which allows us to work within the category of "women" as a *linguistic* rather than a natural kind [of category]. (4–5)

In other words, nature (some "real," unchanging essence) does not determine the collective identity, the sign "woman." A semiotic approach to woman enables an analysis not only of what language is saying (its content, its signifieds) but also of what it is doing (the social effect of its signifiers).

Judith Butler adds to this contingent, semiotic understanding of woman:

> What women signify has been taken for granted for too long. . . .
> In effect, the signified has been conflated with the referent,
> whereby a set of meanings have been taken to inhere in the real
> nature of women themselves. To recast the referent as the signi-
> fied, and to authorize or safeguard the category of women as a
> site of possible resignifications is to expand the possibilities of
> what it means to be a woman and in this sense to condition and
> enable an enhanced sense of agency.   ("Foundations" 16)

Butler is clearly calling for a deconstructive strategy that will open woman up to resignifications. She acknowledges the political necessity of speaking as and for women but also notes that "the minute the category of women is invoked as *describing* the constituency for which feminism speaks, an internal debate invariably begins over what the descriptive content of that term will be" (15). Far from seeing disagreements over the content of *woman* as negative, Butler argues that such rifts "ought to be safeguarded and prized." Therefore, to deconstruct the subject of feminism neither negates that subject nor privileges one understanding of it. Instead, such deconstruction "release[s] the term into a future of multiple significations" (16).

Together, Fuss and Butler offer a strategy for reading the ways in which the sign "essence" is invoked and for analyzing the political effects of the category of woman. This strategy suggests to me a contingent rhetorical analysis of how *sign* and *woman* each circulate in texts that have shaped feminist composition theory. The word *contingent* itself echoes not only Fuss's emphasis on historical contingencies but also Butler's notion of "contingent foundations" for a theory of the feminist and postmodern subject; functioning as both adjective and noun, it is rich in connotations and possibilities. The word also suggests metonymy, since it derives from the Latin verb *contingere* 'to touch.'

Metonymy is a powerful trope for understanding the possibilities and difficulties of the collective identity of woman—partly because of the way it can both contrast with and supplement metaphor. Metaphor typically depends on similarity and congruity; it is used to see something in terms of something else. Metonymy, however, is characterized by contiguity: the sharing of an edge or a boundary. Because in metonymy a boundary delineates a separation as well as a common ground, the trope can be useful for negotiating the border between individual and collective identity. That is, instead of reading or writing narratives of individual women's lives as a paradigm for all members of the category of woman (metaphor), the evidence of experience might emphasize contiguity, shared borders (metonymy).

The shift from metaphor to metonymy is, in fact, one that Luce Irigaray discusses. She posits a "fluid" female language and "impugns the privilege granted to metaphor (a quasi solid) over metonymy (which is much more closely allied to fluids)" (110). But even as she emphasizes fluid metonymy, she asserts that "all language is (also) metaphorical" and that "fluid . . . is by nature unstable" (110, 112) and thus susceptible to being reabsorbed into a solid. Through these seemingly contradictory moves, Irigaray refuses polarities that privilege one term over another. She emphasizes a deconstructive supplementation rather than an opposition:

> How, then, are we to try to redefine this language work that would leave space for the feminine? Let us say that every dichotomizing—and at the same time redoubling—break, including the one between enunciation and utterance, has to be disrupted. Nothing is ever to be *posited* that is not also reversed and caught up again in the *supplementarity of this reversal.*
> (79–80)

Supplementarity is a deconstructive double entendre: it suggests both an addition and a continuing lack; it plays with the concepts of presence and absence, similarity and difference. Consider, for instance, Rodolphe Gasché's explanation of supplements as "pluses that compensate for a minus in the origin" (211). The strategy of supplementarity is consistent with Irigaray's acceptance of both metaphor and metonymy. Metonymy expands metaphor and opens up new interpretations.

Fuss points out that Irigaray's recurrent image of two lips "function[s] as a metaphor for metonymy; through this collapse of boundaries, Irigaray gestures toward the deconstruction of the classic metaphor/metonymy binarism" (66). This deconstructive gesture is important for the ways in which Irigaray, like Butler, safeguards multiple readings of signs, including the sign "essence." For example, Irigaray writes:

> Kiss me. Two lips kissing two lips: openness is ours again. Our "world." And the passage from inside out, from the outside in, the passage between us, is limitless. . . . Are we unsatisfied? Yes, if that means we are never finished. If our pleasure consists in moving, being moved, endlessly. Always in motion: openness is never spent nor sated. (210)

The invitation to kiss is an invitation to open up. It is what Irigaray adds to Fuss's and Butler's (re)consideration of the sign "essence" and the category of woman.

Three Influential Feminist Texts

Because Chodorow's *The Reproduction of Mothering*, Carol Gilligan's *In a Different Voice*, and *Women's Ways of Knowing*, by Mary Field Belenky, Blythe McVicker Clinchy, Nancy Rule Goldberger, and Jill Mattuck Tarule, draw on first-person accounts for their data, all helped make women's narratives visible. In all three texts, individual narratives became the basis for generalizations about the collective identity of woman. As I begin to analyze how each of the three has shaped feminist composition theory, Fuss's work reminds me that "the radicality or conservatism of essentialism depends, to a significant degree, on *who* is utilizing it, *how* it is deployed, and *where* its effects are concentrated." She adds that "essence is a sign, and as such historically contingent and subject to change." For Fuss, factors of time, place, and purpose all affect the "strategic or interventionary value" of gendered identities (20). I contend that the work of Chodorow, Gilligan, and the Belenky collective continues to have a strategic value but that it has lost much of its interventionary (tactical) use for contemporary feminist composition theory.

Michel de Certeau associates strategy with established institutions and a sense of place; strategies are designed to prevent change in an existing order, and thus they resist "the erosion of time." Tactics, in contrast, depends on time, specifically on the "clever *utilization of time*, of the opportunities [time] presents and also of the play that it introduces into the foundations of power" (38–39). Both strategy and tactics affect the production, circulation, and disruption of power.

Although Certeau presents strategy and tactics as oppositional categories, I suggest that in practice feminism—as both an organized institution and a counterinstitutional movement—always functions strategically and tactically. That is, tactical uses of essentialism can disrupt assumptions about gender roles, identity categories, and the intersections of language and material bodies. When the disruptions are successful enough to become visible and bear repetition, they are transformed into strategies. While strategies can be politically useful, they can also be dangerous. When strategies of essentialism resist change, they will become institutionalized unless new, subversive (tactical) uses of essentialism disrupt the order.

The works of Chodorow, Gilligan, and the Belenky collective all had a tactical value when they were published: in 1978 Chodorow challenged long-standing bourgeois assumptions about the sexual division of labor; in 1982 Gilligan resignified Lawrence Kohlberg's theories of moral development to include women; and in 1986 Belenky, Clinchy, Goldberger, and Tarule drew on Gilligan's work to critique educational systems. Repeated citations of these three books have institutionalized a popular concept of the category of woman, which has helped create a newly established set of gender conventions that both feminists and antifeminists appropriate. My purpose is not to diminish the role these texts have played in the past but to look at their usefulness at *this* moment in time—a moment characterized in part by poststructuralist feminist theories. If these texts have lost their tactical force, then it's time to turn to new tactics for challenging conventions about gender and writing.

Chodorow's Uses of Essentialism

When *The Reproduction of Mothering* was published in 1978, it received wide notice both inside and (perhaps more important) outside academe. *Time* magazine gave the book the following brief summary: "Chodorow says that fathers must take over half the parenting and raise daughters with a sense of self derived from both parents" ("Remembering" 52). *Ms.* magazine, in "a sampling of new finds in women's studies," recommended the book, saying it "provides careful psychoanalytic grounding for the radical position that both sexes can and should parent equally" (Bailey). *Contemporary Psychology*, welcoming the text for the way it "sets forth a theoretical basis for that universal and intransigent sexual division of labor in which women mother and men order the social domain," predicted that Chodorow's delineation of "how social structures develop the psychological means of their own development" would remain "important for some time to come" (Gump 657, 658).

The prediction proved accurate. At the moment of its publication, Chodorow's text had a tactical force, acting as one of several isolated movements that disrupted assumptions about gendered roles. Over time, as scholars repeatedly cited *The Reproduction of Mothering* in their feminist critiques of institutions, it became an increasingly visible text. Used to draw attention to the social organization of parenting and the sexual division of labor, it acquired a central position in Anglo-American feminism that has, over time, transformed its use from a tactical disruption of patriarchal gender roles to a strategic essentialism. The text now raises questions about how strategic essentialism functions.

Chodorow's introduction to the book suggests that she resists reductively simple arguments based on biology and favors instead a social-historical approach (8). But the book shows how difficult it can be to maintain the opposition between essentialist and constructionist views.

From her application of object-relations theory to the reproduction of mothering, Chodorow concludes:

> Issues of differentiation have been intertwined with sexual issues. . . . The earliest mode of individuation, . . . the earliest conflicts and the earliest unconscious definitions of self, the earliest threats of individuation, and the earliest anxieties which call up defenses, all differ for boys and girls because of the differences in the character of the early mother-child relationship for each. (167)

She shifts emphasis from the social organization of sex, gender, and family toward an organization that is determined by the mother, by virtue of biological reproduction. Not only does she place the organizing power solely with the mother, but she also omits consideration of the social context of the mother-child relationship. Nowhere does she address ways in which socioeconomic status may influence that relationship, nor does she account for other factors such as race, ethnicity, or environment—an odd omission, given her training as a sociologist. Mother becomes an essence that transcends other conditions.

The effect of Chodorow's mother-child focus is clear:

> Women's mothering, then, produces asymmetries in the relational experiences of girls and boys as they grow up, which

account for crucial differences in feminine and masculine per-
sonality, and the relational capacities and modes which these entail. . . . The *basic* feminine sense of self is connected to the
world; the *basic* masculine sense of self is separate.

(169; emphasis added)

The basic (or essential) power in this passage is ascribed to the
mother. Janice Doane and Devon Hodges point out that the dominant,
powerful mother figure "makes it all too easy to forget why women resist the cultural construction of feminine identity and sexuality" and
thus "has the effect of masking women's subordination" (40). This effect undercuts Chodorow's goal of showing how "women's mothering
is . . . implicated in the construction and reproduction of male dominance" (9). Doane and Hodges attribute the ideological contradictions
in Chodorow's work to her unquestioning reliance on object-relations
theory, which, they argue, "mystifies the social construction of the
mother-child dyad by defining that dyad as an origin" (34). The problems inherent in Chodorow's position are perhaps easiest to see when
she endorses Robert Stoller's theory of a "core gender identity" that is
"best understood as female for both sexes" (151). This return to the
mother as a primal and identifying force effectively minimizes culture's role in constructing gender and identity.[1]

Chodorow marginalizes the social context that she states so as-
sertively in her introduction: the myth of the dominant mother figure
displaces the reality of many women's subordinate socioeconomic position. Chodorow's nonmaterialist image of the powerful mother thus
accounts for its idealistic appeal as a feminist narrative; it emphasizes
power while largely erasing an understanding of significant sources of
power, such as class, race, or geopolitical position.

In rhetorical terms, Chodorow uses personal narratives synecdochically. That is, the experience of one woman often functions as paradigm for all members of the category of woman. Since individual
women's stories stress the same points, they function as partial—but
essential—narratives. Chodorow does acknowledge the criticism of
oversimplification at the end of the book:

Some friends and colleagues have said that my account is too un-
qualified. In fact, *all* women *do not* mother or want to mother,
and *all* women are not "maternal" or nurturant. *Some* women are
far more nurturant than others, and want children far more.
Some *men* are more nurturant than some women. I agree that
claims about gender differences gloss over important differences

within genders and similarities between genders. I hope this
book leads people to raise questions about such variations.
(215)

Although she believes there are "structural and statistical truths about
male-female differences" that cannot be ignored, she goes on to argue
that "it is important not to confuse these truths with prescription"
(215). Unfortunately, her qualifying statements are often ignored. As
Katha Pollitt points out:

> Popularizers of Chodorow water down and sentimentalize her
> thesis. They embrace her proposition that traditional mothering
> produces "relational" women and "autonomous" men but forget
> her less congenial argument that it also results in sexual inequal-
> ity, misogyny and hostility between mothers and daughters, who,
> like sons, desire independence but have a much harder time
> achieving it. (800)

But despite her qualifications, Chodorow does emphasize "truths"
about intergender differences, and she does generalize on the basis of
individual narratives. In response to her hope that her book "leads
people to raise questions," I question her use of narrative as evidence.
How representative is any narrative? How large or small a part of the
category of woman does it represent? It is a question I also pose of
Gilligan's *In a Different Voice*.

Gilligan's Uses of Essentialism

Certeau points out that "the space of the tactic is the space of the other.
. . . It is a maneuver . . . within enemy territory" (37). Gilligan's book
maneuvered within the male-dominated terrain of Freud, Piaget, and
Kohlberg. Her timely contributions to professional exchanges about
psychological development were well and widely received in 1982, and
her work quickly became a focal point for larger feminist issues. An
early scholarly review of her book in *Signs: Journal of Women in Culture and Society* asserts that "Gilligan's research stands among those
significant revisions of traditional scholarship that change the face of
that scholarship as well as of feminist thought" (Benjamin, Rev. 297).
Ms. magazine named Gilligan woman of the year and predicted in January 1984 that she would be "one of our future leaders." The praise was
linked directly to *In a Different Voice*: "a study of contrasting ways of
defining and developing morality . . . predicated on finding that men in

this culture tend to see the world in terms of their autonomy . . . whereas women tend to see the world in terms of connectedness" (Van Gelder 37).

These are the same points associated with Chodorow: autonomous men and relational women. As with Chodorow's work, Gilligan's now occupies a strategic place in Anglo-American feminism. This position, however, has to be considered from a contemporary feminist perspective.

Gilligan's representation of gender roles (or of the sign "essence") needs to be put into a context of use: that is, if her book is deployed as part of a strategic essentialism, how, where, when, and by whom is it deployed?

Like Chodorow, Gilligan is interpreted—and appropriated—too simply. Although her work received academic praise because it "[elucidates] key problems in both male and female development and opens the way to a broader social critique of individualism" (Benjamin, Rev. 298), it has sometimes been used to foreclose such critiques. Susan Faludi argues, for instance, that

> much against her will, Gilligan became the expert that backlash media experts loved to cite. *Newsweek* used Gilligan's book to support its contention that career women pay "a psychic price" for professional success. Retrograde pop psychology books . . . invoked Gilligan's work to bolster their arguments that independence was an unhealthy state for women. Antifeminist scholars such as Michael Levin abused Gilligan's scholarship even further, characterizing it as a reaffirmation of traditional Freudian analyses of the female psyche.   (331)

Gilligan addresses both misappropriations and critics in a response written for a 1986 *Signs* forum on her book. She writes:

> I am well aware that reports of sex differences can be used to rationalize oppression, and I deplore any use of my work for this purpose. But I do not see it as empowering to encourage women to put aside their own concerns and perceptions to rely on a psychology largely defined by men's perceptions in thinking about what is of value and what constitutes human development.
> (Kerber et al. 333)

Despite Gilligan's denunciation of misinterpretations of her work, it's worth asking how it is that *In a Different Voice* has been used by the backlash movement and by feminists alike. This question connects with Fuss's key questions about how the sign "essence" circulates: "Where, how, and why is it invoked? What are its political and textual effects?"

One effect of *In a Different Voice* was a resignification of Freud's, Piaget's, and Kohlberg's theories of moral development. Gilligan argues that those psychologists' often cited studies excluded women. Specifically, she contests Kohlberg's six stages of moral development that center on rules, rights, and autonomy. Not only is Kohlberg's research flawed because his sample excludes women, but, she argues, his conception implies that women are bound to be morally deficient because they are fixed at stage 3, where "morality is conceived in interpersonal terms and goodness is equated with helping and pleasing others" (Gilligan 18). Women's goodness paradoxically marks them as morally deficient on Kohlberg's scale.

As an alternative to Kohlberg's rules-and-rights conception of morality, Gilligan proposes the "responsibility conception," which focuses on the "limitations of any particular resolution [to a moral dilemma] and describes the conflicts that remain"; her theory is marked by "insistent contextual relativism" and a relational concept of self (22). The relational aspects of Gilligan's theory derive in part from Chodorow's study of sex differences in early experiences of individuation and relationships (see Gilligan 8–9, 11). Gilligan builds on Chodorow's work, finding that boys develop "a self defined through separation . . . a self measured against an abstract ideal of perfection" whereas girls develop "a self delineated through connection . . . a self assessed through particular activities of care" (35). In 1982, Gilligan's use of both Kohlberg and Chodorow was insurgent and timely; it was, to use Certeau's term, tactical.

The appeal of Gilligan's work can be traced to the status and complexity it bestowed on behaviors that had been dismissed as indecisive and overly relativistic. These behaviors (which are not necessarily gendered) can, in the light of Gilligan, be seen as complex and vital to social continuity and cohesion. When Gilligan describes the goals of her study, she attempts to avoid essentialism with an appeal to both nature (biology) and nurture (society): "The different voice I describe is characterized not by gender, but theme. . . . Clearly, differences arise in a social context where factors of social status and power *combine with reproductive biology* to shape the experience of males and females and the relations between the sexes" (2; emphasis added). The hope is expressed for new interpretations and a new focus on "the interaction of experience and thought, in different voices and the dialogues to which they give rise, in the way we listen to ourselves and to others, in the stories we tell about our lives" (2).

Gilligan emphasizes social context, but her study, when read through the contemporary lens of poststructuralist feminist theory, nonetheless returns to a biological argument. Throughout her analyses of specific cases, she omits discussion of the "factors of social status and power" that she mentions in her introduction. She favors gendered generalizations. For instance, she draws the conclusion that "while women thus try to change the rules in order to preserve relationships, men, in abiding by these rules, depict relationships as easily replaced" (44). Women, in other words, enact Gilligan's ideal of "insistent contextual relativism" (22) whereas men are bound by rules rather than relationships. Ironically, her contextual relativism fails to consider factors other than gender that might account for—or at least contribute to—patterns of similarity and difference. Gilligan's emphasis of gender differences constructs an undifferentiated woman's voice. That voice—as synecdoche for women in general—is disembodied; Gilligan literally and figuratively elides material differences. Without those differences, the collection of personal narratives and experiences paradoxically objectifies and defines a new set of restrictive conventions, which becomes a strategic rather than tactical expression of women's experience. And these conventions can too easily be used to confirm traditional gender roles.

Despite the inconsistencies in Gilligan's study, it remains popular. Catherine Greeno and Eleanor Maccoby suggest that the book's appeal can be credited to its narratives: "Many women readers find that the comments by women quoted in Gilligan's book resonate so thoroughly with their own experience that they do not need any further demonstration of the truth of what is being said" (Kerber et al. 314–15). Although Gilligan contends that her cases "seem 'intuitively' right to many women" because they reflect common experiences (Kerber et al. 325), I would argue that the narrative appeal results from a reading strategy that emphasizes commonality to the exclusion of differences that might problematize the category of woman.

Belenky, Clinchy, Goldberger, and Tarule's Uses of Essentialism

The four authors of *Women's Ways of Knowing*, like Joans of Arc guided by the sounds of women's voices, have moved into another sphere [education]. Just as the voice of conscience says different things to women than it does to men [in Gilligan's book], the authors found that a different voice speaks to women when they ask themselves what it is they know.   (Neustadtl 38)

The description of Belenky, Clinchy, Goldberger, and Tarule as Joans of Arc is ambiguous in the *New York Times* review of *Women's Ways of Knowing*. Are the writers crusaders? saints? martyrs? Just how different are the voices speaking to women? The reviewer Sara Neustadtl establishes the connection between Gilligan's work and *Women's Ways of Knowing*, then basically summarizes the book by outlining its five epistemological perspectives (silence, received knowledge, subjective knowledge, procedural knowledge, and constructed knowledge). Neustadtl goes on to argue that "the tragedy of those trapped in silence" (the first of the five categories) is not a condition limited to women: "Men in similar families grow up no less inarticulate, no more able to control their circumstances, likewise doomed to repeat their tragedy with their own children" (38). Neustadtl implicitly critiques the way the book emphasizes gender to the exclusion of other factors (such as class position) that affect education and empowerment. Her objection continues to be the major criticism of the book.

To pursue a contemporary critique of *Women's Ways of Knowing* requires an analysis of how the work is used. If it, like Chodorow's and Gilligan's influential texts, buttresses a strategic essentialism, how is that essentialism put into practice?

In an interview with Belenky, Evelyn Ashton-Jones and Dene Kay Thomas ask her about the text's "potential to reinforce gender stereotypes and essentialist definitions of femininity." Belenky acknowledges the fact that "many people . . . classify us with those who see sex differences as immutably rooted in biology" (284), but she seems to reject polarities:

> Mostly, we have a rigid, dualistic way of structuring the world that makes it hard for people to understand that a voice can be associated with gender without being encased in gender. . . . If you study women, you have to call it "women's ways"; if you called it "people's ways," you would meet with criticism about generalizing beyond your data. But calling it "women's ways" is problematic, too, because then men will think, "Well, if women do it and I'm not a woman, then I can't be like that." It's very confusing because we're gendered, but we're also just human beings.   (285)

She recognizes the "rigid" limitations of both dualism and sexual differences, yet she reinforces both with her example. Whether named "women's ways," "people's ways," or (the unstated, alternative category) "men's ways," each option overgeneralizes: the only possibility of difference allowed is that between women and nonwomen. By pointing to the problem in naming the study "women's ways," Belenky underscores the study's polarity between male and female experience. Gender categories become the sole basis for interpreting the data.

The same male-female polarity appears in the introduction to *Women's Ways of Knowing*: "Historically, it has been assumed that the development of women's intellectual potential would inhibit the development of their emotional capacities and that the development of men's emotional range would impair intellectual functioning." Although Belenky and her collaborators go on to say that women have tried to "examine and dispel beliefs suggesting sexual polarities," the authors also suggest that these efforts have too often minimized differences (7).

Women's Ways of Knowing seeks to maintain differences in much the same way that Gilligan seeks to establish a "different voice." Rather than present sites and interpretations of difference, both Gilligan and the researchers in *Women's Ways of Knowing* present individual experience and life stories as explanations in themselves. That is, they use individual narratives to generalize a collective female identity. As a result of this synecdochic reading, gendered experience is privileged as the only meaningful experience. Consider the description of the overall study that is offered in the introduction to *Women's Ways of Knowing*:

> We adopted an intensive interview / case study approach because we wanted to hear what women had to say in their own terms. . . .
>
> Before asking a woman to participate, we told her that we were interested in her experience—and in women's experience—because it so often had been excluded as people sought to understand human development. We told her we wanted to hear what was important about life and learning *from her point of view.*
> (11)

This description collapses "her experience" and "women's experience": the individual substitutes for the collective. First-hand accounts become a way to discern collective truths.

Each chapter begins with a story, either an account of one of the women interviewed for the book or an account taken from a literary source. The Belenky collective, although more materialist than either Chodorow or Gilligan in its consideration of factors such as age, economic class, and education in addition to gender, nevertheless mythologizes women along lines similar to both Chodorow and Gilligan when it emphasizes women's patterns of "connected knowing" and the ideal of teacher as midwife or nurturing mother (217–18). The positive myths of connection, collaboration, and maternal bonding displace the very differences that the book sets out to examine.

In all three studies, the original, tactical use of experience becomes a strategic use that objectifies identity, gender, and difference—and this shift is precisely the problem I am addressing. In Chodorow, Gilligan, and the Belenky collective, the experience of some women leads to generalized claims about all women and, by extension, to opposite claims about all men. Over time and through continued scholarly citations, these three works function strategically to reduce difference to gendered essences that elide critical specifics and render nearly impossible the type of "insistent contextual relativism" that would, as Gilligan idealistically hopes, allow consideration of "limitations of any particular resolution . . . and the conflicts that remain" (22). To consider those limitations and remaining conflicts, this essay questions the role of experience as evidence and the role of personal narrative as argument. It questions the uses to which that evidence and that argument are put.

How Scholars Cite the Three Texts

What are the political and rhetorical effects of appeals to narrative and experience? Chodorow, Gilligan, and the Belenky collective are most often cited, in the context of composition scholarship, with reference to male-female narrative writing patterns or with reference to male-female experiences of both teacher and student in the classroom. In the following examples of feminist composition scholarship, I examine the influence of Chodorow's, Gilligan's, and the Belenky collective's descriptive, experience-based data and conclusions. My purpose is not to find fault with the work of the scholars Elizabeth Flynn, Mary Lay, and Catherine Lamb; their articles are outstanding examples of careful scholarship. I cite them to show precisely how difficult it is to examine consciously a convention that has become so well established as to be transparent.

Experience, in particular, has become a transparent strategy. Joan

Scott's work "The Evidence of Experience" offers an explanation of the appeal of first-hand testimony and suggests the limitations of narrative evidence:

> When the evidence offered is evidence of "experience," the claim for referentiality is further buttressed—what could be truer, after all, than a subject's own account of what he or she has lived through? It is precisely this kind of appeal to experience as uncontestable evidence and as an originary point of explanation— as a foundation on which analysis is based—that weakens the critical thrust of histories of difference. By remaining within the epistemological frame of orthodox history, these studies lose the possibility of examining those assumptions and practices that excluded considerations of difference in the first place.   (777)

Scott's argument might be thought of as antifoundationalist: personal experience, when taken for granted as a type of evidence, often contributes to essentialist arguments.

Elizabeth Flynn's often-cited essay "Composing as a Woman" invokes Chodorow, Gilligan, and the Belenky collective as "especially relevant to a feminist consideration of student writing," because "all three books suggest that women and men have different conceptions of self and different modes of interaction with others as a result of their different experiences" (425–26). She summarizes the arguments of each of the three texts and then applies their conclusions about male-female differences to "narrative descriptions of learning experiences produced in the first of a two-course sequence required of first-year students at Michigan Tech" (428). She finds that those student narratives verify the findings of Chodorow, Gilligan, and the Belenky collective. "The narratives of the female students are stories of interaction, of connection, or of frustrated connection. The narratives of the male students are stories of achievement, of separation, or of frustrated achievement" (428). As a result of these findings, Flynn calls for a new direction in composition scholarship that pursues questions raised by feminist researchers and scholarship and that engages in the type of self-reflective critique that often marks feminist scholarship (425, 431). She also calls for a recognition of women's experience:

> Women's experience is not entirely a distorted version of male reality, is not entirely elusive, and it is worthy of recuperation. We must alert our women students to the dangers of immasculation

and provide them with a critical perspective. But we must also encourage them to become self-consciously aware of what their experience in the world has been and how this experience is related to the politics of gender. Then we must encourage our women students to write from the power of that experience.

(434)

Flynn's call for self-critical examination and new questions for composition studies had tactical force in 1988. The emphasis placed on experience and narratives of experience, however, follows Chodorow, Gilligan, and the Belenky collective, because Flynn also grants experience authority without examining the contexts for that authority. Women's experience assumes a collective, gendered identity that does not allow a full consideration of the politics of gender. Instead, the resultant emphasis on "women students" reinforces the very polarity that Flynn addresses when she calls for "a feminist approach to composition scholarship [that] would focus on questions of difference and dominance" (425). As important a focus as that is, it needs to consider the effect of experiential evidence, and the effect of essentialism, in constructing difference and dominance.

Mary Lay's essay "Feminist Theory and the Redefinition of Technical Communication" examines how common characteristics of and debates in feminist theory affect technical communication, specifically in terms of "the myth of scientific objectivity, . . . new interest in ethnographic studies of workplace communication, and . . . collaborative writing" (348). Offering an overview of feminist theory, she finds that one common theme is the "inclusion of women's experiences" (349–50). Lay explains that feminist research offers women "explanations of social phenomena" and that for them to arrive at these explanations, "the subject matter of feminist research is women's experiences." Because of the centrality of women's experience to feminist research, "feminist critics relate to their audiences by acknowledging their own backgrounds, by investigating experiences that their audiences have, and by inviting their audiences to test feminist investigations against their own experience" (351–52).

Among numerous and wide-ranging examples of feminist scholarship that rely on women's experience, Lay cites Chodorow, Gilligan, the Belenky collective, and Flynn. Specifically, she brings these strands of scholarship into her discussion of collaborative writing. She begins with Chodorow's conclusion that "girls define themselves as 'continuous with others,' whereas boys define themselves as 'more separate and distinct'" (Chodorow qtd. in Lay), then uses Gilligan's extensions of Chodorow and the Belenky collective's idea of women's "connected knowing" (362). Her point is that in the context of collaborative groups "authority or knowing for women is commonality of experience" and that "gender roles, as established in the family structure, influence how men and women relate to the demands of collaboration" (362).

Analyzing the impact of feminist theory on technical communication, Lay considers the effects of context and differing conventions. She raises questions about whether "technical communicators" should, when advocating effective models of collaboration, "stress the similarities or the differences between men and women" and whether it is possible to "avoid the labeling that contributes to dualistic thinking or binary opposition" (366). Despite this analysis of both organizing structures and contextual actions, the strategies of essentialism and experience reassert themselves when Lay uncritically accepts the conclusions of her predecessors, making the assumption that experience is sufficient evidence for conclusions about gender. Lay's essay demonstrates that the oppositions between tactics and strategy are dynamic.

I find that the tacit acceptance of the use of experience as evidence exists even among scholars who seem acutely aware that essentialism should be challenged as a reductive critical position. One example is Catherine Lamb's essay "Beyond Argument in Feminist Composition," in which she tries to "enlarge the sphere of feminist composition by including [experience] in an approach to argument" (11). Lamb takes care to "be as free as possible from the charge of essentialism" (12). Even though she does not directly cite Gilligan or Chodorow (she does cite Flynn and Belenky), she relies on the related work of Sara Ruddick's *Maternal Thinking*. Lamb pauses in her discussion of Ruddick's "standpoint theory" (based on the idea that women, as an oppressed group, must know their oppressor—men—in a way that the oppressor does not need to know the oppressed) to acknowledge the "dangers" in this theory, which "can imply the moral superiority of women [and] easily become essentialist" (16). Lamb continues to invoke Ruddick's standpoint theory, however, "because of the teaching power of concrete *experience* . . . to which the success of a book like . . . *Women's Ways of Knowing* is eloquent testimony" (16). The argument of experience, along with Ruddick's notion of maternal thinking (defined by Lamb as "loving attention . . . the ability to think or feel as the other" [16]), is central to Lamb's proposal of mediation and negotiation as feminist alternatives to "the self-assertiveness of monologic argument"

(17). Despite her aversion to the charge of essentialism, Lamb does not address the essentializing effect of first-person testimony when it is used to construct a gendered identity. As a result, her feminist alternative to monologic argument inadvertently underscores traits that arguments of experience have gendered female, such as the "'attentive love' of maternal thinking" (21). Although she acknowledges the writing context in which the feminist alternative may occur, we need to examine also the experiential context of that alternative.

In Chodorow's, Gilligan's, and the Belenky collective's use of personal narratives and in the way these texts are then cited and circulated in feminist composition scholarship, gender is offered as the only (or at least the primary) site of identification. Devoney Looser, among others, challenges the use of gender alone as a category of identification, arguing that much of feminist composition theory "assumes a stable and/or recoverable homogenized 'woman' and that such 'identity politics' present costs that feminist compositionists may not be ready to pay" (54–55). Identity politics raises important questions about the effect of emphasizing personal narratives in such a way that the personal is generalized to all women. While Looser notes the political value of feminist composition scholarship (including the emphasis on personal narratives) in "getting the category 'women' accepted as an important locus of study in rhetoric and composition," she also calls for an examination of the theoretical foundations for this work (54).

When we examine the theoretical foundations of Gilligan, Chodorow, and the Belenky collective,[2] it is clear that each author gives priority to gender as a category of identification. Their works tend to use narratives synecdochically, focusing on commonality and congruity to the exclusion of contiguity and difference. An uncritical reliance on experience as evidence constructs a type of fixed subjectivity. The use of experience as evidence rests on assumptions that universalize the experience of one instead of exploring differences within and between subjects. The universalizing effect is the result of the transparency of gender: what a woman says is taken as evidence of what women think.

Chodorow's, Gilligan's, and the Belenky collective's works were important for making women's narratives visible, for raising questions about the uses of essentialism, and for calling attention to the ways in which narratives of experience often function as evidence. But it is time to move beyond existing uses of personal narratives and consider new citations and significations.

New Citations and Resignifications

Personal experience is one interpretation of an event, shaped by a subject's positioning and type of agency; it should invite discussion and analysis of the conditions that construct both the event and the narrative. Narratives can be productive sites for acknowledging difference.[3] In rhetorical terms, we should shift from synecdoche to metonymy.

I realize that there is always a danger of metonymy slipping into synecdoche. I like metonymy precisely because of its instability and am proposing the trope as an operational tactic for reading and rereading (perhaps repositioning) narratives. The slippage between positions can be productive: it lends itself to deconstructive analyses that allow us to look at processes of producing both texts and subjectivity.

In *Bodies That Matter*, Judith Butler calls for "contestatory connections" that acknowledge the ways in which identity is constructed through both opposition to and exclusion of other categories (115). Consider how this idea might be extended to Chodorow, Gilligan, and the Belenky collective, whose feminist identifications focus on gender to the exclusion of race, sexuality, class, geopolitical position, and so on. The simple proliferation of new identification categories does not solve the problem. Butler argues that "an economy of difference is in order" to avoid "at the level of identity politics the very exclusionary moves that initiated the turn to specific identities in the first place" (118). Contestatory connections, in other words, provide a point of convergence that erases neither identity nor difference.

Butler links identification practices with "performatives" in speech acts, which are those words or utterances that perform or produce what they say. Their ability to perform relies on repetition.[4] The act of repetition implies that performatives refer to prior acts and become part of a signifying chain. Butler gives the example of a judge who both cites the law and becomes a site "for the reconstitution and resignification of the law" (107). The notion of citationality grounds her analysis of "sexed positions":

> To the extent that the "I" is secured by its sexed position, this "I" and its position can be secured only by being *repeatedly* assumed, whereby "assumption" is not a singular act or event, but, rather, an iterable practice. If to "assume" a sexed position is to seek recourse to a legislative norm, as Lacan would claim, then "as-

sumption" is a question of *repeating* that norm, citing or miming that norm and an occasion to expose the norm itself as a privileged interpretation. (108)

Butler's concept of citing-siting the norm provides a strategy for examining repeated assumptions about the evidence of personal experience for grounding knowledge of women. New discussions of narratives of experience, for instance, might foreground the ways that identity is constructed *and* deconstructed by the opposition to and exclusion of other categories. The possibilities that Butler's notion of contestatory connections opens up may be illustrated by rereading a narrative of knowledge from *Women's Ways of Knowing.* In a section entitled "Real Talk," there is discussion of "constructivist" women's "capacity for speaking with and listening to others while simultaneously speaking with and listening to the self" (145). The writers note how one young woman named Bridget moved from a position of "silence" to "constructed knowledge"; they illustrate her progression with excerpts from their interviews with her as a college sophomore and then four years later. The following passage quotes Bridget "thinking as a constructivist" after she had "finished college and travelled abroad" (144):

> I always was the kind of person who felt I had to entertain people or keep the conversation going. I was brought up to be really wishy-washy, at least by my mother anyway. To be the one who entertains, who supports, who perhaps provides the forum for the discussion, but is never a participant in that discussion herself. I'm still finding it difficult in certain circumstances to truly express what I feel or what I want. But I am trying—at least for my own mental health—to be honest and forthright in my communication with people. That is a big challenge—a big, big challenge! (145)

The writers attempt to locate a single, coherent subject position, then extend that to create a coherent discourse and ideology of women's constructed knowing. They cite Bridget to illustrate that "listening to others no longer diminishes women's capacity to hear their own voices" (145). Once again, they equate one woman's experience to all women's voices, without comment on other factors that may set Bridget apart from some women: her education (a completed college degree), age (early twenties), ethnicity (unstated), and class (implied by her travels abroad). The Belenky collective does not comment on the slips and contradictions in Bridget's narrative. The contradictions, however, provide a way to resist or challenge the synecdochic reading.

Instead of reading this narrative as proof that Bridget "was thinking as a constructivist" (144), I propose a rereading that analyzes how her narrative cites (and perpetuates) cultural assumptions about feminized discourse. By ironically qualifying her statement about being "brought up to be really wishy-washy" with the phrase "at least by my mother," Bridget not only reinforces the stereotype that women's discourse is tentative but also characterizes this tendency as a behavior learned from another woman—her mother. The phrase "at least" implies a contrast to someone else who "brought up" Bridget that reinforces cultural assumptions about family structures and gender oppositions: the non-wishy-washy other is quite likely her father. Another contradiction is found in Bridget's shift from first person to third person when she talks about "the one who entertains, who supports" but is "never a participant . . . herself." The one is female and clearly being cited-sited as an outsider. The distancing use of the third person might be read as resistance to that female role. Finally, Bridget implies a tension between being dishonest and being able "to truly express" what she feels and wants, but she omits mentioning what she thinks. She reiterates and thus perpetuates language that constitutes female subjectivity as irrational. Bridget retreats from these various contradictions by citing an implicit form of illness—the loss of her mental health. This reference, too, repeats a cultural assumption about how women respond to contradictory subject positions: as fragmented subjects, they become mad.

To avoid reading Bridget's narrative synecdochically, I've carefully tried to note Bridget's particular relation to cultural assumptions. I've tried to avoid claims that her narrative is representative of a large group of women or that the presentation of this narrative is typical of *Women's Ways of Knowing*. My goal is not to erase the Belenky collective's reading but to contest it by citing and situating differences and to offer a supplementary, metonymic strategy of reading narratives and evidence.

Yet all uses of evidence—including mine in this essay—are, in some sense, synecdochic; any act of academic citation repeats parts of another's argument to construct a new, whole argument and places the author in a particular social, historical, discursive frame. This citational use of evidence is so interwoven in Western epistemology, discourse, and rhetoric that it is almost inescapable; tropes like metaphor, metonymy, synecdoche, and irony inevitably structure and organize knowledge. Since we cannot escape from language, we can at least move from an analysis of structures to an analysis of actions by foregrounding the role of language in constructing subjectivity and ideology. A contingent rhetorical analysis of citations and tropes emphasizes the intersections between language and ideologies (such as the ideologies of gender); these analyses, in turn, allow an understanding of the transformative shifts between tactics and strategies, places and spaces, production and consumption. Citations of Chodorow, Gilligan, and the Belenky collective, for instance, have repeatedly positioned gender as an exclusionary category, a normative site for women's ways of knowing, reading, and writing. While these citations have made the category of woman visible, the discursive practices that construct gender and experience have become transparent. More recent work in feminism and composition (such as this volume of essays) provides new sites-cites for discussions and differences.

NOTES

I'm grateful to Dennis Allen, Beth Daniell, Susan Jarratt, Susan Sailer, Tim Sweet, and Lynn Worsham for their perceptive comments at various stages of the writing of this essay.

[1]Fuss extends the critique of Chodorow's reliance on object-relations theory by noting that if both sexes "long for a return to the primary [mother-child] union with the female," then everything in Chodorow's work should point "specifically toward a theory of female homosexuality" (48). Not only does Chodorow dismiss lesbianism as rare (Chodorow 200), but her theory does not account at all for male homosexuality; as a result, Chodorow's "theory of mothering is less a critique of compulsory heterosexuality than a mandate for it" (Fuss 48).

[2]The different disciplinary emphases that inform these three studies doubtless shape both their methods and their interpretations: Chodorow is a sociologist who relies on psychology to interpret social patterns, Gilligan is a psychologist who is concerned specifically with the psychology of moral development, and the Belenky collective represents developmental psychology but is concerned primarily with education. I limit my discussion to the authors' uses of experience as evidence, especially those that circulate in composition studies.

[3]For another perspective on this point I recommend chapter 4 of *Sexing the Self*, "Materializing Locations: Images and Selves," where Elspeth Probyn asserts the following: "In recognizing constructions of the self as specific points of view both derived from very local configurations and trained back onto a particular ground, we can begin to open up the analytic possibilities of the self beyond the literary problematic of autobiography as a unifying discourse. . . .

In locating the image of the self that is put forward in a document (or as a document), we can begin to analyse and articulate the specificities of the relation of 'theoretical problems' to 'lived experience'" (101).

[4]The iterability of performatives is not original to Butler. See, for instance, Derrida's response to J. L. Austin in "Signature, Event, Context."

"When and Where I Enter": Race, Gender, and Composition Studies

Shirley Wilson Logan

Only the BLACK WOMAN *can say "when and where I enter, in the quiet, undisputed dignity of my womanhood, without violence and without suing or special patronage, then and there the whole Negro race enters with me."*
—Anna Julia Cooper

Black women have a long history as communication specialists, teaching facility with language to those who needed it most—free and enslaved Africans in America—throughout the nineteenth century. When the educator Anna Julia Cooper addressed the Washington, DC, Convocation of Colored Clergy of the Protestant Episcopal Church in 1886, she was continuing a tradition among black women of public speaking and teaching begun many years before. In her speech "Womanhood a Vital Element in the Regeneration and Progress of a Race," from which the title of this essay is taken, Cooper suggests that if the neglected black woman enters, then a fortiori the more highly regarded members of her race accompany her. But the speech also mentions the unique significance that black women and all women possess when they enter new situations, by virtue of what Cooper calls, in another essay, the "feminine . . . side to truth" ("Education" 60). By claiming for women this special influence, Cooper applies the nineteenth-century suffragist argument from expediency, based on the claim that women were indeed fundamentally different from men and that this different, "feminine side" entitled them to a place in the public sphere (Kraditor 43–74). She gives the Episcopalian leaders a thorough tongue-lashing for the church's failure to attract more than the black educated elite. More significant, she condemns the leaders' neglect of southern black women, "at once both the lever and the fulcrum for uplifting the race" (73). Her post-Reconstruction black women stepped tentatively into the public space occupied by those who had denied them room throughout the century. Black women entering writing classrooms at the end of the twentieth century share common experiences with their nineteenth-century foresisters. And, of course, much has changed.

In this essay, I review briefly the teaching activities of a few nineteenth-century black women. I believe such a review is an important first step toward understanding some of the racial and gender issues facing higher education today. Contemporary discussions about black women educators should be set against the historical backdrop of this deeply rooted tradition, because that backdrop corrects the short-sightedness inherent in the current perception of diversity that sees all difference as ahistorical. This perception too often assumes that people of color are just now beginning to take part in developing and shaping American culture, however defined. I then address some of the issues facing black women professors generally and those teaching writing in particular, using two of my own experiences as examples. I close by suggesting some ways in which the tensions surrounding black women who teach in predominantly white institutions might be converted into catalysts for change.

I am keenly aware that although I was asked to write this essay for a collection on feminism and composition, many of the writing concerns addressed here do not arise strictly from the professor's gender or from the gender of the students. They arise from a conflation of gender and race and subject matter and setting, a conflation that for me is difficult if not impossible to sort out. Marsha Houston reminds us that "women of color do not experience sexism *in addition to* racism, but sexism *in the context of* racism; thus, they cannot be said to bear an *additional* burden that white women do not bear;" instead, they "bear an altogether *different* burden from that borne by white women." Houston characterizes burdens as "multiple, interlocking oppressions" (49). Frances Harper, the nineteenth-century author, lecturer, and women's rights activist, was faced with this kind of burden when she announced to suffrage leaders that she supported the Fifteenth Amendment, which gave black men the vote but not women. She considered sex the lesser question (Stanton, Anthony, and Gage 391). In other words, sex became an issue for her only in the larger context of race. While less certain than she of the ranking of oppressions, I do want to acknowledge confliction. But I still hope that what Jerome Karabel, describing some of bell hooks's insights, calls "a shock of recognition" (27) will be evoked in others who read the following descriptions of classroom encounters, wherever they find themselves, and that it will stimulate future conversations and ultimately effect changes in classrooms and curricula.

Necessary Work

A legion of black women went into teaching before and after emancipation, responding to the need for literacy education in the North and South. In 1836, Mary Ann Shadd Cary, as staunch a feminist as she was an antislavery woman, opened a school for black children in Wilmington, Delaware, then settled in Canada West to teach black emigrants for the American Missionary Association; there she became the first black newspaperwoman, editing the *Provincial Freeman*. Susan Paul, daughter of a prominent minister, ran her own school for blacks in Boston in the 1830s. By 1837, Sarah Mapps Douglass had established a school in Philadelphia, which for a while provided the only opportunity for black women to receive a high school education. Frances Harper taught briefly before launching her career as an antislavery lecturer in 1854. In 1856, Charlotte Forten became the first black teacher of white children in Salem, Massachusetts; she later volunteered to teach free black men and women on the Sea Islands of South Carolina. Cooper, Cary, Paul, Douglass, Harper, and Forten are typical of the many nineteenth-century black women who not only chose a career in teaching but also helped establish schools. Teaching was considered a proper and highly respected profession for black women. According to Dorothy Sterling, most of these women were "northern born, middle class, single, and childless. Almost all were in their twenties, with an above-average education acquired at Oberlin, the Institutes for Colored Youth, or at normal schools near their homes; almost all had taught locally before going South" (263).

The wish that African American teachers in particular be hired for the work of literacy education is already apparent in the 1872 observations of one northern missionary, Charles Stearns. He argued, during Reconstruction, that black teachers were preferable because they would have faith in their students' ability to learn, the students would be more receptive to them, black teachers would understand the students' needs better, and black teachers would serve as role models (qtd. in Alexander 168–69). These advantages resonate today in requests to hire additional African American faculty members at predominantly white institutions, where too many students of color begin, but do not complete, their higher education. According to the

Journal of Blacks in Higher Education, "less than three quarters of black college freshman [enrolled in NCAA Division II and III schools] return to college for their sophomore year" ("Retention Rates").

Evidence of the response to this nineteenth-century call to racial uplift and self-help is clear in Fannie Barrier Williams's 1893 speech to the World's Congress of Representative Women:

> In twenty-five years, and under conditions discouraging in the extreme, thousands of our women have been educated as teachers. They have adapted themselves to the work of mentally lifting a whole race of people so eagerly and readily that they afford an apt illustration of the power of self-help. Not only have these women become good teachers in less than twenty-five years, but many of them are the prize teachers in the mixed schools of nearly every Northern city.   (109)

Such phrases as "prize teachers in the mixed schools" remind us that Williams spoke at a time when evidence of intellectual competence was required and offered explicitly. Similar evidence is perhaps no less necessary today, when phrases such as "bright black woman" are too frequently interjected oxymoronically into academic conversations.

Those pioneer teachers of literacy performed the same role that many writing teachers do today, who, Susan Miller reminds us, are hired to teach composition not to the "already entitled" but to the unentitled and those "only tentatively entitled to belong in higher education" ("Feminization" 45). While the early teachers were not necessarily preparing their students for higher education as it is now understood, they were preparing them for survival in a strange culture. The teaching of the unentitled and the tentatively entitled has been described as foundational, preparatory, preliterate, and, in the view of many today, is "distasteful but necessary cultural work" (46). In the euphoria of nineteenth-century post–Civil War America, blacks optimistically viewed this necessary cultural work as a means of preparing black people to take their place in American society.

A Necessary Presence

The early educators were teaching in settings quite different from those in which black women find themselves today. Most taught a range of courses; they taught not only reading and writing but also geography, Latin, Greek, and mathematics. Today's highly specialized classes satisfy the careerist students' demand for an immediate superficial relevance in every course. Semester offerings now include a proliferation of upper-level writing courses, such as business, technical, medical, and legal writing. Nineteenth-century black women largely taught students with little prior education, of all ages, hungry for knowledge. Black women today typically teach college students with a family tradition of education, in classes where women, too, are perceived as other. Unlike what we now call multicultural classrooms, where the teacher usually belongs to the majority culture, in the classroom under consideration here the students are predominantly white and the teacher is a woman of color.

Another difference between then and now is that today black women are not present in legions. According to the October 1994 survey report of the National Center for Education Statistics, as of fall 1992 only 2.8% of full-time faculty members in English and literature at accredited United States postsecondary institutions were identified as black non-Hispanic female. White males made up 45.2%, white females 45%, and black males 2.1% of the total (United States 14). Of part-time faculty members in English and literature, 2.6% were black female, .5% black male, 61% white female, and 29.5% white male. (The racial-ethnic categories of American Indian, Asian, and Hispanic completed the percentage distributions [16].) Unfortunately, the category of English and literature does not indicate how many primarily teach composition. We do know that roughly two-thirds of all composition teachers are female (S. Miller, "Feminization" 41). These percentages are not surprising. They are evidence of the "hegemonic compromise," about which Miller writes, "As statistics about who writes composition theory and who administers composition programs tell us, neither describing composition as a discipline nor asserting its equality has 'worked' on the actually gender-coded professional circumstances of those who teach writing" (49).

What is also clear is that few English faculty members are black and female, and few of those, if they are tenured or on a tenure track, are likely to teach composition, especially at predominantly white institutions where black women are seen as commodities too precious to use in this manner. (Departmental assumptions about what subject areas are valuable do not support such use.) But since writing takes place—or should take place—outside the traditional composition classroom, we can imagine this scenario: a black female teacher, white students, and students of color having conversations about writing.

In *Teaching to Transgress,* bell hooks recalls her experience as the black female teacher in such a setting. She points out that "the majority of students who enter our classrooms [in predominantly white institutions] have never been taught by black women professors. My pedagogy is informed by this knowledge, because I know from experience that this unfamiliarity can overdetermine what takes place in the classroom" (86). In another section of her book, she contrasts her estranged situation at a white institution with the normative classroom presence of a white male professor, whose casual dress and manner said that he was there "to be a mind and not a body," and she observes that only those in power have "the privilege of denying their body" (137). Describing her own efforts to apply the tenets of Paulo Freire's liberatory education to create an environment where all voices are respected, hooks learns that the professor cannot make a classroom exciting by her enthusiasm alone, especially when faced with this unfamiliarity. Discussions of the need to empower students in a multicultural classroom usually invoke images of the self-isolated students of color sitting in the corner eyeing their white teacher suspiciously or tentatively. But what of classes where most if not all students are white? To what extent might their views be suppressed because the class is taught by a woman of color? Cheryl Johnson calls this situation "the teacher as racial/gendered subject," in which the professor is perceived as a "representation of essentialized black womanhood" (410). The presence at the front of the room is read as a signal that now oral and written expressions of ideas may need to be suppressed lest they offend the person who will evaluate them. All too often my students submit stifled prose that sticks to stock responses to racial issues, issues that beg for critical consideration. The students perceive this kind of writing as safe for them because it is nonthreatening to me. The challenge for the teacher in such a class is to create an environment that encourages the free expression of ideas even when they may be unpopular. This situation is more than merely the opposite of white teacher versus student of color because the reversal of classroom roles by color no longer mirrors conventional societal hierarchies. Elizabeth Flynn reminds us that efforts to encourage women students in particular to write with power and authority can have only limited success because "individual classroom instructors are not sufficient to bring about powerful writing." She argues that "changes in the social and economic order must be made as well" ("Studies" 149). Societal constraints, along with the racial presence of the black female professor, surely limit that professor's attempts to empower her students as writers.

Writing and Outside Interference

The following descriptions of two classroom episodes are based on my experience as a black woman teaching courses in composition and rhetoric at a predominantly white university. They certainly do not represent the whole situation, or even the whole of my experience. And they should not be read exclusively as tales of what Houston refers to as the "triple jeopardy" of race, gender, and class (48)—and, in this instance, for class we should read academic discipline. Indeed, some may consider my affiliation with rhetoric and composition the greatest jeopardy, the second-class status of writing teachers having been well documented. But as the Anna Cooper epigraph to this essay implies, these jeopardies should perhaps be labeled differences instead, differences that can act as a force for change. Further, I hope that for my telling of my episodes I will not be given the essentialist label of the anthropological "native informant" who is presumed to speak for an entire group (hooks, *Teaching* 43).

In a course in advanced academic writing, some of my students had difficulty critiquing a section of "Letter from Birmingham Jail," by Martin Luther King, Jr., which I had assigned for rhetorical analysis. Enrolled in the class were students who had fulfilled the upper-level writing requirement and were seeking further writing instruction; English majors concentrating in language, writing, and rhetoric; and a few graduate students writing theses—all experienced writers. Thus I was especially disappointed to find their responses filled with glowing praise for King and his accomplishments. The students seemed reluctant to suggest that there was any flaw in the writing of a revered leader, reluctant even to support their praise with specific examples. Glowing but generalized praise often masks the condescension that denies a text serious critique. But I suspect that something more than condescension was operating here. Although we had studied various tactics of rhetorical analysis, I think that with King's letter there was too much external societal interference for these students. The difficulty they had with the assignment may have had nothing to do with the racial identity of the instructor, but generalized prose is common when race is involved. Perhaps they feared that any critical comments would be interpretéd as racist.

Describing a similar silence in a communication class during a discussion of "ethnic cultural differences among women," Houston concedes that her students' fear of saying the wrong thing was valid and adds that "in a society where racism, like sexism, remains pervasive, speaking in nonracist ways is difficult, especially when the topic is racial differences" (46). My students may well have been reacting to an instance of what hooks characterizes as unfamiliarity overdetermining the classroom environment. No doubt I could have better explained and modeled rhetorical analysis, a genre that challenges most students. I could have chosen a text by someone or about something less racial, less controversial. But surely, rather than keep silent, we need to engage in democratic conversations about divisive topics like race and gender, and in a variety of public spaces, especially in classes designed to enhance effective communication.

In another course on rhetorical theory, we listened to Fred Morsell's compelling recording of Frederick Douglass's well-known 1852 speech "What to the Slave Is the Fourth of July?" I then distributed copies of the speech and asked the class to identify some of its stylistic features as a way of applying an earlier reading of book 4 of the *Rhetorica ad Herennium*. In response, one female student wrote two dense pages in defense of America, stating that she didn't see why Douglass was complaining about the treatment of slaves. After all, she argued, the Irish immigrants had as many difficulties as the slaves, yet they overcame them. In conclusion she said that if people didn't like this country, they should not have come here. Her response indicated that she had not heard Douglass's speech at all but instead was reacting to contemporary reverberations emanating from the racial nature of the subject. This student had contributed little to class discussions, and her prior papers had not been particularly enthusiastic. Because of my nurturing pedagogical impulse, mixed generously with a lifetime of covert and overt suppression of my opinions, I made no negative comments, afraid that they would discourage the student's future participation.

Susan Jarratt addresses this problem in an essay on feminist pedagogy in the composition class. Stressing the need for a "more carefully theorized understanding of the multiple forms of power reproduced in the classroom," she points out that "differences of gender, race, and class among students and teachers provide situations in which conflict does arise, and we need more than the ideal of the harmonious, nurturing composition class in our repertory of teaching practices to deal with these problems" ("Feminism" 113). It would have been easy enough for me to point out to my student that she had not fulfilled the requirement of the assignment, that is, to identify selected tropes and their uses to persuade. The challenge I faced was to respond constructively to the paper she did write. In my written comments, I suggested that the arrival histories of the two groups—Irish Americans and African Americans—might account for the differences in the two groups' experiences. We met briefly after class to discuss her need to address the assignment. Trying to tap into and rechannel her interest in the speech, I suggested that she reexamine the speech to determine what specific language choices of Douglass might have elicited such a strong response in her. I invited her to make an appointment with me to talk further about how to do this as well as to talk about some of the objections she had raised to Douglass's arguments. She declined the opportunity to revise and chose instead to submit a stylistic analysis of another text, one that in her mind was less controversial.

Cheryl Johnson notes that as more multicultural texts are incorporated into the curriculum, some students may view them "as intrusions on their academic study and actually resent texts which explore racial, ethnic, gender, or religious differences" (411). Although to some extent texts have always explored difference, certainly the differences are embodied to a greater extent today in those who teach the texts. Should I have chased my student down the hallway or called her dorm to demand that she make an appointment? I had given the class a brief introduction to Douglass—most knew little about him—and reminded them that the event of his speech took place before the Civil War and emancipation; but perhaps I should have devoted a portion of a class session to a discussion of African American history. I chose to let my student decide how she wanted to respond to my evaluation of her essay. Her subsequent class participation increased considerably, even though the two of us never had our follow-up discussion of Douglass. True, the remaining course texts were not by or about African Americans. I was not entirely satisfied with the outcome but accepted my student's analysis of a substitute text. I saw in all this a small pedagogical victory, feeling that our encounter helped her realize that I was open to discussion about the *r* word. She was just not ready to have such a discussion with me. I was reminded that teaching, like learning, can never be a neutral act. As Sharon Crowley writes:

> We can look at our students as people who bring the discourses of their communities into the classroom with them. Their discourses are not always pleasant to hear and read, riddled as they may be with racism, sexism, and elitism. But we acknowledge students' languages as their own these days, more profoundly than we used to. And we don't deny the ugliness and alienation of the world outside the classroom anymore, and we don't kid ourselves that our classrooms are, or can be, warm huggy refuges from that world. ("Letter" 324–25)

Acknowledging Difference

In both the courses described above, an assignment asked white students and a sprinkling of students of color to give a critique of a text by an African American, a critique to be read and evaluated by their African American teacher. But black students face this situation in reverse—white author, white teacher—all the time, as they make their way through white institutions. It is interesting that many of my black students struggled with the same two assignments—perhaps for related racial reasons. After describing several black teacher–white student encounters in her literature class, Johnson cautions:

> What may be erroneously suggested here is that the relationship between a black professor and black students would be harmonious because both, supposedly, locate themselves culturally, socially, politically, historically, and intellectually at an all-encompassing black / African-American site. If such a location exists, it is a tentative and unsteady one, affected by time and place of encounter. In other words, there is no fixed African-American ideology; black students may inscribe one or more various, sometimes conflicting, codes onto the body of the black professor such as Afrocentricism, black nationalism, womanism, feminism, assimilation, or other perspectives arising from each student's subjectivity.   (416)

The periodicals *College English, College Composition and Communication, Teaching English in the Two-Year College,* and the *Journal of Advanced Composition* have all featured articles on white students and students of color developing voice in the college classroom.[1] Indeed, the role of race and gender in the teaching of writing needs to be studied from a variety of perspectives. I have been focusing here on just one perspective: black professors, especially black women professors, trying to create in multicultural contexts an environment where students, especially women students, can comfortably express opinions. If we do not consider strategies for constructive critique of the opinions put forth in this triply complex convergence of gender, race, and class, then, as hooks writes, we will "engage in a form of social amnesia in which we forget that all knowledge is forged in conflict" (*Teaching* 31). If we desire peace and harmony in the classroom instead of welcoming dissent, we will be dancing around or smoothing over important issues. In a composition class, where a writer's well-argued opinions often constitute the content, students and teachers may avoid topics that are controversial. It becomes safe to discuss only the "them" not represented in the classroom. We need to devise ways to speak the unspeakable, to talk about and have students write about issues surrounding race and gender, in composition classrooms and in all classrooms.

Joyce Middleton describes a series of "introductory class rituals." To establish a framework for discussion, she "asks students to question unchallenged assumptions about race, literacy, and teaching" (104) and helps them develop a vocabulary for talking about those assumptions. At the beginning of one semester, Middleton had her students read two contrasting texts and discuss some of the issues they raised. One text was an editorial from a local newspaper, filled with "unchallenged racial stereotypes" and "ridiculous analogies" (104). She chose a blatantly racist text to unify the class against material that they would all agree was biased. The second text was an essay by bell hooks in which it is argued that love of blackness is a form of resistance against racism. During the discussion of this piece, tensions emerged as the class struggled with the notion of loving blackness without rejecting whiteness. As a final opening strategy, Middleton had the class work its way through a list of concrete but invisible white privileges. This exercise shed light on hooks's essay. Middleton's framework establishing helped students understand what is involved in unlearning racism. A black woman teaching at a predominantly white university, Middleton employed an up-front approach to the unspeakable, which seemed especially appropriate for that course's subsequent readings. Such an approach can reduce the anxiety produced by unfamiliarity.

Concern for helping students develop voice and authority in the writing classroom should not lead teachers to abdicate their positions as writing experts. But there is a great difference between a teacher who is an authority in the subject matter and one who squelches ideas. I believe that all students have strong opinions about most things and that they will not be afraid to express them in an encouraging environment. Yet many lack the argumentative skills needed to support their opinions and the adaptive skills needed to address different audiences. The students who wrote extended King encomiums instead of the assigned rhetorical critiques may have considered themselves skillful accommodationists, carefully adapting text to audience. The student in the second classroom episode clearly had strong opinions but needed more practice in connecting argument to evidence—and in retrieving accurate evidence. Critiquing the open-classroom movement of the eighties, Lisa Delpit speaks of the continuing need to teach skills "within the context of critical and creative thinking" (384). I am not opposed to teaching skills along with helping students express ideas and find voice. It may be that our students need skills more than ideas. We won't always change their opinions—and perhaps we should not— but we certainly have a responsibility to teach them how to express those opinions and to challenge the assumptions that support them. A facility with language may be the most liberating pedagogy we can offer.

Black women are especially challenged to teach communication skills in settings where they must often first overcome resistance to their very presence. But hooks suggests that rather than attempt to deny identity, we take a closer look at "the presence of teacher as body in the classroom, the presence of the teacher as someone who has a total effect on the development of the student, not just an intellectual effect but an effect on how that student perceives reality beyond the classroom" (*Teaching* 136). A step is surely taken toward achieving our goal of helping students become more effective written communicators when in designing our courses and assignments we pay attention to the interaction among teacher, student, and subject matter in a variety of multicultural contexts. Fine-tuned "introductory class rituals" like those described by Middleton, establishing the appropriate framework for teaching and learning, would also discourage the sort of evasive writing that my students produced. Jarratt sees these "collisions of gender, race, and class" as opportunities for improving pedagogy: "Recognizing the inevitability of conflict is not ground for despair but the starting point for creating a consciousness in students and teachers through which the inequalities generating those conflicts can be acknowledged and transformed" ("Feminism" 119).

Difference can be a force for change. Yet it would be naive to think that the simple presence of a black female teacher guarantees change. Taking exception to hooks's characterization of the movement toward multicultural pedagogy as "tantamount to a revolution," Tom Fox reminds us:

> There's a danger in thinking of multiculturalism as a revolution that has already occurred. The small changes toward more inclusiveness and diversity in our curriculum and pedagogy don't seem anything like a revolution. And even those small changes are in danger of backsliding into monoculturalism. . . . Actually there's been minuscule success in hiring people of color in universities across the country, baby steps toward a more inclusive, more constructive curriculum, pedagogical changes only by a

tiny few, and only a slight increase in the representation of students of color in higher education.   (567)

Still, it is certainly worth exploring and exploiting Anna Cooper's claim that black women enter uncharted territory with the unique and valuable perspective of their race and gender, especially in a time when achieving gender, racial, and communicative equality is critical.

NOTE

[1]See, for example, Gary Olson's interview with hooks; Terry Dean's "Multicultural Classrooms, Monocultural Teachers"; and *Teaching English in the Two-Year College* 21. 2 (1994), a special issue on multiculturalism in the writing classroom, edited by Frederic Gale.

Interrupting Our Way to Agency: Feminist Cultural Studies and Composition

Nedra Reynolds

Feminist writing teachers have long been concerned with questions of empowerment for women students. How can we help them "come to voice," both in a classroom setting, where they will feel comfortable enough to speak, and in their reading and writing, where they will not be silenced by the masculinist codes of academic discourse? This issue becomes even more complicated when postmodern theories of language and subjectivity enter the feminist composition classroom. Postmodernism poses a keen problem for composition, particularly when agency or an active writing subject is involved. Rebecca Moore Howard succinctly explains, "In postmodern[ism]..., the subject does not 'possess' agency, cannot simply 'choose' roles and discourse communities. What, then, would be the point of composition instruction, which attempts to foster control over the writing process or the ensuing written texts?" (349).

Along with many other feminists and a number of composition theorists, I want to resist versions of postmodernism that deny agency to the subject and leave it fractured or dispersed—unable to "foster control" over writing or discourse.[1] Feminists need a concept of agency in order to work and hope for social change; writers need a concept of agency in order to write a page, make a claim, or extend an idea. A number of composition workers are struggling with the challenge of theorizing a postmodern agent, one not limited to modernist or essentialist notions of the writer but one not incapable, either, of action or choice.[2]

The definition of agency that I am working with here includes the poststructuralist concept of multiple and competing subjectivities while also allowing for the possibility of "resistance to ideological

58

pressure" (P. Smith xxxv). Agents are not exactly autonomous, self-aware individuals of the Enlightenment, but they are nevertheless "capable of making their own history" (Trimbur "Cultural Studies" 5). Agents are those who "[speak] as an equal to an authority figure," "[dare] to disagree" (hooks, *Talking* 5), and are bold and defiant in their speech (9). Agency is not simply about finding one's own voice but also about intervening in discourses of the everyday and cultivating rhetorical tactics that make interruption and resistance an important part of any conversation.

My essay explores how interruption, a familiar feature of spoken conversation, might contribute to a theory of agency for women writers. Feminist scholars in philosophy, psychology, linguistics, and, most recently, cultural studies have studied the ways that women's identities or locations function in women's reading and writing practices. In her book *Sexing the Self: Gendered Positions in Cultural Studies*, Elspeth Probyn explores "how we can use our sexed selves in order to engender alternative feminist positions in discourse" (1). Seeking a "tactical rhetoric" to ground discursive practices in materiality and in the everyday, Probyn uses Michel de Certeau's distinction between strategy and tactics, where tactics is "the space of the other . . . [and] an art of the weak" (qtd. in Probyn 86–87). Strategies are institutional, operating from a base to calculate or manipulate power relationships, whereas tactics can occur "in 'the absence of a proper locus,'" in the midst of shifting practices and marginal or multiple sites (87). Interruption might become part of a tactical rhetoric for marginalized speakers and writers—those who are often interrupted routinely as well as those who do not speak or write from a single location.

Interruption has often been interpreted as rude behavior, especially for women and children. In some linguistics research, interruptions are defined as "violations of the turn-taking rules of conversation" that break "the symmetry of the conversational model" (Coates, *Women* 99). Despite the cultural stereotype of women as the talkative sex, sociolinguistic research has demonstrated that most interruptions occur in mixed-sex conversations and that men interrupt women far more than they interrupt one another (Spender, *Language* 43–50). Jennifer Coates summarizes some of the findings: "In mixed-sex conversations men infringe women's right to speak, specifically women's right to finish a turn. Conversely, the fact that women used no overlaps in conversations with men . . . suggests that women are concerned *not* to violate the man's turn" (*Women* 99–101). (Deborah Tannen casts interruption in a more positive light, as supportive overlap that defines a "high-involvement" speaking style [*You* 53–74].) Because being interrupted usually causes the first speaker to fall silent, women in conversations with men are often silenced.

Unexpected interruptions, defined as either breaks or overlaps, by their suddenness or surprise factor force others to pay attention. Many a large-family child learns the lesson of interruption, and that the way to be heard is to talk louder, and if that doesn't work, to shout! Although butting in and yelling louder than anyone else may not be strategies that endure—their effectiveness may be limited to kairotic moments—they can sometimes be satisfactorily interventionist. Through interruption and talking back, women rhetors can draw attention to their identities as marginalized speakers and writers as they also force more attention to the ideological workings of discursive exclusion.

Cultural studies provides an apt beginning for my exploration of interruption and agency. At the Centre for Contemporary Cultural Studies (CCCS) at the University of Birmingham, women's productive interruption occurred in direct response to certain events and exclusionary practices. When their work on gender issues was excluded or marginalized, women associated with the CCCS developed tactics for resistance and opposition: a means toward agency. Cultural studies therefore provides both a specific site of interruption (the Birmingham center) and a set of texts that illustrate interruption in oral and written form. Working from Stuart Hall's metaphor of theory as interruption, I locate interruptive acts of asserting agency in the work of several feminist writers in cultural studies. Feminists who broke into the (male) discourses of cultural studies to take issue with the exclusion of feminism managed to shift the agenda of cultural studies, and their success has been credited with "radically alter[ing] the terrain of Cultural Studies" (Hall, "Centre" 39).

Cultural Studies: Theories of Interruption

A growing number of literary and composition scholars advocate cultural studies as a way of reformulating English studies, but feminists need to interrupt with the reminder that from its earliest days cultural studies has been a distinctly male enterprise and still rests on a canon of works by men: Raymond Williams, Richard Hoggart, E. P. Thompson, Paul Willis, Dick Hebdige, Lawrence Grossberg, Stuart Hall. As bell hooks points out, cultural studies programs "are most always administered by white men" (*Yearning* 125), and issues of race and gender have been secondary, to say the least, in the evolution of cultural studies.

To "break in" to the work of the CCCS, feminists and others had to interrupt its everyday practices and to insist on the legitimacy of their contributions. Three accounts of this transgression come from one of the major male figures on the scene, Stuart Hall, who explains the feminist disruption of the CCCS and feminism's role in cultural studies with metaphors of theory as intervention or disruption. Hall writes about the development of cultural studies as well as about key events in the CCCS that kept interrupting previous or current theoretical work. He traces the genealogy of cultural studies through Hoggart, Thompson, and Williams and their "seminal" texts, which interrupted traditional, old-left Marxism and broke away from institutionalized sociology. Guided by a new definition of culture, the "'culturalist' strand in Cultural Studies was [then] interrupted by the arrival on the scene of the 'structuralisms'"—that is, by the impact of Claude Lévi-Strauss, Louis Althusser, and ideological critique ("Two Paradigms" 64).[3]

Hall claims—in terms reminiscent of Thomas Kuhn and Richard Rorty—that in intellectual work

> what is important are the significant breaks—where old lines of thought are disrupted, older constellations displaced, and elements, old and new, are regrouped around a different set of premises and themes. . . . It is because of this complex articulation between thinking and historical reality, . . . and the continuous dialectic between "knowledge" and "power," that the breaks are worth recording. (57)

Hall asserts that cultural studies constitutes such a break, a break with "the great inadequacies, the resounding silences, the great evasions of Marxism" ("Legacies" 279). Cultural studies interrupted Marxism with a series of contestations: about Marxism's base-and-superstructure metaphor, about the question of false consciousness, and about Marxism's profoundly Eurocentric tradition. By struggling with the problematic of Marxism—Hall calls it "wrestling with the angels"—British cultural studies began its search "to find an institutional practice . . . that might produce an organic intellectual" in Antonio Gramsci's sense (281). Intellectual work proceeds and ideas take hold, according to Hall, through disruption, contestation, wrestling, struggle.

Just as cultural studies of the 1950s broke with the economic, base-superstructure model of Marxism, feminism of the 1970s made a crucial break in the class-bound research of the CCCS. According to Hall, "feminism has provoked a break with any residual attempt to give the term 'material conditions' an exclusively economistic or 'productivist' meaning. . . . It has displaced forever any exclusive reference to class contradictions as the stable point of reference for cultural analysis" (" Centre" 38). In his narrative of the evolution of cultural studies, Hall values the tension that gives cultural studies a richness but that also makes it a site of contention and difficulty. His metaphor of theory as disruption, then, characterizes the workings of the CCCS and cultural studies, where nothing proceeded smoothly or without debate.

In his essay "Cultural Studies and Its Theoretical Legacies," Hall uses a metaphor of theory as noise and speaks autobiographically about the "bad feeling, argument, unstable anxieties, and angry silences" that accompanied the theoretical work of the center (278). Two of the noisiest interventions were concerns of gender and race, and feminism provided an "opportunity" for Hall and other men to discover "the gendered nature of power" (283). Despite his intention to commend the role of feminism, however, a close reading of the following brief passage reveals uncommending metaphors at work in his account of the relation between feminism and cultural studies: "It's not known generally how and where feminism first broke in. I use the metaphor deliberately: As the thief in the night, it broke in; interrupted, made an unseemly noise, seized the time, crapped on the table of cultural studies" (282).

Hall's purpose here is to further his "metaphor for theory: the way feminism broke, and broke into, cultural studies" (283). But what is disturbing to feminist readers is that Hall characterizes this theoretically positive disruption in terms of bodily functions, farting and crapping, and likens any radical alterations to those of soiling or staining. A table—an item that usually marks a center of activity or production—might be littered with food, papers, coffee cups, and other signs of work or daily life. To crap on that table means ruining or defiling the work being done—not forwarding or transforming it. In addition, while noise can mean a great many things, here it seems to contrast specifically with silence: gender and race were noisy because they were not quiet.

Making unseemly noises and messes is a strikingly visceral image for discursive intervention—and a quite different portrayal of the way in which Williams, Hoggart, and Thompson interrupted the mainstream work of Marxism. While those in the New Left "wrestled with angels," feminism was farting in the polite parlor of cultural studies (and I doubt if this is what Gramsci meant by "organic" intellectual). These images read women either as infantile, incapable of controlling their bodily functions, or as rude, ignoring the social conventions.

In addition, Hall's use of "it" as the thief who broke in collapses the actual women involved to a singular object, a unified body. Accounts of the evolution of cultural studies almost always name the founding fathers. Here, however, the women are not named; they are lumped together in a pack—like thieves or wolves. Rude women, then, are denied agency, despite Hall's acknowledgment that feminism radically altered the terrain.

The contradiction is a keen one: Hall wants to value theory as disruption and to acknowledge the ruptures; but if the interruption of feminism is tantamount only to a crap on a table, then his celebration of ruptures refers only to the contributions of men. Such interruption depends on exclusion and domination, on the genesis of cultural studies as the work of British males. Richard Johnson, in fact, objects to Hall's version when he asserts that it is "incorrect to see feminism or anti-racism as some kind of interruption or diversion from an original class politics and its associated research programme. On the contrary, it is these movements that have kept the new left new" (40). While I agree with Johnson, I want to do more than simply dismiss as incorrect Hall's version of interruption; I want to examine how feminist writers have put the idea of interruption into practice.

Feminist Interruptions: Examples of Agency

The pack of women who broke into the CCCS were frustrated by their relegation to the Women's Studies Group, established in 1974 as a response to the isolation two or three women felt in working at the center with about twenty men (Women's Studies Group 11). After ten issues of the journal *Working Papers in Cultural Studies* had appeared, containing only four articles that concerned women, the Women's Studies Group thought it time to try to overcome "women's continuing 'invisibility' in the journal and in much of the intellectual work done within CCCS" (7). These women broke into the publishing end of the center's work and, as Hall describes it, "took over that year's book and initiated a quarrel" ("Legacies" 282).

Taking over that year's book did not happen, of course, without their presenting their case to the CCCS. The introduction to this volume—*Women Take Issue*—outlines their effort to intervene in the CCCS's work and the obstacles they faced. Their success came only when "the CCCS *let* [*them*] do this book" (Women's Studies Group 14; emphasis added). Permission was granted because these feminist researchers were able to prove that their research on women's oppression was sufficiently theoretical and thoroughly economic in its analysis. The results of the interruption were not immediate, but they have been productive.

One of the most productive interventionist feminists associated with the CCCS is Angela McRobbie, who sees the importance of her work as a turn "to the terrain of domestic life," especially for an understanding of femininity and female youth culture (*Feminism* xvii). Her essay "Settling Accounts with Subcultures: A Feminist Critique" is a forceful interruption of the center's concern with class, to the exclusion of gender and race. McRobbie points out that both Paul Willis (*Learning to Labour*) and Dick Hebdige (*Subculture*) fail to use gender as a category of analysis in their studies of working-class boys. "Youth" becomes, metonymically, "male," and neither author acknowledges the ideological construction of masculinity; Hebdige's usage of style, for example, "structurally excludes women" (25). But McRobbie resists simply dismissing these works or "cataloguing the 'absences'"; her purpose, rather, is to do a feminist rereading of these books, to question the extent to which "patriarchial meanings" shape youth subculture for both sexes (25).

The masculinist tradition in cultural studies research—marked by the emphasis on class rather than on gender or race—has left many spaces that need interruption. McRobbie's work prompted others (e.g., Canaan) to reexamine studies of youth subcultures by male sociologists. In addition, the successor volume to *Women Take Issue*, tellingly titled *Off-Centre*, illustrates that feminist work continues to resist the center of the center (Franklin, Lury, and Stacey). By working in subgroups rather than in the mainstream and by participating in collective action, these women recognize the power that a marginal, or off-center, position can yield.

Feminists in more recent years have continued to interrupt the normal discourse of cultural studies by drawing attention to all forms of silencing and then linking the silencing to ideological structures of racism and sexism. *Cultural Studies*, a collection of papers read at the 1990 University of Illinois Conference on Cultural Studies, includes transcripts of the question-and-answer periods following several of the presentations (Grossberg, Nelson, and Treichler). Reading these transcripts gives a great deal of insight into the conference itself; readers who did not attend it can detect some of the "contentiousness" that Hall says is so characteristic of cultural studies ("Legacies" 278).

In these *Cultural Studies* transcripts are powerful instances of inter-ruption, especially by bell hooks, who refuses to participate in the sta-tus quo of most academic conferences. Hooks states, "[the Illinois conference] seems to me to be so much a mirroring of the very kinds of hierarchies that terrorize and violate. The problem is that we can't even dialogue in this space. The challenge to us here is to try and dis-rupt and subvert and change that and not just to sit here and be pas-sively terrorized" (discussion participant; Grossberg, Nelson, and Treichler 171). Later in the volume, after Alexandra Chasin voices her objection to the silencing mechanisms of the conference (293), hooks clarifies: "When I talk about being terrorized, I wasn't talking about the room, or the microphones; I was talking about how the discourse of cultural studies as it was being constructed here was silencing cer-tain kinds of people" (293–94). Hooks's interruptions are an attempt to force conference participants to acknowledge the contradiction be-tween their desire for change and their inept ways of making change happen, a contradiction she identifies in *Talking Back*: "Intellectual radicals who speak about transforming society . . . cannot break with behavior patterns that reinforce and perpetuate domination" (77).

Hooks provides abundant examples of enacting effective tactics and of helping feminists, as Probyn puts it, "elaborate ways of tactically speaking in strategic loci" (87). In her speaking and writing practices, hooks connects her experience and identity with ideological structures of exclusion and marginalization. "Terror" is what she experienced in a white world, where crossing the clear black-white boundaries of her Kentucky hometown meant confronting "that terrifying whiteness" (*Yearning* 41). For hooks, living in a segregated world meant continual anxiety about safety, and that anxiety has given her a way of analyzing the world that startles people, especially white middle-class academics who have never known terror. For hooks, language is a source of ter-ror when it is used against those who cannot talk back. At the conclu-sion of her paper included in *Cultural Studies*, she writes:

Attending a recent conference on cultural studies, . . . I was dis-turbed when the usual arrangements of white supremacist hier-archy were mirrored both in terms of who was speaking, of how bodies were arranged on the stage, of who was in the audience, of what voices were deemed worthy to speak and be heard. As the conference progressed I began to feel afraid. . . . I talked openly about that sense of terror. Later, I heard stories of white women joking about how ludicrous it was for me to say I felt terrorized. (345)

Hooks's interruptions at the conference and in the published text provide one model for emulation, especially in such places as academic conferences, where the physical surroundings—a dais and rows of chairs—imply a hierarchial, one-sided distribution of knowledge and where much of the conversation is inaccessible to those who are the subjects of cultural studies discourse and other intellectual research: for example, working-class youth, romance readers, students. As hooks illustrates, when the mechanisms of cultural studies become responsible for silencing the voices of marginalized others, then cultural studies is obliged to address that exclusion.

The Women's Studies Group interrupted the class-bound research of the center, and hooks interrupted the Illinois conference. Both interruptions began as speech acts, but they were recorded and became written examples of interruption. Such examples are growing increasingly common as postmodernism and cultural studies, to name just two influences, have forced white liberal feminists to confront essentialism and the problem of representation—of speaking for others. Feminists daring to criticize other feminists have opened up spaces for analyzing difference; they interrupted the discourses of feminism in the singular to make possible feminism in the plural.[4] When feminists dare to interrupt one another in public places, the risks are very real. When their interruptions occur in texts that are published and widely disseminated as critique, the consequences deepen. Within these risky spaces, however, writing agents find opportunities.

Interrupting Conversations in Composition

Following through on the implications of feminist agency means, for me, finding specific conversations in composition studies where it is necessary to interrupt a troubling inattention to the influence of feminist theory and politics—conversations that are the result of recent encounters between (male) composition scholars and the discourses of both cultural studies and postmodernism. My act of feminist interruption is not simply "to make the rather dreary charge that [these men are] insufficiently aware of feminism" (Wicke 15). Some of the most important voices in composition today—James Berlin, John Trimbur, and Lester Faigley—have a tendency to ignore work in feminism that might complement or complicate their ideas. Despite the collective efforts of these key figures in composition studies to engage with ideology, history, and difference, they miss opportunities to examine how discourses of postmodernism and cultural studies might work to exclude women and how their own locations for agency are not necessarily locations where women can be heard.

Both Berlin and Trimbur have introduced readers in composition to cultural studies by outlining the convergences and shared interests of the two areas; they note, for example, that both fields are interested in understanding the workings of institutional ideology, in developing demystifying strategies to promote critique and encourage resistance to forms of oppression, and in improving reading and writing practices. Most important, Berlin and Trimbur acknowledge the role of the individual as an agent of change (Berlin, "Composition Studies" 103; Trimbur, "Composition Studies" 130). But their work generally sees agency through a Marxist lens, where issues of work, class, and labor have traditionally dominated to the exclusion of gender analysis. This bias reveals itself in their representations or explanations of cultural studies and the Birmingham center, which make no mention of conflict or the struggle for power. It also reveals itself in their lists of works cited, where feminist scholarship in both cultural and composition studies is glaringly absent. Notable exclusions are Susan Miller's "The Feminization of Composition," Linda Brodkey's study of class and gender in "The Literacy Letters" ("Subjects"), and Sue Ellen Holbrook's labor analysis in "Women's Work: The Feminizing of Composition."[5]

Berlin wrote a number of articles on the intersections of cultural studies and composition, emphasizing the "mutually enriching" possibilities for the two fields, where "our problematics are finally similar and thoroughly compatible" ("Composition Studies" 100). In two of these essays, he refers to Richard Johnson's "What Is Cultural Studies Anyway?," arguing that in any cultural studies approach the entire cycle, or "circuit," of cultural production and consumption must be acknowledged. Berlin says that it is not enough for us to concentrate on the production of ideological images (in the media, for example). We must also analyze the point of consumption: the site where negotiation and resistance are most likely to take place. In his own cultural studies approach, however, Berlin does little more than include a gender unit in his suggested syllabus, and he misses an obvious question about his pedagogical practice: How does the syllabus position women students, especially on a male-dominated, engineering campus like Purdue, when it asks them to read an article about cowboys?[6]

In their introduction to *Cultural Studies in the English Classroom*, which is aimed at a wide readership, Berlin and Michael Vivion portray cultural studies as "tough to pin down" but not as a site of conflict (viii). Introducing readers to their curriculum-centered book, Berlin and Vivion reiterate the usual cultural-structuralist trajectory without mentioning the feminist intervention at the Birmingham center. Only one contributor to their volume acknowledges the role of feminism in the formation of cultural studies: Anne Balsamo argues that the tendency to overlook "the historically specific feminist intervention into cultural studies" becomes "a critical oversight in the recent turn to cultural studies in the United States where the multiplicitous identity of cultural studies is celebrated to the exclusion of its concrete historical specificity" (150).

The exclusion of historical specificity is evident in Trimbur's treatment of cultural studies, despite his commitments to historicizing. The first to articulate the possibilities that cultural studies holds for composition, Trimbur says in 1988 that composition has ignored "the simple fact that teaching writing takes place conjuncturally, in a history we are not free to determine, in concrete settings" ("Cultural Studies" 13). He states that the teaching of writing "must be located historically" and that we need to "see the emergence of composition studies historically," linked to "the struggle for popular and critical literacy" (14). At the forefront of composition's New Left direction, Trimbur is not usually one to ignore history or to downplay dissensus, yet he commits the very oversight that Balsamo warns against: he presents the history of cultural studies to readers in composition—who in 1988 were largely unfamiliar with it—without acknowledging the conflicts and battles of its development. Such a conflict-free narrative would be like writing a history of modern composition studies without noting the struggle for its legitimacy and acceptance that took place in many English departments. Berlin and Trimbur simply do not acknowledge the radical changes wrought by feminism's intervention into cultural studies, I think because they followed the rhetorical pattern of so many cultural studies narratives, which walk neatly through the "seminal" texts of the all-male trinity of Hoggart, Williams, and Thompson.[7]

Postmodernism has had a much less chronological development than cultural studies has; it is nevertheless difficult to find feminist engagements with postmodernism represented in the work of Berlin and Trimbur. For example, in his article "Composition Studies: Postmodern or Popular," Trimbur is cautious about seeing postmodernism "as a theoretical breakthrough" (118). Along with many feminists, he is concerned that "the overriding sense of contingency in postmodernism can dissolve the rhetor into a function instead of the agent of discourse" (119). Trimbur follows the art critic Hal Foster's distinction between reactionary postmodernism and resistant postmodernism, but he fails to note any of the feminists who have also resisted post-modernism (122).

If Trimbur recommends cultural studies as one way to retain agency (130), Lester Faigley recommends the work of Jean-Francois Lyotard as one possibility for an ethical writing agent. Faigley's award-winning book *Fragments of Rationality: Postmodernity and the Subject of Composition* constructs a convincing argument that composition studies, in its firm modernist foundation, has managed to resist the implications of postmodern theories. Faigley represents postmodernism through feminist contributions and articulations (Jane Flax, bell hooks, Iris Young) much more than do Berlin and Trimbur, but his heavy reliance on Lyotard throughout the book proves troublesome for feminist readers and rhetors. First, Lyotard's war on totality and his argument to eliminate metanarratives leaves women without a totalizing theory of patriarchy or a way of analyzing global oppression (Ebert, "Difference"). Second, Lyotard's insistence on the agonistics of discourse raises immediate questions about women's access to the parry and thrust of academic argument. Finally, with his concluding paragraphs, Faigley reinscribes the authoritative signifier of the Euro-centric male.

To accept Lyotard as "the norm for postmodernism," as Faigley often seems to do, means to ignore the "radically different notions of politics in postmodernism" (Ebert, "Difference" 898, 887). The feminist theorist Teresa Ebert situates Lyotard in ludic postmodernism—roughly, where language is play and signifiers are free-floating—rather than in resistance postmodernism, where language is social struggle (887). Lyotard's project of eliminating totality is problematic for feminists, who must struggle against the totalizing effects of patriarchy, against the celebration of pluralism and the local that does not include analysis of "the global relations of patriarchial oppression" (902).[8]

Lyotard informs much of Faigley's chapter "The Networked Classroom," in which the on-line discussions of Faigley's students challenge our liberal notions of the classroom as a site of consensus and community. Interpreting the transcripts of those discussions, Faigley explains Lyotard's view of conversation as "inherently agonistic," his view that "to speak is to fight" (185). Faigley goes on to narrate instances of hostility in his classroom and the alarming aggressiveness of the comments, especially when male students outnumber female students (189). Even if we agree with Lyotard that, in Faigley's paraphrase, "agonistics is the inevitable condition of everyday life where . . . the best we can do is allow everyone to speak," much more needs to be done to provide women and other marginalized speakers with the tactics necessary to participate in that discourse arena (Faigley 199). In Lyotard's language games, therefore, where phrases are constantly in dispute, linkages are absent, and all discourses are incommensurable; the metaphor of argument as war remains dominant, making male rhetors raised in a patriarchial culture much more comfortable with agonistic discourse than female rhetors are (see Lakoff and Johnson 4–6).

The conclusion of Faigley's *Fragments* concentrates almost exclusively on Lyotard. The culmination of the book, unfortunately, rests on a single male figure instead of being dispersed among the number of fragments that appear throughout the book—the voices of students on *InterChange*, for example. (*InterChange* is a conferencing program designed for synchronous online discussion by several participants.) While Faigley also acknowledges criticism of Lyotard (238), his conclusion centers composition's sense of ethical agency on an authority that is endowed by the birthright of gender and the tradition of philosophy.

Collectively, Berlin, Trimbur, and Faigley have charted important new territory in composition studies, and they would probably agree that criticizing one another is a vital part of "the intersection of critique and utopian possibility" that a cultural studies informed by postmodernism might occupy (Trimbur, "Cultural Studies" 12). However, because these influential male scholars in composition have such power to shape the direction of the field, the need to interrupt them becomes even more urgent.

Interruption and Agency

Hall's metaphor of theory as interruption offers possibilities for exploring agency, but his narrative of women's contributions to cultural studies makes interruption only an "unseemly noise." By linking women's interruption with belching or farting, Hall diminishes the political potential of interruption while also minimizing the risk it involves. But interrupting patriarchial discourses holds far greater risk than transgressing a point of etiquette does. For hooks as a young girl, it meant punishment, ridicule, even the threat of being declared mad, "the destiny of daring women born to intense speech" (*Talking Back* 7). Women who interrupt may be hit, lose their jobs, or be punished in a number of insidious ways.

If we work, however, to "elaborate ways of tactically speaking in strategic loci," we may be able to situate interruption in a larger tacti-cal rhetoric that emphasizes everyday acts of public discourse. Inter-ruptions define the daily lives of working women who must negotiate second shifts, child care, and sometimes blurry divisions between self and other, between work and home, as they try to join conversations or concentrate on acts of reading and writing. The practical question remains, then (as it always does): How? How can women and other marginalized speakers and writers interrupt the very discourses and practices that exclude or diminish them? How can a theory of interruption help feminist rhetors analyze the workings of discursive exclusion?

Interruption is most effective in the spaces where physical presence heightens the effect—at conferences, in classrooms, around tables. Those of us who teach writing or women's studies classes have the op-portunity to discuss interruption directly—to share with students the research of linguistics, to analyze the possibilities for shifting power, and to encourage women and other students to interrupt the domi-nant (usually male) members of the class. We can also model interrup-tion for students, both as a tactic of resistance and as overlapping support for a speaker.

Despite the obvious role of interruption in oral discourse, it seems necessary in the academy to pursue the implications of this tactic in written discourse as well. Feminists in composition studies might want to investigate the kinds of interruption possible in written texts and the reader-writer relationship. Such investigation might lead to a cultivation of postmodernism-inspired discourses that offer other forms of participating in intellectual and political discussions besides the formal essay or written Standard English (the *InterChange* tran-scripts Faigley provides are an excellent example of another form). We need to offer students more and greater means of resistance to the thesis-driven essay, rigidly structured paragraphing, and the reductive emphasis on coherence and clarity that still determine so much of aca-demic writing and the service-course ideology of composition pro-grams. For composition we need to rethink radically the forms of writing we find acceptable. The result might be the breakdown of some of the rigid boundaries that separate life and politics inside and outside the academy.

Those of us working at the intersection of feminism and composi-tion can explore, without enforcing either silence or complicity, how interruption emphasizes discontinuities. Interruption, contributing to a cultural studies emphasis on the everyday, resisting theories of sub-jectivity that diminish action or choice, and negotiating between speech and writing, offers a tactical, practical means toward discursive agency.

NOTES

[1]Feminists who offer reasons for resisting postmodernism are Ebert; Wicke and Ferguson; Morris (11–23). See also Giroux ("Modernism" 2–3, 19–22). A composition theorist who resists some versions of postmodernism is Trimbur ("Composition Studies").

[2]For discussions of modernist or essentialist notions of the writer, see Brodkey ("Modernism"); Clifford; Faigley, especially 13–20 and 156–62; S. Miller, *Carnivals* 84–104. Mortensen and Kirsch's Braddock-award-winning article on authority and agency in composition offers a dialogic model of authority informed by an ethics of care. Ewald and Wallace focus on agency in the classroom in a hermeneutic study that interprets classroom discourse about a specific incident. See also Howard.

[3]Hall explains that the culturalist strand began with the work of Williams, Hoggart, and Thompson, which glorified the "low," especially the working classes, and moved the definition of culture away from great art toward the everyday. The structuralist strand, which interrupted culturalism, was based primarily on the work of Lévi-Strauss and caused a turn to analyses of ideology and hegemony.

[4]In her essay on *Hustler* magazine the feminist Laura Kipnis dares to criticize other feminists, pointing out that in Robin Morgan's radical feminist stance on pornography there is no ability or effort to acknowledge the specificity of class location. "Has feminism," Kipnis asks, "in arrogating porn as its own privileged object, foreclosed on other questions?" (373–74). She charges that "anti-porn feminism lapses into bourgeois reformism" (389). Bell hooks criticizes another feminist when she points out lapses in Meaghan Morris's often-cited bibliography of feminists "doing" postmodernism (Morris 17–23), noting especially that "there are no references to works by black women" (*Yearning* 24).

[5]Arabella Lyon suggested, in her presentation at the 1994 CCCC, that feminists should begin counting the citations of women's scholarship in the bibliographies of published texts—and then refuse to cite the work of men who ignore feminist work. If feminists do count the citations by Berlin and Trimbur of women's scholarship, they won't find more than one or two.

[6]The article on cowboys is offered as an example of a cultural studies approach in two of Berlin's essays, "Poststructuralism, Cultural Studies, and the Composition Classroom: Postmodern Theory in Practice" and "Poststructuralism, Semiotics, and Social-Epistemic Rhetoric: Converging Agendas."

[7]The trinity trajectory shows up in all three of the Hall essays, to one degree or another; in Kobena Mercer's answer to a question following his talk (447); and in Slack and Whitt 574–77.

[8] Jennifer Daryl Slack and Laurie Anne Whitt, who write on ethics and cultural studies, claim that cultural theorists influenced by postmodernism have gone to great lengths to avoid " 'humanist,' 'essentializing,' 'moralizing,' 'classical' positions" but that the price paid is serious when this avoidance closes down discussion of, for example, human nature, responsibility, or the concept of totality (584).

The Costs of Caring: "Femininism" and Contingent Women Workers in Composition Studies

Eileen E. Schell

Lorie Goodman Batson contends that when we speak of women in composition studies—their varying interests, desires, motivations, and political affiliations—we often appeal to a common female identity that levels differences and creates alliances where there may be divergences (207–08). As identity categories become increasingly fragmented and contested in postmodern thought, it is important for feminists in composition "to begin challenging the privileging of singular political identities" (Wicke and Ferguson 7). Poststructuralist and postmodern critiques of identity politics necessitate that we reexamine previously unchallenged assumptions about women students and women teachers.

In particular, the argument that feminists in composition should favor what Elizabeth Flynn refers to as "femininist" principles or the "recuperation of those modes of thinking within the field that are compatible with a feminine epistemology" ("Studies" 143) needs to be reexamined. According to Flynn, a feminine epistemology is an approach to language study "characterized by modalities of relatedness and mutuality, indistinct boundaries, flexibility, and non-oppositional styles" (147). In this essay, I examine the limits of femininist thought; I critique arguments that advocate a feminist pedagogy based on an "ethic of care," which is a set of principles that Nel Noddings refers to as a reliance on an ethical subject's "feelings, needs, situational conditions," as a "personal ideal rather than universal ethical principles and their application" (96). It is my contention that femininist pedagogy, although compelling, may reinforce rather than critique or transform patriarchal structures by reinscribing what Magda Lewis calls the "woman as caretaker ideology," the "psychological investment women

74

are required to make in the emotional well-being of men [and others]—
an investment that goes well beyond the classroom into the private
spaces of women's lives" (174). While I do not wish to discredit femininist pedagogy, I do wish to question the ways that an ethic of care
may prevent feminists from addressing one of the most serious gender
problems we face in composition studies: the relegating of women to
contingent (part-time and non-tenure-track) writing instructorships.

"Femininism" in Composition Studies

Beginning in the latter half of the 1980s, femininists in composition
have created a discourse on pedagogy that perpetuates feminine values and principles (Caywood and Overing; Phelps and Emig; Flynn,
"Composing" and "Studies"; Frey, "Equity"; Rubin). In 1987, Cynthia
Caywood and Gillian Overing coedited the anthology *Teaching Writing: Pedagogy, Gender, and Equity,* the first book-length work on feminist writing pedagogy. Drawing on the work of feminists Nancy
Chodorow, Carol Gilligan, and Sara Ruddick, several volume contributors (Daumer and Runzo; Frey; Goulston; Stanger) advocate a pedagogical approach rooted in Noddings's ethic of care: a process of
ethical decision making based on interrelationships and connectedness rather than on universalized and individualized rules and rights.[1]
Weaving together strands of liberal and cultural feminisms, the editors contend that feminist pedagogy revalues the experience of women
students and encourages individual voice and personal growth in the
writing classroom (Caywood and Overing, Introduction xi). In "Transforming the Composition Classroom," Elisabeth Daumer and Sandra
Runzo urge feminist teachers to help their students "unearth" their authentic voices by encouraging them to "search out untraditional
sources, often the forms of writing which have not been granted the
status of literature because they are either personal (journals, letters,
diaries) or community-based (Blues, spirituals, work songs)" (56). In
this formulation, female students' subjectivities are represented as
buried treasure, which must be brought to light with the assistance of
the feminist teacher. Thus the theory of subjectivity in *Teaching Writing* is grounded in Enlightenment notions of the self-governing, autonomous individual.

   Cultural feminism, as represented in *Teaching Writing,* entails a radical transformation of pedagogical relationships. "Cultural feminism,"
writes Linda Alcoff, "is the ideology of a female nature or female

essence reappropriated by feminists themselves in an effort to revalidate undervalued female attributes" ("Feminism" 408). Following nineteenth-century ideals of femininity, cultural feminists argue that feminine values have been denigrated and superseded by masculine values such as aggressiveness, confrontation, control, competition, domination, and physical violence. To reverse the perpetuation of harmful masculine values, cultural feminists contend that all people— men and women alike—should emulate feminine values: nurturance, supportiveness, interdependence, and nondominance. In addition, cultural feminists deemphasize a model of communication based on argumentation and endorse a rhetoric of mediation, conciliation, and shared authority. Alcoff warns that, although many women have developed invaluable skills and abilities in response to patriarchal restrictions, feminists should be wary of advocating "the restrictive conditions that give rise to those attributes: forced parenting, lack of physical autonomy, dependency for survival on mediation skills" (414). Furthermore, Devoney Looser cautions that theories of gender identity that presume "a stable and/or recoverable homogenized" female subject "present costs that feminist compositionists may not be ready to pay" (55).

The happy marriage between cultural feminism and expressivist composition studies, however, is evident in many of the essays in *Teaching Writing*. As Wendy Goulston indicates, process theories of composing rely on qualities associated with a "female style" (25). In fact, Caywood and Overing locate their volume at the "recurrent intersection" between feminist theory and expressivist writing theory: the privileging of process over product; the encouragement of inner voice, exploratory or discovery writing; collaboration; and the decentering of teacherly authority (xii–xiii). Caywood and Overing find that "the process model, insofar as it facilitates and legitimizes the fullest expression of individual voice, is compatible with the feminist revisioning of hierarchy, if not essential to it" (xiv).

Unlike expressivist pedagogy, femininist pedagogy consciously embraces "maternal thinking," a term borrowed from Sara Ruddick's landmark essay "Maternal Thinking" (Daumer and Runzo 54). According to Ruddick, feminists should strive to bring the patterns of thinking characteristic of the social practices and intellectual capacities of the mother "in[to] the public realm, to make the preservation and growth of all children a work of public conscience and legislation" (361). In Ruddick's theory of ethics, maternal thinking is governed by three interests: preserving the life of the child, fostering the child's growth, and shaping an acceptable child (348–57). To accomplish these maternal interests, the mother must exercise a capacity for "attentive love," the supportive love and caring that allows a child to persevere and grow (357–58). Applied broadly to human relations, maternal thinking offers a radical alternative to a theory of ethics based on a concept of individual rights (see Perry).

Applied broadly to the feminist writing classroom, maternal thinking encourages writing teachers to create a supportive, nonhierarchical environment responsive to students' individual needs and cultural contexts (Daumer and Runzo 50). The maternal writing teacher "empowers and liberates students" by serving as a facilitator, a midwife to students' ideas; she individualizes her teaching by fostering "self-sponsored writing"; she decenters her authority by encouraging collaborative learning among peers (49). In "The Sexual Politics of the One-to-One Tutorial Approach," Carol Stanger borrows Gilligan's theory of women's moral development to argue for a model of collaborative learning that encourages students to build knowledge through consensus, not competition (41). In "Equity and Peace in the New Writing Classroom," Olivia Frey, like Stanger, endorses a "peaceful classroom" based on "understanding and cooperation," not on competition and aggression: "Group work and peer inquiry . . . discourage harmful confrontation since through cooperative learning students discover how to resolve conflict creatively and effectively" (100). Both Stanger and Frey eschew hierarchical forms of discourse in favor of discourses grounded in mediation and negotiation.

Overall, contributors to *Teaching Writing* suggest that a classroom based on an ethic of care can counteract patriarchal pedagogy's "emphasis on hierarchy, competition, and control" (Gore 70). They also appear to agree with the premise that feminists are better equipped to achieve a nonhierarchical and noncompetitive classroom because they possess the nurturing, maternal qualities to facilitate such a change (70). Yet will the maternal stance work for all women teachers and students, including those who are white and working-class, African American, Latina, or Asian? Caywood and Overing admit that their volume "may not meet some of the particular needs of minority students" (xv), implying that maternal teaching is best suited for white middle-class women. Although the volume omits the important perspectives of minority women and teachers, it nevertheless has served as the starting point for conversation about feminist pedagogy in composition studies (xv) and an inspiration for further feminist pedagogical models based on an ethic of care.

But what are the ethical, emotional, and material costs of a pedagogy based on an ethic of care? If teaching writing is considered women's work—underpaid and underrecognized—how might femininist pedagogy make it difficult for feminists in composition to address gender inequities in academic work, particularly the preponderance of women in part-time and non-tenure-track positions?

The Hidden Costs of an Ethic of Care

Ethnographic studies and surveys of feminist classrooms demonstrate that students, both male and female, expect their women teachers to act as nurturing mother figures (Friedman, "Authority" 205). There is often conflict between that expectation and the teacher's need to be taken seriously as a teacher and intellectual (205). Research on gender bias in student rating of women teachers, conducted by Diane Kierstead, Patti D'Agostino, and Heidi Dill, reveals that

> if female instructors want to obtain high student ratings, they must be not only highly competent with regard to factors directly related to teaching but also careful to act in accordance with traditional sex-role expectations. In particular . . . male and female instructors will earn equal student ratings for equal professional work only if the women also display stereotypically feminine behavior.　　　　　　　　　　　　　(Kierstead et al. qtd. in Koblitz)

If a feminist teacher adopts a maternal stance, she may better conform to her students' expectations. But what if her pedagogy favors critical challenge and intellectual rigor, not overt encouragement and nurturance (Friedman, "Authority" 207)? Neal Koblitz reports that if women teachers give challenging assignments and exams and follow rigorous grading policies, students are more inclined to give them lower ratings. A study of teaching evaluations at the University of Dayton indicates that "college students of both sexes judged female authority figures who engaged in punitive behavior more harshly than they judged punitive males" (Elaine Martin qtd. in Koblitz).

The research that Koblitz cites shows that for women teachers caring is not merely a natural instinct or impulse, it is a socially and historically mandated behavior. "Caring," writes the feminist philosopher Joan C. Tronto, "may be a reflection of a survival mechanism for women or others who are dealing with oppressive conditions, rather than a quality of intrinsic value on its own" ("Women" 184). Women

who do not occupy positions of power often adopt a posture of attentiveness or caring accompanied by "deferential mannerisms (e.g., differences in speech, smiling, other forms of body language, etc.)" as a
way to appease and anticipate the needs of those in power (184).[2]
Rather than view caring as solely a natural act, we can productively
view it as a form of "emotional labor," a category that the feminist
philosopher Sandra Bartky defines as the "emotional sustenance that
women supply to others." It is the labor of "feeding egos" and "tending
wounds": "The aim of this supporting and sustaining is to produce or
to maintain in the one supported and sustained a conviction of the
value and importance of his own chosen projects, hence of the value
and importance of his own person" (102). Bartky characterizes emotional labor as a continuum occupied on the one end by commercial
caregivers, who perform "perfunctory and routinized [caregiving] relationships," and on the other end by "sincere caregivers," who direct
"wholehearted acceptance" and emotional support toward the objects
of their caregiving (116).

Not surprisingly, academic women often feel compelled to direct
their energy into caring labor: teaching, advising students, and performing lower-level administrative duties. As one tenured woman faculty member observes in Angela Simeone's study of academic women:

> I think the great trap of young women today is that there is a sort
> of subtle pressure to be compliant, to not assert themselves intel-
> lectually, to spend . . . more time with students than the men do,
> to be motherly and nurturing, to be on a million committees, not
> to be a power within the university but to just do the drudgery
> that has to be done, to be compliant in every way. And then they
> don't get tenure and they fail. They don't say no to these de-
> mands, and these demands are demands that are much more put
> on women.   (36)

Many administrators and full-time faculty members believe that
women make ideal candidates for teaching writing because the same
qualities necessary for motherhood—patience, enthusiasm, and the
ability to juggle multiple tasks—are qualities that effective writing
teachers possess (Holbrook 207). The belief that women's essential
nature is to marry and mother is reinforced consciously and unconsciously throughout the institutions of hegemonic culture: the
schools, government, religion, and family life. These institutions—or
ideological state apparatuses, to use Louis Althusser's term—structure
the social relations that interpellate human subjects (81). Through

sexual-role socialization in the family, schools, and churches, women learn to channel their energies into nurturing forms of labor: teaching, nursing, social work, and mothering.

This sexual division of labor charts a predetermined pattern for many women's lives, what Nadya Aisenberg and Mona Harrington call the "marriage plot": "The central tenet of the plot, of course, is that a proper goal is marriage, or, more generally, the woman's sphere is private and domestic. Her proper role within the sphere is to provide support for the male at the head of the household of which she forms a part" (6). The marriage plot carries over into the public sphere, where a woman's proper role "is still to be supportive—either to an employer . . . or in some cases to a cause" (6). The marriage plot requires that women's roles, even in academic work, be supportive and nurturing. Women should be satisfied and fulfilled by low-paying, low-status teaching jobs.

The marriage plot is particularly pervasive in composition studies, where a large group of contingent women workers "nurture" beginning writers for salaries that rival those of underpaid waitresses. Sue Ellen Holbrook's history "Women's Work: The Feminizing of Composition Studies" and Susan Miller's "The Feminization of Composition" and *Textual Carnivals* call attention to the prevalence of this caretaker ideology. Miller's metaphorical analysis of the hierarchical, gendered constructions of teaching illuminates how institutional scripts cast women teachers as nurturers (*Carnivals* 137), thus making it problematic for feminists to continue advocating nurturant behavior as a form of empowerment.

According to Judith Gappa and David Leslie, women make up only 27% of all full-time, tenure-track faculty members in American colleges and universities, yet they make up 67% of all part-time faculty members. In the humanities, 67% of part-time positions are filled by women, whereas 33% of full-time positions are filled by women (25; see also Burns 21). Bettina Huber reports that of a cohort of 1,674 women who received PhDs in English between 1981 and 1986, 56% found tenure-track appointments by 1987, whereas of a cohort of 1,475 men, 77.8% did (62). Some women choose to teach part-time because it affords them the flexibility to raise a family or care for aging parents, to pursue a writing or artistic career, or to run a home business. Others are less than happy with their contingent status. Some women turn down full-time employment to avoid relocating a family or a partner already holding a full-time job. Others seek part-time work (often several part-time jobs pieced together) because they cannot find full-time work in an overcrowded job market.

Although conditions of employment vary, universities and colleges often hire contingent writing faculty members on a semester-to-semester basis through "informal interviewing and appointment procedures" and without the benefit of contractual job security (Wallace 11). Many administrators hire contingent faculty members a few weeks or even days before the semester begins, as soon as enrollment numbers materialize for first-year composition. When part-time faculty members are hired, their "research, creativity," or previous academic employment is often not valued (11). Once hired, these teachers may receive little or no training or work orientation. And the criteria for assessing their teaching are often ill-defined (13).

Keeping in mind these grim facts about the gendered nature of contingent writing instruction, we need to assess how theories of feminist pedagogy based on an ethic of care may reinforce the labor patterns that feminists critique. Socialist feminist analyses of women's work in nurturant occupations may help in that assessment.

Socialist Feminism and Sex-Affective Production

Like cultural feminists and liberal feminists, socialist feminists examine how patriarchal socioeconomic relations subordinate women's interests to the interests of men. Unlike cultural and liberal feminists, however, socialist feminists (Michele Barrett, Sandra Lee Bartky, Zillah Eisenstein, Ann Ferguson, Heidi Hartmann, Alison Jaggar) argue that sex, class, and racial oppression maintain the gendered division of labor. Moreover, socialist feminists critically examine women's labor, analyzing the costs and benefits of the ideology of nurturance. The socialist feminist philosopher Ann Ferguson has argued that contemporary American women, despite differences of race, class, and sexual orientation, have in common "a sex/class connection organized by the sexual division of unpaid labor in the family household as well as wage labor, the gender bias of the patriarchal state, the mass media and the public/private split of family/household and economy" (8). Although Ferguson seemingly essentializes women's labor, she emphasizes that class identity highlights differences among women, since individual women belong to overlapping classes that are often in conflict with one another: family class, sex class (organized around the gendered division of labor), race class, and economic class (119). Within these different class positions, women are expected to engage in forms of labor that involve the function of caring or sex-affective production, "that human physical and social interaction which is common to human sexuality, parenting, kin and family relations, nurturance and social bonding" (7–8).

Sex-affective production is characterized by "unequal exchange," in which women often receive "less of the goods produced than men" although they work harder and spend more time producing those goods: "The relations between men and women can be considered exploitative because the men are able to appropriate more of women's labor time for their own uses and also receive more of the goods produced" (132). Since sex-affective modes of production are largely unpaid, underpaid, and underrecognized forms of labor—such as mothering, nursing, and teaching—they are essential to the successful functioning of a late-capitalist economy. Moreover, women's involvement in nurturant labor is made to seem natural by discourses on gender and work claiming that women choose "inferior work status" (Bergmann, "Feminism" 23). The feminist economist Barbara Bergmann explains:

> If a person doing the [career] choosing is female, the person's choices are seen as powerfully conditioned by her "home responsibilities." This line of thinking leads to the view of women's inferior position in paid work as a benign and necessary adaptation to biological and social realities, and in no way due to biased and malign behavior on the part of employers. (23)

Maria Markus describes a "second tier" of work for women in the "less attractive, less creative, and usually less well-paid branches" of the professions. Women who end up in the second tier tend to be " 'accused' of not 'planning their careers,' of not 'keeping their eyes open to the next step' but instead of burying themselves in the current tasks and awaiting 'natural justice' to reward them for working hard." Furthermore, women's lesser "agility" in professional careers includes their "lower mobility" as a result of family attachments and women's tendency to focus on human relations (105, 106).

In English studies, a second tier of work exists for women in the form of contingent writing instructorships, and such positions epitomize the paradox of sex-affective production. On the one hand, emotional rewards—a "psychic income"[3]—keep women invested in teaching; on the other hand, many contingent women writing instructors recount experiences of exploitation and express feelings of alienation. This paradox supports Bartky's claim that women may be epistemically and ethically disempowered by providing nurturance for others while they receive little compensation—emotional and material—in return (117). Women's so-called innate, instinctual desire to nurture and care for others brings them a psychic income—personal fulfillment and satisfaction—yet that psychic income is "the blood at the root" (A. Ferguson) of women's exploitation as underpaid workers.

To understand the costs as well as benefits of an ethic of care in feminist writing pedagogy, I conducted primary research on contingent women writing instructors' attitudes toward their work, exploring the contradictory forces that surround their involvement in writing instruction. My research reveals that a pedagogy based on an ethic of care is simultaneously empowering and disempowering: it offers psychic rewards while exacting a distinct emotional and material price from women workers.

Contingent Labor as Sex-Affective Production

In the fall of 1992 and spring of 1993, I interviewed a dozen lecturers (both full- and part-time) who held semester-to-semester teaching contracts in the first-year writing program at the University of Wisconsin, Milwaukee, where I worked as a teaching assistant and assistant writing program coordinator. The interviewees were white women ranging in ages from twenty-five to fifty-five; most had master's degrees in literature or education, and some had completed credits toward the doctoral degree. The women of ages twenty-five to thirty-five had five to seven years of teaching experience in community colleges or state universities; the women of ages thirty-five to fifty-five had taught for ten to fifteen years in community colleges, state universities, or public and private elementary and secondary schools. I conducted the interviews in an open-ended manner, allowing the responses to determine the order of the questions. Each interview lasted approximately ninety minutes and was taped and partially transcribed. To allow these women to speak candidly and without fear of institutional reprisal, I have omitted their identities. (I also surveyed essays and articles on women's experiences as part-time and non-tenure-track faculty members to broaden the perspective of my interview project. And as a former part-time faculty member, I drew on my own experiences.)

In the interviews, I investigated how contingent women faculty members describe the costs and benefits of their work, and I paid particular attention to their "workplace emotions," a term used by Carol Stearns and Peter Stearns, who research "emotionology," the history and sociology of the emotions (7–8). Stearns and Stearns define emotions as socially constructed, historically specific responses rather than as transhistorical and transcultural essences. In a separate essay, Peter Stearns describes how nineteenth-century industrialization brought technological displacement, inflation, management impersonality, white-middle-class downward mobility, and the increasing isolation of unskilled workers (149–50). In the early-twentieth-century office, management began to suppress anger and impose a standard of surface friendliness, particularly among white collar workers and those who worked "in a variety of service industries including the airlines and branches of social work" (156). Because of societal expectations and management policies that mandate friendliness and nurturant behavior, workers in caring professions increasingly experience emotions like anger, cynicism, and frustration in response to a loss of autonomy, increased work hierarchies, management domination and surveillance, job instability, lack of promotion, and specific forms of workplace discrimination.[4]

In my interviews with part-time women writing instructors, the concept of workplace emotion helped illuminate a split between the instructors' feelings about their classrooms and their feelings about the institutions that employed them. Both the interviewees and the writers of published narratives revealed that while they liked, even loved, to teach, they nearly all had negative feelings about their working conditions and their relation to the institution at large. In the classroom, they felt in control, valued, and alive; in the institution, they often felt invisible and alienated.

The separation between institutional space and classroom space mirrors the attitude that teaching is a private or individual activity and research a public activity. In an account of her experiences as a part-time writing instructor at the State University of New York, Stony Brook, Clare Frost characterizes this public-private split: "I may be a misfit in the academy but not in my classroom. For me it's not a job, it's a calling. The pain of being an adjunct is not inflicted in the classroom, but in the hallowed halls of academe. My struggle to be seen and heard in this discipline is also a struggle to have faith in myself and what I'm doing" (66).

In both the published narratives and the interviews I conducted, women writing instructors reported passionate feelings about teaching and described a sense of connection and satisfaction; they identified their teaching roles as supportive, nurturing, and facilitative. One interviewee characterized herself as a midwife: "I think they've got little baby writers in them that are going to be born. I'm helping the student who has had *x* number of bad encounters with writing give birth to that infant writer inside." Many of the interviewees remarked that they continue to endure exploitative working conditions because they enjoy teaching. Frost writes:

> I love the teaching of composition. I enjoy seeing my students use writing to tap into themselves, some for the first time in their lives. I glow when some of their final evaluations say that the course was better than they expected it or that their attitudes about writing have improved. For me, getting to know a new group of young people each semester and seeing what they can accomplish in a few short months is exhilarating. I don't find their writing boring, because I don't find them boring.   (66)

One woman, in her late forties and with over ten years of teaching experience, argued that the students, not the institutional setting, offered her psychic rewards: "The students give a lot back to me. The institution doesn't give me much. I get a paycheck, I get an office, I get a nine-year-old computer. I don't get much support from the institution." The attachment to teaching is bittersweet because many contingent teachers are isolated from professional networks. Nancy Grimm, a formerly part-time writing teacher at Michigan Technological University, describes the unstable nature of part-time labor:

> For seven years I have taught part-time. I give conference presentations. I publish a little. I even direct the local site of the National Writing Project—one of the department's few graduate level offerings. But at this university I will never be full-time, and I will never be hired for more than a year at a time. My part-time teaching load fluctuates each year. More than once, I have made less money than I made the year before. My teaching load—and consequently my salary—depends on how many gaps the department has to fill. I am going nowhere, but to work effectively I can't let myself confront the issue too often.   (14)

The key issue for contingent women faculty members who wish to participate in research and scholarship is "work time"—the way in which students and teachers circulate in the organizational structure of English (Watkins 4–6). In composition studies, the work time of intellectuals (specialists, practitioners) is directly affected by the research-teaching division, a split predicated on the difference between the creation of knowledge and the perpetuation of already existing knowledge or know-how. Teachers perpetuate what Antonio Gramsci has characterized as the "pre-existing traditional, accumulated intellectual wealth," whereas scholars create new forms of knowledge (307). Scholars, Evan Watkins writes, are classified as professionals "understood to work at the very frontiers of knowledge, at the edge of a 'heart of darkness' where expertise . . . [is] tested in the most demanding situations" (104).

Teaching writing, of course, resides on the low end of the research-teaching binary. Not only is writing instruction devalued, but it also requires substantial time and emotional energy from the teacher. The CCCC "Statement on Principles and Standards for the Postsecondary Teaching of Writing" acknowledges that writing instruction is labor-intensive:

> The improvement of an individual student's writing requires persistent and frequent contact between teacher and student both inside and outside the classroom. It requires assigning far more papers than are usually assigned in other college classrooms; it requires reading them and commenting on them not simply to justify a grade, but to offer guidance and suggestions for improvement; and it requires spending a great deal of time with individual students, helping them not just to improve particular papers but to understand fundamental principles of effective writing that will enable them to continue learning throughout their lives.   (335)

The labor-intensive nature of writing instruction makes it difficult for contingent faculty members in composition to take part in scholarly conversations. Mary Kupiec Cayton argues, "The material conditions of participating in the conversation that is academic scholarship include the ability to devote oneself to it wholeheartedly—at least at certain points in time." Borrowing Kenneth Burke's metaphor that scholarship resembles a parlor conversation, Cayton likens contingent faculty members to parlor maids who are busy "attending to the necessary chores that will free the guests for conversing." Because their teaching responsibilities—and often family responsibilities—remove them from the parlor conversation that is academic scholarship, contingent women faculty members often "play a supporting role rather than the role of the participant," and as a result they hear and understand less "of what is transpiring inside the parlor" (655). Frost attests to the difficult choices they must make regarding their work time:

> After family responsibilities and more than thirty hours a week spent directly on the teaching of three sections of composition, I

have to think carefully and pragmatically about how I'm going to spend the precious remaining time. . . . For the sad truth is that even if I become more knowledgeable—read theorists, attend conferences, present papers, take additional courses—I will receive no additional institutional recognition of any sort. I will not receive a penny more in remuneration for the courses I currently teach, nor will I become eligible for a full-time position or additional employee benefits. In fact, no practical or professional benefit will result. (63–64)

One of the interviewees, an experienced instructor with a background in ESL and teaching experience at several institutions, commented that, while she felt the writing program administrator and his assistant valued and respected her work as a teacher, she was invisible to the rest of the university: "As far as the rest of the school goes, I don't even think they know who I am. I'm just someone filling a hole, and they don't know about my experiences, they don't know about my ideas, I know they don't know who I am, they don't care who I am, they just want someone in there teaching classes."

She referred to herself as an interchangeable part, "not even a person—just a cog" in the university machine. Another interviewee described the university as a machine that consumes human labor: "A friend of mine once said the institution wants to chew you up and when they're done with you, they'll spit you out." She commented on her expendability: "You know there will be five more people standing in line to do what I do, and they'll love doing what they're doing just like I love doing what I'm doing."

For those interviewees who had been working for many years as contingent writing instructors, the overwhelming response to their professional situation was a growing and hardening cynicism. One woman stated that she had learned not to expect any rewards or recognition from the university: "I think I'm just very hard-nosed and resigned. I just say 'I like my job, I'm good at my job,' but I don't have any expectations. I don't expect any recognition. I'm just jaded and sort of hardened to anything like that." As Cynthia Tuell relates, contingent faculty members are like handmaids:

We clean up the comma splices. We organize the discourse of our students as though straightening a closet. When it's straight the "regular" professors teaching "regular" courses don't have to pick through the clutter and can quickly find the suit that suits them. When we can't manage to scrub them clean, we are called on to

flunk out the great unwashed before they sully the orderly classrooms of the upper divisions. As handmaids, we are replaceable
and interchangeable. . . . As handmaids, we serve the needs of
our masters, not the vision we may have of ourselves, of our
work, or of our students.   (126)

For many women, the cycle of contingent teaching constitutes a form
of exploitation sweetened by emotional or psychic rewards.

Although teaching composition has been thought of as women's
work for the past seventy years, we have only begun to question the
larger socioeconomic structures that channel women into contingent
work.[5] As feminists in composition studies, we need to understand
how femininist arguments for an ethic of care may reinforce the cycle
of sex-affective production, in which women work hard but appropriate few professional rewards for themselves. By studying women's
work narratives, we can gain alternative visions of our disciplinary realities and begin to rethink fundamental assumptions about our disciplinary identities and the structure of academic work. Ultimately, we
can work on multiple levels—national and local—to organize coalitions that improve the working conditions of our colleagues who are
non-tenure-track writing instructors.

Addressing Professional Inequities

Although we—feminist teachers and intellectuals—may exercise an
ethic of care in our writing classrooms, we may fail to exhibit an anal-
ogous ethic in our relations with non-tenure-track faculty members.
Unlike Susan Miller's "sad women in the basement" (*Carnivals* 121),
some of us work on the first floors of English departments, where we
serve as writing program administrators and as directors of writing
centers, writing-across-the-curriculum programs, and graduate programs in rhetoric and composition. Many of us train and supervise
graduate teaching assistants and serve as dissertation advisers, holding power and prestige unimaginable to women writing teachers of
previous generations.

But our privilege does not mean that we are exempt from the threat
of sexual discrimination and sexual harassment. Some of us on the
tenure track feel exploited and underappreciated; some of us have
been denied tenure and feel that our work in writing pedagogy and
rhetorical theory has been undervalued; some of us have been pushed
into administering writing programs as untenured assistant profes-

sors and must fight to maintain time for our scholarly work. Our experiences resonate with those of the women scholars who pioneered composition studies and who tell us of the great personal and professional price they paid to achieve professional recognition in a fledgling subdiscipline (see Crowley, "Three Heroines").

Empowered financially and professionally yet subject to sexual discrimination and sexual harassment, women academics occupy contradictory roles (see Luke and Gore, "Women"). Evelyn Fox Keller and Helene Moglen find that academic women, because of their historically marginal positions in higher education, "continue to feel the oppression of past struggles and the ongoing burdens of tokenism" (26). Uncomfortable with newly won power and embattled by the criticisms of hostile colleagues, they may not realize the privileges or advantages they do have (28). Nor are they "immune to the problem of competition"; in an economy of scarce resources, where "influence and power are by definition in limited supply," women must compete with one another for positions, committee and teaching assignments, teaching awards, and book contracts (22). Academic women also directly and indirectly benefit from the exploitation of other women's labor, particularly the labor of non-tenure-track faculty members. Even as I write this essay, I am benefiting from the exploitation of contingent faculty members at my institution. My research load—and the research load of three dozen other tenure-track faculty members—is made possible by the labor of approximately forty part-time and full-time non-tenure-track writing faculty members, two-thirds of whom are women. I call attention to this issue to illustrate the deep contradictions—tensions and discontinuities—of academic life. While many of us work to alleviate inequities in our classrooms, we are nevertheless complicit in gendered inequities that are often invisible or appear natural to us. Feminist research in composition studies, however, can serve as a site for exposing, questioning, and changing academic hierarchies that are considered natural. The continuing presence of women in contingent writing instructorships can become a site of activism for feminists in composition.

I am not alone in calling for better working conditions for contingent writing instructors. The CCCC has addressed the problem of contingent labor through its 1989 "Statement of Principles and Standards for Postsecondary Writing Instruction." Adapted from the 1986 "Wyoming Conference Resolution"—a grass-roots petition calling for improvements in the working conditions for exploited writing faculty members—the CCCC statement is "based on the assumption that the responsibility for the academy's most serious mission, helping students to develop their critical powers as readers and writers, should be vested in tenure-line faculty" (330).[6]

Although the statement acknowledges that "most teachers of writing are women and that many more of them are people of color than are tenure-line faculty" (CCCC Committee 336), it does not address the specific barriers to success women face in academic work: racial and sexual discrimination, sexual harassment, and the gendered division of labor.[7] Neither the "Wyoming Conference Resolution" nor the CCCC statement deals with the larger social and economic structures that channel women into contingent labor. The problem of contingent labor in composition studies is not just a professional issue that we can correct by eliminating contingent positions and hiring more full-time faculty members; it is a gender issue, and thus a feminist issue, tied to larger systems of exploitation. To ignore this problem is to ignore one of the largest gender inequities in English studies.

Feminists in composition must find ways to alleviate this problem through collective action. Two groups in the CCCC, the Committee on the Status of Women in the Profession and the Coalition of Women Scholars in the History of Rhetoric and Composition, offer sites for promoting the professional development and equitable treatment of women faculty members in composition. In addition, the yearly CCCC feminist workshop offers a forum for women to meet and discuss feminist research, pedagogy, and professional issues. At the 1995 CCCC feminist workshop, Women in the Academy: Can a Feminist Agenda Transform the Illusion of Equity into Reality?, presenters spoke about family and partner choices, part-time labor, administrative work, ageism, sexual orientation, race, ethnicity, and class issues. Workshop leaders Jody Millward and Susan Hahn distributed a mission statement entitled "Other Choices, Other Voices: Solutions to Gender Issues" and proposed that the CCCC, NCTE, American Association of University Women, and MLA conduct an investigative survey of the employment, underemployment, and professional choices of women in ESL, essential skills, and composition. They urged the organizations to establish an ethical code of hiring that would consider the traditional practice of hiring from the outside rather than promoting from within; the high teaching load and lack of institutional support for nonliterary fields; the overreliance of institutions on temporary contracts and part-time positions; recommendations for health and retirement benefits; recommendations for flexible careers, including job sharing, part-time tenure, and flexibility of tenure deadlines; maternal-leave policies and spousal hiring; the establishment and enforcement of sexual harassment policies; the enforcement of policies to prohibit discrimination based on ethnicity, age, marital status, sexual orientation, and number of children. In addition, members of the workshop drafted a statement on affirmative action to be presented to the CCCC Executive Committee.

Efforts to combat the problem of gender and contingent labor on a national level emphasize consciousness-raising and general organizing strategies, but local organizing may be a better way to change specific institutional climates. On university campuses across the country, faculty women's coalitions have offered many academic women the opportunity to act collectively and speak out against sex discrimination, sexual harassment, and the general exploitation of women faculty members.[8] For instance, on nonunionized campuses a local departmental or university-wide women's coalition could conduct a study of the working conditions of non-tenure-track women faculty members across campus, offering both a statistical analysis and testimonial accounts of hiring practices, salaries, evaluation procedures, contract renewal, fringe benefits, and professional development opportunities. Armed with such a report and a comparative analysis of working conditions at peer institutions, a women's coalition could influence departmental and university administrators to improve the working conditions, salary, benefits, and professional development opportunities for non-tenure-track women. Moreover, faculty women's coalitions provide psychological support for women, a designated space for women to meet and receive professional advice and mentoring (for coalition models see Childers et al.).

A major obstacle confronting women's coalition building is the meritocracy ideal—the individualist "work hard and you will succeed" mentality that fails to acknowledge power relations and hierarchies among women. Many powerful women faculty members see their achievements as individual efforts and hesitate to help other women, particularly non-tenure-track faculty members. Bernice Johnson Reagon characterizes the problem: "Sometimes you get comfortable in your little barred room and you decide you in fact are going to live there and carry out all of your stuff in there. And you gonna take care of everything that needs to be taken care of in the barred room" (358). For women the academy can operate as a barred room where a few enter while others are left outside. As we feminists in composition studies gain intellectual capital and institutional clout, we must not merely advance our individual careers and unquestioningly perpetuate the hierarchies and inequities of disciplinary culture; we must find ways to critique and transform the inequitable labor situation for non-tenure-track women faculty members, many of whom are our former students. While working at the material level—in local university and college settings and through professional organizations—we also need to reassess the theories that guide our feminist practices. Although femininist writing pedagogy deserves recognition and praise, we must ask if an ethic of care will enable us to improve and transform the working conditions and material realities of writing teachers. We need models of feminist thought that reassess rather than reinscribe the costs and benefits of the ideology of nurturance. Socialist feminist analyses enable us to see the costs of nurturant labor and help us make self-conscious choices about our investment in femininist pedagogies. Without acknowledging differences among women, the costs of maternal pedagogy, and the gendered constructions of teaching, theories of femininist pedagogy may reinscribe the woman-teacher-as-caretaker ideology, a time-honored role that has often limited and circumscribed women's mobility and creativity.

NOTES

I thank Lynn Worsham for the term "contingent workers" and for her intellectual guidance in the formulation of this essay.

[1]See Mary Field Belenky, Blythe McVicker Clinchy, Nancy Rule Goldberger, and Jill Mattuck Tarule's description of a "caring" or "connected" pedagogy in chapter 10 of *Women's Ways of Knowing* ("Connected Teaching"). See also Noddings.

[2]See also Tronto's analysis of an ethic of care in *Moral Boundaries*. For a general overview of the philosophical and political debates over an "ethic of care," see Larrabee.

[3]"Psychic income" is a term used in economic theory to describe the nonmonetary rewards of labor. For a feminist assessment of the psychic costs of a psychic income, see Gillam.

[4]For an insightful discussion of pedagogy and schooling as a site for the education of emotion, see Worsham, "Emotion and Pedagogic Violence."

[5]For an informative survey of the problem of part-time labor in composition studies, see Slevin. For general accounts of contingent academic employment across the disciplines, see Emily Abel; Gappa and Leslie; Leslie, Kellams, and Gunne; Tuckman and Tuckman; Tuckman, Vogler, and Caldwell.

[6]The CCCC statement advises that no more than ten percent of a department's course sections be staffed by part-time faculty members (CCCC Executive Committee 333). The statement, however, has been criticized by part-time teachers who object to the recommendation that departments transform part-time lines into tenure-track positions and impose "severe limits on the ratio of part-time to full-time faculty" (333). Part-time faculty teachers accused the statement of favoring research faculty members and discrediting practition-

ers, "those whose expertise has developed outside the typical, traditional scholarly track" (Gunner, "Fate" 117). They argue that the Wyoming resolution has been transformed from an argument for improved working conditions for contingent faculty members to an argument for hiring PhDs in rhetoric and composition. But neither side has fully examined the implications of the relation between gender and part-time status, and this is where feminists can make an important intervention.

[7]Regardless of my criticisms of the CCCC "Statement," I would like to acknowledge the important work of Sharon Crowley, James Slevin, and other former members of the CCCC Committee on Professional Standards who have brought the issue of non-tenure-track labor to the attention of tenured faculty and administrators.

[8]Faculty members who wish to address the problem of gender and part-time labor should consult the professional statements about reasonable contingent working conditions: Modern Language Association; AAUP Committee; AAUP Subcommittee; CCCC Executive Committee; CCCC Committee; Robertson, Crowley, and Lentricchia (on the "Wyoming Conference Resolution"); Wyche-Smith and Rose (on the "Wyoming Conference Resolution"). General guides to improving the working conditions of part-time faculty members through organizing efforts can be found in Gappa; Gappa and Leslie; Tuckman and Biles; Wallace. Journals and newsletters devoted exclusively to contingent instructors and the improvement of their working conditions are the *Adjunct Advocate, Professing: An Organ for Those Who Teach Undergraduates,* and *Forum: The Newsletter of the Part-Time Faculty Forum for the CCCC.* Helpful general guides to organizing women's coalitions are Bannerji et al.; DeSole and Hoffmann.

Argument and Composition

Suzanne Clark

In the first part of this volume, the writers take an unsentimental look at the category of woman and raise questions about feminist differences. They are particularly concerned with a line of argument in composition studies that has associated women (in their writing and in the profession) with a limiting, too narrow feminist agency. The writers' critique has a twofold purpose: first, epistemological, to articulate a more workable approach to the idea of feminism in composition; second, political, to define a less circumscribed and monocultural feminist subject. The feminist argument that emerges is neither a scientific positivism nor a challenge to the fathers; it is, rather, a discursive, historically situated epistemology.

Of course, the feminist situation itself has historical and cultural aspects that ought to be taken into account. In some respects, feminists challenging a certain kind of feminism in composition represent a luxury: women now have a sufficient number to play out the anxieties of influence so familiar in the battles of male critics. That is not to say that feminist battles are or should be (or even could be) the same as the male challenge to the fathers. The feminine in composition is very much complicated by the fact that earlier generations of feminists include many who have built a career on the margins. It is not surprising that an allegiance to the "ethic of care" idea developed in the context of feminism in composition. But that approach did not provide a definition of woman that could stabilize a field of inquiry in composition studies—precisely because it was too arbitrarily stable, too distant from the rhetorical, and did not take differences among women sufficiently into account. The essays here overcome the ethic-of-care immobility not merely by attacking but also by exemplifying, supplementing, interrupting, citing. They succeed in elaborating a more flexible, generously inclusive, and yet more critical feminism. But only partly.

The writers may be willing to give up too much. Laura Brady critiques the use of narratives of experience by feminist theorists: the Mary Belenky collective, Carol Gilligan, Nancy Chodorow. Brady argues carefully that narrative is a transparent convention, that these theorists have made unwarranted generalizations, that they employ a metaphoric strategy of reading that reinscribes feminism into the context of male-female oppositions. What really troubles Brady about the ethic-of-care theorists is not that they use narratives but that they make assumptions about knowledge and individuals that she wants to challenge. Like many of us, she is suspicious of the dominant assumptions about woman. She prefers the philosophical approach represented by Judith Butler. Butler is more appropriate to feminists in composition, however, not because she eschews narratives but because she argues on behalf of a theory that is rhetorical, discursive. Butler's notions of performativity, citation, and iteration ought to make sense to us—if we already take seriously the idea that most of what we know is the result of persuasive argument and discursive articulation rather than a matter of absolute proof. But if we have such an idea, we also know that narratives aren't transparent and that we don't need to be afraid of them.

Eileen Schell addresses the most pressing problem created by totalizing definitions of woman: that an ethic of care reinforces the exploitation of women in less-than-professional categories of employment. In particular she examines Cynthia Caywood and Gillian Overing's influential volume on feminist pedagogy, *Teaching Writing*, and its use of the care ethic and cultural feminism. The idea that maternal thinking, through its decentered, nonhierarchical approach, will challenge hierarchical and oppressive teaching practices is problematic. What are the hidden costs of a maternal ethic? Students expect care and evaluate harshly if it is not forthcoming. The teachers' labor, in other words, is the work of caring, and their labor is exploited. Caring is far from natural: it takes time, it is learned, and it is associated with subordination. Schell conducted primary research, interviewing parttimers about the costs and benefits of care. Her study will make a very interesting book. And the research shows that the genres of the care approach—narrative, interview, oral history—are potent forms of argument that don't necessarily reinforce the politics of individualism they seem to assume.

Part of the debate over cultural feminism and the ethic of care involves institutional affiliation. The closer we come to women-centered enclaves in the university, the more dominant the ethic of care appears to be: in women's studies, in education, in social services, in health, in counseling. In these disciplinary arrangements of power, epistemological issues arise. Social science and its empiricism underlie the disciplines informed with the ethic of care, but writing is associated with English departments, not with social science. The rightness of that association is perhaps blurred by the cold war development of English departments, which eschewed rhetoric as they embraced the New Criticism and raised aesthetic barriers against social, historical, and (above all) political topics. Nonetheless, English departments' continuing association with a rhetorical epistemology is expressed by a commitment to literary theory and to questions of interpretation—if not by a commitment to teaching argument. And a rhetorical epistemology has much to offer.

Feminism, in fact, has more to gain by this association with rhetoric than by an association with knowledge claims that are positivistic. The university continues to function according to principles of reason defined by disciplines despite the interdisciplinarity of issues of difference and despite the increasing influence of the rhetorical-critical turn taken by the social sciences. The problem with the ethic of care is that it is based on claims that do not involve ethical issues—for instance, the claim that women naturally choose nurturing practices and forms of attentiveness to others. Caring about children is ethically desirable but, alas, not naturally assumed by either men or women. Departments of English, biology, and sociology address this problem differently. A rhetorical discipline is especially well suited to address the relation of texts to ethics and to resist the dangers of reductive essentialism.

I have some reservations about taking a posture that appears critical because it opposes sentimentality (see Clark). Such a positioning of the critical reproduces the fault line—gendered—that opposes rationality to irrationality and also opposes both intellectuals and the working class to middle-class domesticity. So implicated in the formations of the bourgeoisie is the figure of the domestic woman—as Nancy Armstrong argued in 1986—that any attempt to stand outside middle-class ideology is likely to involve a rejection of nurturing maternal identity. But I don't think it is possible for anyone to step outside the dominant culture and institutions in this way. If critique must locate itself in discourse, it is important to throw doubt not on the nature of woman but on the epistemological claim that a culture-free natural state is at all discernible. What feminists require, then, is an epistemology that includes the mediations of the cultural situation—in other words, a rhetorical analysis that addresses cultural history.

Cultural history can ignore neither the specific history nor the mobility of this rhetorical analysis. For example, several of the writers in part 1 of this volume cite Elizabeth Flynn's "Composing as a Woman" to make their case for a more critical, less reductive, concept of the feminine. But who is the subject of Flynn's text? Flynn herself has followed the direction of their argument. Her February 1995 *College English* review of publications in feminism and composition makes distinctions among feminisms, particularly between the cultural feminism that is most in question here and a postmodern feminism that questions generalizations, binaries, and essentialist categories—an approach she endorses. Her ongoing work, in other words, does not exemplify the excessive certainty of early feminist characterizations of woman; rather, it exemplifies the way much feminist work mobilizes the uncertainty produced by historical change. To the extent that critique itself introduces excessive stability, critique enacts the essentialism it would avoid—though perhaps such transitory assertiveness is necessary in the thesis-making constructions of argument. The difference between the Flynn of "Composing as a Woman" and the Flynn of the 1995 review illustrates the danger of taking woman out of history, text out of context. It illustrates the danger of losing sight of the rhetorical situation.

Abandoning the rhetorical approach is fatal, since that approach is the best contribution to feminism that women in composition can make. However strong the pressure is to prefer analyses over the difficulties of history, contemporary feminist theory has been forced again and again to confront the sudden appearance of ghosts from the past. The resurrection of feminism and other social movements in the sixties brought back figures that had been lost to historical memory. In the seventies, women didn't know there had been hundreds of women writing before the nineteenth century. Even *Uncle Tom's Cabin* was absent from most classes in American literature and fading from memory. In the mid-nineties, we support a teaching diversity that seems new only because we don't remember that a long history has been foreclosed. Shirley Logan writes in this volume that "a legion of black women went into teaching before and after emancipation," teaching white as well as black children. Difference, without the knowledge of traditions, can take on an abstract, oversimplified character. So it is extremely important to think about an inquiry into feminism and composition as a situated knowledge, a knowledge shaped by forces that may be invisible, the ghosts of forgotten histories that inhabit discursive practices. Women's participation in discourse may leave an uncanny remainder because the logic of gender has operated by a suppression of women's rhetorical history. Woman haunts us because a victim seems essential.

To escape the haunting, the writers who begin this volume have changed their focus, appropriately, from phantasm to language informed by a material history—discourse. Disagreement, however, reappears around narratives of personal experience. At stake is the evidentiary force allotted to narrative as it defines experience. Postmodernism, skeptical about any master narratives, is equally skeptical about narratives of the self. Still, as Frederic Jameson has argued, we need to read narrative allegorically as well, in an effort to posit the real as a function of political struggle. It makes a considerable difference not only to argue that black women are making increasing contributions to teaching writing today but also to demonstrate that the work of black teachers has been part of our cultural history. A revisionary history rewrites founding assumptions.

Nedra Reynolds, reviewing the history of cultural studies, shows that it has been male-dominated and that there have been interventions by feminists. Both a composition studies informed by practitioners and a rhetorical studies informed by theory have ineluctably to do with gender: rhetoric has been male-dominated for millennia, and cultural studies seems uneasy about its feminist encounters. The disciplinary problems of composition studies, particularly feminist composition studies, have a great deal to do with the more general problem of agency. A too confident reply to the question of whether women can speak at all seems not only essentialist but idealistic, unhelpful, and naive, and yet the most naive reports of personal experience do more than interrupt the conversation. At the same time that stories of personal experience invoke and re-cite determinant categories of identity, reproducing the very position of womanhood they wish to disturb, such stories also produce an excess not easily retrofitted as the norm. What is excessive about the stories teachers tell? That is the question that feminism should ask of composition studies. What refuses, despite the sometimes daunting applications of straitjacket pseudo-sciences, to be contained?

It is difficult to talk about the practice of teaching, perhaps because at the intersection of personal experience narratives and pedagogical institutions it is the institutional economy—and institutional narrative—that seems to prevail. And if the institution does not script the narrative, the most powerful of Louis Althusser's ideological state apparatuses in the United States, the family, does. Family narratives provide the motif of the nurturing mother. But that the mother motif emerges in stories of personal experience told by women should not prevent us from taking an interest in the stories or from paying attention in them to what puzzles rather than to what confirms the repetition of family relationships. If the struggle is between two institutions that have both been male-dominated—the academy and the family— what emerges in the conflict of discourses may exceed both.

There are dangers in acquiescing to the idea that what part-timers do is exploited labor or, worse, subaltern labor, reproducing the dominant power relations and ideology in the very practice of teaching writing. One danger is imagining that other labor escapes exploitation and late capitalism. Another danger is denigrating the political value of alternative forms of academic work. There is a certain destabilizing effect of the feminine that is truly progressive and challenging to the academy; the disgust provoked by the ethic of care ought to alert us to the issues of identity and abjection that continue to accompany the feminine. And what challenges will not be rewarded: why is anyone surprised?

To designate women's teaching as reinforcing the patriarchy by a maternal ethic of care, hence reactionary, and as exploited for its weaknesses rather than mistreated for its strengths is to argue that part-time teachers are not doing what they should: entering the critical debate. Of course they should, if they can, find the time to do so. But the insistence of the patriarchy on a rhetoric of war is notorious; even as we go to battle, perhaps we ought to think about genres of peace as well. Being privileged and complicit positions us in the white light of middle-class guilt—wouldn't we do better to think about a more dialectical position? That is, rather than make a futile effort to separate the analytic and differentiating function from the synthetic and connecting function, we would do better to think them together, dialectically. Perhaps this is only to signal that the title of this section is appropriately plural: feminisms for composition.

Critiquing the "Culture" of Feminism and Composition: Toward a Red Feminism

Deborah Kelsh

As Eleanor Burke Leacock (in her 1972 introduction to Friedrich Engels's *Origin of the Family, Private Property, and the State*) and Frigga
Haug (in her 1995 essay "The Quota Demand and Feminist Politics")
have argued, discussions of women's workforce equity are explosive
precisely because they raise an issue that few want to address: If
women are to be included in the workforce according to their percentage in the population, then many men and women of privilege will
have to take a reduction in their working day—and therefore in pay—
to meet their social responsibility of contributing to the subsistence
care of humanity. That contribution is now largely unpaid or underpaid in the categories of domestic and service-sector work. The difficulty of bringing feminist concerns to the foreground in composition
studies—a difficulty Elizabeth Flynn ("Studies" 137) and others (e.g.,
Brannon 458) have called attention to—is an index of how that project
also powerfully calls into question the entire division of labor under
late capitalism. By continually pointing out the devaluation of women
in composition as well as the devaluation of composition itself, the
feminism-composition project always implicitly—and sometimes
explicitly—interrogates the division of labor whereby people are constructed to undertake the subsistence care of humanity (Mies calls this
"super exploitation" [48]) necessary for exploitation and are therefore
conditioned by it. But largely absent from the essays I am responding
to is an explicit critique of the late-capitalist division of labor that conditions knowledge production (Marx, *Contribution* 11–12), a feature of

subsistence care insofar as one needs to argue and write effectively in order to participate in a critical citizenry.

This absence is curious for two reasons. First, the feminism-composition project has worked to advance analyses of the ideologies controlling women in late capitalism, analyses quite close in approach and findings to classical Marxist analyses (see Holbrook; Tuell). Second, to varying degrees the writers in part 1 of this volume call for critique that will connect their analyses to economic structures. In short, the feminism-composition project raises questions and issues that point to the theorization of a third-wave feminism for all women, not just white, middle-class women, a feminism that includes as well those male objects of patriarchy who are coded as female or feminine because of their constructed interest in caring for people's basic needs. The feminism-composition project, while poised to assist in the development of a global, third-wave feminism, has so far failed to engage the knowledges of historical materialism—of which Marxism is the most developed form—that would enable it to do this. In my following remarks I explain not only why this contradiction exists but also why it is dangerous to allow it to stand without critique.

The advancement of a third-wave feminism for all objects of patriarchy is repeatedly thwarted by ideological pressures on women in composition (as on women elsewhere) to forgo or truncate classical Marxist analyses. These ideological pressures proceed from the assumption that we are now in a "post-Marxist" age (Laclau and Mouffe 4), in which reproduction—how we reproduce ourselves and our species—is a wholly cultural matter. It is noteworthy that the ideological pressure to refrain from Marxist critique both stems from and is legitimized by theories advanced and celebrated in the more privileged strata of English studies—literary study and critical theory—which benefit greatly from the ongoing oppression and exploitation of composition teachers. This interested advocacy of certain theories has led me to reconsider the possibilities that classical Marxism offers for women in composition and composition teachers in general—both to explain the prevailing conditions of oppression and exploitation and to change them.

I cannot address all the objections to a Marxist-feminist analysis here. But I do want to advance several critiques that will, I hope, serve as cautionary reminders to all of us in composition that taking up the most current theories may be precisely what prevents us from transforming our circumstances. As Karl Marx and Friedrich Engels note in *The German Ideology*, "The ruling ideas are nothing more than the ideal expression of the dominant material relationships" (64), that is, ideologies that secure our acquiescence to the many demands capital places on us in its pursuit of profit. There is no reason to think, given the poststructuralist emphasis on the way contradictory elements traverse a single site, that the postmodern academy and its theories—even its many theories of resistance—do not participate in the production and dissemination of the ideas of the ruling class. Marxist critiques must also be circumspect about the interests they serve, as Rosa Luxemburg repeatedly argued. But the point is, "ruling ideas" can appear in the guise of radical critique claiming liberatory potential. One consequence of such disguise is that a bourgeois theory such as post-Marxism may be widely accepted as liberatory, and indeed it may even repeatedly point out inequity (Marx and Engels, *Ideology* 108–09). As with the feminism-composition project, however, that apparently liberatory theory may in fact pressure people to forget or dismiss the knowledges necessary for transforming—rather than simply pointing out—inequity. The pressure of bourgeois knowledge on a group becoming more acutely aware of its exploitation produces the sort of contradiction evident in the feminism-composition project, where historical materialist arguments are dropped when they are needed most—dropped at the very moment when their inclusion might compromise acceptance of the project, which has encountered difficulty in achieving legitimacy.

To a certain extent, composition recognizes that mainstream theory—which dismisses Marxism—can be dangerous for composition to use. Susan Miller alluded to the danger in her 1993 CCCC talk, cautioning that perhaps composition should curtail its intellectual "affair" with cultural studies ("Tracing"). Jeanne Gunner has pointed out that "the CCCC has been seduced by what might be called 'MLA values'" ("Fate" 119). But such recognition should be more explicit, since it is precisely the prevention of explicit theorization that contributes to the ongoing exploitation of women in composition, of composition teachers in general, and of all objects of patriarchy. This effort extends the Marxist-feminist project of "red feminism," which, as Teresa L. Ebert argues, takes "cultural and ideological practices"—including the dissemination of theories that block explanation of exploitation—to be "primary sites for reproducing the meanings and subjectivities supporting the unequal gender, sexual and racial divisions of labor, and thus a main arena for the struggle against economic exploitation as well as cultural oppression" ("Critiques" 147).

Classical Marxist theory, which is necessary in enabling compositionists to struggle against economic exploitation and cultural oppression, is now roundly rejected by leading feminists. Michele Barrett has rejected Marx for Michel Foucault (*Politics* vii), Judith Butler clearly supports a "postmarxist" position ("Poststructuralism"), and Drucilla Cornell sees the Marxist paradigm as inadequate (*Accommodation* 153). And leading postmodern theorists—Michel de Certeau, Ernesto Laclau and Chantal Mouffe, Mark Poster, Slavoj Zizek—reject both the production paradigm and Marxist critique.

The blanket rejection of Marxism by people who represent themselves as poststructuralists and postmodernists is radically at odds with poststructuralist and postmodern principles proclaiming the dividedness of entities. These principles should enable us to take up and extend theories capable of explaining the exploitation that conditions our thinking, not insist that we reject them out of hand. I find this total rejection of Marxism to be symptomatic of postmodernism's totalizing tendency, which—quite unself-reflexively—levels the charge of totalizing at Marxism. At the core of current theory is a dangerous blind spot.

The general rejection of historical materialism by leading feminist and postmodern theorists can work—and has worked—to prevent exploited people from coming to the class consciousness necessary to transform the capitalist system of exploitation, in which one class, the capitalist class, virtually owns the majority of the people on the planet, the working class. To give but one example of the prevention of working-class consciousness: historical materialism has been publicly decried as "dated" (Hill) and "crude" (Maltby) by the referees of the journal *College Literature*. Such public demonization of Marxism can be seen as a threat made by those in positions of privilege against those they exploit. The veiled message is, If you dare to take up a theory that can explain how the class I identify with exploits the class you belong to, I will threaten your employment by labeling your work dated and crude. It is understandable, then, that none of the essayists in part 1 of this volume engage in a historical materialist analysis. They do not want to lose their jobs, opportunities for promotion, or a chance for inclusion in projects. Moreover, as an effect of thirty years of public and academic retreat from Marxist analysis, they may partially agree with the referees' assessments. But to the extent that any of us see the "inequitable labor situation" (Schell, this volume) to be a problem, it is necessary to question dominant theories through a return to historical material analysis.

The essayists take up a broadly cultural materialism in which differences are effects of signification only and not of the division of labor. The points they make are insightful, carefully thought through, and

based on the most up-to-date scholarship. I do not question their intellectual abilities or the value of their arguments. Indeed, cultural critique is an important feature of classical Marxist analysis. What I
question is the class interestedness of the scholarship that current academic conventions, together with the economic conditions of today,
virtually bind these theorists to use. The conventions prevent cultural
critique from being extended so that we may consider how cultural
materialist critiques are conditioned by the mode of production in
which we must all participate to sustain our individual and collective
existence. The link between culture and the economic is critical in the
construction of a feminism that argues, in Jennifer Cotter's words, for
freedom from exploitation for "women all over the globe" (6) as well as
for freedom from exploitation for all objects of patriarchy.

There are two problematic aspects of the feminisms argued in part 1
of this volume. First, the writers embrace cultural materialism, in
which signification processes determine both the subject and the
knowledge the subject has access to. But this embracing displaces the
classical Marxist understanding of class—the binary division of
labor—as that which constructs subject and knowledge (Marx, *Contribution* 11–12). It thereby limits the reach of cultural materialist feminisms to only those women who have the material security to imagine
that what they think does not depend on how they fulfill their subsistence needs. Laura Brady's emphasis is on resignification; Shirley Wilson Logan advocates facility with language as a form of liberation;
Nedra Reynolds locates agency in speech, specifically the development
of rhetorical strategies; and Eileen Schell transmutes the division of
labor into narrative structure to be overcome. Such local and discursively based resistance is effective for improving the lot of women who
already have ties to academia, however tenuous those ties may be. It
allows such women to construct themselves in or according to written
documents (grant proposals, Supreme Court decisions) and in terms
of certain historically produced features of themselves—experience,
gender, race, age—features that capitalism can no longer deny that it
has used to exploit and impoverish many people. Capitalism, if it is to
survive, must not appear to be discriminatory. And indeed, since it
does not concern itself with discrimination per se—only with the advantages it can derive from previous and historically produced biases
(Marx, *Process . . . Production* 20, 106, 339)—it is more than happy to
make use of a few linguistically privileged people to appear congenial
to all.

Cultural materialist paradigms produce models for freedom for
some people only. Feminisms that advocate local resistance depen-

dent on the materiality of language are unable to provide an effective way to free "women all over the globe" from exploitation. All women simply do not have access to the literacy skills required to increase their options. But even if they did, and the social imagination was strongly affected by their representations, would all the world's women then be able to lift themselves from poverty and exploitation? No. Capitalism requires that many people must be exploited and many more kept in poverty if surplus value—profit—is to be accumulated (*Process . . . Production* 672–73, 842–43; *Process . . . Whole* 300, 309–10). This means that capitalism must be confronted as a ruthless system, not as a system that simply needs to be more open. Resignification only increases the distinctions capitalism can use.

Seventy percent of the world's 1.3 billion people living in poverty are women (Koch). Women's multiple differences are systemically organized by late capitalism to benefit the few. Moreover, "wages for women workers in multinational industrial enterprises in developing countries typically range from a minimum of 5 to 25 percent of wages for similar jobs and workers in their western industrialized home countries" (Intl. Labour Organization, cited in Safa 77). How will the many women on the planet whose daily focus is on staving off hunger, on gaining access to food, be helped by feminisms that argue for liberation in language rather than for liberation from exploitative labor arrangements?

I sense throughout these essays that the writers are aware of this limitedness of currently privileged feminisms. Schell cautions that we must not end up helping only our careers; she urges that we "find ways to critique and transform the inequitable labor situation for non-tenure-track women faculty members." Recognizing the limits of the feminisms she is bound to advocate, she works to go beyond them. But that she can extend her concerns to non-tenure-track women faculty members only and must call for rather than theorize efforts to critique and transform institutional structures is symptomatic of the power of the dominant discourse to contain efforts at transgression.

The tactic of interruption, as Reynolds theorizes it, is important and indeed necessary for academic women to adopt, precisely to critique the ideologies that are containing efforts to construct third-wave feminism. That is why cultural materialism is a necessary feature of any feminism, as well as of historical materialism. However, when interruption is employed independently of a critique of the binary system of class—which is the most fundamental concept of historical materialism (Edgell 4)—it not only becomes a tactic that risks legitimizing the interruption of critical discourse by conservative discourse but also constructs a feminism that is ultimately for some women only. Reynolds's theorization of interruption in fact belongs to a long line of interruptions that has, as her own account indicates, moved steadily away from a binary understanding of class. In short, then, the first problematic aspect of the feminisms argued from in part 1 of this volume is their displacement of a binary understanding of class and their consequent ineffectiveness in arguing for freedom from exploitation for women globally.

The second problematic aspect concerns the local effectiveness of the feminisms. Even if one claims, with poststructuralists, postmodernists, postmarxists, and so forth, that local, middle-class effectiveness is the best we can accomplish without moving to a totalizing system, local feminisms cannot explain the mechanism by which patriarchy works with capitalism to depress the wages and life opportunities of many men. Even Susan Miller's and Miriam Brody's rich cultural articulations of the feminization of composition do not specify why men's wages and potential in the field are sometimes truncated. Feminism must argue for freedom from exploitation not only for all women but also for all objects of patriarchy. Classical Marxism, reinvigorated through confrontation with postmodern tenets, can produce a red feminism that addresses the interests of men as well as women in composition.

Postmodernism, the current cultural logic of late capitalism, is distinguished by indeterminacy of meaning, reversal of existing hierarchies, and substitution of one element for another in a given series (Rosenau 13–14). These elements allow for and indeed legitimize the transcoding of features across traditional boundaries—high and low culture, men and women. In doing so, these elements provide capitalism with rationalizations (ideologies) for multiplying previously sanctioned and naturalized sites of exploitation. Such rationalizations work to naturalize, for instance, the exploitation of some men on the basis of presumably inherent or even historically produced tendencies toward nurturance. It is important to recognize that these postmodern rationalizations are decidedly complicit with the development of capitalism. As Marx and Engels argue in *The Communist Manifesto*, "Difference of age and sex have no longer any *distinctive* social validity for the working class. All are instruments of labour, *more or less expensive to use, according to their age and sex*" (88; emphasis added).

In late capitalism, the logic of postmodernism encourages the fragmentation and dispersion of gender differences across gender lines in order to create subjects that are "less expensive" as "instruments of labour." (This is not to argue that men do not enjoy, in general, greater access to socioeconomic resources.) We need a feminism that can explain the local transmutation of gender features that allows for the feminization of a specific field, including both the women and men in it, as well as the ongoing exploitation of women. Red feminism allows for the possibility of such an explanation, which is especially important for the field of composition, whereas none of the local and cultural feminisms presented in this part even raises this issue.

Classical Marxism offers important concepts from which to develop a third-wave feminism—a red feminism capable of freeing all objects of patriarchy from exploitation. The most fundamental of those concepts is a binary understanding of class. Regrettably, that concept has been systematically eroded over the past half century at least. We should be wary of the move to dismiss Marxism in favor of postmarxist theories. In February 1996 the Lehman Brothers investment banking firm sponsored the First Annual Education Industry Conference. Analysts observe that "this meeting may well be remembered by historians as the day 'for profit' education came of age" (Cooper and Doyle 48). Marx has argued that "a schoolmaster is a productive labourer, when . . . he works like a horse to enrich the school proprietor. That the latter has laid out . . . capital in a teaching factory, instead of a sausage factory, does not alter the relation" (*Process . . . Production* 558). In short, it is not a matter of entering the conversation. We are already in it, whether we are silent or not. The goal we seek in and through that conversation should be a human society for all human beings.

PART II

Specifying Locations

Let It Pass: Changing the Subject, Once Again

Pamela L. Caughie

> *Writing courses . . . have become the last bastion of defense of traditional humanism against radical (post)modern critical theory. . . . The "self" ultimately is the cognitive domain upon which the practice of writing . . . is grounded.*
> —Mas'ud Zavarzadeh and Donald Morton

This essay attempts to intervene, theoretically and pragmatically, at a critical moment in our profession, as English studies (both literature and composition) in colleges and universities across the country increasingly is becoming cultural studies. The transformation of the 1980s and 1990s in the social, philosophical, and political bases of what has been known traditionally as the humanities is due partly to the academy's efforts to acknowledge diversity by institutionalizing multiculturalism and various studies programs (women's studies, gay studies, ethnic studies, composition studies) in response to the influx of nontraditional students since the 1970s and partly to postmodernism's efforts to theorize difference and to destabilize the categories of identity on which those studies programs are founded.[1] And when theories that deconstruct the self converge with various studies programs (including composition) that revive it, anxiety arises over the positions we find ourselves in as scholars and teachers in the newly configured university.

Today scholars in composition, particularly those who are feminists, increasingly identify their work with the practices and objectives of a cultural studies paradigm.[2] Cultural studies, as I use the term, designates an array of cross-disciplinary inquiries, including feminism and poststructuralism, that make the construction of the subject in cultural institutions and social discourses central to their investigations. These new methods challenge assumptions that inform traditional pedagogies in composition and women's studies programs: for women's studies, the pedagogy of nurturance and consciousness-raising, where women learn to "come to voice" in the safe haven of the feminist classroom; for composition studies, the pedagogy of expressive realism, where writers learn to refine their language in order to express more clearly a self or position formed extradiscursively (Bauer and Jarratt 154–55; Faigley 112; Zavarzadeh and Morton 16). Mas'ud Zavarzadeh and Donald Morton argue that most writing courses are "firmly grounded in the 'self' of the writer-student" and "based on the notion of the subject as a rational, coherent individual who, at times, is present to himself" (15). Susan Jarratt shows that the pedagogies associated with both cognitive and expressivist approaches, which make individuals and their experiences and beliefs the focus of the course, have served to shore up the liberal humanist concept of the self (*Rereading* 91). It follows that writing courses may offer the most resistance to a postmodern critique of the subject. Not surprisingly, the primary site for debate in composition scholarship today, says Lester Faigley, is the subjectivity of the writer, which in turn "concerns larger cultural conflicts over the question of the subject" (225).

To the extent that cultural studies makes issues of identity formation and subject positions central not only to its object of study but also to its method of inquiry, it would seem to offer a pedagogy for working through the tensions between, on the one hand, studies programs like composition and women's studies, often devoted to a humanist concept of the subject as "source and agent of conscious action and meaning" (P. Smith xxxiii–xxxiv) and committed to opening this subject position to previously marginalized groups, and, on the other hand, various postmodern theories, including feminist and composition theories that reveal that humanist subject as the effect, not the origin, of representation and seek to vacate that subject position.[3] Concerned with "the complex ways in which identity itself is articulated, experienced, and deployed" (Nelson, Treichler, and Grossberg 9), cultural studies requires its practitioners "to include in their critical view the conditions of their own existence" at the same time that it identifies itself "polemically with certain social constituencies"— namely, blacks, women, workers (Bathrick 323, 325). Given that these values have historically motivated feminist inquiries, cultural studies could be said to promote a feminist pedagogy. With its emphasis on "the materialist dimensions of culture" (Schilb 174) and "the politics of location" (Faigley 218), the cultural studies classroom becomes a site of both cultural intervention and continual self-critique. To practice cultural studies is, as Susan Suleiman writes in another context, "to implicate yourself, your self, in what you write" and in what you teach (2).

Yet however strong, however sincere our commitment as English professors to certain social constituencies and to continual self-critique, when ethnicity becomes "the new frontier, accessible to all" (hooks, *Yearning* 52); when men become feminists and straights become queer; when African American studies and women's studies become cultural studies; when a prominent feminist can write, "I began to wonder whether there was any position from which a white middle-class feminist could say anything on the subject [of race] without sounding exactly like [a white middle-class feminist]. . . . In which case it might be better not to say anything" (N. Miller, "Criticizing" 364), then something has gone wrong. Rather than resolve the conflict between traditional programs and postmodern discourses, a cultural studies pedagogy puts its practitioners in a double bind created by the tension between the desire—indeed, the imperative—to speak as or for members of a particular social group and the anxieties and risks such a practice incurs. A writer who deliberately assumes another's position risks being accused of unconsciously doing so.[4]

In recent writings, I have used the metaphor of passing to describe our subject positions in postmodern culture and in cultural studies classrooms. Passing traditionally refers to the social practice of assuming the identity of another type or class of person for social, economic, or political reasons. Passing denotes mainly, though not exclusively, the practice of light-skinned African Americans assuming a white identity. The practice is generally implicated in a racist social organization. The painful psychic consequences of passing attested to in many narratives are corporeally depicted in Agnieszka Holland's film *Europa, Europa*, based on Solomon Perel's autobiography. The protagonist, a German Jew, in an effort to conceal his identity from his Nazi companions, pulls what remains of his foreskin over the tip of his penis and ties it in place with a piece of thread.

In its traditional sense, passing often carries pejorative connotations of deception, dishonesty, and betrayal (see V. Smith). When used metaphorically, with the operative *as*, passing can apply to a variety of situations in which one impersonates another identity, perpetrating a fraud on the public. But for me, passing (without *as*) figures that always slippery difference between standing *for* something (having a firm position) and passing *as* something (having no position or a fraudulent one), between the strategic adoption of a politically empowered identity (as when some blacks pass for white) and the disempowering appropriation of an identity that presents a potentially threatening difference (as when some men pass as feminist); and between what one professes as a teacher (the positions one assumes in the classroom, often as spokesperson for another's position) and how one is actually positioned in a society, institution, discourse, or classroom. Marked by a discrepancy between what one professes to be (and what one professes, as a writer or teacher) and how one is positioned, passing is risky, but also unavoidable, for there is no taking a position without passing.

I offer passing not as a solution to the double bind elaborated above but as a descriptive theory of its dynamics. Passing, unlike the more common expressions "speaking as" and "speaking for," disrupts subject positions. To clarify the difference between these two ways of conceptualizing the problem, I want to compare two sentences that appear on the same page of Linda Alcoff's essay "The Problem of Speaking for Others," which analyzes many of the issues and impasses described in this essay. Alcoff, who first proposed the concept of positionality for feminism as a way of defining the subject by social location rather than by essential attributes,[5] explains that the problem of speaking for arises from the recognition that the social location of the speaker has bearing on the meaning and truth of what the speaker says (an insight, says Alcoff, that women's studies and African American studies were founded on) and the recognition that some privileged locations are "discursively dangerous" no matter what the speaker's intentions (6–7). Recognizing the danger but opposing those who would retreat from the practice of speaking for, Alcoff offers criteria for distinguishing between responsible and irresponsible representations of others. These criteria take the form of imperatives, the primary one being that if you do speak, you must examine the effect of your social location on what you say (24–26).

Alcoff's insistence on self-critique combines a materialist focus on specific locations with a postmodern understanding of the discursive character of subjectivity. The "mediated character of all representations" (9) is acknowledged in these two sentences:

> When I speak for myself, I am constructing a possible self, a way to be in the world, and am offering that to others, whether I intend to or not, as one possible way to be.

When I "speak for myself" I am participating in the creation and reproduction of discourses through which my own and other selves are constituted. (21)

Alcoff seems to be saying much the same thing in these two sentences, yet the quotation marks around "speak for myself" in the second make the (dia)critical difference. In the first sentence, "I" takes for granted that it can speak for itself, assumes that it can occupy a subject position, assumes even that there are subject positions to be occupied. In the second sentence, "I" is performative, constituted in and through the practice of speaking, through the act of invoking an "I." The second sentence reveals that the "I" of the first, and the subject of Alcoff's imperatives, is a seduction of grammar (Butler, *Bodies* 6). The one who writes the first sentence forgets the "I" of the second, writes as if one could be immune to the effects of performance.

The impasse that emerges in the conflict between Alcoff's two sentences gives rise to the structural dynamic that I term passing. Even if we acknowledge our social locations as multiple and unstable, shaped by specific histories and subject to various representational technologies, whenever we talk of subject positions and self-critique, we talk as if we were immune to performance, and thereby we resuscitate in practice (in grammar) the very subject we dismantle in theory. In this sense, not just traditional writing courses but the practice of writing itself may resist the radical insights of postmodern theories, putting us all in the position of passing when we speak for ourselves and others. Passing is neither something we do (as in performing a role) nor something we are (a subject position we must account for) but a way of naming and conceptualizing the interpersonal, psychopolitical dynamics that for many of us structures the experience of reading, teaching, and writing in English classes today.

In this essay, I engage broader cultural and pedagogical debates over the nature of the subject by working though the dynamics of passing. That dynamics is exemplified in a particular exchange on this issue among feminists, in two student responses to the 1934 film *Imitation of Life*, and in Fannie Hurst's novel, which inspired the film. My purpose is not just to demonstrate how certain theoretical debates in feminism might inform our understanding of the subject for composition and critical pedagogy[6] and not just to argue for a performative concept of the subject against those in feminism and composition who find that concept suspect. More important, I want to show how taking a certain position on the subject—whether we are feminists, cultural critics, or writing teachers—is not the same as taking responsibility for the subject positions we assume and put into play in the classroom.

The Subject in Feminism

> *The question of women as the subject of feminism raises the possibility that there may not be a subject who stands "before" the law, awaiting representation in or by the law.*
> —Judith Butler

Two prominent debates among feminists in the 1990s have centered on the viability of postmodern theories for feminist politics and on the political implications of white feminists' use, in their writing and teaching, of black women's writings. These debates are not unrelated. Black and white feminists alike have accused white feminists of exploiting the "fractured public identities" (Berlant 121) of African American women to promote a new commodity of postmodern subjectivity. Whereas in the 1970s white feminists were accused (fairly) of ignoring in their theories the writings and experiences of black women, today they are accused of turning to black women's writings and bodies to rereferentialize or rematerialize an increasingly abstract and disengaged theoretical feminism. In the 1970s, before the convergence of forces that instituted cultural studies in the United States academy, there were two responses to the charge of neglecting black women's writings: one was to correct that oversight by adding the particular oppressions faced by black women to a universal and liberationist theory of gender oppression; the other was to admit, as Patricia Meyer Spacks did in *The Female Imagination*, that a white middle-class woman could not theorize about experiences she hadn't had (Carby 9). In contrast, cultural critics, who problematize the very boundaries of social identity on which such responses rest, are more likely to attend to "the operations of race in the feminine" (Elizabeth Abel 471). Today we hear less about the failure of the (white) female imagination to project itself into experiences that it is estranged from than we do about the exposure of white (female) desires in that very effort—to speak as or for black women.

Two articles by white feminist critics exemplify not only what cultural criticism asks us to do (speak on behalf of certain social constituencies while engaging in self-critique) but also the double bind created by that imperative. Margaret Homans's "'Women of Color' Writers and Feminist Theory" and Elizabeth Abel's "Black Writing,

White Reading: Race and the Politics of Feminist Interpretation" both critique the positions assumed by white feminists in their use of black women's texts, and both authors are, to differing degrees, self-conscious about their own positions as white feminist critics writing on black women's texts. These two essays provide a good opportunity to analyze the dynamics of passing in cultural criticism and critical pedagogy.

Homans criticizes three postmodern feminists (Diana Fuss, Donna Haraway, and Judith Butler) for the way they appropriate black women's writings: these theorists use texts by "women of color" (Homans's quotation marks) to figure a postmodern subjectivity that critiques "bodily or biological based theories of gender" and identity (82). In doing so, they ignore how the works they appropriate position themselves on both sides of the identity debate, simultaneously invoking a natural, already existing, identity and revealing an awareness that such an identity is always "in the process of being made" (79). Citing only the postmodern aspects of the texts they appropriate, these theorists, Homans charges, downplay the texts' ambivalence (79). Homans revalues the naturalizing tendencies of the texts, the ways in which women of color reclaim themselves as embodied subjects. These texts promote a concept of identity as embodiment; they construct the black female body as natural (86). To use them as examples of postmodern theories of the subject, which for Homans are theories of *dis*embodiment, is to deny their claim to the natural while *re*embodying theories of disembodiment; it is to make women of color do the cultural work they have always done—namely, embodying the body for white culture (73).

Homans contrasts Donna Haraway's use of Sojourner Truth with Alice Walker's appropriation. Haraway urges us to be *like* Sojourner Truth, who in Haraway's essay becomes a figure for a "nongeneric, nonoriginal humanity" (qtd. in Homans 78). For Haraway, Homans says, the body of the black woman is a "resource for metaphor" (77). In contrast, Walker achieves a "personal identification" with Sojourner Truth; indeed, Walker claims to *be* her. Whereas Haraway's figurative language is "an alibi for dematerializing the [black] female body" (78), Walker's personal identification is, for Homans, a way of (re)claiming that body. In Homans's reading, Walker and Truth stand before the law (of representation), bearing an unmediated relation to the black female body. Both women embody this body naturally, as if their identity were so close to nature that it didn't pass through the filter of cultural discourses, those "powerful institutionalized rhetorics that provide the terms in which to represent the self as a subject in relation to others" (Brodkey, "Pedagogy" 138). Yet the ambivalence Homans notes in black women's writings would also suggest an awareness of the filter, of the constructed nature of subjectivity.

Abel's critique of Barbara Johnson follows the same lines as Homans's critique of Haraway. Abel argues that Johnson ignores in Zora Neale Hurston's writings "a possible belief in, or desire for belief in, a black identity" (480), because Johnson understands race as rhetorical rather than literal. Johnson says that representations of a black essence operate in "specific interlocutionary situation[s]" and are "matters of strategy rather than truth" (qtd. in Abel 480). Abel argues that by dereferentializing race, Johnson displaces "a discourse on race" with "a discourse on positionality," a move that enables the white deconstructionist to write *as* the black novelist—not only "in the manner of" (for Abel compares Johnson's and Hurston's techniques of framing their essays) but "in the subject position of" as well. For if race is only a matter of figuration, then a white critic can assume the position of a black writer. Drawing on Johnson's critique of male philosophers who position themselves as women, Abel points out that although Johnson might philosophically position herself as a black woman, she cannot do so politically. Failing to make this distinction, she risks "dislocating race from historically accreted differences in power" (482–83).

Both Homans and Abel demonstrate effectively that adopting a certain theoretical position on the subject (in this case, a reputedly postmodernist position) is not the same as taking responsibility for one's own subject position enacted in one's writing, and to this extent they advance one argument I am making about passing. But what particularly interests me are the solutions they offer to the problem of writing across racial differences, the ways in which they try to save themselves and (white) feminist criticism from passing in the pejorative sense.

The "cultural problematic" Homans uncovers in white feminist writings on black women's texts is both "a problem of race relations in the academy" and part of "the widespread debate over the uses of postmodernist theory for feminist political practice" (76). The troubling question, she acknowledges, is whether this cultural problematic authorizes or invalidates (or both) her position in her essay. While Homans never explicitly returns to this question, she does imply an answer: Homans comes close to suggesting that white feminists should have nothing to do with—or, at least, should do nothing with— the writings of women of color. Ironically, this answer would put Homans in the position of passing as a black feminist, because she does use black women's writings. But the difference between Homans and the feminists she attacks does not lie in the fact that they use black women's writings to defend their positions on the subject; it lies in the very positions they take. Homans's theoretical stance is that all women share the cultural position of embodiment, which is devalued because the symbolic register (figuration) depends on the exclusion of "the female (maternal) body" (literalness) (Abel 484). Thus it is precisely the construction of the black female body as natural that not only makes tenable Alice Walker's claim to be Truth but also enables Homans to use Walker to represent a theory of embodied subjectivity while at the same time exonerating herself from her own criticism of white feminists who use black women to embody their theories. Homans claims she uses black women's figures of embodiment rather than make black women figures for her position on embodiment (which happens to coincide with theirs).

Yet Homans's effort to reclaim or reliteralize the black woman's body in order to argue against postmodern feminism, questioning "the political utility of arguments that dissociate feminism from the body" (87), not only fails to save Homans from charges of appropriation but actually implicates her in an act of passing far more audacious than the examples she cites. Characterizing postmodern feminists as the exploitative white mistresses using black women to do their work for them, Homans casts herself in the role of the domestic. As she puts it, black women in her essay "are working . . . for themselves at least as much as for me. Perhaps it could even be said that I am working for them" (87–88). The metaphor of domestic service allows her to pass not only as a domestic (working for others) but also as a black woman speaking as and for black women in her essay and in the feminist debate on the subject. In the name of reclaiming an embodied position, she embodies another's position and then uses that figurative position to attack a theory of figuration. Her performance (her assumption of an identity) comes into conflict with the literal identity she would assume (take for granted).

I do not mean to deny the value of Homans's essay; rather, my point is that the incompatibility between her rhetoric and her meaning, between her performance and her theory, results from the same cultural problematic that she identifies as the problem to be solved. By failing to interrogate the ways in which this cultural problematic inflects her writing, the ways in which *she* may be passing, she displaces the general fear that the essence of feminism (not just a shared concept of woman but also the idea that women share the same position) is at risk in postmodern culture with the more specific anxiety that some people (women of color) are being denied the opportunity to represent themselves because other people (white feminists) have unfair access to the means of representing theory in the academy and unfair access to race as, in bell hooks's words, "the new frontier" (Poovey, "Feminism" 35–36).[7] I do not dismiss the anxiety, but I question the effort to allay it by reclaiming the body in the name of women of color.

In calling for "thick descriptions" as a more viable feminist practice (496) and in engaging the writings of feminists of different theoretical persuasions, Abel at least potentially directs her attention to feminism as an institution rather than to a certain kind of feminism. Analyzing the writings of Johnson, Homans, and Susan Willis, she argues that no matter what theoretical position they take, their readings across racial lines are marked by white desires. Whereas "privileging the figurative enables the white reader [Johnson] to achieve figurative blackness" (to speak *as*), writes Abel, "privileging the literal enables the white *woman* reader [Homans] to forge a gender alliance" across race (to speak *for*) (485). Black and white *writers* meet in shared figurality for Johnson; black and white *women* meet in shared literality for Homans. Both feminists, Abel argues, use black women to legitimate their positions (486). Race is, in each case, "a salient source of fantasies and allegiances that shape" white women's reading of black women's writings (497). All these efforts to read across racial lines are, for Abel, forms of passing, and, in the end, all passing fails, because "our inability to avoid inscribing racially inflected investments and agendas limits white feminism's capacity either to impersonate black feminism, and potentially render it expendable, or to counter its specific credibility" (497). Instead of attributing racial investments to particular feminists only, Abel calls on white feminists to provide "thick descriptions" of black women's texts and to engage in continual self-critique.

In the opening of her essay, Abel practices self-critique, embarrassingly exposing her "racially inflected investments" (497) in her reading of Toni Morrison's story "Recitatif." Here we see that for Abel, self-critique depends on the confessional, and the confessional "I" is the guilty "I." The guilty "I"—whether Abel's or Nancy Miller's or René Descartes's—finding that it is not what it thought (i.e., that it is a fraud), tries to master the self (Worsham, "Emotion"), which hails us back to the Enlightenment notion of the subject before the law. The belief that we not only can but must rid ourselves of unruly (white) desires before we can write responsibly about others (blacks) is not unlike the desire for an unmarked position that characterizes Enlightenment discourses. Both rest on a belief in the self-determining, rational subject of humanism (Poovey, "Feminism" 37). The assumption behind Abel's call for an alternative practice for feminist criticism is that an honest account can be given by honest individuals, who are coherent, comprehending subjects (Poovey 42). The subject in feminism, for Abel as for Homans and Miller, is already there, constituted by her (racial) desires and exposing herself at every turn.

Passing, in these analyses, is a charge to level against others, an illegitimate subject position, or a practice to be consciously avoided through persistent self-critique. Isolating categories of identity like race and gender from other social determinants, as Abel and Homans tend to do, does not invalidate the insights provided by their analyses, but it does mean that neither woman is capable of analyzing the way in which passing originates in the cultural problematic that Homans identifies as a problem of race relations in the academy and as a consequence of postmodern theory and culture. Suffering guilt for exclusionary practices of the past and feeling anxiety about the precariousness of identity in postmodern culture, some white feminists seek comfort in confessions aimed at reclaiming the subject in the name of those who have in part brought about this crisis of identity, in feminism and in the general culture: women of color. Indeed, self-critique in the form of the confessional seems to intensify the tendency for white writers to use black people as "a way of talking about and a way of policing matters of . . . repression . . . and meditations on ethics and accountability" (Morrison, *Playing* 7). For this reason, Abel, who in her essay connects her critical project with Morrison's in *Playing in the Dark*, cannot help participating in the very practice she seeks to expose.

Failing to account for the postmodern context of her own analyses, Abel misses the point of her call for thick descriptions of "a cultural economy which constructs the feminine within the domain of racial difference" (Wiegman 323). If there is a tendency for white feminists, in Robyn Wiegman's words, "to circulate 'racial difference' as a commodity in our own discourses, pasting over the white bourgeois woman who occupies the center of theoretical paradigms with images of black women whose historical and material specificity we thereby render indecipherable" (as Abel and Homans argue), then, continues Wiegman, "the future of feminism depends on revealing the inadequacies of its most privileged theoretical category"—namely, women (326). Revealing those inadequacies is precisely the task of postmodern feminism, insofar as postmodernism is understood as a historical and cultural imperative, not narrowly conceived as a theory of identity.

I have discussed this debate over the subject in feminism at some length for two reasons. First, at least insofar as it gives rise to efforts to expose the passer and to a form of self-critique that entails "policing the identity line" (Wicke 30), the debate can have the effect of making students unwilling to risk themselves in their writing (or, in Suleiman's terms, to run the risk of being contemporary), thereby rendering them incapable of analyzing the import of postmodernism for the multiple subject positions any person can inhabit and the multiplicity of subject positions that make up the body politic (see P. Harper 90–91). Like the more traditional composition studies, known as current-traditional rhetoric, which feminists have long opposed, these recent debates can make students feel that they must get it right, say the right things, make the right moves, and avoid revealing too much of themselves. Yet what women's studies and composition studies have historically sought to do is precisely to allow more exposure of the self in writing. Feminism and composition studies, insofar as each identifies itself with a cultural studies pedagogy, must resist efforts to reclaim "a sovereign, self-aware consciousness at the center of any composing act" (Crowley, *Guide* 32), in practice as much as in theory, by shifting attention from the individual writer to the scene of writing, to the possibilities and constraints of the rhetorical and cultural situation in which writers find themselves (34, 46). For, and this is my second point, passing as a politics of positioning (not a new theory of identity but a response to the problem of identity) is an effect of the institutional and cultural realities in which we teach and write. As Amy Robinson argues, "In an academic milieu in which identity and identity politics remain at the forefront of a battle over legitimate critical and/or political acts, the social practice of passing offers a productive framework through which to reimagine the contours of this debate" (716). For if cultural studies is about nothing else, it is about revealing the ways in which what appears as natural, a given, is historically and culturally produced. When we structure our writing and reading assignments, we need to tap into those opportunities for passing that have become available in the current cultural studies climate.

Class Notes: An Interlude

> *Women have rarely been composers. But we do have one advantage. We're used to performing.*
>
> —Laurie Anderson

Midway through a writing-intensive core course in the Harlem Renaissance, I showed the film *Imitation of Life*, a melodrama based on the popular novel by Fannie Hurst. I asked the students to respond in their journals to the relationship between the two mothers, Bea Pullman and her live-in domestic, Delilah. One woman, who asked me not to share her response with the class, clearly expressed the anxieties created when a humanist concept of the subject comes into conflict with a critical pedagogy:

> I am not even really sure if this is supposed to be an important part of the movie but it got me thinking. It's the "friendship" between Aunt D. and Miss B. The reason I am a bit confused is because I am not sure I am supposed to take it at face value. Here is the way I saw the friendship: I believe it was an honest to goodness one. . . .
>
> The confusion lies here. Being that this is a class on African Americans, I am not sure if I am not looking, or should be looking for hidden reasons (as far as color goes). Because Aunt D. did not move out and buy her own house after she came into some money, am I to think this had anything to do with color? See, I believe it does not. I myself am someone who enjoys taking care of others. It has always been a part of my nature. Did Aunt D. stay because this too was a part of her nature or because since she was black she felt she would not be in her "place" if she did not stay and take care of Miss B. and her daughter? Perhaps this was not a color issue. Just wondering.

The confusion, the hesitancy, the qualifying quotation marks all suggest that the student has learned that "an honest to goodness" response is not to be trusted, that what comes naturally to her may be culturally produced. But her language also reveals a strong desire to believe in a natural self, to assure herself that her desires belong to her and that they are "not a color issue."

In contrast, another woman, who was more than willing to share her response, clearly showed that she had learned the lesson of cultural criticism:

> The characteristics given to Delilah were many of the same characteristics attributed to the mammy stereotype. All of her tendencies were described as being "natural." For example, Delilah said that it was "natural" for her to raise children. This idea goes back to the notion that mammies have an overwhelming maternal instinct. It was also interesting to see how Delilah was made to be asexual or not involved in any sort of sexual relationship. . . . In other words, Delilah's instincts were maternal not sexual.
>
> It was interesting to see how they portrayed Delilah as being

the faithful servant. This stereotype, made up by white America, helps defend the ideology that African-Americans are perfectly satisfied in their subservient position. This is apparent when Mrs. Pullman tells Delilah that she could stop working and be fairly well off but Delilah cannot bear the thought of not taking care of Mrs. Pullman. We are to assume that Delilah cannot live independently of a white person. This was important because it made the audience more comfortable with the relationship between Delilah and Mrs. Pullman. This reassured them that Mrs. Pullman was not taking advantage of Delilah.

This woman has no anxieties, in part because her own position in relation to the material she is writing about is not an issue for her. The first woman risks putting herself, her self, into the text (something women's studies and African American studies students are often encouraged to do) and as a result feels like a fraud. The second woman unmasks the first woman's response, showing that those "natural" responses are "ready-made reflections which promise a false identity" (Lydon 219).

However much these two journal responses offer conflicting ways of reading the place of the natural in our concepts of the subject, the writers hold similar notions of themselves as writing subjects. The first woman wants desperately to believe in her authenticity and in her authority to speak; the second woman simply assumes these. Although the second woman mastered better than the first the lesson of reading and writing presented in a critical pedagogy, it was the first woman who in this course came to change her notion of her self as a subject through her writing. For, as her rhetoric painfully reveals, she implicated herself, her self, in what she wrote and as a result undermined the authenticity of that "I."

I am not saying that the first student was the better reader because she put herself into the text. Obviously, at this point in the course, the second student was reading with more sophistication. But the first reader at least came to experience, through the act of writing, the self-displacement advocated by so many people writing on pedagogy. In other words, there is more than one way of getting it right, or wrong. The kind of argument the second student makes, while intellectually and politically astute, does not require anything of her, makes no demands on her subjectivity; the first reader's response does. Whereas the first reader sought, and failed, to suppress her whiteness, which emerged through her writing as a category of analysis, the second student implicitly suggests through her writing that she can and must disavow her whiteness in analyzing whiteness as a racialized identity. That disavowal reinforces the belief that knowing can be separate from experience (see Harding, "Who Knows?").

Changing the Subject

> *Now I'm* loud. . . . *This is why I usually get along with African Americans. I mean, when we're together, "Whooo!" It's like I feel totally* myself—*we just let everything go!*
> —Camille Paglia

Few white women have so repeatedly attracted charges of passing as has Fannie Hurst, over some sixty years of criticism. What made Hurst's representation of black women so controversial, sparking a lengthy debate in the pages of *Opportunity* magazine, was that Hurst actively supported and promoted black artists, such as Zora Neale Hurston, her secretary for a time. Hurst brought the controversial issues of passing and racism to wide public attention through her 1933 novel, *Imitation of Life*, which served as the basis of screenplays for two films. *Imitation of Life* was "one of the first screen dramas that linked issues of race, gender, and sexuality" (hooks, *Yearning* 3–4). Yet the racist representations of Delilah (the mammy) and Peola (the tragic mulatta) and their relationship to Bea (the mistress) fostered the charge that Hurst was merely passing as a friend of the black race, that her identity as a white liberal was a fraud. Hurst did not help dispel this view when, in her response to Sterling Brown's attack on the film, she made the patronizing suggestion that blacks should be grateful to her because the film "practically inaugurates into the important medium of the motion-picture a consideration of the Negro as part of the social pattern of American life" (Letter) or later, when she wrote an editorial speculating on the notion "If I were a Negro" ("Sure Way").[8] Not surprisingly, Brown's reply expressed no more gratitude for the white woman's efforts than does bell hooks's sarcastic response to Camille Paglia's comment cited in the epigraph above: "Naturally, all black Americans were more than pleased to have Miss Camille give us this vote of confidence, since we live to make it possible for white girls like herself to have a place where they can be 'totally' themselves" (*Outlaw Culture* 84).

The question of whether white women are writing on behalf of black women, making black women's experiences and desires known to a white public, or are appropriating black women's experiences for their own needs and interests—for example, to become more comfortable with their racial and gender identity at a time when many are suffering deep anxieties over the insecurity of that identity—links Hurst's writing of the 1930s with feminist debates of the 1990s. Partly for this reason, I include *Imitation of Life* (both the novel and the 1934 film) in my African American studies course on the Harlem Renaissance as well as in my women's studies course on the construction of femininity in twentieth-century Anglo-American culture. Written at a time of increasing concern about the number of white women entering the workforce and the number of black women leaving domestic service, especially as live-in help, the novel expresses the ambivalence that attends systemic social change. Working through the complex relations among race, gender, sexuality, and class in this novel can provide a way of coming to terms with our own forms of passing in contemporary culture.

On the one hand, through the phenomenal business success of Bea Pullman (who passes as "B. Pullman, business man" [124]), the novel celebrates a mother's escape from domesticity into "a market economy, where she supposedly can own her own labor" (Wiegman 309). On the other hand, the novel appeals to the nostalgia for the lost mother and for the security she represents. Bea domesticates commercial space, fashioning her waffle houses as wombs, kennels, and "safe havens" (134, 149, 161, 235–36). Clearly the novel appeals to the public's "racial nostalgia" (Berlant 122) for the lost mammy in the character of Delilah; at the same time it gives Delilah some of the most explicit statements about the operations of race and racism in American society. But the novel is most interesting to me because it shows (as the two film versions do not) that in times of anxiety over women's changing social roles and identities—such as Hurst's depression era or our own postmodern moment—the need to return women to the (maternal) body becomes all the more urgent.

What is offbeat about Hurst's novel is that in it the maternal, traditionally assumed to be women's natural role, is exposed as a cover for racism and sexism in American society, precisely because the maternal is linked with the inability to pass. Hurst's novel, like the 1934 film, ostensibly suggests that racism can be overcome if women band together on the basis of their shared condition of motherhood. Yet, as the second student quoted above clearly understood, this friendship between the white and black mothers only sentimentalizes racist social practices. But while the film's sentimental ending invites this reading, the novel actually explodes it.

The place in the novel where the maternal is revealed to inhibit passing is the moment (not included in the films) when we find out that Peola, who passes as white, has had herself sterilized. To pass, she must reject the possibility of motherhood—giving birth to a dark-skinned child could expose her as a fraud—just as she must demand that her dark-skinned mother (Delilah) "unborn" or disown her own child. One cannot pass as a mother. This lesson is reinforced when at the end (again, this is not included in the films) Bea, whose business success has been driven by her desperate need for domestic security, is deprived of the home she has spent a lifetime dreaming for, planning, building, and furnishing. That home is occupied by her daughter, now married to the only man Bea ever loved, her business manager, who is eight years her junior, Frank Flake. This bitterly cruel punishment for the working mother makes the novel seem complicit with a patriarchal agenda. Yet the interdependence of the racial and maternal discourses suggests a different reading.

The novel actually exposes the nostalgia for the mother that I spoke of earlier, because Peola does not return home at the end to throw herself on her mother's coffin, as she does in both screen versions. She passes completely in Bolivia with her white husband. The focus at Delilah's Harlem funeral is instead on Frank's discomfort in the presence of so many black people. "Didn't know there were so many in the world," he says. "There can't be any darkies left anywhere." "Except one," the narrator reminds us in a parenthetical aside. "In her white man's jungle" (Hurst, *Imitation* 329). This reference to Peola (one of the few narrative intrusions in the novel) reminds us that the passing and the maternal plotlines are chiasmatically linked. Bea, too, is living in the white man's jungle, the world of business. By having Peola disappear from the novel, Hurst leaves open the possibility that Peola has successfully disrupted cultural identities and identifications, eliding the effects of race on social relationships and personal identity. That such elision is threatening in a highly racialized society is one reason the film versions have Peola return home to reclaim her racial identity. But the subversiveness of Hurst's novel actually turns on Peola's sterilization and the link between passing and motherhood. For if Bea is punished at the end, as Peola is not, it is precisely because Bea has tried to pass as a mother. Although Peola's sterilization may well imply that passing is unnatural, an impersonation of white womanhood, the sterilization also allows female desire to be detached from maternal desire, and that detaching makes it possible for the cultural production of femininity to proceed apart from the reproduction of mothering and the reproduction of mammies. The "natural" basis of female identity is thus undermined (Poovey, "Abortion" 243), as well as the basis for female bonding across racial differences.

Hurst lets the black woman pass, which could, as Sterling Brown charges, reinforce the myth that all black people want to be white. Yet the very representations that Brown uses to argue that Hurst's novel is racist—and the novel is—function as well to locate racism in the cultural production of femininity rooted in the maternal. Hurst's narrative suggests (1) that the idealization of the maternal is one way white patriarchal culture disavows the threat posed by passing women and (2) that the racialization of the maternal is more pervasive in the psychoanalytic narrative of subjectivity than the occlusion of women within the symbolic register (Homans's position). It is not a feminist project, Hurst suggests, to reclaim the maternal or the black woman's body. You have to let it pass.

Let It Pass

> LOUIS: *I'm not racist. Well, maybe I am.*
> BELIZE: *Oh, Louis, it's no fun picking on you; you're so guilty.*
> —Tony Kushner, *Angels in America*
> (Chicago production)

Passing disrupts subject positions, as speaking for or as does not. The precariousness of identity, which, as Mary Poovey ("Feminism"), Judith Butler (*Bodies*), and Jennifer Wicke say, has come to characterize our postmodern moment, is precisely what the first student experienced in writing on *Imitation of Life*. In the end, taking a position on the subject had less importance for her writing than did changing her own subject position. For her, doubts and hesitations meant that she could no longer take her self (as referent) for granted. She learned through her writing that the subject position from which one speaks and writes is never secure. Having no secure position to return to is precisely what distinguishes passing without the "as" from "passing as." Coming to terms with the precariousness of one's identity opens up the possibilities of passing or, in Toni Morrison's words, "becoming," that "process of entering what one is estranged from" (*Playing* 4)—which may not be those labeled "other" but the "self" that we have long thought our own. The first student, by her halting efforts to come to terms with gender identity as racially inflected, came to work through her personal identifications, which the second woman, savvy as her response was, never seemed to do in her writing. The second woman found a secure position from which to write; the first woman wrote herself through precarious positions.

In the end, both women received an A in the course, but the first woman, I believe, learned something more than the lesson of cultural criticism that the second student mastered so well. The first woman learned about the nature of writing, its supplementary logic. As Crowley explains:

> Writing never exactly substitutes for speech [for speaking for or as]. . . . But even more profoundly, writing never gets it exactly right; it never imitates or copies what would be said or thought exactly, but instead goes off under its own steam, does its own thing. Supplements never substitute exactly; they always differ from, and defer, realization of the "real" thing.   (*Guide* 14)

Writing for the first woman was a performative process that provided an experience of subjectivity as passing, an experience that the second woman's discourse rhetorically suppressed. If we are always passing, even or especially when we seem to inhabit our natural position, it is not just because our social location is complex, multiple, and shifting, as Alcoff says (although it is); it is also because that subject position, once represented, is always to some degree an effect of the scene of writing.

The point of all this for pedagogy is that we need to provide our students with strategies and occasions for working through rather than taking up subject positions. Such strategies and occasions are especially important whenever we make whiteness visible as a racial category, available for critique and open to delegitimation; reconceive concepts of essence and experience in the aftermath of poststructuralist theories; and engage the politics of identity in postmodern culture and (multi)cultural studies classrooms.[9] In other words, the double bind created by the discrepancy between what we profess and how we are positioned and between the demands of a critical pedagogy and the constraints of postmodern culture cannot be resolved only in the register of theory; it must also be confronted performatively. My readings of the critical essays, the student responses, and the novel are intended to alert us to those moments when passing is happening in our classrooms and our writing so that we can exploit the analytical, political, and ethical possibilities it creates.

It is not that I would reject self-critique by whites writing on race or by men writing on feminism. But I would argue that self-critique can be effective only when we do not attempt to reclaim the body or to resuscitate the humanist subject (Poovey, "Feminism" 38). Self-critique without a postmodern effort to detach concepts of identity from their metaphysical foundations leaves us with a choice between the confessional and the fraudulent. The problem is not self-critique. The problem, as Mary Poovey writes in another context ("Feminism," esp. 38), is that the humanist subject continues to be produced as a solution to the cultural problematic that would place us all in the position of passing. The more passing becomes the very real possibility opened up by our interrogation of subject positions, the more we need to make it illegitimate. Yet that cultural problematic cannot be elided by seeking a more authentic position. You can't get out of passing by attempting to reclaim the subject, the "real thing"; you have to let it pass.

NOTES

The subtitle alludes to a paper by Nancy K. Miller, "Changing the Subject: Authorship, Writing, and the Reader" (ch. 5 in her *Subject to Change*), in which she argues that a poststructuralist concept of the subject does not work for women.

[1]*Postmodernism* has become a shorthand word to refer to a number of social, cultural, and theoretical movements of the 1980s and 1990s that have altered profoundly our experience of and thinking about identity in Western culture. Postmodern theory erodes any faith in a stable, coherent self, in a universal foundation for knowledge and truth, and in language as a transparent medium of communication. *Difference*, as it is used by postmodern theorists, attempts to account for the role language plays in categorizing and distinguishing among groups of people by binary oppositions. *Diversity* acknowledges variety without attention to how language produces differences. See Penticoff and Brodkey 124.

[2]On composition and women's studies courses as cultural studies, see Faigley; Schilb; Worsham, "Emotion" and "Writing"; Balsamo and Greer. On cultural studies, its relation to cultural criticism, and its institutionalization, see Poovey, "Criticism"; Graff and Robbins; Berlin and Vivion; Smithson and Ruff.

[3]On the notion of the subject in composition studies, see Zavarzadeh and Morton; Harkin and Schilb, esp. Clifford in that volume; Jarratt and Reynolds; S. Miller, *Rescuing*; Faigley.

[4]On the issue of who can speak in the classroom, see Fuss (esp. ch. 7) and hooks (*Yearning* and *Teaching*, esp. her critique of Fuss in ch. 6).

[5]Alcoff's positionality is an effort to mediate between humanism's autonomous subject and poststructuralism's depersonalized subject by defining the subject in terms of its external contexts and historical experiences. Posi-

tionality conceives the subject's position as "a place from where meaning is constructed, rather than simply the place where a meaning can be *discovered* (the meaning of femaleness)" ("Feminism" 434).

[6]"Critical pedagogy" refers to the activist nature of teaching in the shift to cultural studies. Derived from the work of activists like Paulo Freire and pragmatists like John Dewey, it is a commitment to intervention in public life and an understanding that knowledge must be critical and transformative. Critical pedagogy concerns itself with questions of subjectivity and agency in postmodern culture. See Aronowitz and Giroux, *Postmodern Education* 117–18; George and Shoos 201–02; Jarratt, "Feminism" 107–17.

[7]Poovey analyzes various defenses against the pervasive fear that the nature of the human is at risk in postmodern culture. I borrow from her description to account for how postmodern feminist theory prompts defensive responses in some feminists afraid that it eliminates the body. On the notion of identity at risk in postmodern culture, see Poovey, "Feminism"; Wicke; Butler, *Bodies*.

[8]Hurst passed in other ways. To experience lifestyles she wanted to write about, she engaged in impersonation. She once took on the role of a shop girl in her father's factory so that she could write about working-class life in one of her novels. To create a place for her, Hurst's father fired an employee. This example should suffice to warn us of the dangers of overgeneralizing about the value of passing. There's passing and there's passing (Butler, *Bodies* 130).

[9]On the problems that can arise in the classroom whenever we engage in the interrogation of whiteness and other racialized identities, see AnnLouise Keating, especially her observation that students often conflate representations of whiteness with white people. (Such conflation is evident in the first student's response, quoted above, when she refers to my course in African American literature as "a class on African Americans.")

"Ye Are Witnesses": Pedagogy and the Politics of Identity

Wendy S. Hesford

In 1903, the American Board of Commissioners for Foreign Missions of the Congregational Church erected the Memorial Arch on the Oberlin College campus to commemorate the American missionaries who died in the 1899 Boxer Rebellion in north China. Oberlin College was a particularly suitable site for this memorial, having a tradition of religious and political reform and missionary zeal since its founding in 1833 ("Boxer Uprising"). Ninety years after the erection of the arch, in the fall of 1993, the inside of its semicircle was spray-painted with the words "Death to Chinks Memorial." On the outside of the crescent sides were the words "Dead chinks, good chinks." These graffiti appeared in a climate of racial tension. In the space of a few weeks, anti-Muslim graffiti were found on the door of the Muslim Student Association, graffiti against blacks appeared in the men's room in the college gym, and two wooden crosses were burned in front of one of the student housing co-ops. The combination and proximity of these incidents on the small, insular, and politically liberal Oberlin campus created an atmosphere of tension and concern.[1]

At first, local newspapers referred to the graffiti on the arch as a defacement. The assumption was that the graffiti were an anti-Asian hate crime committed by a member of the white community. But when an anonymous letter by a self-identified Asian American student, published in the college newspaper, claimed responsibility for the graffiti on the memorial, the defacement began to be seen in a different light. The purpose of the graffiti, according to the letter writer, was to draw attention to the politics of commemorative practices and to the racial politics on campus. The graffitist argued that the arch "glorified white accomplishments" and made no mention of the "thousands of Chinese who were killed or raped" (Letter). But instead of unifying the community in the fight against institutional racism and the monumentalism of Western imperialism, the graffitist's signature as an Asian American unsettled existing conceptions and elicited conflicting claims of authority and authencity from different communities. Many white students felt that they had been unfairly positioned as perpetrators of the hate crime. A number of Asian American students felt that the graffiti reinforced essentialist racial politics by generalizing the Asian American standpoint. A number of feminists sympathized with the graffitist's antiracist position but thought that her public suppression of gender identity (in the letter, she did not identify herself as a woman, but the fact became known eventually) had missed an opportunity to reimage Asian American women as activists and thereby challenge the stereotype of Asian women as docile and subservient. And some people felt that the graffiti were insensitive to the sacrifices of the Oberlin missionaries who died in the rebellion and to the grief of family members still in the community.

The graffitist's disclosure of identity and the responses to it raise critical questions about how the community perceived both the graffiti and the arch. Who has the authority to interpret graffiti? Who has the authority to construct whose history? Is one group's interpretation more authentic than another's? Is each group obliged to have its own historians and critics? Finally, how can we acknowledge and respect the experiences, values, and culture of different communities and envision forms of commonality?

Feminists have long been engaged in analyses of women's struggles for voice in the academy. But the graffiti prompt us to consider how intersections of gender, race, and national identity shape those struggles. If feminism is to remain an active and vital force in the academy, feminists must acknowledge the political and cultural boundaries that distinguish forms of protest from crimes of hate, must see how the slippage between these opposed discourses currently shapes students' struggles for power and a sense of place. Beyond the specific concerns of one small campus, the arch incident shows that the interrogation of past events and their representation are imbued with notions of authenticity and the creation of identity.

At Oberlin, the incident prompted certain groups to solidify their identity positions. The graffitist's disclosure of identity reinforced many white males' sense of victimization and self-righteousness. The sad irony is that her graffiti reified a racial position—white defensiveness—that the graffitist hoped to dislodge. In an era defined by a plethora of conflicts related to identity; by the blurring of national, cultural, and disciplinary boundaries; and by backlash against reforms that benefit women and men of color (e.g., affirmative action), it seems more pressing than ever to focus on how social differences intersect and are mobilized in campus politics and to examine the consequences of that intersection and that mobilization for particular communities.

Mary Louise Pratt's notion of the contact zone helps us understand how historically oppressed groups negotiate identities and imagine communities in the context of institutional power relations. Pratt defines contact zones as "space[s] in which peoples geographically and historically separated come into contact with each other and establish ongoing relations, usually involving conditions of coercion, radical inequality, and intractable conflict" (441). When applied to the academy, Pratt's concept of the contact zone challenges images of colleges and universities as stable and unified cultural sites where the principles of cooperation and equality obtain. In fact, colleges and universities are sites where the contradictions of power, politics of representation, and construction of historical memory are made visible. Collisions and conflicts among students illustrate how power is expressed and contested through written, spoken, and symbolic representation.

In this essay I offer a close reading of the untidy intersection of gender, race, national identity, and negotiations of power on the Oberlin campus during the fall of 1993. I also call on academic feminists to reinterpret their activist roots, to investigate the dynamics of campus activism, and to bear witness to and keep alive the vitality of intervention and disturbance in their classrooms and scholarship. Many feminists have been trying for some time to bridge the divisions between classroom and community and to engage questions of agency and conflict in their composition teaching and scholarship (Brodkey and Fine; Ellsworth; Flannery; Jarratt, "Feminism"; Kirsch; Lu), and I have been one of them (Hesford, "Autobiography" and "Identities"). But it was not until the fall of 1993, when I was teaching an introductory writing course entitled Gender, Race, and Language, that I discovered the potential of feminist teaching as a form of activism and the role that an analysis of campus politics and student activism could play in the writing classroom.

My reading strategy of the events on the Oberlin campus and of the narratives, both written and spoken, that emerged during and immediately after the burning-crosses incident and the arch incident is shaped by encounters with materialist feminism and postmodern theories of subjectivity and language. Materialist feminism emerged in the late 1970s from feminist critiques of Marxism and its inability to sufficiently address women's oppression. Early materialist feminists, focusing on women's oppression and patriarchal economic social arrangements, tended to "search for central commonalties" among women (Nancy Hartsock, qtd. in Crosby 133). Materialist feminists of the 1990s continue to focus on women's economic and social oppression, but they also engage questions of difference and acknowledge the exclusivism of the idea that women share a collective oppression (Crosby 135). Postmodern theories of subjectivity and language have provided materialist feminists with useful frameworks to critique the totalizing category of woman and the racist imperialism in mainstream Western feminism.[2] Significantly, critiques of feminism's (white feminism's) exclusions have not led materialist feminists to abandon politics or the notion of human agency. Particularly important for feminist pedagogy in composition studies is the materialist feminist rethinking of the concept of agency. Materialist feminists of the 1990s and postcolonial feminists, whose work is often associated with materialist feminism, see agency as it is shaped by historical practices, positions, and discourses. Chandra Talpade Mohanty reads the autobiographical subject in ways that demonstrate how experience and social action are mediated by institutional systems, historical frameworks, and material relations (146). Materialist feminists see individual subjects not as determined by forms of social mediation and therefore lacking agency but as complex and often contradictory sites of representation and struggle over power and resources (Newton 8–9). Rather than view women's oppression and resistance as founded on universal principles, we should view them as social phenomena formed by the contested histories of nationality, race, and gender identity. The arch incident at Oberlin College exemplifies materialist-feminist arguments about how language encodes social relations of power.

My interest in representations of power and resistance in the academy and in how the projects of activism can enrich feminist teaching and pedagogy scholarship prompts a return to and reinterpretation of the activist roots of feminism. My return is not a journey of simple nostalgia. The history of women's activism in the United States is fraught with contradictions and significant absences. The woman's rights movement in the mid to late nineteenth century was organized by college-educated middle- and upper-class white women, many of whom took a stand against slavery as an institution but did not challenge directly the hierarchical relations of race and class in American society (hooks, *Ain't* 124). Although some white woman's rights advocates were antiracist, many supported racial segregation and advanced their causes at the expense of blacks. For instance, some used slavery as a metaphor for their own oppression, a tactic that deflected attention away from their privileged race and class. Similar patterns characterized white feminism through the 1970s and 1980s; much of it failed to address differences among women and the simultaneity of oppressions based on race, gender, class, sexual orientation, and national identity. As in the original woman's rights movement, the category of woman was synonymous with white woman (Crosby; A. Davis; hooks, *Ain't*; Lorde, *Sister*).

Given the exclusivism of the woman's rights movement and the limiting concept of a universal feminist standpoint, academic feminists today might wonder what we can learn from retracing our activist roots. Indeed, why should we look back at all? First, to reject outright feminism's activist roots is to ignore the important role that the woman's rights movement played in developing gender consciousness and empowering women (even if mostly middle-class white women) to see themselves as agents capable of organized resistance. Second, to forget feminism's white-centered roots is to ignore how they were contested historically, how women whose interests were not reflected in that movement carved out new spaces from which to speak. Academic feminists can learn from the failures of early feminist activism. But, as Susan Stanford Friedman cautions, "We should be aware of the ways in which feminist histories can narrativize the past of feminists such that other feminist histories are discounted or discredited" ("Making" 18). The woman's rights movement and critiques of its exclusivism can provide us with powerful tools to examine critically our actions and narratives of resistance and to recognize the ways privilege finds "ever deeper places to hide" (Elizabeth Spelman, qtd. in Newton 163). If our actions, like the stories we tell about them, are historically mediated, shouldn't we reflect on the forms of mediation so that we can become more active in their transformation?

Framing Institutional Memory:
The Hidden Transcript

The Memorial Arch is a granite, semicircular colonnade that stands in neoclassical fashion at one of the entrances to the town square. Inscribed on the face of the archway in the center are the words "Ye Are Witnesses." On one of the crescent-shaped sides, it reads, "The Blood of Martyrs the Seed of the Church." Walking through the arch, a person can see bronze plaques embedded in the granite wall to the right and left. These plaques list the names of the Christian missionaries from Oberlin killed in the Boxer Rebellion in Shandong Province. The Boxers, wanting to drive foreign influence from their land, first rose against their neighboring Chinese Christian converts and then against the foreigners. Approximately thirty thousand Chinese Christians were killed; the number of non-Christian Chinese who perished is unknown (Jacobson).[3]

Historical photograph of the Memorial Arch, Oberlin College. Photo courtesy of Oberlin College Archives, Oberlin, Ohio.

If we read the graffiti on the Memorial Arch as a historical and ideological phenomenon, we must recognize how language shapes historical memory and foreground the national logic and martyrology that anchors the kind of witness that the monument announces. Whose history does the monument represent? Who has access to the monument and its particular history? What role do particular witnesses play in generating certain historical memories? How do these memories shift according to the way the witnesses define themselves? To deconstruct the arch's imagined audience, viewers must first read through the expectations of its designers and the values that the arch celebrates. Viewers must acknowledge the Western declaration that the killed missionaries were martyrs. The phrase "ye are witnesses," a declaration and an exhortation, refers to both the martyrs and the present viewers as witnesses. Martyrdom means "to witness," "to testify that Jesus is the Son of God," and "to refuse to renounce one's faith in the face of persecution and death" (Hevia 319–20). Missionary discourse on the Boxer Rebellion maintains that the missionaries in China had "suffered and borne witness to their belief and had all led pious and exemplary lives" (320–21). Thus those who died could be considered martyrs from various Protestant vantage points. The New Testament Christian Gospel narrative of suffering, death, and resurrection is expressed on the crescent sides of the arch in the proverb mentioned above, "The Blood of Martyrs the Seed of the Church," and in three other inscriptions: "If We Died with Him We Shall Also Live with Him"; "More than Conquerors through Him That Loved Us"; "Neither Count I My Life Dear unto Myself."

In the early twentieth century, missionary discourse often constructed the Chinese subject as uncivilized, barbaric, and believing in magic (magic was the Christian appraisal of the Boxers' polytheistic religion). This view of the Chinese draws on an essentialist rhetoric of race that conflates skin color with intellectual capacity and character (Frankenberg). Many American missionaries saw the Chinese as people capable of becoming civilized if converted to Christianity. To the Boxers, missionary imperatives were imperialistic acts that reduced Chinese cultural space and made Asia coextensive with the United States. Neither reading is completely accurate; each suppresses important cultural and historical contradictions. First, the Memorial Arch at Oberlin does not reflect the range of American sentiments toward either missionary work or China. Second, missionary work is complicated by the contradictions between religious universalisms and national particularities. Third, the feudalism of the Qing dynasty certainly marginalized the peasants by denying them access to social wealth, but the anti-imperialist and anti-Christian struggles among the Chinese were not necessarily directed against that feudalism. The Boxer slogan "Uphold the Qing; exterminate the foreigners" was not logical; "supporting the Qing could never mean getting rid of the foreigners" (Jikui 110). The Qing dynasty itself "had become the complete slave of imperialism" (Minghan 38). Ding Minghan writes, "In those days when China occupied a semicolonial status, and the Qing dynasty had become the tool of imperialists who controlled China, it was impossible to attack imperialism without also attacking feudal rule" (34). Thus, if the arch represented an uncontested history, the graffiti initiated a reinvestigation of the constructed nature of that history and its contradictions.

On Sunday morning, 7 November, the arch was spray-painted. College building and grounds maintenance crews were alerted that afternoon and soon thereafter covered the graffiti with brown paper. They were unable to remove the paint from the arch, because they did not have the staff and because the cleaning chemicals would not work in the cold (Rafter). The act of covering the graffiti set the tone for what was to follow from the administration and some faculty, who saw the graffiti as vandalism. At a general faculty meeting, a tenured white male called the graffiti on the arch an act of lawlessness and urged the college to reevaluate its vandalism policy. A tenured woman of color said that this response showed indifference to struggles of subordinate groups and minimized the graffiti's political challenge as a form of activism.

Graffiti are almost always a coded version of what James Scott calls the "hidden transcript" (14). Scott defines the hidden transcript as nonhegemonic, subversive discourse generated by subordinate groups and concealed from certain dominant others. Hidden transcripts are usually presented in a way that will not jeopardize the speaker or actor. Graffiti "[have] become the medium of an urban and mostly black male subculture." Urban graffiti are largely personal signatures identifiable as trademarks or monograms only to the initiated (Warner 397, 398). The graffiti on the arch, unlike typical urban graffiti, were not accompanied by a personal signature. The phrase "death to Chinks memorial" refers to the lives that the monument fails to remember and to the consequences of the meanings that the monument generates. The graffiti on the arch were hidden transcript made public, a subversive act generated by a member of a subordinate group. But at first they were interpreted by most as an anti-Asian hate crime. The community's lack of understanding or dismissal of the graffiti's potential as counterhegemonic discourse shows the ineffectiveness of the use of this medium for protest and the blurring of the boundaries between activism and hate crimes. In addition, the graffiti, like the original inscription of the arch, are coded by national rhetoric and national boundaries. The word *Chink* is a racial slur that Westerners use to refer to Asians. Both the graffiti and the original inscription assume a Western audience.

The arch had been protested before by members of the Oberlin College community: during past commencement processions, a number of students and faculty members walked around the arch instead of under it in protest of its exclusions. But this was the first time that the college community's interpretation of the memories generated by the arch became part of the memorial itself. The gift from the class of 1994 to the college was a pair of plaques—in both English and Chinese—dedicated to the Chinese who died in the Boxer Rebellion. The English translation of the inscribed poem by Du Fu reads: "I am Grieved by the War / and have not Slept. / Who has the Strength to Right Heaven and Earth?" Reactions to the plaques varied. Some students and alumni said that the plaques were "a token concession," an "effort to appease concern regarding unequal representation" and to "silence voices expressing their rejection of imperialism which is linked to expansion of capitalism and the perpetuation of racism." Others expressed "dismay that the people involved in killing the Oberlin missionaries now share the monument with their victims" ("Class"). In short, the Oberlin community continues to struggle over the meanings of the arch and its construction and over its mediation of historical memory. The following semester, the Oberlin Memorial Shansi Association organized a symposium to educate the community about the Boxer Rebellion and the interventionist aspects of making history. The symposium and the struggles on the Oberlin campus during the fall of 1993 demonstrate that "the shape of memory cannot be divorced from the actions taken in its behalf." For if we were "to remain unchanged by the recollective act," as James Young observes, "it could be said that we have not remembered at all" (*Texture* 13–15).

The Memorial Arch graffiti followed racist incidents on the campus. A week earlier, two wooden crosses were found burning in front of the Harkness student housing co-op. According to the residents, scarecrows on the crosses were burned in anticipation of Halloween and the yearly Bike Derby (Rafter). Regardless of its intent, the act had racist meanings. That the co-op members allowed the cross burnings to continue revealed their cultural insensitivity to the historical significance of the sign and to its potential harmful effects on certain groups on campus and in town. Many students and faculty members perceived the cross burnings as part of a historical totality, in contrast to their response to the words "death to Chinks memorial." But those who witnessed the graffiti and those who witnessed the burning crosses were both engaged in reading history's narrative in the process of a rearticulation formulated around issues of cultural identity and notions of authenticity (Hennessy 99).

Imagining the Academy as a Public Space

The arch graffiti, the cross burnings, and the general increase of racial epithets on campus led four hundred students to hold a rally to protest institutional racism, to create support for a hate-crimes policy, and to urge the administration to address the situation immediately. "Oberlin in the long run is about changing attitudes, ending racist mentalities. It's about making you accountable for your actions. You write 'chink' on the wall, you are accountable for that," one student at the rally said.

"We didn't pay all that [tuition] to be called niggers and chinks," another student commented. Organizers of the demonstration, primarily women of color, said that it was an opportunity for students of color to voice their concerns. A few white students tried to join the list of scheduled speakers but reportedly were not permitted. At the rally, one of the leaders said, "Their voices have been heard. . . . Now it is our time to speak." "That is not acceptable," someone from the crowd yelled (Tryselaar, Kearney, and Schneider 7).

Afterward there was a meeting advertised for "all people of color." Students of color organized it to develop a collective response to the rise in racial tension on campus. A number of white students and a journalist attending the meeting were asked to leave. They were accused of being antagonistic and of trying to take control of the meeting. All but one student left, a white male. He was asked several times to leave but refused; then he intentionally gagged himself with a bandanna. The student's actions may have been based on an idealized image of Oberlin as a unified community in which individuals equally share power. The students of color experienced his presence not as an act of unification but as an act of control. The self-gagged white student failed to understand the legitimate need for students of color to create a space to voice experiences silenced by dominant groups in the academy. Using a tactic that oppressed groups have used in their struggle for freedom, the student implied that he was himself a victim. This appropriation assumes a common humanity on white-centered terms and thus averts white eyes from the realities of power (Frankenberg 143). Unlike the graffiti on the arch, his act contains no hidden transcript. On the contrary, the persistence of the white male's performance of silence is symbolic of dominant groups' attempts to police and monitor the hidden transcript. His visible gesture restricts the meaning of free speech to the curtailment of his individual rights and renders invisible the forced segregation and silencing of people of color. The white male's symbolic self-gagging and his forced removal from the meeting bolstered reverse-racism arguments on campus, cast him as a martyred defender of free speech, and silenced other positions in the ongoing dialogue about race. The next day, the white male student reported a fire in a garbage can outside his dorm room and the words "Racists must die" spray-painted on the wall, with an arrow pointing to his door (Riccardi). That he had been ejected from the student-of-color meeting prompted the president of the college to acknowledge heightened racial tensions on campus and to denounce the use of physical force. The president's rhetoric, like the student's symbolic gesture, was color-blind. Basing his sense of community on the idea that all its members are historical equals, the president argued for the "non-exclusion of individuals on the basis of race, versus feelings of solidarity." Documents from his office painted the image of Oberlin as a unified community. In a letter addressed to the college community, he wrote:

> Over the past ten days the Oberlin campus has witnessed a number of alarming examples of hateful graffiti and symbolic acts. . . . We all regret these recent examples of crude hatred and hurtful bigotry. We are all demeaned by such acts, but I want to extend a hand in particular to anyone who feels intimidated by these objectionable signs and to anyone in whom they arouse *fear*. For the foreseeable future, I authorize any such person to call Campus Security to be driven or accompanied by a campus security officer on or off campus as needed.   (Starr)

This statement reduces the significance of institutional abuses of power by shifting the focus to individual acts of intimidation. Through his use of the collective *we*, the president suggests that the entire Oberlin community has been demeaned. But the historical fact is that we are not all equally demeaned. I would ask, Who constitutes the community at Oberlin? Were the privileged injured, or were they horrified by the witnessing of injury?

In a letter from the president, the dean of the college, and the dean of students, the administration stated, "Whatever the outcome of any judicial process [regarding the incidents surrounding the removal of the white male student from the student-of-color meeting] it is important that the College at this time reaffirm its commitment to free speech, openness, mutual respect, and fairness" (Starr, MacKay, and Penn). The administration said that the principles of free speech and nondiscriminatory practices can coexist—a laudable sentiment—but the administration did not look closely at the conflict between an unbending defense of the First Amendment and the college's goals of equality, diversity, and an environment safe for all students, faculty, and staff. The administration's idea of free speech was abstract and did not recognize that in certain contexts freedom of speech can interfere with the rights of others, that in the case of hate speech the competing values of liberty and equality are at stake (Matsuda 47). The administration's absolutist interpretation of the First Amendment erased the historical reality of racism and sexism at the college.[4]

A number of positions offered by faculty members during an open forum later that week contrasted with the president's letter. A tenured African American woman, characterizing the college, used *we* differently. She began her presentation with an autobiographical statement: "Today, I come to you not only as a faculty member, but also as one of the precious few African-American faculty members on this campus, and even further as one of only three tenured African-American female persons in the *history* of this college" (Jones). She spoke of the "tyranny of Oberlin's liberal reputation," the gap between the real Oberlin and the mythical Oberlin, and the barriers that African Americans continue to face in the academy. She said:

> We are outraged that administrators, faculty, and a majority of students spend more time defending what we perceive to be racist acts, and denying our reality. . . . Solving issues of racism and oppression is *not* offering to talk with victims or providing escort services. . . . It is *not* sprinkling black students throughout a white campus like pepper dots to educate the majority about diversity and multiculturalism. . . . Whenever folks hear the name Oberlin College, the image of a sort of paradise of liberal thought, free speech, and multicultural existence is raised in a very positive way. . . . [This] mythology . . . functions as a mask behind which administration, faculty, and students hide. (Jones)

This professor's strategic use of *we*, unlike the self-gagged student's use of a rhetoric of race to portray white males as collective victims of the politics of students of color, bears a relation to the graffiti on the arch. The Asian American student used the phrase "dead Chinks, good Chinks" to point out the underlying nationalism, essentialist racism, and exclusionary rhetoric of the monument—how it commemorates only the death of the missionaries from Oberlin, not the thirty thousand Christian and countless non-Christian Chinese who died in the Boxer Rebellion.

Another speaker at the open forum, a tenured white male, exposed the administration's depiction of Oberlin as a neutral zone even further by imagining the academy as a place where individuals and groups continually negotiate their identity and sense of community. This speaker grappled with the contradictory aspects of his own location and the fracturing of power in the institution.

> I speak as a gay man. Like so many people at Oberlin I am the victim and the beneficiary of multiple positions. I know the pain and the anxiety caused by discrimination. The kick-in-the-gut feeling of violation when my office door was spattered with homophobic epithets, and the sense of being alone with only a few friends to whom to turn. . . . But I also speak as a member of the

College Faculty Council and, in a very committed way, as a member of the beloved community of Oberlin. . . . Majority members of the community need to be especially aware that invocation of free speech—a basic human right—must be coupled with an awareness of how power and privilege may distort what is often taken to be a neutral right.   (Koppes)

These excerpts from faculty speeches at the open forum point out the extent to which the dominant view of free speech at Oberlin inflects the image of the academy as a "fairness zone" (DeMott 131).

Critical race theorists suggest that one way to respond to the increase of hate crimes on American campuses is to develop policies that narrowly define hate speech. Speech that infringes on public order or that incites violence (e.g., "fighting words") is not covered by the First Amendment and thus is unlawful on college campuses. The problem, as Charles Lawrence points out, is that most college policies fail to recognize that racist speech does not always lead to violence. Targets of sexist, heterosexist, or racist speech often avoid escalating the conflict by internalizing the harm done them. The fighting-words doctrine also "presupposes an encounter with two persons of relatively equal power" and is therefore blind to the particular cultural experiences and discursive practices of women and men of color (69). Mari Matsuda is careful to distinguish between the freedom to criticize institutions and hate speech directed against the least powerful in the community. Like other critical race theorists, she argues for a narrow definition of unlawful racist speech. Speech is racist, she argues, if a message of racial inferiority is directed against a historically oppressed group and if the message is persecutory, hateful, and degrading (36). Matsuda recognizes that there may be difficult cases. At the University of Michigan in the early 1990s, there were more than twenty cases of whites charging blacks with racist speech. In one instance, a black student was punished for using the phrase "white trash" (Glasser 8). Matsuda attempts to counter such measures with her narrow definition of hate speech and her focus on power relations and the specificity of the historical context. Thus the intention of critical race theorists is not to avoid the larger issues of equality or to undermine the First Amendment but, rather, to ground the First Amendment in the experiences of victims of oppression.

A broad definition of hate speech might equate the graffiti on the Memorial Arch at Oberlin, particularly the phrase "death to Chinks memorial" (a criticism of the institution), with the burning crosses (a clear message of hatred to African Americans). Rather than equate these acts, Matsuda would consider the status of the target of the hate crime, the crime's historical context, and the amount of freedom the perpetrator enjoys. Critical race theorists view hate crimes as part of larger historical patterns; they imagine the academy as a contact zone. In contrast, the Oberlin administration looked at racial conflicts and hate crimes on an individual basis instead of seeing them as historical patterns of exploitation. It is debatable whether hate-speech codes can adequately address the problems of racism and violence on our nation's campuses. But critical race theorists offer an approach to policy that moves beyond a liberal discourse of rights toward a discourse of responsibility.

Students Speak Out: The Pedagogical Implications of Personal Testimony

> I am a person of Color and I am threatened on this campus.

> I am Asian American. I do not have the privilege of ignoring this. I am threatened.

> I am a black woman of Color and a senior here and I feel very threatened.

These statements are transcripts of students' oral testimonies presented at Oberlin College during a speak-out held after the graffiti appeared on the Memorial Arch and crosses were found burning in front of a student co-op (Transcript). More than six hundred students gathered in one of the old dormitory dining rooms to exchange views about the racist incidents and the administration's handling of events and to explore ways people could work together for institutional change. Few professors and administrators attended. Some students talked about the need for a hate-crime policy and for greater institutional support of students of color and the Office of Multicultural Affairs. But most related personal experiences as political testimony. Their accounts reminded the community that the recent incidents occurred in a historical context of institutional racism. Thus many students, particularly students of color, used the speak-out as an opportunity to make the hidden transcript public.

After a number of students of color had testified to feeling threatened on campus, a white male student stood up and said:

> This is not just about race. This is not just about color. This is about how people look at one another. . . . A lot of people look at one another through a very cloudy filter that shows only their

> skin colors: we look at each other as black, white, Asian, Latino.
> My filters are clean. I look at each person as individuals and see
> them as who they really are.

Putting forth the idea that all human beings are essentially the same,
he was attempting to erase identity categories. According to him, it
would be racist not to act in a color-blind fashion.

Insofar as students' testimonies gloss over differences in a racially
defined group, they are essentialist. But essentialism practiced from a
place of resistance is not equivalent to essentialism practiced by dominant groups. Whereas the self-gagged white male student positioned
himself as representative of the victimization of white males, students
of color used essentialist tactics to reveal situated practices of racism.
The particularity of their testimonials exposed the falseness of the
neutralizing rhetoric of the administration and others in dominant positions. Later that evening, an Asian Indian male student invoked the
dominant discourse of essentialist racism (the view that natives of
Africa, Asia, and the Americas are biologically inferior) to show how it
could be used against whites. "The only people who have been threatened and harassed this past week have been white," he said. "What
kind of animal do you think this white person is?" he asked, to a cho-
rus of hisses. This student used the language of the colonizers to write
the discourse of reverse racism.

The color-blind rhetoric of the administration and the reverse-
racism standpoint expressed by the self-gagged student both contrast
with calls for white students to recognize their privilege and to work
toward institutional change. An African American female at the speak-
out exclaimed, "It's time that your white comfort be threatened. It's
time that your class privilege (whatever color it is) be threatened. It's
time that your apathy and inaction be threatened." Then a white female student approached the microphone and urged listeners to consider the inadequacy of essentialist analyses of white power and
privilege:

> I am a white student and I feel threatened on this campus. . . .
> [The] hate towards white people [is] just as frightening and ab-
> horrent as the words written on the arch against Asians. . . . I am
> a descendant of one of the few survivors in my family who had
> not been tortured, or tortured and murdered, robbed or de-
> graded, or been the recipient of one of the horrors of the sadistic
> mind conjured during the persistent elimination of the Jews dur-
> ing World War II. Yet, a generation later, I still bear the insults: a

swastika being painted on my house, of having my mailbox blown up, as well as having the windows of my house smashed in on a regular basis. I am certainly not a stranger to the hurt and anger that comes along with anti-Semitism and I am personally involved in searching for a place which will lead to all forms of future human harmony.

Her articulation of cultural identity suggested that the dominant class views her as an outsider at the borders of whiteness (Frankenberg 230). She had pointed out the limitations of a black-and-white analysis of cultural marginalization historically and in the present setting.

Students spoke for two hours. One might argue that their use of personal testimony displaced the larger analysis of social inequalities they intended to resist. Yet the public staging and repetition of identity positions put forth in personal testimonies had an important pedagogical impact on the community. Student use of personal testimonies challenged and made visible the unacknowledged positions of dominant groups. In contrast to the president's "I," which spoke on behalf of a presumed collectivity, the "I" of the student testimonials expressed social affinities and recognized its outsider status among privileged discourses (Nichols 183). Much as the graffiti presumed a witness, the amplifying resonance of testifying turned both speakers and listeners into witnesses: speakers became witnesses of themselves and their position in the academy, and listeners became witnesses of the speakers' witnessing. The word *testimony* derives from the Latin *testi* ("witness"). As Young points out, "To testify is literally 'to make witness'— an etymological reminder that as witness and testimony are made, so is knowledge" (*Writing* 19). The graffiti incident and the speak-out taught students the power of language to shape action. Their testimonials, a creation of the contact zone, connected autobiography with political resistance (Pratt 446).[5]

Linking the Classroom and Community through a Pedagogy of Witnessing

The politics of language and identity highlighted in my analysis of the fall 1993 events on the Oberlin campus yields a range of pedagogical discourses. The color-blind and power-concealing rhetoric that the president and self-gagged white male student adopted (e.g., "We are all the same blood") translates into writing pedagogies and literacy projects that do not recognize power imbalances in communities and writing cultures. Pedagogies that conceptualize difference only as a matter of individual choice are based on the principles of cultural assimilation and personal responsibility, both of which are basic tenets of classical liberalism. Standpoints that ignore inequality can translate into practices that are far more conservative, practices that regulate the curriculum through corrective measures and domesticate historically oppressed groups by constructing pedagogies of language control, standardization, and normalization.[6] For example, instead of grappling with the increasing cultural and linguistic diversity on our nation's campuses, the new right has called for a return to the "great books" and the establishment of a common culture (A. Bloom; H. Bloom; Hirsch). Many multicultural writing pedagogies say that their objective is to integrate the works of groups historically oppressed, but many reproduce the status quo, simply adding more voices to the curriculum while preserving the language and values of the dominant group.[7] Similar patterns characterize early feminist pedagogies of writing, especially those that tried to validate women's experiences but ignored intersections of gender, race, class, sexuality, and national identity (see Hesford, "Autobiography"). Feminists should develop writing pedagogies that reflect the experiences and languages of traditionally oppressed groups and simultaneously bear witness to social constructions of whiteness and to the way such constructions shape reader-writer and student-teacher relations.

I urge feminists to develop activism-oriented pedagogies that recognize the intersections of social differences and the links between classroom and community rhetorics and that locate teachers and students at those intersections as cultural agents who extend and revise the practices of democracy. I do not advocate that feminists use their classrooms as political platforms but, rather, that they enable their students to understand better how institutions function so that the students can be more active in the history and transformation of those institutions.

Feminist teachers and activists in the academy must recognize how power and resistance are historically and discursively constructed at the crossroads of social differences and must use this knowledge to develop more reflective and democratic learning and writing communities.

During and immediately after the arch incident and cross burnings, many students said they had lost precious study time and undergone severe emotional stress. I invited students in my two introductory writing courses—Gender, Race, and Language; Basic Composition—to integrate their experiences into their course work. I encouraged them to examine how different theories of race, gender, and ethnicity and contesting narratives of community shaped the debates on campus over free speech, hate speech, and institutional racism. I wanted to create a pedagogy that framed the classroom and the campus as places of learning and rhetorical analysis, as places that made students reflect on their assumptions and positions in the community. To enlarge, as Henry Giroux puts it, "the range of cultural significations that can be taken up as classroom texts" (*Pleasures* 119), I had my students examine the campus events as textual and material phenomena. They clipped out articles, letters, and editorials from campus publications and listened to tapes of the speak-out and forums. Some students worked with Mary Louise Pratt's essay "Arts of the Contact Zone" to investigate the contesting rhetorics and power relations enacted in those spaces. I found Ruth Frankenberg's *White Women, Race Matters: The Social Construction of Whiteness* particularly useful in getting my white students to move beyond guilt and toward a historical understanding of whiteness that did not situate it beyond ethnicity, privilege, or struggle.

I encountered difficulties. White defensiveness, expressed by students in both oral and written exchanges, was a challenge pedagogically. Leslie Roman defines white defensiveness as "the relativistic assertion that whites, like 'people of color,' are history's oppressed subjects of racism" (71). One student in my introductory writing class that semester—I'll call him Stan—said during a class discussion that he felt excluded and unfairly positioned by students of color as the white male enemy. Like the self-gagged student, he felt he was a victim of reverse racism. Stan decided to write an essay about this experience and share an early draft of his paper, sarcastically titled "White, Middle-Class, Heterosexual, Adopted, Republican, Good-for-Nothing Male," with the class, which had only one other white male. (The students in this class had a range of cultural backgrounds: African American, Asian American, Latin American, Indian, Afghan.) In his first draft, Stan wrote, "White heterosexual males have a unique burden, to carry the shame of their descendants." He said he felt "completely shunned out and alienated" during the rallies on campus and was "enraged" over the meeting designed specifically for students of color.

During a class workshop, students raised questions that further antagonized Stan. An Asian American woman asked him what he had done to prove that he was not a stereotypical white male. I guided the class to move beyond personal criticism and look more closely at the principles and language informing Stan's position, to use the conceptual frameworks that I had introduced earlier in the course. We discussed the consequences of Stan's conflation of ethnic identity with race, a position that denies his whiteness. I should point out that there are personal psychological issues that inform Stan's observations about race. For instance, Stan writes about his experiences as an adopted child who has no knowledge of his own cultural heritage. As he puts it, "I have no history and thus feel alienated when it comes to race." After class, Stan told me that his classmates had convinced him that his argument was weak and his conclusions unsubstantiated. But he seemed even more defensive. I realized that his defensiveness might grow along with his awareness. I suggested that he talk with other students about their perceptions of or experiences as white men at Oberlin. The problem, as I saw it, was that Stan had positioned himself as the enemy and assumed the passivity of a victim. My objective was to get him to examine his defensiveness and realize also that he was generalizing the white male experience. Stan seized the opportunity and interviewed other male students at Oberlin about their responses to the recent incidents on campus. He then revised his paper, now titled "Perceptions of the White Heterosexual Male at Oberlin College." After Stan interviewed twenty students, seven of whom he identified as white heterosexual males, his conception of the white male community seemed to harden. A number of white males confirmed his position. One claimed that people at Oberlin expected him to be ashamed of who he was. This student, whom I will call Ben, continued, "Somehow, it was my responsibility to constantly feel apologetic for the foolishness of long since dead whites and the racist whites found throughout the world." Ben's testimony led Stan to conclude that such "outside pressure" was responsible for and justified Ben's indifference to the plight of minorities.

Stan's analysis of the evidence he gathered was not consistent. He reported that a black gay student, whom I will call Derek, felt that "we are all subject to the society that the white heterosexual male has created—a society in which white heterosexual males are privileged because of their race, sexuality, and gender." After providing examples of what Derek called the "destructiveness" of white heterosexual males, Stan made the following statement: Derek "doesn't believe we should blame individuals. He believes in educating individuals. . . . He doesn't believe in revenge or oppressing the white male." Stan said, "I agree, but he is still making negative generalizations of the white male as the greedy oppressor." Stan was unable to see the contradiction in his agreeing with Derek's analysis of the cumulative actions of individuals while disagreeing with Derek's historical grouping of white men.

I pointed out to Stan the gap between Derek's concept of oppression and Stan's understanding of race. By focusing Stan's attention on his own narrative of whiteness, I hoped to enable him to take a step beyond the essentialist discourse of reverse racism and recognize the historical inaccuracy in his equating his inaction and silence with the silences imposed on historically oppressed groups. It was not my intention to invalidate Stan's feeling of alienation, but it was my pedagogical responsibility to weigh his claim of victimization against a structural analysis of his social location. I wanted Stan and other students in the class to bear witness to the particularity of their struggles, privileges, and agency, to foster in my students the capacity to investigate historical events and experiences that may be dissonant cognitively and culturally.

A pedagogy of witnessing can help develop students' ability to interrogate those neutral legal principles and conceptualizations of the academy that are based on the imperatives of the white, Anglo, male world. A writing course with that pedagogy prepares students to respond to situations of conflict when they arise on campus, and it shapes student activism. I do not intend to reduce institutional racism, classism, heterosexism, and sexism to representations that are one more text to deconstruct. Rather, I invite students to investigate language and its relation to the material realities and systemic patterns of subordination. A pedagogy of witnessing strives for both critical reflection and action; it works against "cultural monumentalism" (Giroux, *Pleasures* 151) and calls for an interrogation of the past and the present as living history (Giroux, "Multiculturalism" 340).

The challenge for faculty members is to examine forms of institutional racism, sexism, ethnocentrism, and heterosexism at work in their classes and curricula. But curricular interrogation and revision alone cannot transform power relations in the academy; we must reinforce pedagogical changes with institutional reforms that give groups full participation in the project of re-creating democracy. The challenge for administrators is to look at hate crimes as part of a historical totality, to break away from binary models of difference (black-white, male-female) that ignore the complexity of racial and gender politics in America, and to use policy as an instrument of liberation, not domination. And we must recognize when the categories of equality and free speech collapse. We must "[draw] links between movements for social justice and our pedagogical and scholarly endeavors and [we must expect] and [demand] action from ourselves, our colleagues, and our students at numerous levels" (Mohanty 162). What is at stake is not simply a struggle over words in the contact zone of the academy but also a struggle over a whole range of institutional practices and social relations.

NOTES

I thank Ann Cooper Albright, Matthew Cariello, Jan Cooper, Leela Fernandez, Wendy Kozol, and the editors of this volume for their helpful suggestions and challenging questions. I also thank Adrienne Jones and Clayton Koppes for kindly giving me written copies of their speeches for this research.

[1]Oberlin College was the first coeducational institution of higher education in the United States (1833) and the first to admit African Americans to degree programs on an equal basis (1835) (Bigglestone). Despite its focus on equal access, Oberlin retained traditional divisons of labor. For example, its women students in the nineteenth century were expected to prepare themselves for motherhood and wifehood. Such traditions did not go unchallenged. Early Oberlin women activists included Antoinette Brown Blackwell, Lucy Stone, Mary Church Terrell (Fletcher; Solomon; Spain).

[2]For critiques of Western feminism see Alarcón; Barrett, "Meanings"; Brooks-Higginbotham; A. Davis; Ebert, "Ludic Feminism"; Hennessy; hooks, *Ain't*; Lorde, *Sister*; Spivak, *Post-colonial Critic*.

[3]There are three phrases of Oberlin's involvement in Asia. The first was the missionary phase. The second was the establishment of the Oberlin Shansi Memorial Association, which oversaw the secularization of educational work, the development of middle schools in Asia, and the establishment of an agricultural department and a research center in China. The third was mutual educational exchange. Currently, the association offers fellowships to any member of the Oberlin graduating class to teach English in Asia for two years. Students may apply to teach in universities in India, Indonesia, Japan, or the People's Republic of China (Carlson).

[4]First Amendment absolutists support unconditional protection for speech in all circumstances. See Smolla on the differences between absolute absolutism and qualified absolutism, especially 23–27.

[5]A now classic example of the use of autobiography as a medium of social protest is the Combahee River Collective's manifesto opposing racism of white middle-class feminism. As Sidonie Smith points out, autobiographical manifestos issue a call to action and foreground group identification over individuality (160–61).

[6]See Mohanty, "Race," for a compelling analysis of race management pedagogies and practices in the academy. For critiques of the rhetoric of equality and community in composition pedagogy see Chordas; J. Harris; Shirk.

[7]See Giroux and McLaren; McCarthy; and Thompson and Tyagi for more detailed discussion of institutionalized multiculturalism and the politics of multicultural education.

Equivalent Students, Equitable Classrooms

Christy Desmet

We the Jury: The Metaphor of Classroom as Courtroom

A number of years ago, I served on a jury for the first time. A young white woman's purse had been snatched, and an even younger black man was on trial for the theft. A piece of pure chance raised the stakes for both parties. The purse in question had contained $600, which made the crime a felony, not a misdemeanor. The jury, sequestered in a back room containing one table and a tiny rest room, was composed of four white men, four white women, two African American women, and two African American men. We conferred for seven hours. Periodically we took anonymous votes on small slips of paper but never came close to a consensus. Each time the jury was almost evenly divided, half of us voting guilty and half not guilty. Our group became even more discouraged after we revealed our positions to one another. The white men had consistently voted guilty, while the African Americans of both genders had consistently voted not guilty. The white women's slight wavering accounted for the small variation in numbers for each vote.

When we discussed openly the basis for these positions, it became clear that we came to this story with very different experiences and attitudes toward the law. Race and gender seemed to exacerbate the differences. One white male juror, a father of three, said, "I just know that young man is guilty and I can't let him back on the street." A black woman who taught middle school suggested that the prosecuting attorneys were relying on prejudice when they insinuated that the boy's grandmother, an elderly woman on public assistance, could never have provided the defendant with the $250 found on his person by police. With the dinner hour hard upon us, we began using the small

153

slips of paper to vote for our favorite pizza, when the judge declared a mistrial and sent us home.

I found this foray into American justice thoroughly disheartening, at least until I saw the same rhetorical situation repeated, with a difference, in my freshman composition classroom. In the spring quarter of 1994, I taught a beginning writing class centered on logic and argumentation. We had read a brief essay by Robert L. Rose entitled "Is Saving Legal?" Written in an evenhanded, journalistic style, it concerned Mrs. Capetillo, a woman on welfare who had inadvertently broken the law by saving money for her daughter's college education. (Her savings account had exceeded the $1,000 legal limit for individuals receiving public assistance.) In our discussion, the three African American students in the class (two women and one man) united in their defense of Mrs. Capetillo, the welfare mother from New York who had aspirations for her daughter's education. Their argument was based on the primacy of the mother-daughter bond and on a firm belief that Mrs. Capetillo's daughter deserved a chance to break out of the cycle of poverty that had put her mother on public assistance in the first place. The other students energetically voiced the opinion that individuals are responsible for knowing and upholding the law. During our discussion, the class, like my jury, was divided along racial, but also along ethical, lines.

What finally focused our debate in a useful way was one student's ability to imagine the material existence of Mrs. Capetillo. Kim, one of the African Americans, responded firmly to another student's suggestion that Mrs. Capetillo was not trying hard enough to get a job. Kim spoke at length of how much time and effort are required to satisfy a family's basic needs under conditions of poverty. Trying to make nutritious meals on a hot plate and without a refrigerator and trying to care for children while holding a job that did not pay enough for day care worked against Mrs. Capetillo's desire for independence. To care properly for her daughter, Mrs. Capetillo had to accept public assistance. As the one student in the class who had been reared in Atlanta public housing and who was attending the university on an athletic scholarship, Kim spoke with authority. More important, she translated the evidence of personal experience into a coherent defense of the welfare mother.

When Kim came to Mrs. Capetillo's defense, taking a strong ethical position that challenged existing alliances among students in the class, she introduced into the debate a feeling of risk coupled with a need for commitment. As the class addressed seriously the danger a trial posed to Mrs. Capetillo and her family, a new mood was felt. Kim and several others seemed to feel that they, like Mrs. Capetillo, had been put at risk, since the newly personalized tone of the discussion made abstract generalizations about welfare reform impossible. Members of the class began to argue with a sense of urgency, to commit themselves to a verdict either of guilt or innocence. The class had experienced what I would call a judicial moment. Like my jury, we recognized what was at stake. Unlike the jury, we moved through abstract positions to a clearer sense of ethical priorities if not a consensus.

The resemblance between my frustrated jury and this successful class discussion has led me to rethink the usefulness of judicial metaphors for composition pedagogy. As Patricia Bizzell has argued, the popular image of courtroom debate provides students with a powerful and sometimes pernicious model for the exchange of ideas. She suggests that the media represent ideas as self-evident and public debate as a series of stated positions, a shouting match rather than a reasoned dialogue, and concludes that students have problems with academic discourse because they have grown up in the kangaroo courts of *Oprah* and *Crossfire* ("Ethos").

Although writers like Bizzell recognize the currency of judicial metaphors for intellectual exchange, feminist pedagogy has traditionally rejected the characterization of a teacher as a judge (of writing or of student opinion). Feminist jurisprudence, however, can provide composition pedagogy with a useful perspective on the metaphorical equation between courtroom and classroom. Feminist theorists of the law have long sought to reconcile an ethics centered on the subjectivity of individual women with a global politics of gender. Theorizing about power relations, feminist jurisprudence argues that the judicial subject is defined by negotiating the distance between a person's particular circumstances and the place assigned to that person by a system of legal definitions. Two concepts deriving from debate among theorists of law make that negotiation possible. The first is equity, as it has been defined by Martha Nussbaum ("Equity") and implied in the work of other theorists. According to Nussbaum, equity is a principle of mercy, a leniency that goes beyond the law but is nevertheless necessary to the ethical functioning of law itself. The law may define a woman as a murderer when a jury convicts her of killing her husband, yet the principle of equity points to mitigating circumstances that make the label of murderer inadequate to define her legally. In this sense, equity depends on close and sympathetic attention to narrative detail, an effort to show how stories contradict categories.

The other concept is equivalence, which has been defined most clearly by the legal theorist Drucilla Cornell ("Gender Hierarchy," "Sex-Discrimination Law," "Sexual Difference"). The notion of equivalence, building on equity's attention to detail, revises existing legal categories. For instance, equivalence argues that because pregnancy is not a disease, pregnancy leave for women should not be treated exactly like sick leave for conditions such as cancer in men. The law should establish, between conditions for leave from work, an equivalence that attends to differences among groups of people without denying their common identity as employees. In developing the metaphorical equation of court to classroom, I suggest that feminist jurisprudence can provide the foundation for a utopian vision of classroom praxis that reimagines relations among teacher and students without denying real discrepancies of power.

Gender, Power, and the Panopticon

Much recent discussion of composition pedagogy centers on issues of power. Feminist theorists in particular have examined how pedagogies that in theory should empower student writers re-create the hierarchies they seek to dismantle. Pedagogies that valorize writers' private experiences and those that offer them access to public discourse have been equally vulnerable to this charge. Susan Jarratt, for instance, shows that although Peter Elbow's expressivist pedagogy endows the ideal reader with traditionally feminine virtues—openness, empathy, and even passivity—Elbow's decentered classroom could put women students at a double disadvantage by asking them to mime behaviors already assigned to them by cultural fiat ("Feminism"). At the other end of the spectrum, Sandra Stotsky seeks to enfranchise students by inviting them to participate in civic discourse, but she recommends a code of professional decorum that promotes stereotypically feminine character traits. According to Stotsky, students of public discourse should show respect to their subject matter, their readers, and other writers. They become passive and self-effacing, deferring to the opinions and expertise of others. Ironically, participating in public discourse under Stotsky's rules may constrain women writers already trained in civility rather than authorize them to speak out or act up.[1]

With both Elbow and Stotsky, a refusal to classify writers by gender obscures the operations of power in the writing classroom and the academy in general. Michel Foucault's classic study *Discipline and Punish* helps define power relations in composition pedagogy by linking the emergence of the modern prison with the highly regulated schools of eighteenth-century France. Both institutions feature a rigid and detailed mechanism for disciplining subjects that works by obscuring the source of power. The subjects of this discipline are subject to those who have power over them precisely because the subjects can be observed without their being able to see those who orchestrate their behavior. In the *école militaire*, masters presided over meals from a dais that permitted them to survey all their charges at once (173). Toilets also had half doors so that the heads and legs of students could be seen at all times. According to Foucault, prisons perfected the art of disciplining even more thoroughly than the schools did by obscuring completely the sources of power. Jeremy Bentham's prison plan epitomizes for Foucault the way in which discipline depends on invisible power. In Bentham's prison, separate cells are illuminated so that the isolated prisoners can be seen without their seeing the observer, who watches everything from a central structure called the panopticon.

Foucault connects the development of these institutions to a more global judicial transformation, in which the judge's power and responsibility for punishing social transgressions are dispersed throughout systems. No longer is punishment a concrete matter, decreed by individual judges and carried out on the bodies of prisoners by executioners locked in a personal relationship with them by virtue of physical and spiritual proximity. In Foucault's analysis, the disappearance of the judge—the diffusion of the judge's power and responsibility throughout an impersonal structure—doubly disempowers those caught in the discipline mechanisms, including those caught in the "pedagogical machine." Feminist teachers who unilaterally refuse to play judge in their classrooms therefore may occupy the panopticon unwittingly. In this case, it would make sense for them to work with rather than resist judicial metaphors for classroom praxis.

The Subject of Violence in Jurisprudence and Composition Theory

Establishing an analogy between class and court begins with Foucault's recognition that relations of power are founded on acts of violence, violence that forms of discipline can obscure but do not eradicate. Working with judicial metaphors for classroom practice therefore means recognizing and taking responsibility for pedagogical violence. Feminist pedagogues have expressed discomfort with the violence implied by such metaphors but have not resolved the ethical problems entailed by denying the existence of that violence. Olivia Frey writes, "In too many old writing classes, the student perceived the teacher as the judge on the side of the system, upholding the rules even at the expense of the student" ("Equity" 100). Feminist writers like Frey have defined the classroom as a peaceful place, where the teacher acts as facilitator, mother, or mediator—anything but a judge. Catherine Lamb, for instance, recommends mediation and negotiation as feminist species of debate that allow power to be shared in a benign way. For Lamb, equity in the classroom is achieved by rejecting violence and refusing judgment. Violence, however, is pervasive in the academy. Lynn Worsham argues that even emancipatory pedagogy may subject students to violence. She writes that "the specific goal of pedagogic work" is to train individuals for their appropriate place in a "hierarchy of social relations." In that structure, pedagogy "retains its authority precisely through violence, through its power to conceal and mystify relations of domination" ("Emotion" 125). Pedagogy may deny but cannot destroy the panopticon.

Feminist jurisprudence, in contrast, takes as its starting point the palpable reality of the law's violence. Robert Cover, whose work is not explicitly feminist but congenial to and formative for some feminist writers, acknowledges that legal acts of all kinds are violent, involving relations of domination and subjection that result in real suffering: "A judge articulates her understanding of a text, and as a result, somebody loses his freedom, his property, his children, even his life" (203). As the judge interprets the law to render a sentence, "she also acts— through others—to restrain, hurt, render helpless, even kill the prisoner" (213). Thus judge and defendant become like torturer and victim: they share a world only by virtue of their diametrically opposed experiences of the act of punishment.

Mitigating Violence: Equity and the Ethics of Narrative

Robin West, among other legal writers, attempts to mitigate the harshness of law's violence by emphasizing the importance of storytelling to justice and therefore to the distribution of punishments. Narratives, she argues, give us access not only to objective facts about any action but also to the subjective life of the actors: "When we tell stories, we not only convey information, but we share a piece of history; we expand not only our knowledge of what happened, of what someone did, but also of why and how they did it, of how it felt, why it seemed necessary, how it fit into a worldview." West imagines legal stories functioning to break down "barriers between persons from different backgrounds to reclaim and honor the traditions of our past, to empathize with others, and to actually build upon, rather than simply rest upon, the bonds of community" (425). Ultimately, by telling and listening to legal stories, we all share responsibility for the criminal's fate as well as for the criminal's violence.

The interest in the power of storytelling expressed by West and other critical theorists of law is paralleled in composition theory. For some time now, ethnographic studies and literacy narratives have given us stories about the subjectivity of individual writers, especially those living on the margins of the academy, stories that record their pain and punishment under the academy's laws. Mike Rose's *Lives on the Boundary* offers a number of such stories. There is Marita, who was "on trial" for an act of plagiarism. She had copied the work of others because she knew that academic writing proceeded by citation but she did not know how to position herself in academic discourse. There is Andrea, a student struggling through chemistry, who carried a backpack weighing twenty pounds, was anemic, lacked sleep, and drove her car into a tree. Rose's vignettes of his students' intellectual life dramatize the kind of bodily pain and suffering that Cover insists is inflicted by the law. Rose's rhetoric encourages us to understand the life and motivations of those on the margin and also to take responsibility for their failures.[2]

Although literacy narratives often tend toward tragedy, composition studies researchers and practitioners have expressed strong faith in the power of stories to confer worth and agency on student writers. May Soliday advocates the use of literacy narratives that allow students to shift imaginatively between stories and vocabularies from different arenas in their lives. Especially striking is Lynn Bloom's narrative of her efforts to find a voice as teacher and writer. Bloom's autobiographical piece culminates with her telling a class of students—who disagreed about what happens in Joyce Carol Oates's story "Where Are You Going, Where Have You Been?"—a personal account of how she, too, narrowly evaded rape in a foreign country. Bloom's and Oates's narratives, it turns out, provide a vocabulary of resistance for one student in the class, who returns home to face and evade a rapist in her own kitchen. Bloom's message is that literacy narratives like these, shared between teacher and students in a writing class, can literally save lives.

Feminist jurisprudence suggests, more skeptically, that narratives can serve widely divergent political purposes. Legal theorists, including many feminists, have turned to the notion of equity to define an ethics for interpreting those judicial stories. At least since Aristotle, equity has been defined as a principle of fairness grounded in a close examination of circumstances behind a crime.[3] Although the question of whether equity belongs to the law or supplements the law has long been debated, in both cases equity involves not only interpretation but also a willingness to engage in interpersonal relations. Aristotle's *Nicomachean Ethics* and *Rhetoric* define equity as an attempt to honor the lawmaker's original intention or, the alternative, to adjust general laws to specific cases. In the first kind of equity, the judge engages imaginatively with the law's author; in the second kind, with the convicted criminal. Historically, the sympathetic relationship during sentencing between criminal and judge or jury—the second kind of equity—has proved more problematic in Western judicial systems (see Hoffer 17–21; Foucault, *Rivière*).

Martha Nussbaum insists on the emotional basis of equity. She considers equity an act of mercy, a leniency that results from weighing mitigating circumstances more heavily than aggravating circumstances. Basing her definition on ancient philosophy and in opposition to current Supreme Court opinion, she argues that Aristotle's equitable person "is characterized by a sympathetic understanding of 'human things'" ("Equity" 94). According to Nussbaum's reading of Aristotle's *Rhetoric*, an ability to understand events in all their narrative particularity—which allows a judge to adjust general laws to specific cases—depends on sympathetic understanding of the person who committed the crime: "One must . . . see things from that person's point of view, for only then will one begin to comprehend what obstacles that person faced as he or she acted" (94). In *Love's Knowledge*, which discusses the philosophical function of the emotions, Nussbaum subscribes to the Aristotelian view that emotions, which are "composites of belief and feeling," play a role in practical reasoning. Intellect alone reinforces habit; emotion, in contrast, makes us responsive to new and different situations (78–79). Thus emotion plays the same role in individual choices that equity plays in the judiciary, adjusting universal laws to particular cases.[4]

Nussbaum's "emotional knowing" (285), rooted in particular situations and entailing relationships with particular persons, combines objective knowledge (of events and circumstances) with subjective knowledge (of persons and characters). To this extent, Nussbaum's vision of equity answers the feminist philosopher Lorraine Code's

call for an understanding of knowledge that breaks down the opposition between objective knowledge, traditionally characterized as
masculine, and subjective experience, traditionally characterized as
feminine.

Nussbaum makes two important contributions to the discussion of
intersections between feminist pedagogy and feminist jurisprudence.
The first is her insistence on the subjective dimension of judgment, the
need for mercy grounded in sympathy and related emotions. She
thereby permits us to imagine a classroom that accepts emotion and
experience without denying the institutional power structures of the
academy. The second is her notion that equitable judgment is an act of
reading. She thereby makes interpretation of texts and actions a paradigm for the general understanding of the classroom as courtroom.
The problem with Nussbaum's judicial vision is her mechanism for
ethical reading. Preferring the realistic novels of the nineteenth century, she sees reading as a free and democratic activity, an opportunity
for our absorption into the life of a fictional other that transcends differences of class and history.[5] She therefore denies the violence that
upholds law and the cultural inequalities that make equity necessary
to justice.

Escaping Essentialism: The Politics of Equivalence

What Nussbaum's description of equity lacks is an acknowledgment of
power, of the panopticon's invisible influence. To address the unequal
power relations that characterize public institutions and therefore
condition the stories about individuals "on trial," a number of feminist
thinkers begin by critiquing the notion of equality under the law. Elizabeth Wolgast argues that while equality of the sexes should remain a
political goal for feminists, the notion of equality itself ignores relevant differences among people and the existence of multiple social relations.[6] Martha Minow, however, shows that recognizing difference
does not in itself ensure equitable treatment for all individuals under
the law. She argues that the binary opposition between equality and
difference puts women and other marginalized individuals in a double
bind, which she calls the "dilemma of difference" (20). Ignoring difference in the case of subordinated groups means reifying a false neutrality; focusing on difference can stigmatize those who deviate from the
norm.

Minow offers as an example the politics of education in San Francisco public schools. During the 1960s, teachers taught their classes in

English. A group of parents charged that their children, who spoke largely Chinese, were being deprived of an equal education. "The parents pushed the courts to consider whether according the same treatment to people who differ—to the students who speak English and to those who speak Chinese—violates commitments to equality" (19). In 1974, the Supreme Court, agreeing that the Chinese students suffered from unequal treatment, directed the school system to rectify their language deficiencies. Emphasizing difference turned out to stigmatize the Chinese students, by segregating them in separate language classes for part of the school day. At the same time and using comparable rhetoric, parents of children with disabilities claimed that their children were also suffering from unequal treatment and demanded that students with physical or mental disabilities be mainstreamed. Again the school systems complied, but this time they erased rather than exaggerated differences among children in a school. The dilemma of difference, according to Minow, is a paradox in which difference can be stigmatized both by being privileged and by being ignored.

Faced with this dilemma, some feminist thinkers recommend abandoning the language of legal rights altogether. Feminist jurisprudence, assuming the inevitability of courtroom conflicts, focuses instead on the problematic nature of the equality-difference dialectic in specific cases.[7] Drucilla Cornell, analyzing sex discrimination in the workplace, argues for a concept of equivalent rights rather than equal rights. Under a program of equal rights, "the wrong of sex discrimination is not the imposition of stereotypes per se, but the imposition of stereotypes when they are not 'true'—that is, when the stereotypes are not an adequate description of the actual life of the person" ("Sex-Discrimination Law" 147). Thus, if a job requires employees to lift two hundred pounds and a particular woman can lift two hundred pounds, to deny her that job may be treated as sex discrimination.

What interests Cornell more are instances in which the stereotypes are true. For example, the difference drawn between men and women according to women's capacity and desire to bear children has resulted in a situation where women are expected either to embrace an ideology of sameness—men and women working under exactly the same rules—or to accept the stigmatization of their difference, such as derailment onto the "mommy track." A principle of equivalent rights deconstructs the dilemma of difference by recognizing relevant differences between women and men without either requiring women to show that they are like men for legal purposes or forcing women to accept inequitable treatment based on those real differences. Under a system of equivalent rights, a woman could receive pregnancy leave not by analogy to the leave a man would receive for a heart attack or cancer but on the basis of her special condition or her "lived individuality" (154).

By advocating that feminists pursue equivalent rather than equal rights, Cornell echoes the philosopher Elizabeth Spelman's position that categories such as male, female, white, and African American have significance only in larger contexts of classification. For example, if we divide Americans into four categories (African American, European American, Asian American, and Hispanic American), then subdivide each category according to gender, we focus primarily on differences within an ethnic group, and by that schema differences among women are not obvious. If we start instead with male and female, then subdivide according to ethnicity, we observe more clearly differences within the broad categories of men and women. We recognize four distinct kinds of women.

The categories that we use to define people in relation to one another Spelman calls doors (142–58). At each step of classification, one must choose a door. In judicial situations, categorical systems have particular force. For example, in the Congressional hearings on the nomination of Clarence Thomas to the Supreme Court, which despite Joseph Biden's protests to the contrary functioned as a loosely constructed trial, Thomas's insistence that he was being lynched as a black male transformed Anita Hill into the white woman whose sexuality provoked the lynching (see Fraser). This judicial episode and Spelman's feminist perspective both underscore the hidden politics behind all classifications. Spelman reminds us that "we get different pictures of people's identities and of the extent to which one person shares some aspect of identity with another, depending on what the doors are, how they are ordered, and how people are supposed to proceed through them" (146). For both Cornell and Spelman the important question is "Who controls the doors?" (see esp. Spelman 146–47).

Cornell imagines two ways to expose and challenge the hidden sources of power constructing the doors that define public identity. First, she analyzes skeptically the ethical foundations of law itself. Second, she defines the political goal of feminist jurisprudence as a revision of Aristotelian friendship, a move that connects her belief in the efficacy of deconstruction with her effort to affirm the value of women's lived individuality ("Sex-Discrimination Law" 154). Both approaches suggest the possibility of legal activism through deconstructive reading.

In "The Violence of the Masquerade," a more theoretical essay about judicial ethics, Cornell begins with Jacques Derrida's deconstruction of the law's moral authority. Derrida suggests, in his "Force of Law," that law does not equal justice precisely because law rests on a "mystical foundation of authority," a phrase he borrows from Montaigne. Law rests on a mystical foundation because nothing legitimizes the law but law itself: applications of the law are justified by reference to the law, which is in turn justified by reference to conventions and previous legal fictions rather than to any foundational truth. The search for the law's origin recedes infinitely into the past as the quest for justice stretches impossibly into the future. Thus law is ultimately illegitimate. For this reason, Derrida concludes, as Robert Cover did, that all legal acts are violent ("Force" 15).

If all legal acts are violent, then the law is inherently political and concerned with power. Cornell develops this observation into a mandate for deconstructive reading as legal activism. Acknowledging "the uncrossable divide between law and justice" ("Violence" 1049) and recognizing that interpretation is itself a kind of violence, she explores the ethics of reading law deconstructively. She uses Derrida's surprising assertion that while the law rests on a mystical foundation that precludes it from being just, "deconstruction is justice" ("Force" 15). That is, justice exists only as an aporia, an interpretive impasse that disrupts the symmetrical equation between the violence of injustice and the violence of the law that corrects injustice. Thus justice, like all deconstructive acts, is eternally deferred.

Since the problem of injustice cannot be resolved, we are all responsible for the law's violence. Although deconstructive reading unmasks the law's meaning as undecidable, we are not allowed to rest smugly in a state of interpretive superiority. Derrida speaks of a "responsibility without limits" (19). Cornell concurs that we are left "with an *inescapable responsibility* for violence, precisely because violence cannot be fully rationalized and therefore justified in advance" ("Violence" 1049). Ironically, to realize that the law's violence rests on a fictional foundation is to become implicated in its violence. For this reason, Cornell feels that the inexorability of the law despite all challenges to it is a horror story.

Derrida responds to this horror story by erasing the distance between universal law and particular cases: "Each case is other, each decision is different and requires an absolutely unique interpretation, which no existing, coded rule can or ought to guarantee absolutely" ("Force" 23). Derrida's just judge improvises, reinventing the law in each and every case. Cornell translates Derrida's vision of an improvisational equity into feminist terms by appealing to the psychoanalytic concept of the masquerade. If Derrida argues that the law's mystical foundation obscures the law's dependence on violence, Cornell, in more strongly gendered language, characterizes the law as violence dressed up as justice. She uses a critical vocabulary that leaves room for feminist activism.

Cornell's phrase "the violence of the masquerade" operates by the logic of chiasmus: while a masquerade is a kind of violence, violence is a kind of mask. With this rhetorical gesture Cornell draws on the Freudian and Lacanian notion that femininity is a mask that conceals woman's lack. But feminist psychoanalysis reveals the lack that defines woman—her failure to possess the phallus—to be a rhetorical construct. Femininity is not something real but a mask or fiction that legitimizes masculine identity by functioning as its opposite. The idea that femininity is a mask is also double-edged. On the one hand, the masquerade denies women an essential identity. On the other, it can provide women with opportunities for agency through improvisation. If femininity is a masquerade, the argument goes, then a woman can "play the woman or not as she so pleases" (Wright 243–44).[8]

Although Cornell does not define clearly the term "masquerade," in *Beyond Accommodation* she recommends Luce Irigaray's idea of mimesis as an antidote to repressive constructions of gender, and I would argue that in this context "masquerade" and "mimesis" are closely related if not synonymous. Cornell argues that "we must work through the metaphors of the feminine" (146), citing Irigaray's belief that at least initially one "must assume the feminine role deliberately" (Irigaray 76; see Worsham, "Writing"). Whereas a masquerade is a condition, mimesis is a strategy, evaluating rather than merely reproducing the sex-gender system described by psychoanalysis (Cornell, *Accommodation* 148). Further, mimesis turns woman's status as object in relation to masculine subjectivity to an advantage by allowing her to identify with other objects and so achieve an "ethical relation to otherness" (148). More concretely, woman's ambiguous status in the masquerade—her lack of any identity outside improvisation—permits her to embrace rather than passively absorb the other (149). Thus redefining "masquerade" as "mimesis" allows Cornell to figure the performance of feminine identity as a positive political action.

Cornell's focus on the dynamics of the masquerade and on mimesis as a political strategy that can disrupt the violent operations of binary thinking has implications for composition studies. Other writers have defined students' relation to the academy in terms that recall the masquerade. Peter Elbow, although using a different critical vocabulary, defines academic discourse as a form of masquerade that hides the mystical foundations of its authority through rhetorical sleight of hand. He writes, "The very thing that is attractive and appealing about academic discourse is inherently problematic and perplexing. It tries to peel away from messages the evidence of how these messages are situated as the center of personal, political, or cultural interest" ("Reflections" 141). Training students to produce academic discourse is therefore an act of violence dressed up as justice.

Some composition theorists respond to the violence and mysticism surrounding academic discourse by focusing on the liberating potential of mimesis. David Bartholomae offers mimesis as an enabling strategy for basic writers, who in his opinion might "need to learn to crudely mimic the 'distinctive register' of academic discourse before they are prepared to actually and legitimately do the work of the discourse, and before they are sophisticated enough with the refinements of tone and gesture to do it with grace or elegance" (162). Although Bartholomae emphasizes the advantages of learning to play by the academy's rules, some feminist writers have embraced mimesis as a more revolutionary strategy, imagining a writing classroom in which *écriture féminine* shatters the facade of patriarchal discourse (Junker) or at least a classroom in which writing as a woman is possible (Howe; Annas; Frey, "Darwinism").

Mimesis in composition studies, as a strategy of either accommodation or resistance, has remained largely a technique, a local tactic rather than a means for evaluating institutions or for defining ethical relations between self and other. From the standpoint of Cornell's feminist deconstruction, mimesis as a local tactic or mere technique simplifies the relation between writer and the academy by failing to confront the existence of the panopticon at the center of educational institutions. Bartholomae comes close to assuming that basic writers can be legitimated by a system he implies is neutral. By the logic of the masquerade, however, others who seek access to the academy will, without a systemic change in the academy, always be in disguise. They will never become authentic (or, at least, authenticated) scholars. Conversely, in a writing classroom that culminates in graded products there can be no triumphant escape from academic discipline. At this point, Cornell's use of masquerade-mimesis as a deconstructive strategy becomes helpful because it seeks to achieve political change without denying the sex-gender system that prevents isolated legal reforms from being revolutionary. Cornell's deconstruction seeks to refigure gender relations or, in Spelman's terms, to alter the system of doors that defines public identity. Thus the politics of equivalence completes the work of equity, providing a context in which the narratives that

give voice to lived individuality can affect symbolic relations in the
public sphere.

A Politics of Friendship in the Writing Classroom

The question remains how a dialectic between equity (respect for lived
individuality) and equivalence (disruption of existing institutional categories) might affect classroom praxis. Cornell's understanding of jurisprudence depends on a revisionary notion of community. Her
strong faith in the feminist's ability to embrace the other might seem
sentimental. Joseph Harris reminds us that in composition studies as
well, *community* can easily become "an empty and sentimental word"
(13). But the recognition of violence that Cornell brings to jurisprudence allows her to imagine a masquerade that is dynamic rather than
progressive, centered on an ethical imperative rather than on a dream
of perfect social harmony.

Cornell concludes her response to Derrida's essay "Force of Law" by
evoking Monique Wittig's myth of the Amazons in *Les guérillères*. If the
Amazons overthrow patriarchy and create a new state, Wittig asks, do
they not reinstate patriarchy by re-creating the state? Cornell answers
that the Amazons are protected ethically by their less-than-complete
understanding of their action. The Amazons' inability to see clearly either past or future—to penetrate the mystical foundation of authority—is what makes their action revolutionary. They emphatically do
not occupy the panopticon. Thus, in Cornell's rewriting of the Amazons' myth, the restrictiveness of the masquerade become the masquerade's political strength. Cornell's version of the Amazons' story
might be attractive to many teachers of composition, who according
to Susan Miller ("Feminization") and others occupy the devalued feminine position in the academy.[9]

In response to Derrida's demand for a "responsibility without limits," Cornell defines public life as a "politics of friendship," a phrase
she takes from Derrida. In his essay "The Politics of Friendship," Derrida proposes that "we are speaking first of all from within the tradition of a certain concept of friendship, within a given culture, let us
say ours, in any case the one on the basis of which a certain 'we' tries
its luck here" (634). Such a friendship, according to Derrida, is a tentative, provisional, contingent thing: "Friendship is never a given in
the present; it belongs to the experience of waiting, of promise, or
of commitment" (636). Although friendship is directed toward the

future, it also involves a sense of excessive responsibility grounded in past relationships. To enter into friendship in Derrida's polis is, paradoxically, to be on trial. For this reason, friendship can exist only as a politics, an action rather than a state of being.

Cornell remakes Derrida's politics of friendship into a masquerade where the psychoanalytic construction of gender provides the model by which fragmented subjects—not only women but also cultural others of various kinds—can maneuver within existing social hierarchies. In her essay "Gender Hierarchy, Equality, and the Possibility of Democracy," she begins with Jacques Lacan's observation that since gender identity is constructed through language, there can never be a complete identification of oneself with one's gender. In Cornell's formulation, Derrida's intervention into the Lacanian system translates Lacan's observations about psychology into juridical philosophy and reminds us that there is continual slippage in the use of language. That slippage mandates a recognition of the contingency of identity in any given situation. Because identity is contingent, Lacan's definition of woman as lack has no essential force. To the contrary, Cornell reaches a politically optimistic conclusion: "Derrida argues that the performative aspect of language which defines gender roles cannot be thought of other than through their performance. As such, the signifier has no essential determining power, and with language, we can play at what we become and not simply submit to determinations whose origins would reside outside that language" ("Hierarchy" 257). Derrida's performative ethics is therefore simultaneously a politics, a vision of civic friendship that resists masculinist stereotypes in the act of evoking them.

Cornell revises Derrida's politics of friendship in a way that is both more forceful and more guarded than Derrida's line of argument. Although she praises Derrida for recommending supposedly feminine virtues like care, gentleness, and an "appreciation of heterogeneity" (258), she stresses that the phallic economy exiling women from public life is pervasive. Elsewhere she cites bell hooks's belief that racism also operates according to a "phallic logic" ("Difference" 131). By envisioning a polis whose structure is fluid, Cornell emphasizes even more than Derrida does that friendship is an effect of politics. Her imaginary court, unlike that of other legal writers, has no judge; there is no fixed place for an authority who decrees the appropriateness of mercy or who hands down opinions that reconfigure legal categories. Power may be dispersed in Cornell's judiciary, but it is not hidden. The partial vision that deconstructive reading offers of the relation between universal laws and individual cases—the partial understanding that characterizes the Amazons' revolution—denies all members of the system the comfort of prescribed roles. As Cornell puts it, we are all responsible for the law's violence.

I would suggest that in the writing classroom, as in Cornell's decentered court, "a certain 'we' tries its luck here" on a daily basis. Within the terms established by Cornell's politics of friendship, the equation between court and classroom offers itself as both a description of existing conditions and a utopian metaphor for classroom relations. In the anecdote that began this essay, I argued that Kim demonstrated equity by showing leniency to Mrs. Capetillo, the hapless welfare mother in our textbook. Kim recommended mercy for Mrs. Capetillo because Kim identified with her experience and had sympathy for her plight. But Kim behaved equitably also by unfolding Mrs. Capetillo's case in all its possible particularity, detailing the daily problems of preparing dinner and of arranging for child care. At the same time, Kim moved the discussion beyond identity politics by aligning herself with a woman different from her in race and geographical region. Demanding respect for Mrs. Capetillo's lived individuality, she applied the principle of equivalence and challenged the stereotype of the welfare mother who does not enter the workforce.

In that judicial moment, Kim's intervention achieved something like what Patricia Williams calls the "hard work of a nonracist sensibility," which she describes as "the willingness to spoil a good party and break an encompassing circle, to travel from the safe to the unsafe" (129). Yet that moment also did not take place, since the students' essays that resulted from the discussion, although to my mind stronger in argument and firmer in prose style than any previous productions, were less than revolutionary in their political sentiments. A pedagogy based on equivalent rights, as described by Cornell, focuses not only on the importance of lived individuality but also on the rhetoric of equivalence that gives lived individuality significance in the public sphere. It must be utopian rather than essentialist. As Cornell reminds us in *Beyond Accommodation*, revisionary metaphors are necessarily utopian. My exploration of the classroom as courtroom is also utopian, envisioning a classroom that acknowledges the panopticon without assenting to its replication. A pedagogy based on a feminist politics of friendship aims, finally, to create what Kenneth Burke calls the "dancing of an attitude" (11), a desire for community that respects lived individuality rather than legislates homogeneity in the classroom.

NOTES

A number of people helped this essay become a reality. Susan Jarratt and Lynn Worsham offered a careful reading and intelligent editorial suggestions. Patrick McCord and Clai Rice read the manuscript, argued with its premises, and helped me revise the argument. Aaron Parrett and Marisa Pagnattaro helped identify key problems in the comparison between the law and composition pedagogy. Most important to my understanding of feminist pedagogy, however, has been the continued conversation and friendship of the "lady rhetoricians," especially Kathy Houff, Parker Luchte, Deborah Miller, Kris Sieloff, and Rochelle Glenn.

[1]Christy Friend gives an intelligent assessment of how Stotsky denies relevant differences between students in the name of promoting equality in the classroom.

[2]Many literacy narratives articulate a relation between individual pain and loss and unwritten social laws. Linda Brodkey's account of her socialization into academic success is structured around sewing as a healing metaphor but also chronicles her loss of communication with her working-class father ("Writing"). Another powerful account of culturally derived pain in the writing class is by Carole Deletiner. And Elizabeth Chiseri-Strater's study of the public and private discourse of students records moment by moment their frustration and their struggles to find a place in the university.

[3]For a good general definition and history of equity, especially in the American judicial tradition, see Hoffer.

[4]But Nussbaum does not use the term *equity* in this context. See "Equity."

[5]Relying on Adam Smith's *Theory of Moral Sentiments*, Nussbaum assumes a nearly complete identification of readers with characters that ignores differences of race, class, and gender—differences that have preoccupied feminist thinkers. She writes, "Identifying with a wide range of characters from different social circumstances and concerning oneself in each case with the entire history of their efforts, the reader comes to have emotions both sympathetic and participatory toward the things that they do and suffer." But she also claims that the reader's distance from the circumstances in which the reader participates imaginatively and emotionally makes the reader's judgments "neutral" ("Equity" 110). Thus Nussbaum overvalues at once subjective experience and objective knowledge.

[6]Wolgast's discussions of case law are by now outdated, but her discussions of equality and of the uses and limits of Aristotelian friendship as a model for judicial relations remain highly useful.

[7]Carol Smart, focusing on legislative reform, identifies four problems with using the concept of rights as a feminist legal strategy: (1) rights oversimplify complex power relations; (2) an appeal to rights can be countered with an appeal to competing rights; (3) the burden always falls on the individual to prove that her rights have been violated; and (4) rights formulated to protect the in-

dividual against the state, or the weak against the strong, can be appropriated by the powerful (144–45).

[8]Elizabeth Wright's dictionary of feminism and psychoanalysis provides a useful summary of writing on the masquerade after Freud.

[9]In "The Feminization of Composition," Miller makes the point that composition teaching is always already a feminized occupation. Judith Bechtel argues that the hierarchy subordinating composition teachers to literary scholars makes questions of equity central to all discussions of rhetoric and composition.

Women on the Networks: Searching for E-Spaces of Their Own

Gail E. Hawisher and Patricia Sullivan

I don't know how many people saw that 1950's television show, _Queen for a Day_. I used to watch it as a little girl. Four or five women would come on TV and tell horrible stories about their lives—too many children, no money, no jobs, no husbands (or no-good ones), evil in-laws. Then the audience would pick the "Queen for a Day." Baroque music would come on, a red carpet would be placed at the new Queen's feet, and the Queen, usually crying, would walk up to her throne. There she would learn from some triumphant man (glad to help her out) what her prizes were: chief among them, as I recall, were a Maytag washer and dryer. Even at the age of six I thought something was a little bit *off* about this, that a Maytag washer and dryer weren't going to solve the Queen's problems. But I was most interested in watching the losers, the other contenders, the ones who *didn't* have the most horrible stories after all. They'd be brave, nice (trained to be nice and brave), sad but not that surprised. After all, they'd never really expected anyone to care, or so it seemed to my six-year-old self. Now somehow all of this is hooked together in my mind. Do we expect the computer to be like the Maytag, making everything better for all of us, making each and every one of us Queen for a Day? I think I'd like that but don't imagine I'll get it.
(LF, 14 Nov. 1994)

These words, written by one of the participants in our study of a group of academic women and their online lives, convey the spirit of the participants' conversations about computers and e-spaces.[1] Many of the women participate often, even daily, online, searching for an e-space to call their own. Do they become queen for a day? Do they gain the recognition and acceptance they seek? Activity on the networks is only just now claiming the attention of feminist theorists, who have much to contribute to an understanding of the online environment as a new social and political location. Electronic networks, neither egalitarian utopias nor sites devoid of power and influence for women, offer women a way into the male-dominated computer culture. But gaining access to this culture means that women must confront issues of gender and power in the construction of their views of e-space.

This necessity is not new. As Dale Spender has argued, each new information technology—writing, print, and now electronic—tends to exclude women from positions of influence (*Nattering*). When writing became part of Western culture, few women were scribes and fewer yet authors. When print was in its ascendancy as a primary communication medium, women tended not to be in positions of power in major publishing companies. In the information age, as electronic media take center stage, women are being similarly excluded.[2] As the backbone for the delivery of cyberspace is being debated nationally, women have not been among the policy makers who are setting the agenda for the National Information Infrastructure or for its educational counterpart, the National Research and Education Network. Few women today are editors of online journals, a publishing venue increasingly important for gaining academic credibility. If women are underrepresented in the shaping or use of electronic environments (i.e., e-spaces), how can the new networks accommodate women's cultures? This was the question that motivated our inquiry. But as the study evolved, we focused more on existing e-spaces than on policy making for future e-spaces, because we realized that online space is both complex and little explored. By examining how a group of women constructed an e-space and how they critiqued other online contexts, we seek to provide a basis for further discussion of how women activists might transform e-spaces into sites for productive feminist change.

In composition studies, e-spaces brought with them a new enthusiasm for teaching and working with computers. For the first time, writing instructors could use a social technology that provided a forum for previously unheard voices, in effect an egalitarian space. Michel Foucault might have characterized e-spaces as utopias, "sites with no real place . . . present[ing] society itself in a perfected form," or as heterotopias, "simultaneously mythic and real contestation[s] of the space[s] in which we live" ("Spaces" 24). In his discussion of cultural sites in "Of Other Spaces," Foucault contrasts utopias with heterotopias, which are countersites where culture is represented, contested, and inverted. Though writing before the advent of e-spaces, Foucault describes the countersites as places that "suspect," "neutralize," or "invert" the very relations they are meant to "designate," "mirror," or "reflect" (24). Viewed as utopias, e-spaces present a vision that corresponds to social constructionists' goals of a decentered writing class where communities take shape. Viewed as heterotopias, e-spaces for teachers can transform writing classes, subverting dominant power structures and traditional classroom roles.[3]

Many compositionists place their hope in a utopian e-space as an egalitarian forum. Writing of electronic classes, Thomas Barker and Fred Kemp maintain that because "body language, intimidating or distracting appearances, voice and intonation, aggressive or distracting speech mannerisms, quick- or slow-wittedness and all the paraphernalia that allow physical context to . . . inhibit the pure exchange of ideas" are missing from electronic discussion, what is said becomes more important than who says it (21). Diane Langston and Trent Batson note that "in computer-based working groups . . . social roles become . . . blurred [and] participants who don't generally dominate face-to-face interactions are likely to speak more strongly when communicating on-line" (146). Others argue that electronic environments can create productive classroom communities. Having used computer networks to teach writing at the University of Michigan, Ann Arbor, Delores Schriner and William Rice report that "far from making the class more impersonal, [networks] fostered a strikingly close community in one of the nation's largest universities" (476). Such visionary and utopian images of e-space reflect the high expectations that continue to accompany computer networks in the writing class.

There is also research to support the applause that comes from scholars' experiences with electronic discourse. The claim for egalitarianism grows largely out of studies that Sara Kiesler and her colleagues conducted at Carnegie Mellon University, research that began in 1984 and continues today (see Sproull and Kiesler for an overview of it). Kiesler and her colleagues regard networked discourse as an efficient medium for communicating information but as a deficient medium for constructing a social space, since the contextual features that mark face-to-face communication are missing (Eldred and Hawisher). Networked discourse may be ideal for the business settings that Kiesler and her colleagues study, because it facilitates information transfer, but those working in composition studies turn the research to a different end. If participants cannot see one another in electronic settings, they argue, and therefore are unaware of paralinguistic cues such as voice, facial expressions, and dress, students are less likely to judge one another by differences of race, social class, age, sexual preference, disabilities, and gender. Thus many writing instructors who hope to decenter their authority and transform their classes into egalitarian sites for learners and, by extension, for others on the nets apply to composition theory the findings of this social science research.

Although Kiesler's model continues to influence perspectives on electronic writing classes, recent studies of women and technology have begun to question the adequacy of egalitarian narratives for describing e-space. Feminists studying technology and writing often represent women online as victims. Not only have several articles appeared in the popular press—the *Village Voice*'s "A Rape in Cyberspace . . ." (Dibbell), *Ms. Magazine*'s "The Strange Case of the Electronic Lover" (Van Gelder), *Vogue*'s "Terror On-Line" (Gill)—but also television news shows, such as *Dateline NBC*, have focused on incidences of stalking and sexual harassment. Because of the attractiveness of the egalitarian narrative and the persuasiveness of the research that supports it, feminists have needed powerful stories of gender deception, violence, and harassment to counter prevailing notions about the utopian possibilities of e-space. One of the earliest and most poignant stories is Lindsy Van Gelder's "The Strange Case of the Electronic Lover." In this 1985 report, a male psychiatrist in his fifties posed online as a woman who was crippled and mute as a result of an accident involving a drunk driver. Joan—or "Talkin' Lady," as the psychiatrist was also known—became a CompuServe celebrity, giving much advice and support to disabled women. Many online participants came to love her as a sister—and sometimes as more. When participants discovered the deception, their trust in the online utopian community was shattered. "The Strange Case of the Electronic Lover" alerts us to the dangers of e-spaces. As one woman who was duped noted, "Although I think this is a wonderful medium, it's a dangerous one, and it poses more danger to women than men." Van Gelder adds that "maybe one of the things to be learned from [the event] is that we have a long way to go before gender stops being a major, volatile human organizing principle—even in a medium dedicated to the primacy of the spirit" (375).

As feminists in technology have shown, stories of gender deception, violence, and harassment are not limited to commercial networks like CompuServe. Cheris Kramarae and H. Jeanie Taylor report that women on *Systers*, a computer science network, often experience harassment in other e-spaces (54). Even in spaces devoted exclusively to women's issues, such as the "Electronic Salon" for Lewis and Clark's Gender Symposium, a 1992 weeklong conference, women appeared to be increasingly shut out as men came online and began to dominate the discussions (Ebben and Kramarae 17). Studies analyzing the on-line discourse of academic lists such as *Megabyte University* (comput-ers and writing) and *Linguist* (linguistics) or newsgroups such as soc. women (sociology) find that women make fewer and shorter contribu-tions than men and that both men and women respond more fre-quently to men's postings than to women's (Selfe and Meyer; Ebben), thereby reinforcing the offline status quo.

Nancy Kaplan and Eva Farrell argue that despite emerging publica-tions detailing how women in e-spaces are "ignored, silenced, even abused," most published studies neglect other stories of "women [who] persist despite the barriers to entry and the problems they find" (6). In other words, studies haven't yet paid enough attention to the complex negotiations women must engage in to establish presence in a particular e-space. Our study is about a small group of academic women who persist.

The Research Process

Much of our methodological guidance came from Liz Stanley and Sue Wise's landmark treatise on feminist sociology, *Breaking Out, Again,* and Sandra Harding's *Whose Science? Whose Knowledge?* Patti Lather's *Getting Smart* and Shulamit Reinharz's *Feminist Methods in Social Research* also contributed to our thinking. Our work had much in common with other feminist studies in composition (particularly Gesa Kirsch's study of professional women's publications), but they could offer little guidance in the area of online research. (A number of textual studies have examined electronic text from feminist perspec-tives—for example, Selfe and Meyer; Herring; Ebben; Herring, John-son, and DiBenedetto—but they typically deal with found texts, those that are transcribed or printed, rather than with online interviews or texts in the making.) Neither was the metadiscourse about method in composition studies extensive enough to guide our decisions about structuring an approach to study a new domain—an e-space.

Thus we drew on sociology, especially the work of Stanley and Wise, for our direction. We focused on the relationship between researchers and participants, on the emotion we could expect to feel as we con-ducted the research, on disclosing our own positions as a part of the research, on acknowledging the different perspectives of researchers and participants, and on understanding the power we held as re-searchers (Stanley and Wise 23). Further, we agreed with Lather that a primary goal of feminist research is to empower, to improve the lot of the participants, and thus we attempted to structure our study so that participants could not only address issues we foregrounded in the interviews but also set their own agendas. Recognizing the importance of balancing our research goals with the interests of the participants, we turned the later online discussion over to them for the airing of topics they valued.

The study took place entirely online. We sent e-mail invitations to about fifty women in composition studies. If they agreed to participate, we told them that they would receive two electronic interviews and be expected to contribute to woman@waytoofast, the discussion group we set up for the study.[4] We sought diverse voices in composition. Because of Kirsch's findings about the solidarity in academic ranks,[5] we invited women from all levels, full professor to graduate student. We also tried to locate participants who were geographically dispersed, of differing ages, of various ethnicities, and of different degrees of experience with online communication.[6]

After thirty-two women agreed to participate, we sent them a first online interview. Thirty responded. We read it and crafted a second interview that followed up on the first, asking them further questions. We tried to personalize the second interview as much as possible to make the online exchange resemble more an interview than a survey. After twenty-nine interviews were completed, we began an online discussion with twenty-seven of the women; it ran for twenty-eight days and yielded 227 messages—a volume of mail that caused a number of justified complaints, considering the women's busy lives. The discussion, however, was not directed by us; no prodding was needed. And when we did ask questions, the participants felt no compunction about ignoring them if the issues did not fit into their agendas. A number of participants wrote with enthusiasm about having, as one called it, an "all-girls forum," and pushed at its edges more persistently than we expected. As the discussion was winding down, one woman requested that we ask everyone what they liked and disliked about the discussion. This question framed the final interview (with thirteen now), which we treated as their analysis of the online discussion. Thus the entire study was conducted online, with the listserv discussion and final analysis directed by the participants.

E-Spaces: Mapping the Territory

Our interest in how these women constructed and negotiated e-space led us to identify moments when they felt a gain or loss of power, when they felt silenced or celebrated, when they successfully resisted misrepresentations of their identities. Moments like these marked power and lack of power, being silenced and resisting; they were often foregrounded as critical and sometimes sensational negotiations on the net. Yet there were other, more ordinary exchanges that revealed how the women inhabited e-spaces daily, how they saw e-space and what they valued in it.

As James Porter and Patricia Sullivan argue, and as Edward Soja demonstrates in his analysis of Los Angeles, the terrain of a particular site requires the multiple mappings of time, space, and culture. Such varied and simultaneous mappings of e-space resist a totalizing vision because of the many paradoxes at work in shaping electronic contexts. Yet the sensational and mundane moments in the e-spaces our participants negotiated provide a sense of how these women map e-space, a sense of their utopian (or egalitarian) visions of e-space, and a sense of how their experiences challenge or resist current notions of the boundaries of e-space.

How Did the Participants Map E-Space?

The women wrote frequently of their desire for a space of their own (and time to spend there), a desire both physical and psychic—alluding to Virginia Woolf's wish for "a room of one's own" and bell hooks's longing for publication space for African American women (*Talking* 150). They longed for e-spaces arranged to their liking. Though we did not directly ask what would characterize an ideal or utopian or even an acceptable e-space, the women presented rich scenarios depicting how e-spaces should function.

There was a range of opinions: some women wanted e-spaces to be a supportive community; some wanted them to be sites of scholarly discussion about composition studies; some wanted them to ease the burdens of professional or personal isolation; some wanted public discussions to take on the comforting qualities of personal e-mail; some wanted fun and escape from their day-to-day, overworked lives; some wanted efficient forums for the exchange of professional information.

When we asked about memorable online experiences, they told us both of establishing and maintaining personal connections and of communication that contributed to their professional lives. From the first, they doubted the existence of utopian e-spaces. They spoke repeatedly about the types of online discussion they had experienced rather than about the electronic culture they desired. They observed that current electronic discussions often lacked depth or were boring; at the same time, those discussions tended to minimize or ignore the women's contributions to the conversation. Even worse, several women found themselves attacked when they entered into lively intellectual debate. That experience made some feel unsafe.

Both those who wanted a nurturing environment and those who wanted an efficient space were disappointed by the electronic discussions held on the listservs to which they belonged. When they used electronic discussion to keep current with professional issues, they were frequently disappointed by the slow pace or by the superficiality of the commentary.

> Professional: Seems a shortcut to being introduced to a field (women's studies, gay studies, witchcraft, semiotics), and a way to keep up with current topics in teaching writing, again easier than reading whole journal articles. But it gets more boring than journals when old topics come round again for new list members and with minimal variation. (DB, 11 Oct. 1994)

> I too find that lists are "seductive but generally unsatisfying." I'm going out on a limb to say that lists are a little like conversations (and sessions) at conferences: intense but fleeting. The emotional experience of connection may itself have importance—great importance. No one expects more than one or two ideas or contacts to rise to consciousness in the months following. Lists improve in some respects the conference intensity, because you can return a few days later with more questions. But the "conference" may have gone on to other things. For those who subscribe to stay in touch with others they already know f2f, the conference analogy may hold in another respect: you get to make and hash out concrete proposals, etc., more easily. But on lists others may get the idea that they are merely spectating. (TI, 14 Oct. 1994)

The women also felt that much of the online discussion talk shut them out:

> Generally, I [see my comments as being] ignored more than overtly put down—but to me being ignored is a put down.
> (DB, 17 Oct. 1994)

> I think women get less airtime. Specifically, our comments are picked up less often and thought through less by the group.
> (LF, 12 Oct. 1994)

Feelings of exclusion became particularly strong when the women encountered overt hostility:

> I was very nervous about the class, somewhat computerphobic, anxious to be very smart. I did all the reading meticulously. . . . The putdown was so light—my own insecurity magnified it. One of the guys in the class told me that obviously I didn't know anything about computers, judging from one of my posts. We were talking about Artificial Intelligence and I'd been running with the idea of computers and creativity. I guess I was trying so hard to keep up with a dominant thread I called techie talk that such a remark was shattering. I feel silly telling you—I can't account for my extreme reaction (running to the bathroom several times during class and crying and being furious for weeks).
>
> (TS, 20 Oct. 1994)

or violent attacks:

> Recently, I got involved in a very heated discussion on [a listserv] about sexism in computer ads, and the role of women in technology. Several times I was violently accused of oversimplifying points, and when I reviewed my own comments, I never made the sweeping generalizations that one person in particular accused me of. . . . In addition, I was also told I had misread a theorist I used to make a point, and then was one-upped by another person.   (LC, 3 Oct. 1994)

Many of the women attacked in discussion were concerned with how gender may have been a factor in the treatment they received. "Sometimes I feel talked down to—not sure if it is because I am a woman or if it is related to ways I phrase questions and responses" (DB, 17 Oct. 1994). A few participants masked their gender online to find out if it made a difference in how they were treated. One woman replaced her first name with an initial. When asked whether that had any positive effect, she replied that it did and then explained that women's names are often perceived as "frilly." She received more respect when she used businesslike initials. Interestingly, she thought the move to initials did not so much erase her gender as place it in the background. In fact, few of our participants ever thought that their gender was erased from their contributions to an e-space, and this opinion supports the feminist challenge to the idea that e-space is egalitarian. Unlike Kiesler and her colleagues, who argue that e-space reduces social-context cues (flattening hierarchies and masking gender), the women experienced themselves and saw themselves perceived fully as women, online or offline.

Although it may seem that the interviews produced a dark vision of electronic discussions, many participants talked positively about what would constitute a healthy culture for an e-space. By and large they wanted comfortable, hospitable, friendly, and welcoming spaces, especially the women who were coming to the nets from a position of isolation. One woman wanted politeness (a place where people were thanked), another wanted an e-space free of harassment, and another wanted an e-space free of lesbian or gay bashing. Some wanted minority issues addressed by the majority. Some wished for all participants to be acknowledged rather than dismissed. In many ways their remarks were the opposite of the criticisms they lodged against the current e-space culture. They also wanted to be able to feel like gendered women, to have fun, to relax, to be able to play, experiment, and express emotions. One participant wanted e-spaces to feel homey and "make the net less a public space." But the women also wanted information and ideas in a speedy fashion. And they wanted to be able to withdraw from participation without experiencing guilt.

Did the Participants Construct Utopian or Heterotopian E-Spaces?

The online discussion on woman@waytoofast enabled us to examine the kinds of talk and responses the women valued. Did the discussion (and the e-space constructed) reflect the women's utopian visions for online communities? Or did the list function as a countersite, a heterotopia, of one sort or another? Both utopian longings and heterotopian inversions appeared frequently in the sometimes competing discourses of the participants.

Woman@waytoofast was not an attempt to construct an e-space for women; it was an occasion for a group of women in composition studies to discuss how they would like an e-space constructed and to model the kinds of values and actions they might expect of e-space participants. The discussion enacted the participants' earlier complaints about e-space at the same time that it captured several key features prized by the women. It foregrounded the women's multiple visions of e-spaces. It gave voice to the longing for action that many participants had, as speakers contemplated the types of actions women might take to confront problems in living online.

The women's first postings, their discursive introductions for woman@waytoofast, show how they thought this collective should act. Everyone enjoyed and valued them. The introductions, first, were welcoming; second, they gave information about participants' online literacy, scholarly interests, teaching interests, and enthusiasm for talking with other women; third, they invited immediate response; and, fourth, they gave every member a reason to write about herself without fear that self-disclosure would be pompous or vain. The responses to those initial postings were particularly instructive.

> [In her introduction] Tina talks about her entry into computer use as a response to a course requirement, and I've had a few other students who also found e-mail that way. But there must be other ways to get a departmental community inspired to use e-mail. I hear Linda alluding to the technophobia abroad and have faced that in environments from undergrad classes to graduates who can't forward to me electronic versions of thesis chapters, to colleagues (one called yesterday) who have real trouble with the concepts of computer interaction while doing their best by rote.   (KE, 11 Nov. 1994)

> The waytoofast pace of this list prompts me to post with haste. . . . I too am an RWS [returning woman student]. At home I have long been surrounded by techie males, which shapes me into a more gendered person than is probably necessary or prudent. Like Penny and Dee, I have recently had an online "experience" that was upsetting and now, as I gain more distance, that I find intriguing. I am still on the list, I think partly from not wanting to leave victimized and pitiful and partly because so long as I retain some intellectual distance it is a place to experiment. The very idea of having to intellectualize the whole thing (keep a distance) terrifies me as I do it.   (TS, 13 Nov. 1994)

Friendly responses like these demonstrate genuine interest in others' words—a characteristic that infused the discussion. KE and TS responded supportively to introductions that expressed anxiety. Most women were careful to mention the names of the authors of previous postings and apologized if they got a name wrong or could not remember it. Such gestures underscored their commitment to recognizing the participants in the discussion rather than appropriating their words or silencing them. The care with which they referenced one another also extended to quoting. The quoting was not done in an acrimonius way. Although there were disagreements and a few sharp exchanges, there was never a message that systematically deconstructed another person's words—the kind where a few lines of the original message are given, then a rebuttal, then a few more original lines, followed by more rebuttal, and so on. The woman@waytoofast introductions fit many of the criteria for ideal e-spaces later specified in the interviews: they were welcoming, disclosing, polite, inclusive, and often personal. They went far to begin to build a community.

In the twenty-second posting, a participant made a general remark about being attacked elsewhere online, introducing a controversial topic. In three hours, two women addressed the issue—one by adding her own story of abuse:

> Several males publicly tore apart my message line by line, pointing out not only how stupid my question was, but how ignorant I was not to know that essayists fictionalize all of the time. Only one male asked why people were getting so angry over a question that he saw as asked in good faith and as important to any teacher even mildly interested in values or ethics in the classroom. I did answer twice, explaining several misperceptions I had noticed and attempting to clarify my problem. When the private mail became overwhelmingly nasty, I gave up and resorted to the silence we talked about earlier. (I almost forgot: one man said I obviously had not read his book.) Since then I have not posted to that group, choosing instead to discuss any further issues with people I know will engage in a good-faith discussion. (CP, 14 Nov. 1994)

The other woman told of a woman "being made into hamburger before my eyes" yet tempering her anger by suggesting that perhaps the incident was a misunderstanding that would not have happened in more intimate and friendly confines. The responses "Me too," "Yes, I know of it," and "Could it be a misunderstanding?" indicate a divergence of opinion in the subsequent discussion about attacks. The discussion included storytelling about violence and abuse, expressions of support for those who had been attacked, and an extended consideration of what kinds of actions might be taken to counter online verbal assaults. This topic resurfaced several times over the twenty-eight days. There was also denial that some attacks had taken place:

> Some of what has been described as attacks or flaming strike me as not necessarily meant that way by the group. I recognize, I

think, one of the situations described and I don't remember the discussion as being as personalized as the writer represents here. I'm not talking just about intentions/perceptions, nor am I trying to suggest that the writer is misrepresenting what happened in this discussion. BUT it does seem that this printed text (that often seems verbal but finally isn't) can be read by the participants very differently and that we have relatively little experience in "marking" the tone of these comments so that they can be read with somewhat more assurance that we really have been insulted.   (NN, 14 Nov. 1994)

While few participants voiced open disagreement at the time, our final query showed that talk of online abuse against women had disaffected some women. In their final comments, these women cited the discussion about online violence as the reason they disconnected; for them the talk was not constructive—it was old ground, it was too anecdotal, it represented misconceptions of e-space. In retrospect we realize that this was a turning point: woman@waytoofast lost the interest of some of its participants while riveting others. Explaining this complex response, particularly in the light of the strong commitment the participants made to the study, is not easy. At first glance, the topic that triggered the disharmony—harassment online—is one we would have expected to unite women. The women involved, all writing teachers, often must deal with online harassment when they teach in computer classrooms, so the problem cannot be dismissed as irrelevant to their professional lives. One explanation, as NN's response implies, is that many women were not new to networking and had experienced situations in which the text they wrote was misconstrued or they themselves had been offended when the sender had not meant to offend. Thus it is reasonable to surmise that those participants were tolerant of slippages in communication in online forums. Possibly some of them viewed e-space as a collection of texts and therefore not personally threatening. The women in technology, living their lives in male communities, may also have been desensitized to masculinist discourse. Such women, accustomed to receiving condescending advice and to having their words dismissed in face-to-face contexts, might accept similar treatment in e-space. Finally, we should note that discussion in a technology listserv does not thrive when agreement comes too easily from all quarters. From our experiences with listservs (Hawisher is listowner for *WAC-L* and Sullivan is listowner for *Purtopoi*), we've learned that topics that attract controversy, passion, and many postings invigorate the discussion at the same time that they increase the number of people who sign off the list.

Most other reasons that women gave for dropping out of our conversation were connected to the women's offline responsibilities. The day-to-day business of their lives caused several to disengage from the discussion temporarily (note also that both the NCTE Convention and Thanksgiving holiday intersected the twenty-eight days that woman@waytoofast was active), and some never regained their enthusiasm for the talk.

Participants had been emphatic in their interviews about wanting congenial e-spaces where others would respond to them with consideration, and many found such a space. Although some saw themselves as frequently misunderstood or thought that others were insensitive toward their views and feelings—in some cases toward their lesbianism—most participants were pleased with the dynamics or the content of the discussion. One participant expressed her mixed feelings about the list this way:

> Being on this list has helped me realize that I'd begun to take for granted the fact that because of the internet I am able to join groups where my issues and my life can be shared with and validated by others (especially as they relate to lesbianism). Being on this list reminded me of what my life was like before I was out and had support from my professors and other grad students as well as before I began to explore the internet and found supportive communities. . . . I think that a strong and very important community was formed through this list and there are certainly women on the list whom I would like to meet face to face.
>
> (MB, 31 Dec. 1994)

Another was surprised by her positive response to the discussion:

> I liked the people on the list: they had interesting things to talk about and were full of energy and ideas. I liked hearing about different ways with computers at different institutions—and different politics, modes of dress, and problems. I often ended up spending more time reading the list than I had intended to. I especially liked hearing about how this writing fit into their lives— what they had just been doing or what they had to leave to do. It gave me an image of all these busy, caring women, engaged in lots of neat stuff.
>
> (ND, 12 Dec. 1994)

When asked what she liked, another said:

> I think the participants on woman@waytoofast did a great job in
> trying to come up with alternative strategies to respond to any si-
> lencing techniques over the nets—something that is helpful for
> all of us who are on-line almost every day. It's challenging to de-
> velop new ways of successful communication over the net, one
> that establishes the right of everybody to participate without hav-
> ing to fear any kind of retribution. This discussion group was one
> of the groups that felt "safe"—nobody was out to find something
> wrong with what I said, nobody insisted on establishing a hierar-
> chical order—grad students, faculty. That was rather refreshing,
> I have to admit.   (TH, 2 Jan. 1995)

Foucault would not have considered woman@waytoofast a fully
formed community that had both understandable shape and function.
Thus we cannot apply rigorously his categories of utopia or heterotopia to this e-space. Yet we see in it the possibilities for a group to
function as a heterotopia of crisis, that is, as a shelter for those who
are experiencing crisis in their online lives. Such a heterotopia would
not be of interest to all women, because Foucault's crisis heterotopia is
connected with stages of passage in life and is therefore not useful to
all people at all times. The welcoming atmosphere, the effort to hear
everyone's words, the empathy for those who have been battered in
other online forums are all characteristics of an e-space that shelters
and supports.

How Did Participants' Experiences Challenge Foucault's Categories?

Although it is tempting to claim that woman@waytoofast occupied
one of Foucault's heterotopian sites and to see it as a countersite to the
typically male e-spaces we normally must negotiate, Foucault's categories do not fully accommodate the complexities of this discussion
group. One way Foucault's utopia and heterotopia fail as an explanation of our study's electronic discourse is that Foucault excludes internal spaces from his analysis. He focuses on external (public) spaces
rather than internal (private) spaces and thus on public cultural institutions. But our participants liked to mix public and private matters in
ways that blurred his distinctions. In fact, this blurring in e-space sug-

gests that woman@waytoofast is an interesting site for studying the challenges feminists have posed to the public-private binary.

In *Situating the Self*, Seyla Benhabib contends that the distinction between public and private spheres has been drawn in ways that confine women to issues of the good life, of values, of nongeneralizable interest and exclude them from issues of justice. Until recently private issues (childcare, housework, nurturance, care of the sick, reproduction) have been treated as natural and unchanging aspects of human relations, both prereflexive and inaccessible to discursive analysis, but women have begun struggling to make these private issues public. Benhabib argues that massive changes in societal roles during the past century have created a tension between the established public-private distinction in political theory and the actual practices of contemporary society.

In the e-space we studied, the private was continually and unselfconsciously becoming public while the public was becoming private. The customary distinctions between the two were often disregarded. The women relied on public e-space to connect with family, build relationships, and sustain aspects of their lifestyle. They also used the e-space to conduct business, discuss research, write collaboratively, carry on committee work, and discuss the ways that dress and personal appearance reflected a woman's understanding of her professional culture.

Women's use of e-mail for the maintenance of personal relationships is not surprising. Most people who contend that women take to e-mail and gravitate to networks think of women as stereotypically social and personable (Matheson). The women in our study valued staying connected with family, friends, and colleagues through technology, and several discussed how they first participated in online communication as a way to keep personal and family connections strong:

> When my son was traveling out east, I made contacts via e-mail with others (friends of friends) and made arrangements for him to stay on different campuses. It would have been very tough to do that via phone or regular mail. (DI, 5 Oct. 1994)

> When I developed premature labor (with my second child) and a score of other pregnancy problems (I've tried to repress from memory!), I clearly had to stay in bed accompanied by monitors and other injections/instruments. Scores of folks "reached out" to

me via e-mail. (My husband situated the computer near my
bed—the Mac cord/keyboard nicely reached over my large
belly—and I can easily type without seeing a screen all that well.)
People gave me prayers and encouragement—over the net. It
gave me that ongoing connection with the world—and helped me
put things in better perspective as others shared about difficulties they faced.   (BE, 12 Oct. 1994)

But these women led online lives that precluded a neat division into
public and private, in much the same way that their jobs precluded a
neat division into public and private. The women praised their ability
via e-mail to maintain and extend their collegial connections.

Six women including myself, most of whom had never met each
other, worked steadily for about three weeks to write our [CCCC]
proposal. We never met f2f about this writing, even if some of us
had this opportunity; we did it all online. A few of the women
who had never worked this way online were amazed and thrilled
at our electronic accomplishment.   (DB, 8 Oct. 1994)

At the same time, the women were unhappy about the increased and
invisible work attached to online activities. Many talked of receiving
several hundred messages a day and feeling guilty about ignoring messages:

I get 200–250 messages a day. I have to deal with management of
my list, respond to the computing center and other business, and
correspond with grad students who are writing their dissertations. I also watch a number of lists for news about new Internet
resources. I read headers and delete most of it. I read everything
related to [the listserv I manage]. It takes me two to four hours
every third day or one to three hours every other day.
                                                    (RT, 11 Oct. 1994)

The strain of maintaining their participation in e-space while
conducting all their professional duties and keeping personal commitments sometimes overwhelmed them. When it did, an interesting fusion of public and private took place. The period preceding
Thanksgiving provides an interesting example. ND began by noting
how much trouble she had remembering people online. Then she
wrote:

```
      XXX
      X  X
      XXX  X  XXXX
         X XX        XX    /
         X            XXXX
         X                X
         X            X
         X            X
         XX          XX
            |  |
            |  |
            /  /
```

Well, it wouldn't have to be realistic photos or even faces. Pick an image. I know that this involves even more rhetorical choices, but I know that I'm not the only person in the world who isn't very word-oriented and something visual to hang a message on would help me a lot and others too I think. Why do electronic lists have to be so tyrannically verbal and linear? That's a pretty dorky bird I managed to construct above. . . . I'm not sure that faces would make people act nicer, more friendly, etc. That wasn't really what I was aiming at anyway; I was thinking more about having a conversation which is so much easier if you have some way of remembering who's talking and what they said a few minutes ago. We can't all be Darwin or Einstein or Austen. Besides, they got great big turns, conversationally speaking, and great big turns are more memorable. I know it brings back in the issues of gender, and status, and agism, and all those other things that go with ftf communication, but I don't think they are absent anyway.   (ND, 22 Nov. 1994)

Less than an hour later, KE added:

```
   (%%%%)
 (%%%%%%%%)
 (%%%   %%%)
 (%% * * %%)
 (%% : %%)
 (%     %)
 (%     %)
```

In Marge Piercy's _He, She, It_, an older woman cruises the information networks giving herself a sexy young identity. Here's mine. The curly hair is accurate at regular intervals when the perms are new.

Karen (I'm not getting older, just better.)
(KE, 22 Nov. 1994)

Then followed:

> Interesting ideas about the need many of us (visually oriented) folk have to see some kind of image (signature?) that will help us remember who is who on the net, when we haven't met them in person. Karen mentions the idea of re-creating our images ala Madonna, and Tina says that the point of MUDS & MOOS is to fictionalize oneself. (I hadn't realized this—I just experienced my first MOO last week! Used my <blush> real name). . . . Well, I'm totally illiterate about how to do any e-art beyond some basic emotions, so instead I'll do the other postmodern thing, and rip off a piece of e-art recently mailed to me, "manipulate it," and pass it on to you here:

```
                          ,+*^^*+___+++_
>  . . . . . .             ,*^^^^        )
>  Happy              *                .
                   _+*              ^**+_
>  Thanksgiving .        +^    __++*+_+++_,      )
> .         . _+^^*+_   (   ,+*^ ^     \+_     )
> .        . {   ) ( ,(  ,_+—+—,   ^)   ^\
>  .      . { (@)  }f ,( ,+-^ __*_*_ ^^\_ ^\    )
>    . . {::,-/  (_+*-+^^^^^+*+*<__++_)_  )  )   /
>    . ...(/ (  (    ,__  ^*+_+*) <  <   \
>        U _/  )  *—< ) ^\——-++_) ) )   )
>      (   ) _(^)^^)) ) )\^^^^^))^*+/ /   /
>      (  / (_))_^))) ) ))^^^^^))^^^)_/  +^^
>      (  / (^))^)) ) ) ))^^^^^^^))^^)    _)
>      *+__+*   (_))^) ) ) ))^^^^^^))^^^^^)____*^
>      \       \_)^)_)) ))^^^^^^^^^^^))^^^^)
>      (_        ^\_^^^^^^^^^^^^))^^^^^^^)
>      ^\___        ^\_^^^^^^))^^^^^^^^)\\
>        ^^^^^\uuu/^^\uuu/^^^^\^\^\^\^\^\^\
>        ___)>___)>___ ^\_\_\_\_\_\)
>        ^^^/^\_^^/^\_^   ^(\_\_\_\)
>        ^^^ ^^ ^^^ ^^                    (NE, 22 Nov. 1994)[7]
```

For some, the faces, picts, or e-art, as the women called them, were fun and foregrounded woman@waytoofast as a safe place in which to play—an e-space where they might risk seeming foolish. Yet they immediately connected the personal and playful aspects of e-space with serious, professional, and scholarly thought. E-art, used as a platform for self-representation and for self-critique, was also used to cantilever the discussion into the areas of how one represented oneself in e-space or in one's department, as a job candidate or as an untenured faculty member. This fluid movement among the tropes of the public and private demonstrated how our discussion group challenged Foucault's cordoning off of internal space from cultural examination.

The fluidity did cause anxiety in participants and observers. Some commented that their lives held little time for play, and the drawing of pictures demanded more than they had to give. In the final interview, one woman said:

> While I found much of the conversation on waytoofast interesting, I was annoyed at the length of some of the responses and their frequency. . . . I thought the images that got created to go with the names were a bit corny and much too time consuming to imagine really doing. . . . I don't have the time and the energy it takes . . . to develop relationships with people (most of whom you will never meet). It is simply more than I have available to me at the moment; there are sooooo many people I need to have relationships with in my face-to-face life that virtual relationships seem secondary. (NN, 12 Dec. 1994)

We don't make light of this response or others like it. For women graduate students there are the pressures of writing the dissertation, for assistant professors the incredible demands of seeking tenure, and for tenured women the many meetings and responsibilities that go with the security of tenure. One such responsibility is to make the university a more hospitable place for junior colleagues. Online and off, the strains of women's academic lives take their toll. Thus the playful responses of some to those pressures (which started during a holiday) were seen by others as another responsibility.

E-space also allows a glimpse at a more metaphoric distinction between public and private forums. As one woman related on woman@waytoofast, she used a MOO (a multiuser virtual space) to explore how her gender affected the ways that others responded to her. She entered the MOO as a neuter person.

> I wandered into the women's room. . . . It was very relaxing— couches everywhere, colorful costumes, women lounging about complaining about cramps ("I have cramps the size of Texas!" "I have cramps the size of California!"). Well, when the group noticed me they *kicked me out* because I was neuter. I was very

crestfallen by this experience, which has stayed with me an inordinate length of time. "They're all men anyhow," I thought as I straggled off. But I was truly stunned and hurt to have my gender taken away, even though *I* made this choice.

(LF, 12 Oct. 1994)

Of course, women cannot abandon their gender, no matter how reduced the social context cues may be. But e-spaces such as MOOs allow them to cloak that gender in order to problematize it and thus see what was once invisible to them. Although MOOs are public spaces, some of the most private disclosures can occur there. The feel of the e-space LF describes is one of a behind-closed-doors, private, all-girls' discussion, and yet this illusion is created inside a public space.

Are these blurrings of public and private a temporary phenomenon that might accompany the current lack of knowledge of the conventions of e-space? Or is the collapse of the private-public division already so accepted in e-space that attempts to resist it will fail? Are these blurrings an enduring characteristic of e-spaces, which are always in flux, always fast, always ephemeral? At the very least, the image of e-spaces given by woman@waytoofast supports the challenge of Benhabib and other feminists to the dominant culture's notion of public space. For these women, the professional and the personal became juxtaposed or conflated. The women's exchanges were made powerful by the women's display of emotional reactions. For some women, discussing things they could never talk about in public was liberating; for some, identifying the ways in which their personal presentation disciplines their professional lives was political; for some, talking about how clothing rules change for the academy in various parts of the country was fun. Not all viewed the discussion through the same lens; not all were excited by breaking the professional taboo of discussing clothes online. But all were aware of how the topic moved across the boundaries of professional and private, and at some level they found such movement appropriate for e-space.

We began this study of a group of academic women, hoping to learn about their online lives—about how they interact with the range of electronic communication media available to them. Our aim was to articulate the difficulties they face as women academics in composition studies who are asked to participate in an increasingly online world. Through individual interviews and a month-long group discussion, we documented the long and hard working hours of the women compositionists, online and off; the sometimes inadequate and unfriendly reception of the women's online contributions; the persistence the women bring to online participation despite the pervasive gender disparities; and the women's disagreements about e-space. We also collected long and thoughtful contributions to discussions on silencing, on online violence, on the nature of online communication, on the problems of access, and on appropriate online feminist actions. But there is much more research and theorizing to be done.

A key question is, What constitutes feminist action in e-space? The e-spaces shown here—spaces that serve as professional forums, as collaborative working environments, as an opportunity to keep in touch with family and friends, as playgrounds, and even as masked balls on occasion—can also function as spaces for political action. Benhabib reminds us that with women entering the public sphere, issues once considered private (care for the young or the elderly; wife abuse) have become topics for political debate.

As our study unfolded, we became increasingly aware of the importance and difficulty of mapping these e-spaces as contested sites open to the influence and actions of women. We looked at how our participants talked about taking action—when they would act, what moves they would make, the actions they would expect others to take, and so on. We focused on a proposal for action to combat attacks against women online. After a considerable number of postings, one of the participants summed up the discussion:

> So far we seem to have identified only three ways of dealing with net evil: silence, patience (soon abandoned as too time and energy consuming), and bitchiness. Surely we can invent other subject positions on line that refuse what Nancy calls the will to win (I think this is one reason we go silent—we refuse to play the I win / you lose game). I haven't done this successfully, by the way, but I think of it as something a bit like Lyotard's [game] theory—except with a large measure of political intention and caring not for the offenders but for the integrity of the electronic space. When caught in uncomfortable situations we might think of ways to unbalance the offenders, to forge alliances with other dwellers, but above all not to cede. I wish I had examples of how this might be done; I don't. (TS, 14 Nov. 1994)

Another woman followed with this statement:

Silence is a form of resistance, but change requires doing some toe-stepping ourselves. Rather than the high heels that have traditionally defined, limited and basically tripped us up, I say we all find more sturdy shoes to keep us rooted in the conversations to construct new knowledge and to improve our status as women, graduate students, and compositionists.   (LC, 14 Nov. 1994)

Another participant added, almost with a sigh:

I don't know. Academic life hurts women, still hurts women, may be designed to systematically eject those of us who discover and believe other ways of knowing and learning.

(LF, 14 Nov. 1994)

Trying to bring the discussion to closure, one participant wove these responses together with her own approach:

My experience seems to be more like Lisa's—although I know there is sexist behavior on the nets—and indeed, in the world everywhere—it really doesn't seem to flavor my activities there strongly, especially with e-mail, at a conscious level too often. I seem to work consciously to ignore it at some level. As for tactics—Tina et al.—I think this gets at one of them at least for me. Women set their own "tolerance" regulators, each of us at the level that we can handle—and then we live our lives. For many of us—this doesn't amount to silence, or patience, or bitchiness— but a series of small, continuous, potent gestures that say, "You will not run my world the way you want to; I will shape my life, too, in the ways that I want to and can." This is one of the things I like most about women—just because they're not talking, doesn't mean they're not acting, and acting effectively, as agents of change.   (DT, 15 Nov. 1994)

Though there was ultimately no agreement about how the women would handle future attacks on themselves and others, the intense discussion led many to decide that some sort of action was necessary— that silence could not be a strategy on the nets, because it went without detection. Interestingly, a tactic for combating online gender inequities grew out of the women's participation on woman@way-toofast. After the twenty-eight days of the listserv, we agreed to keep the list open for those who might have an announcement from time to time. Two or three women signed off, but most decided to stay on.

There's been little activity on the list, with one notable exception. In May 1995, a woman encountered a participant's posting on a new list-serv set up to accompany a conference; the posting was being dismissed as irrelevant and wrong. The woman sent a public message to the list to support her colleague, then posted the equivalent of an electronic SOS to woman@waytoofast, describing the situation and asking others to join in. One woman posted a message in minutes, and soon several women from our study entered the conversation and were able to counter the masculinist discourse in such a way that the wrong-headed postings stopped. There was a tremendous feeling of power in the knowledge that support was only an e-mail message away. When several of the participants met in person at the conference, they agreed that this action had been a liberating experience and that it gave the group a tactic it planned to use again. Woman@waytoofast continues to function as an emergency space where women can go for help. Is this particular e-space an emerging heterotopia of crisis situated somewhere between a women's shelter and a fire station run by women? Not yet.

With Carol Stabile, we agree that feminists must harness the new technologies to serve their own just political and social goals. Though women do not always know how to harness e-spaces as sites for feminist power, it is our contention that women's participation in e-space will necessitate a rethinking of public and private space. Ideally we would like e-spaces to be cultivated as gardens are cultivated—through mediation, persuasion, and acts of kindness—to create a rich and fertile ground for collective feminist action. For Foucault, the garden is a thousand-year-old heterotopia, where "all the vegetation" of the world is "supposed to come together in this space, in this sort of microcosm." The garden can support multiple contradictory sites, but ultimately it represents "the totality of the world" ("Spaces" 25–26). E-space can never represent the totality of the world; no space can. But e-space can give the women who participate in it an opportunity to act, to gain presence, to dispel images of the queen for a day—to claim that space as their own.

NOTES

We thank all the participants, who gave so generously of themselves. Those who wish to be named are Claire Alexander, Kristine Blair, Marilyn Cooper, Margaret Daisley, Jennie Dautermann, Sibylle Gruber, Carolyn Handa, Mary Hocks, Susan Hilligoss, Kitty Locker, Susan Romano, Donnalee Rubin, Cynthia Selfe, Ann Marie Mann Simpkins, Elizabeth Sommers, Ilana Snyder,

Pamela Takayoshi, and Joan Tornow. We also thank Lynn Worsham for her candid reading of our early draft; members of the women's reading group at Purdue University (Margie Berns, Margaret Finders, Patricia Harkin, Janice Lauer, and Shirley Rose) for their insight and encouragement; and Sibylle Gruber, Paul Prior, and Ann Marie Simpkins for their instructive readings of our draft.

[1]For quotations from the interviews of our study, the authors' initials given are pseudonymous. E-spaces are the electronic spaces people construct through participation in online discussions, through construction and use of Gopher and the World Wide Web, through browsing library catalogs online, through building hypertexts, through sending and receiving electronic mail. Though writing using a word-processing program or a page-layout program might technically be considered constructing or inhabiting an e-space, we see e-spaces as cultural constructs. Thus we restrict our use of *e-space* here to those online activities that involve networked connections with people or places.

[2]The following statistics on the use of the Internet come from the Sixth World Wide Web User Survey, conducted in 1996 by the Graphics, Visualization, and Usability Center at Georgia Institute of Technology (this ongoing survey gives information on the age, affiliation, education, occupation, income, gender, politics, and geographical distribution of Internet users). Of the users, 31.4% were female, the average age was 34.9 years, and 93% reported that English was their primary language (Graphics).

[3]For a description of electronic discussion in two undergraduate writing classes, see Faigley's chapter "The Achieved Utopia of the Networked Classroom." After Lester Faigley held his first class in a networked classroom, he prized what he viewed as the realized student-centered class. Subsequently, however, other classes led him to question that utopian vision. At times, he saw networked communication creating "the space that allows mute voices to speak and gives opportunities for resistance to the dominant discourses of the majority" (199), but the discourse occasionally grew more agonistic than he would have liked. At other times the discourse moved toward a consensus he finally saw as "politically desirable" rather than "repressive" (199). Thus his view of e-spaces seems to fit Foucault's notions of both utopias (Faigley's first class) and heterotopias (Faigley's later classes).

[4]This listserv ran from 10 November to 7 December 1994. A listserv group is an electronic discussion distributed to each of its members via e-mail. It was originally scheduled for three weeks, but technical problems pushed it into November (and into the NCTE Convention and Thanksgiving). Thus we let it continue through the first week of December. We started the discussion by posting instructions and calling for introductions. We intended to pose a question for participants every two or three days (a question about power, or a report on interview findings, etc.), thinking that we would need to stoke the conversation. The discussion, however, needed no added attention.

[5]Kirsch, interviewing women from different academic disciplines, found

that the academic rank of those women and whether or not they were tenured accounted for more similarities among the women's attitudes toward writing and authority than did disciplinary affiliation (anthropology, education, history, nursing, and psychology) (see ch. 3).

⁶Invitees were chosen from members of listservs associated with composition studies (e.g., *MBU-L, W-Center, Purtopoi, WAC-L, WPA-L*). The women came from fourteen states and two foreign countries; six were graduate students, three were instructors, one was an adjunct professor, eight were assistant professors, seven were associate professors, five were full professors; two did not give their age, two were born in the 1930s, twelve in the 1940s, seven in the 1950s, six in the 1960s, one in the 1970s); they started using e-mail at different times—six between 1980 and 1985, fourteen between 1986 and 1989, nine between 1990 and 1994. Three of the women were members of racial minorities. Two taught at two-year colleges.

⁷MOOs are virtual textual spaces (MOO stands for "MUD, Object-Oriented"; a MUD is a Multiuser Dungeon). Like e-mail, they are conducted on the Internet, but with MOOs participants create virtual rooms, cafes, hotels, or other e-spaces in which they interact with one another. One of the most popular MOOs for rhetoricians is the *Netoric Cafe*, a part of *MediaMoo*, which was created by Amy Bruckman in 1992 at MIT. Participants commonly take pseudonyms, select a gender (female, male, neuter, sometimes more than one gender), and enter into the spirit of the MOO of their choice. For a more complete description of MOOs, see Bennahum.

The Practice of Piece-Making: Subject Positions in the Classroom

Ellen M. Gil-Gomez

I don't want to derail my readers before I start, so let me preface this discussion by mentioning that my essay was inspired by the working title of this section, which was "Practices," not "Specifying Locations." It was the original categorization that caused me such difficulty. While the editors have chosen to focus on the multiplicitous voices of the authors and on the varied sites of their discourses, I feel it is still important to respond to the creation of feminist practices, because the essays actually connect them with subject positioning. I hope my editorial reenvisioning of these essays will not distort the aim of this section but, rather, call attention to the work in progress of these feminist editors and authors—the processes of their visions. I hope this dual focus will make the numerous examples of piece-making more evident.

It's like pulling teeth. This is the phrase I repeat to myself while staring this response in the face. I am amazed at how many times I have started and restarted, written and rewritten, this essay. Finally I've realized that I must explore the forces behind my problem if I'm to get anywhere.

I've read the following words of Gloria Anzaldúa many times and now feel a complete affinity with them, an affinity that is more than intellectual. Anzaldúa describes her writing blocks thus:

> Blocks . . . are related to my cultural identity. The painful periods of confusion that I suffer from are symptomatic of a larger creative process: cultural shifts. The stress of living with cultural ambiguity both compels me to write and blocks me. It isn't until

> I'm almost at the end of the blocked state that I remember and recognize it for what it is. As soon as this happens, the piercing light of awareness melts the block and I accept the deep and the darkness. . . . And once again I recognize that the internal tension of oppositions can propel (if it doesn't tear apart) the mestiza writer. (*Borderlands* 74)[1]

The block I am experiencing is related not only to my cultural identity as a mestiza writer but also to the power of the many other ambiguities that, as a feminist of color, I am confronted with daily. These ambiguities exist in both my personal and my professional life and have come to a head with this project. Astoundingly, it has been my consideration of a feminist practice of composition that has caused the darkness Anzaldúa describes.

Thus I begin with some of the dynamics involved with my blocked state so that, first, I can write something and, second, I can illuminate what I believe is the paradox of feminists' creating "practices." Christy Desmet implies this type of catch-22 when she describes Drucilla Cornell's use of Monique Wittig's *Les guérillères*. Desmet asks, "If the Amazons overthrow patriarchy and create a new state, . . . do they not reinstate patriarchy by re-creating the state?" I am asking myself the same question as I consider feminists creating practices. I now believe that this writing block reflects my wrestling with my conceptions of what feminist practice might be and with the question of whether it's possible to create a practice that liberates the classroom from its patriarchal roots. Therefore, I have begun my own cultural, academic, and personal journey with this project, and I hope that my difficulties and reflections not only aid in my discussion of these essays but also result in a wider discussion of what it means to be a feminist teacher. I take these first steps into my darkness.

I've been fighting my block, hoping that, if I could just sit down and read these essays one more time, the ideas would come. Instead I've been seeing fragments and pieces, and pulling teeth. My baby daughter is responsible for my attempt to build bridges instead of pulling teeth. One afternoon she threw up on both of us, cried, kicked, and refused to be comforted. Finally, she settled down enough for us both to strip off our dirty clothes and sleep. As she slept, I realized that I must also give up my fight against my fragments and instead of denying them and considering them in conflict with this project, I must write about them. Before I could build a bridge to these authors, I had to make peace with the pieces of myself.

I have a strong desire to make connections. I know that this desire is not peculiar to me, but I can't help feeling that as I learn to be a feminist of color in the academy (and at home), I'm fighting a losing battle against fragmentation. Even the bridge that I attempt to build when I'm confronted with any two things is multiplicitous. At this moment I intend the bridge to reflect my competence, to connect helpfully and meaningfully these women's words, and at the same time to illustrate the legacy of the bridge metaphor that Cherríe Moraga describes. She discusses the problems she had when she attempted to sum up what *This Bridge Called My Back* intended to do, as she found herself faced with the task that I am faced with now: to be bridge builder and bridge at the same time. She writes:

> In writing [these concluding remarks], I fight the myriad voices that live inside me. The voices that stop my pen at every turn of the page. They are the voices that tell me here I should be talking more "materialistically" about the oppression of women of color, that I should be plotting out a "strategy" for Third World Revolution. But what I really want to write about is faith. That without faith, I'd dare not expose myself to the potential betrayal, rejection, and failure that lives throughout the first and last gesture of connection. (Moraga, Preface xviii)

While inhabiting this position of bridge, I feel that strands of myself are falling away and that I am "exposing myself" to the existence of "practice."

Reading these women's essays, I had a string of experiences that highlighted my feelings of fragmentation. I could not help reading the essays, then, through the lens of these experiences.

I was supposed to defend my dissertation in May 1995, and afterward my family was to travel to my parents' home for a few weeks to relax before I started the new school year as an instructor. As it turned out, some members of my dissertation committee had problems with my dissertation, and even though I did successfully defend it, I had major revisions of it to complete at my parents' home. I had also just received the essays that I am responding to here. After working on my revisions all day, I would read these essays at night. The deadlines for both projects were the same day. This meant that I was locked in an upstairs room with a computer as I watched my family, whom I hadn't seen for many months, through the window. The pieces of graduate student and PhD candidate, of personal and professional, of mother and daughter, were pulling on me so hard, I finally spent an evening alone crying and couldn't understand why.

The next day, my fair-skinned, red-haired, blue-eyed mother, my dark-featured baby daughter, and I went out to shop for baby clothes. We left the middle-class neighborhood where my parents live and drove to an inner-city Goodwill store near my mother's workplace. I see nothing incongruous about this, as my mother comes from a working-class family (midwestern, Norwegian American, Lutheran) and my father, though born into an upper-class family (South American, Catholic), grew up in working-class conditions after a failed governmental coup. Both have instilled working-class values in me, though they live in a middle-class, southern California city. At Goodwill, my mother and I dug through the three-for-a-dollar bin while the mainly Mexican immigrant shoppers stared. They saw me as a white woman and were distrustful of my presence in their neighborhood. I felt that my Hispanic heritage had taken a backseat at this moment and that it was my class privilege that they saw. As I looked at my mother's white hand and my darker hand dig through the clothes in the bin, I felt my working-class values and my middle-class privilege collide.

Later in the afternoon, I was pushing my daughter in a stroller on the driveway as my mother pushed my fair-skinned, blond-haired, blue-eyed nephew. One of the neighbors stopped to chat with my mother about the neighborhood news. Before he left, I heard him ask my mother how much her new nanny, clearly meaning me, charged to look after her grandchildren. My mother was aghast at this question, but I only laughed, reflecting how I'd always felt when someone questioned the fact that I was her daughter. What was new for me this time was that the man didn't believe that my daughter was my daughter.

A few moments later, a dark-skinned young woman walked by pushing three fair-skinned, blond-haired children in a stroller. I assumed because of her clothes, her behavior with the children, and her age that she was a nanny. I watched her pushing the children around the manicured lawns and wondered what she thought of me as she avoided my eyes and stared at the sidewalk. I couldn't help feeling guilty for and amused by the assumptions I had just made.

Who am I? When? Where? From whose perspective? During such moments I feel that I am dangling by a thread of knowing myself. I feel like a patchwork quilt engaged in a civil war. Looking back now, I think that I was trying to hold the pieces together so that I could finish my dissertation. As if, to write academically, I had to be a unified self. But my environment was challenging me at all times by questioning the self

I was trying to create, and it seemed that the more I tried to embody this competent person, the more the pieces separated and fell apart.

These pieces remained on the floor as I tried to respond to the essays about feminist practices of teaching composition. They challenged me, disrupting my ability to respond to them in a safe, distanced way. They continue to challenge me as I write this, because they all focus on the paradox that disrupts me: they speak of how feminist classrooms can be created. They have emphasized an awareness of my paradoxical subject position (my specific location) as a feminist teacher; they force me to risk myself in order to join the dialogue.

I am intrigued by the fact that the authors don't prescribe methods. Instead they build bridges between theory and practice, between implication and application. It seems most poignant to me, then, that these women suggest that creating feminist practices is inherently disruptive to simple methodology, hierarchy, and subject position.

These essays don't stand as a monolith. They don't sit quietly and definitively next to one another or to me; rather, they dramatically illustrate that a feminist practice of teaching composition challenges the static nature of creating practices. All the authors, to varying degrees, raise the issue of subject position within and without the composition classroom, thereby illustrating that a successful classroom is a site of critical awareness. The dialogues among these essays question position and show that teachers need not seize authority to create a strategy but that questioning the meaning and content of "practice" is itself feminist practice.

The authors imagine different paradigms of subject positioning that speak to teachers of composition: Pamela Caughie discusses passing, Wendy Hesford describes a pedagogy of witnessing, Desmet speaks of a feminist politics of friendship, and finally Gail Hawisher and Patricia Sullivan talk of e-spaces. Though different, they all clearly articulate a need for revisioning the feminist classroom, and they all, directly or indirectly, emphasize the importance of subject positions in that dynamic. What engages me most in these essays is how the authors view the subjects they position as well as the positions they are subject to. And this is how I interpret what it means to specify locations.

Desmet argues that the subject position of the feminist teacher is of primary importance to her students' success. She emphasizes that a feminist teacher must choose how she'll position herself in her inevitable role as judge. Desmet implies that even though she and her students are connected and restricted by the dictates of "the law," they all have free-moving subject positions that are able to engage in a conversation framed by equity and equivalence. The main goal here rests with the feminist teacher and with how she negotiates the metaphor of classroom as courtroom.

Hawisher and Sullivan, who are concerned with female subject position in e-space, applaud this new possibility for the feminist teacher to create a space of her own. They present the tightrope that stretches between the freedom of one's subject position in cyberspace and the varying positions one remains subject to. By claiming that e-space is not a utopian site, they suggest that it is inflected by social context and subject position. They also suggest that even though "women cannot abandon their gender, no matter how reduced the social context cues may be," our subject as teacher predominates over the other subjects we position. Again, it is up to the teacher to "harness e-spaces as sites for feminist power."

Caughie's discussion of passing speaks to the fragmentation I have experienced, to my difficulty in claiming a whole subject position. She says, as I do, that we cannot ignore this fragmentation; rather, we should emphasize that fragmentation *is* our subject position. She states, "The more passing becomes the very real possibility opened up by our interrogation of subject positions, the more we need to make it illegitimate. . . . You can't get out of passing by attempting to reclaim the subject." Her method of accepting the ambiguity of self in and for the classroom is a useful one. Clearly it challenges the creation of spaces of our own that rest (somewhat) securely on our identities as women. But she feels that teachers can "provide [their] students with strategies and occasions for working through rather than taking up subject positions." This may be easy in some teaching contexts, but in my 99.9% white classrooms, students don't allow me to provide them with anything. We need to focus on the fact that our subject positions are also subject to the positions that our students force on us. Some teachers might walk into a classroom and be visually classified by their students as one of them. My experience is that I'm usually seen as not one of them and that I must earn my role as teacher. It takes me a lot of energy to show my students that I can teach them something. An observer might doubt that this hostile class is a feminist one and see the problem as more than just a discipline issue.[2]

I therefore agree with Hesford's call for feminists to recognize more deeply how societal contexts in the academy affect the subject positions of students and teachers, because such recognition would create a more useful and meaningful feminist classroom. Such a feminist classroom would read the entire university community and presumably develop in students a strong critical awareness of themselves, other persons, and discourses. Clearly parallel to this reading of university and the speaking of the autobiographical is the reading of subject positions and identity constructions.

Focus on the intersections of numerous identifiers separates Hesford's vision of the classroom from those of the other authors. I feel that the pieces of my identity are better accounted for in Hesford's vision. I don't feel that Hesford would see an overwhelming value in creating spaces "of our own"; rather, she insists on the specificity of individual context in order to develop the critical thinking of teachers and students. She wants all her students "to bear witness to the particularity of their struggles, privileges, and agency, to foster in [them] the capacity to investigate historical events and discourses that may be dissonant cognitively and culturally."

I find all these essays useful, because they incorporate subjectivity in the potentially dogmatic composition classroom. They are concerned with how we as teachers can and should function in the composition classroom, but none of them focuses clearly on how we first need to change our visions of ourselves in order to do so. Having read the essays through my fragmented vision of myself, as the pieces of myself constantly threatened to break apart and reform, I suggest that the ambiguity of identification that these women show is actually central to any feminist practice. We must challenge ourselves to risk our identities along with our students', because we cannot expect our students to challenge the stability of their identities and ideologies while we simply "provide" and "enable" our students with opportunities to do so.

I have found that engaging in "piece-making"—that is, nurturing my fragments and accepting the conflicts they raise inside me—is beneficial to the classroom. We must be willing to have our authority as teachers challenged by our students instead of assuming the privileged status of truth tellers. We must be willing to reveal our pieces. Piece-making requires constant effort and often anguish, but in my view it also would bring feminism into composition with dynamic force by dismantling the "master's house," to borrow Audre Lorde's phrase (*Sister* 112), with truly feminist tools.

NOTES

[1]A mestiza is a woman of Mexican Indian and European ancestry who therefore embodies the paradox of something that should not exist: the amalgamation of the conquered and the conqueror. Anzaldúa describes her: "Cradled in one culture, sandwiched between two cultures, straddling all three

cultures and their value systems, *la mestiza* undergoes a struggle of flesh, a struggle of borders, an inner war. Like others having or living in more than one culture, we get multiple, often opposing messages" (*Borderlands* 78).

[2]There is a tendency, in analyses of classroom dynamics, for white teachers who are teaching a mostly white population to disregard the visual differences that make some students instantly combative toward teachers of color. A few years ago, I gave a paper describing this dynamic. I was fascinated by the response of my collegues. Without fail, graduate students of all colors and faculty members of color empathized with this position, whereas white faculty members dismissed it as due to my age and (lack of) position.

Celebrating Dis-eases of Women at Waytoofast

Margaret Morrison

A queering of my writing and reading processes—of my life processes—began early; pressures mounted on me early on to be a normal and acceptable, 1950s-style Pontiac-and-washing-machine girl —and I seemed to me to be nothing of the sort. Indeed, when I was in my teens and twenties, two of the many psychiatrists I went to for severe depression diagnosed my dis-eased me as being, besides depressed, "schizoid" and "polymorphous perverse." As if I were expandable, a protean ooze, a perverse leak! Of course, I sought a cure—and not just because I thought controlling the leak would help me deal with the intolerable pain of depression. Despite my "aberrations" and as one effect of those "aberrations," I was spoken by the very systems of the masculinist signifying economy that were speaking the shrinks, and the categorical imperatives of that economy demanded that I be not a polymorph but a closed, stable, integrated, and unified thing. No one suggested that my depression may have been, in part at least, an effect of various regulatory regimes' attempting to superimpose discourse grids (including Judith Butler's "corporeal significations" [*Trouble* 136]) on my polymorphous perversity and schizoidness. No one suggested that my dis-ease was precisely that precariousness and fluidity of subject positioning the masculinist signifying economy (that trap of a binary system) finds so dangerous to its rigidly potent efficiency. Fortunately, however, the process of my polymorphing into polyethoi (Victor Vitanza used the term in a conversation with me) continued, and still, after all these years, I'm perverse, incommensurate, complex, strangely funny, and difficult as hell to control.

Naturally, too, over the years I've been alert to signs of other leaks, to intractable exscriptors "fly[ing] the coop" (Cixous 344). Our dis-eases of the phallogocentric bear trap that keeps us gridded and gripped, cooped and recooped, may be effects of chance, counterlogics, desire, or the perversely polymorphous. Polymorphing in reading and writing, the "I" may be slipping messily among and exceeding the voyeuristic-exhibitionistic, public-private, inner-outer . . . (those ubiquitous, ridiculous poles!). My purpose is not to plug, cure, control, slap putty over leakiness or signs of fluidity or signs of the perpetual displacement of identity; instead, my purpose is to work at self-overcoming walls and closures (of gender, race, etc.) and to perform affirmative crumblings of the subject's integrity (Butler, *Trouble* 136). Pamela Caughie seems to be calling this fluidity, this performing as pastiche (cf. Butler, *Trouble* 33, 138; *Bodies* 12–16), passing or the disrupting of subject positions. But more on Caughie soon.

Together in their signs of dis-ease—their hesitations, their riveting instants of disorientation—the essays in part 2 generally suggest possibilities for a feminism that is not merely a reactionary feminism. Even the few reactionary moments in the essays—moments in which the writers assume the defined, stable humanist selves the masculinist economy so loves, for example, or moments in which the writers seem to want to engage in the same old revengeful, binary-flipping fisticuffs (you punched me so I punch you so you punch me)—even these moments expose the very dis-ease they seek to conceal or defeat. For when a writer speaks as though she knows who women or other categories of people are and assumes, speaking thus, that the subject as positioned is desirable, the excess polymorphing beyond the bounds of the subject as positioned, this leakiness, can be read deconstructively—as dis-ease.

Christy Desmet draws an analogy between courts and classrooms, attempts to apply feminist jurisprudence to feminist pedagogy, and endorses not an absoluteness of application of the law but equity and equivalence applied as intractable finitudes. Because mitigating little stories (that illustrate what Desmet calls equity in Kim's defense of Mrs. Capetillo, the welfare mother who saved too much money to send her daughter to school) exceed the law, the storytellers require mercy, a leniency that goes beyond the law, an ethics for the law. Like rumors or babblings, little stories (not metastories or Jean-François Lyotard's metanarratives [xxiv]) undermine the law's intentions because they ooze through the law's grids; the little stories (lived individuality) do not speak unequivocally—they leak.

In addition, the law itself passes (or masquerades) as just when it can't be just, having no origins, no absolute foundation, no legitimating grounds beyond its own fiction; a law only refers to other laws.

Thus, in Desmet's redescription of Derrida, justice proves to be an aporia based on law's undecidable meaning; that is, justice is an interpretative impasse and eternally deferred. The Nietzsche calls mercy "the self-overcoming of justice," and one of his central themes was that "man be delivered from revenge" (*Genealogy* 73; 2nd essay, section 10). Likewise, though Desmet doesn't write about this directly, because judges are never identical with themselves, their interpretation too of the law becomes problematic, suspect; they are always already an unclosed slippage (a slippage that includes men and women). Thus not only the law but also judges mask "mystical foundations of authority" (Desmet's use of Elbow). Even when judges attempt to honor the lawmakers' original intentions by adjusting general laws to specific cases, neither lawmakers nor judges can retrieve original intentions exactly.

Desmet's little stories impel a kind of public-private blurring of the sort that makes the woman@waytoofast group in Gail Hawisher and Patricia Sullivan's essay also uneasy, precisely because the women of that study were oscillating on the Internet between public and private in ways disruptive of the subject as positioned. Desmet also suggests that what she calls equivalence disrupts institutional categories, a disrupting that begins with those little stories and goes on to challenge the monoliths of supposedly stable concepts like welfare mother. Her principle of equivalent rights is not a principle of one-to-one equality; it recognizes the impossibility of such an ideal. Instead, the principle is based on a recognition of the differences involved in lived individuality, which in fact expose categories as monoliths that mask power relations.

Because of our partial understandings in the classroom and in the court, Desmet seeks an ethical politics, or Drucilla Cornell's politics of friendship, that enables us to recognize and ameliorate the violence of authority (as in the authority of academic discourse). Equity's little stories effect mitigation partly because of judges' (or teachers') willingness to converse with the storytellers and to acknowledge their being with or being in common with the storytellers (see Heidegger's *mitsein* [162]; or, as Diane Davis puts it in her discussion of Jean Luc Nancy's *The Inoperable Community*, "being as always already being-with").[1] The feminist politics of friendship in and out of class respects this kind of being-with.

In recounting and critiquing the specific instances of racism at Oberlin College, Wendy Hesford has done us all a service by exposing complex, critical debates on free speech and hate speech. These debates have taken place on campuses around the country as American educational institutions "grappl[e] with . . . cultural and linguistic diversity." That the debates are occurring at all seems to indicate a general, ongoing dis-ease at universities, perhaps having to do with confusion over the destabilizing effects of converting uni-versities into multi-versities, where power proliferates. The diversity (or multiversity) and free-speech debates, Hesford suggests, occur between two broad groups that establish a binary:

Centered people. The new right, composed mainly of white, heterosexual men, calls for (1) traditional standards of excellence, the canon, and (2) the establishment of a common (phallogocentric and phallocratic) culture. Though Hesford doesn't say so, this common culture sounds like some women's dream of a common language: the dream of controlled synthesis and unity, a fascist dream to which women are as susceptible as men.

Marginalized people. Traditionally excluded groups, who share the values, experiences, and language of materialist feminists and radical critical educators, urge institutions to think more accurately through a discourse of multiculturalism, feminism, and critiques of the canon.

The fisticuffs between these two groups, a reactionary chain reaction, as Hesford describes it, developed at Oberlin after discoveries of cross burnings and racist graffiti. The Oberlin president assumed the problematic attitude that the academy transcends the cultural identities of its members, and a group excluded a white male from attending and speaking at one of its meetings and later threatened him. During speak-outs, participants voiced a general confusion over free speech and the contexts of power imbalances that might make it harmful.

As a result of the events at Oberlin, Hesford seems to endorse a definition of hate speech—a reacting, vengeful, generally degrading kind of speech—narrowed to apply only when hate speech is directed against historically oppressed or subordinate groups. Thus instead of affirmatively forgetting (though not unproblematically forgetting) a past that cannot be changed, Hesford (like Mari Matsuda) authorizes herself to weigh claims of "victimization against a structural analysis of . . . social location." Furthermore, in regard to Stan, a white male heterosexual student in one of her classes, she deems that "inaction and silence" occurring from a position of privilege cannot be equated with the silences experienced and "imposed on historically oppressed groups." Though, as a critical theorist of race, she claims not to be avoiding the larger issues of equality and the First Amendment, she seems to be making use of the same essentializing tactics that she argues racists have used historically to oppress marginalized people. In authorizing herself to weigh the claims of those who speak, she also seems to see herself as speaking from metaphysically secure lodgings. Meanwhile, the struggle for equal power only validates old phallocentric systemics.

To put the matter a little differently: If, according to the logic of Hesford's (through Matsuda's) definition of hate speech (and the notions of free speech it implies), "Racists must die" is not hate speech, must we then value the lives of racists less than the lives of marginalized people? The same logic applies to "Die, pigs," whether the pigs are cops or male chauvinists. In addition, isn't the call among some neoconservatives for color blindness in the wake of reverse racism simply another tit in response to a Hesford-Matsuda tat in an ongoing, binary-flipping exchange that only continues to trap us all in the masculinist signifying economy? Aren't we simply watching an old-style, bloody cockfight that the owners of the game always win?

As a polymorphing dykey queer who has followed the meanderings of such widely diverse groups as Queer Nation, ACT UP, and, more recently, increasingly outspoken gay male conservatives, I'm certainly in far more sympathy with the aims of the marginalized groups of feminists and radical critical educators than I am with the aims of various kinds of conservatives. But I wonder how often those in marginalized positions of the power binary are appropriating the masculinist signifying economy simply to reverse the equation or flip the binary (however historically based and legitimate their claims of pain). I also question the ethics of such a move. Would it be ethical of me to employ a strategic essentialism—to light fires in the garbage cans of straights and call for the death of all heterosexists (my call not in the narrow definition of hate speech), because I was fired from a job once for being out as a lesbian and because queers have been bashed in various ways for centuries? Isn't a strategic essentialism still essentialism? And how politically effective would such an action be if heterosexists once more simply reversed the equation I reversed? Wouldn't we all be back to square one of the same old game? Isn't this just a trap some marginalized groups fall into, a trap set by the very economy they think they are overturning when all that they are really doing is setting themselves up for a return to the master-slave relationship? "The effort to identify the enemy as singular in form," Butler writes, "is a reverse-discourse that uncritically mimics the strategy of the oppressor instead of offering a different set of terms" (*Trouble* 13).

Stan's friend Derek may be right: Educate white men but don't op-

press them (I'm not sure how that's a contradiction, as Hesford suggests it is, but, in any case, I live nearly every moment of every day
with contradictions). Men like being oppressed no more than women
do—and, as we've seen from the actions of the Gingrich Congress and
from Stan's friend Ben, men are just as likely as women, blacks, and
gays to react, if not more likely. Guilt about past wrongs, blaming, revenge—don't these just make all of us miserable and accomplish absolutely nothing, except to keep us enslaved?

In contrast, Hesford's autobiographies, like Desmet's mitigating little stories that exceed the law and help us arrive at mercy, help open
up, reframe, and renew discussions, recognize contesting points of
view, and offer reconfigurations and redescriptions for a being-with
others, not in the past, but now and in the future. Instead of rooting
ourselves more deeply in the eerily tit-for-tat monotone of phallogo-
centrism, why don't we seek to fly the old coop in little stories (not
metastories), in art and artifice, in desire's traces in writing, and in
laughter (Stan himself seems to know that he's laughable when he ti-
tles his paper "The Good-for-Nothing White Heterosexual Male")?
Why don't we seek something else, whose cacophonous effects might
possibly shiver and crack the old signifying economy's monotone, put
a little tempo in the rhythm, and send us stealing and flying away?

Time and space on the Internet increasingly seem to offer possibilities for cracking the phallocracy and its stifling signifying economy.
Hawisher and Sullivan sketch a picture of excited, enriched, confused
women on the Internet, where e-spaces are already hailing and transforming their being and becoming in ways neither they nor we can
begin to imagine. As Cynthia Haynes has indicated, in opening up to
technology we're inviting, among other things, "the re/production of
new genres (like hypertext), new tropes (like speed), [and] new morph-
ings of identity (like agents or emissaries)" (qtd. in D. Davis). One can't
really generalize about so diverse a group of women as those surveyed
by Hawisher and Sullivan, but the study indicated that on the Internet
the women were struggling with postmodernist dis-eases made more
manifest by cyberspace: the blurring of categories (public-private,
genders) and the flux, fastness, and ephemeralness of life. One month
of the experiment didn't seem long enough to gauge how the Internet
was really hailing these women: it would be interesting to return to the
same group of thirty compositionists in ten years and inquire about
their changes in attitudes.

E-spaces impinged on the women in ways that problematized their
subjectivities (for "what is said becomes more important than who
says it"), whereas the women had little control over the e-spaces. The

essay contains other uneasy (dis-easy) contradictions about life in waytoofast. Although e-spaces resist totalizing schemes; require multiple mappings of the old tropes of time, space, culture, identity, and so on; and cause familiar boundaries to slip, become displaced, and blur, the women in the project "experienced themselves and saw themselves perceived fully as women, online or offline." Hawisher and Sullivan say, for example, that many of the participants' remarks were "the opposite of the criticisms they lodged against the current e-space culture" but that the women also "wanted to be able to feel like gendered women." Likewise, although some of the women played or experimented with gender roles and other posings, passings, or masqueradings on the Internet, where there are no extralinguistic clues to identity, like gestures, voice, dress, and so on, others felt threatened or deeply offended by such masquerades. (In fact, some of the women viewed the ruses as a deception, a betrayal of a stability they had come to depend on, despite the fact that the stability itself is a ruse.) It is interesting that clothes, always a semiotic instrument of identity or masquerade and one that moves back and forth across the public-private divide, were a topic of interest among the participants, even though— or perhaps because—it doesn't matter how you are dressed when conversing with a friend or conducting business in e-space.

Finally, during the course of the project, the greatest source of anxiety articulated was violence—women's being ignored, silenced, attacked, harassed—on the Internet. Early on, violence became a theme and, curiously, split the women. Complaints varied: that men and women responded more frequently to men's postings than to women's; that women made fewer and shorter postings than men; that more often than not men minimized, ignored, or put down women's contributions; that men accused women of oversimplifying or misreading postings. A couple of the women, however, suggested that those who felt they had been treated violently could be mishearing or mismarking the e-mail transmissions. Although gender slippages do become more pronounced in e-spaces, many of the comments about violence on the Internet sounded essentializing. But the question of women's speaking in general, on the Internet and elsewhere, remains complex for women trapped in a masculinist signifying economy. "Where do women go in dis/order to speak?" Vitanza asked once, and the question is precisely to my point and immensely difficult to answer. It certainly was clear that the women in the project sought an ethics of caring on the Internet (as they might offline) similar to the ethics of lived individuality and friendship that Desmet calls for and similar to Heidegger's *mitsein*.

Caughie attempts to contribute to the conversation among feminists and compositionists about the subject by working through what she calls the dynamics of passing (which differs from "passing as" or "passing for"). In the classroom she urges her students to keep "working through rather than taking up subject positions." In her discussion of a journal assignment based on the two mothers in Fannie Hurst's *Imitation of Life,* Caughie describes her first student as conflicted over the relationship between the two women: the student hesitates, has doubts, and, as a result of the discussion in the class, stutter-steps over her old self as a dependable referent. Unlike the second student, who takes a strong position and writes brilliantly, the first student indicates the precariousness of her subject positioning. Caughie says the first student is passing; I would say the student is leaky and polymorphing. Some teachers, parents, or shrinks might ask the first student to firm up, get a grip, become an integrated and stable self that can take and assert positions. Caughie urges her to keep passing, not to allow herself to be deluded into becoming a fixed identity.

As a child, I could pass as a boy or as a tomboy (e.g., I could beat the boys at sports). Nevertheless, I was required to wear dresses with scratchy crinolines to school, that is, to assume the clothes that marked me as a stable identity, a girl. This might have been a form of what Caughie describes as traditional passing as. Passing, for her, is something else. It's not speaking as or dressing up in the clothes of a category one has interpreted or assumed from social webs of discourse or from such linguistic and political representations as professional woman, lesbian, and so on. Rather, it is the jiggliness, the dynamic itself of constantly slipping in and out of subject positions, so that one never knows who or what one is with any certainty or how one is being perceived. It's the act of constantly polymorphing, though I would doubt whether through polymorphing I or my actions would (or should) ever become accountable, as Caughie puts it. Instead, one constantly enriches and affirms life by continuing to be mobile.

Those moments when I pass as a presumptive straight woman might be a more accurate example of traditional passing as. But if I venture into certain dyke bars, however much they feel like home, I might also have to pass, paradoxically, as a lesbian, simply because there is no one, original, stable sexual identity called lesbian. What complicates this paradox still further, of course, is that some lesbians try to pass as butch or femme, while others squiggle around as a sort of femmy-butch or a butchy-femme or both or neither exactly—a problematizing of categories of gender. Likewise, in Caughie's example, Peola, Delilah's light-skinned mulatta daughter who passed as white, might have to pass as a black woman in her own home—a problematizing of the category of race.

Unlike traditional passing as, Caughie's passing goes with what she calls "the precariousness of one's own identity," the recognition that the "subject position from which one speaks and writes is never secure." Caughie's passing is similar to Diane Davis's space of "productive indecision" (ch. 3) or Toni Morrison's becoming, that "process of [constantly] entering what one is estranged from" (*Playing* 4). The dynamic of passing, Caughie suggests, is driven by a non- or counterintuitive logic that opposes a masculinist binary logic. Of course, we're always easily seduced back into the illusions of the apparently stable humanist subject, the "I" with which or through which we usually think we speak rather than the "I" that can never really be represented because the "I" that "I" attempt to represent is always already something else. The distance between the two is approximate to what Nietzsche called "pathos of distance" (*Good* 201). Thus one might say that we are always already passing; we cannot not pass. Despite this, because the pressure is tremendous to seek authentic subject positions, passing constantly becomes vulnerable to metaphysical lodging. But, however unnatural, inauthentic, or illegitimate we may appear in our teaching and writing by shifting precariously through subject positions—and whatever our dis-ease in so shifting—the ethical stakes are too high not to keep polymorphing perversely.

I say let's keep doing that queer, cacophonous little dance of differences.

NOTE

[1]I was reading the final chapters of Davis's dissertation as I began work on this essay. Though it's difficult to account for the many overlappings of Davis's spirit and beautiful theoretical redescriptions as they have criss-crossed me and intervened in my own critical vocabularies, it's not difficult to thank her for enriching my reading and writing.

PART III

Exploring Discontinuities

Riding Long Coattails, Subverting Tradition: The Tricky Business of Feminists Teaching Rhetoric(s)

Joy Ritchie and Kate Ronald

I do believe that people need to know their histories, and one of the most neglected parts of the history of English is its rhetorical, hence its political, roots. The story of this discipline is the story of how rhetoric has moved from the heart to the margins of English studies, a story all about elitism, and the move from people to texts. And I believe that not knowing this story, not knowing the historical context of one's work, leaves a writing teacher isolated, helpless, frustrated. I hope we can use this history to examine, critique, and improve the current contexts in which we work, read, write, and teach.

(Kate's syllabus, Composition and Rhetoric, spring 1994)

Are we going to read any women soon?

(Jennifer's journal, Composition and Rhetoric, 4 Feb. 1994)

Working from a rhetorical and linguistic perspective, we will attempt to see in what ways women have been excluded from the rhetorical tradition, how they have used and accommodated to traditional rhetoric, but also how they resisted and subverted tradition and, in the process, reconceived rhetoric and used it to change the world. The course is framed with questions of our own rhetorical practice, as it is and might be. In our discussions, reading, and writing, I hope we will discover new perspectives from which to understand our own writing.

(Joy's syllabus, Rhetoric of Women Writers, spring 1994)

Why aren't we seeing more new forms of writing? Is it possible for women to write experimentally inside the academy? . . .

217

> Almost sixty years after this book [*Three Guineas*] was published
> it's still a reality. As far as I can tell in most of my classes, we're
> still following along in "this procession of the sons of educated
> men." Most women's education still uses age-old words and
> methods. . . . I know part of the point of this course has been to
> help us appreciate the contributions women have made to
> rhetoric and to see that women's rhetoric is multiple not singu-
> lar, but I still feel like what bell hooks says is true. This language
> I'm using to get ahead "carries the scent of oppression."
>   (Thelma's journal, Rhetoric of Women Writers, 20 Mar. 1994)

These voices, our own and our students', embody the tensions inherent in teaching rhetorical history in a feminist framework or using
rhetorical theory to explore writing by women. Jennifer and Thelma
are students speaking about issues of authority and marginality, forms
of discourse and power, and the cultural purposes that shape all
rhetorical relations. Their voices highlight the difficulties of theorizing
a women's rhetoric or identifying and teaching a feminist rhetoric,
whether in or against the historical canon of rhetorical practice, pedagogy, and theory. Yet as women trained and working in rhetoric and
composition, we see these tensions as productive sites for complicating our thinking about rhetoric in general and about women's discourse in particular. Examining rhetorical theory and feminist theory
together, especially in relation to historical and current practice, expands and unsettles conventional definitions of effective teaching and
writing.

This essay explores the tangled relations among feminist theory,
feminist pedagogy, the canon of rhetoric, and emergent women's
rhetorics. It examines two particular sites where these complexities
were played out for us in dramatic ways: a graduate seminar entitled
Composition and Rhetoric and an undergraduate-graduate course entitled the Rhetoric of Women Writers. It considers questions we have
lived with over the past several years, questions prompted by Audre
Lorde: Can we use the master's tools to rebuild the master's house?
(*Sister* 112). Why and how should teachers teach rhetorical history,
which excludes or at best marginalizes women? How can teachers
counter that tradition by teaching the history and practice of women's
rhetorics? Can there be women's rhetorics without traditional rhetoric? How can a feminist pedagogy help avoid essentializing women or
reproducing existing power relations, whether it addresses traditional
rhetorical history or women's rhetorical choices? How can feminist
pedagogies put in motion intersecting dialogues that involve students

in what Lynn Worsham calls "the ongoing criticism of everyday life" ("Writing" 101)? These are not easy questions, especially as they play out in the pragmatic contexts of classrooms, where students like Jennifer and Thelma have challenged us to avoid oversimplifying the gendered nature of rhetoric or artificially separating women's discourse and feminist agendas from their historical contexts and legacies.

Feminist theories offer alternative stances for working in and against the male-dominated canon of rhetoric, for questioning assumptions about the relationships between readers and writers, for demonstrating ways of rereading rhetoric, and for expanding received definitions of discursive authority and effective communication. Feminists have used a metaphor of marginality, of bringing women's voices from margins to the center and of standing on the margin to reread the core of Western epistemology and rhetoric. Focusing on the rhetorical sites where women study, teach, and write, to see where these metaphors break down, our essay explores shifting centers and shifting margins, arguing that the center may sometimes be a place of recovery and resistance, and the margin, if conceived more as a fixed location than as a fluid zone, may sometimes work to reproduce and reinscribe domination. Our experience teaching the above-mentioned courses as feminists has shown us that although it is fashionable to speak about living or writing on the margins, locating, naming, and fixing sites of discourse is much more complicated than is sometimes presented in feminist or rhetorical theory.

Employing a feminist pedagogy that locates theory and practice in the immediate contexts of women's lives and that models for students a resistant, critical stance toward monolithic descriptions of discourse and gender destabilizes conventional thinking about gender and rhetoric, about what is marginal and what is central. Such a pedagogy has led us to acknowledge and resist our authority as teachers, to decenter it continually with our students' voices. Our attempts to teach rhetoric as feminists have changed our rhetorical choices as teachers. Our conception of audience, the appeals we use to persuade, and the ethos of our voices become part of the rhetoric we and our students examine. Because our essay grows out of this dialogue between theory and practice, we have chosen to represent our thinking here with excerpts both from our journals to students and from their journals in response to the reading and classroom dialogue. This practice of writing to and with our students is a key element in our teaching, and we have adopted it as a feminist practice in all our classes. Our journals and students' journals combine public exploration and public demonstration of our knowledge about the course materials with private analysis of connections between the rhetoric we are studying and personal lives and issues. These dialogues, between us and our students and among all of us and the rhetoric we're studying, help us avoid some of the risks of single-voiced thinking in our classrooms, enhance the possibilities for reexamination of students' and teachers' ideas, loosen the moorings on what is marginal and what is central, and call into question whose coattails we're riding.

Recovery and Resistance as Feminist Practice: Reading the Rhetorical Canon

> I feel compelled after reading your journals to once again say something about the canon of rhetorical history that we are looking at. I've chosen this canon, and so have Bizzell and Herzberg, and we shouldn't forget that this is a *deliberate selection* on my part. I could have chosen otherwise—to explore the neglected sophists, as scholars are just beginning to do, to find the alternative voices from women and other cultures, as scholars are doing too. But I've selected on two principles: (1) these are the texts that survived and influenced rhetoric in each period, and (2) these are the texts that still influence us today, whether we know it or not. I certainly don't mean to hold Plato or Cicero or Campbell or Burke up as the authority on rhetoric or on teaching. I simply want to remind myself here, and you all, that what we make of this stuff is more important than the stuff itself.
>
> (Kate's journal, Composition and Rhetoric, 30 Jan. 1994)

> When I waxed ecstatic about getting a historical perspective, you reminded me to consciously resist these readings, including Bizzell's. It's an important reminder for me. It's so difficult for me to learn to trust my own feelings of resistance. I do think it has to do with the pattern of stifling we develop as women studying under mostly male professors, who demonstrate in countless ways that they will brook no disagreement. Then, of course, when the topic is classical rhetoric and the page is sprinkled with names like Plato and Aristotle, cultural conditioning is so strong that I'm inclined to feel I should be sitting awe-struck at the feet of anyone who claims authority in the field. So a reminder now and then of the need to resist is well-placed.
>
> (Gladys's journal, Composition and Rhetoric, 31 Jan. 1994)

Much work by feminists in rhetoric has focused on recovering silenced voices in history and rereading canonical accounts of rhetoric's role in the discipline (Glenn, "Author" and "Sex"; Jarratt, "Performing"; Bizzell, "Opportunities"; Swearingen). The Composition and Rhetoric seminar, which Kate chose to teach historically, was designed more for rereading the tradition than for recovering women's voices. It engaged students in exploring the forces that have shaped writing teachers' work and still shape the contexts in which writing teachers teach. Her goal was to use rhetorical history to help teachers locate their work and see it in radically new ways. She was teaching the canon in order to subvert it. But her defense of the course three weeks into the semester points to the tensions inherent in studying the male rhetorical tradition. Kate worried all semester about offering a seminar with an overwhelmingly male, traditional reading list. She questioned her decision not to recover more women's writing. Yet it is clear from both Kate's and Gladys's journals that the course functioned as recovery work in other ways—the recovery of rhetorical history in the first place as a feminist, subversive practice in the discipline of composition.

Recovery work always exists in a politically charged context, and the impulses toward recovering composition's history come partly out of the constant need to defend and legitimate composition's existence alongside literary studies in departments of English. A sense of isolation persists where literary theory and literature still hold the center and composition is still considered a new field, necessary but ancillary. Kate's course is a political attempt to recover the history of rhetoric for her students. Most of these students are teaching assistants in a PhD program and have been assigned to teach first-year composition courses. They take Kate's course because they are completing a concentration in rhetoric and composition. But many of them are not writing dissertations in this area; their main interest is elsewhere—creative writing, women's literature, Willa Cather.

Too many graduate students (and faculty members) in English regard teaching composition as an apprenticeship they must serve until they are anointed as literature teachers. In this sense, the teaching of writing is much like "women's work" in the profession, largely carried on by underpaid and overworked teachers. It is the dirty work, the dues they pay until they are educated and powerful enough to get out of the freshman composition course. So Kate offered a history of rhetoric course, first of all, as an act of recovery and celebration. If teachers understood that their work in first-year composition classes was part of a long and rich tradition of serious thinking about invention, audience, style, and form; if they realized that teaching writing was always bound up with theoretical assumptions about epistemology, the structures of culture, and issues of class and power, then perhaps they would be better able to locate their work in a profession that tended to devalue it.

Susan Miller argues that "this view of lower-status female identity . . . is embodied by composition studies. . . . Composition remains largely the distaff partner in a socially important 'masculine enterprise,' the cultural maintenance of linguistic dispositions of power and enfranchisement" ("Feminization" 40). It seemed logical, then, to offer a course that explored how this identity was created, historically and politically, even though Kate worried about the risks of valorizing an oppressive masculine enterprise. Yet Miller complicates the site for this course by arguing that reclaiming and revisiting rhetorical history is not good enough and in fact may be dangerous: she suggests that teaching the history of rhetoric often signals inadvertent "approval of traditional academic privileges embedded in the fabric of hegemonic 'traditions.'" She warns that the desire to place composition in an "intellectual, academic Big history, where it will accrue entitlements from 'authority and the ancients,'" also "sustains the hierarchies and privileging mechanisms that those in the field complain of so often" (50).

If it's a tricky and dangerous business to teach rhetorical history, why would a feminist want to do so? We would answer that a feminist has no choice. Rhetoric is here, has always been here, and to ignore its authority and power leads to the kind of marginalization and lower-status identity that Miller says the history of rhetoric describes in the first place. We would answer further that what matters most is how one teaches this tradition, how one models a context for rereading and resisting its influence and power. Rhetoric can become a feminist practice even when women's texts are not the subject of the course. Rhetoric can be re-dressed, not repaired or rectified but radically altered as feminist practice.

On the surface, Kate's seminar looked traditional: a chronological run through rhetoric in one semester, with heavy emphasis on the classics, then a century a week. All the big names were there, and Kate ordered the authoritative book for the course, Patricia Bizzell and Bruce Herzberg's *The Rhetorical Tradition*. But every week, through her journals and her questions in class, Kate included a critique and a resistance to the tradition the course was studying. She did not present this history as a seamless progression, ever upward, ever better, leading to the present renaissance in composition. On the contrary, she showed students that composition was not a new field at all but an old one, whose history had always been implicated in the relations of discourse to power, status, and privilege. She did not teach Aristotle, Quintilian, George Campbell, or Hugh Blair simply as the forefathers of composition, the thinkers whose coattails the students were riding; she also re-dressed these thinkers by examining the material, social, and gendered contexts of their teaching and writing. She offered readings of the major figures in rhetoric that put their assumptions and legacies into question.

In other words, Kate focused on the places where politics and rhetoric converged, particularly on the split between literature and rhetoric that Miller situates at Harvard in the late nineteenth century and on modern composition's emergence as the legacy of that rupture ("Feminization" 44). Current students of composition, Donald Stewart reminds us, do not know that the methods by which they were taught to write, the practices they hold dear in their own classrooms, and their troubling relation with concepts like standards and good writing come directly from one of the most hegemonic and elitist moves in rhetorical history—what Miller describes as the "winnowing" of those less entitled to be in the academy and the adoption of the view of composition as something the "best men" escape from ("Feminization" 44, 45).

Some feminist theorists warn that looking to composition's history to find or prove equality with literary studies only reproduces the hierarchies that such a study attempts to overturn (Ballif; S. Miller, "Feminization"). Kate and her class negotiated this tricky territory all semester. But the feminist purpose and feminist practice that operated in the course were an important counterbalance to the danger of reproduction that Miller describes. Two central practices in this seminar made all the difference in how the history of rhetoric was read and reread: (1) at each step, connections were drawn to the material, social, professional, and personal contexts in which each member of the seminar wrote, read, taught, and lived; and (2) Kate modeled and the students adopted a resistant stance even as they worked through the history. Each act of historical recovery, then, became a site for trying on varied rhetorical stances, for experimenting with and altering their fit with the students' emerging beliefs about teaching and writing.

Although the seminar was roughly organized as a chronological survey, it set into motion intersecting dialogues. Primary texts from Bizzell and Herzberg's book were read always with and against current research in composition and rhetorical theory, particularly feminist research. Even the primary texts of the male rhetorical canon functioned for students as sites from which to examine their own literate histories and their practices as teachers. Kathy wrote in her final journal for the class:

> I was surprised to see how my 20th century ideas have come from such a long history . . . to see the history behind what I've been taught and the way I've been taught. I'm really wrestling with what my purpose as a teacher of writing will be . . . to develop my poetics as a writer, and my own ethics of teaching. This course has tangled my thinking. I'm creating a complicated philosophy of teaching and writing, not a simplistic or formulaic one.   (Kathy's journal, Composition and Rhetoric, 11 Apr. 1994)

Kathy's complicated thinking resulted from reading Plato on the ethics of rhetoric and Blair on taste in writing, coupled with her close observation and analysis of her practice as a writer and teacher. It may seem odd to think of reading classical rhetoric as feminist practice, but the history of rhetoric allows this feminist reclamation, allows teachers to join the conversation and examine its language. Gladys's journal early in the semester shows how reading the history can be empowering:

> This all has gender associations for me as well. The longer I worked with students—mostly women, who, for countless reasons, had been "under served" by the educational system earlier in their lives—the more I was willing to recognize and resist the societal mindset that separated those of us at work in church basements and dark, unheated community centers from those who were engaged in the professional theoretical conversation. Now that I'm working to maintain a credible identity in both groups, I thirst not only for theory, but for historical perspective. Without the history, I'm a latecomer to a conversation in progress. Every unknown reference serves to silence me and to underscore, at least in my own mind, my position as a outsider.
> (Gladys's journal, Composition and Rhetoric, 17 Jan. 1994)

It is important to remember that this seminar was actively engaged in recovering, for these students, a history they did not know. Jennifer

began to see the complicated ways in which what had been suppressed
was also suppressing her:

> I like the whole idea of the sophists and classical rhetoric; I
> mean, I've gotten through at least three philosophy courses and
> almost a Masters in English and I know practically nothing about
> them. My feminist recovery instincts just go wild for anything
> that has been suppressed for over two thousand years (even if it
> was written by a man!). This is a tradition I am coming out of
> and working against simultaneously.
> (Jennifer's journal, Composition and Rhetoric, 17 Jan. 1994)

The course focused on rhetoric as a part of history but also as a determining agent in the scene in which these teachers and students
worked. Gladys, who explained how she longed for a historical perspective that would allow and invite her into academic conversations,
wrote halfway through the course:

> This whole concept of the effects on rhetoric of the social situa-
> tion and the individual's potential to influence it is so new to me.
> How have I missed it when it is so central to our current class-
> room concerns of public/private language and criteria for admis-
> sion into various "discourse communities"? It's all part of the
> problem of working from unexamined assumptions, I suppose.
> No, that's a little too strong. It's more closely associated with fail-
> ing to identify and trace back to their roots the theories by which
> we operate.
> (Gladys's journal, Composition and Rhetoric, 28 Feb. 1994)

Gladys shows how examining the historical roots of composition and
rhetoric can help students interrogate the rhetorical (political) sites of
their writing and teaching. Throughout the semester, through journals
and discussion, the class overthrew most of rhetoric's cherished idols,
using them for their own agendas. In an interview, Kathy commented,
"Kate wasn't protective about the disciplinary issues that connected to
this class. Rhetoric became a tool with which to critique the establishment and the hierarchies that exist in academia." We emphasize that
the feminist teaching practice in this course, which might have seemed
on the surface a very traditional seminar, made all the difference for
students engaged in teaching and theory building. With students'
voices in dialogue with tradition, Kate's seminar fulfilled Miller's conditions for studying history productively rather than reductively or

simply as a reproduction of existing power structures: "By raising a different voice in an active conversation about the feminized, actual, historical, and symbolic status of composition professionals and their students, we can . . . begin to reveal existing counterhegemonic structures in the field's existing practices and intellectual positions." Miller argues that change in composition will depend on "openly consolidating the field's resistance to the cultural superstructure that first defined it" ("Feminization" 51). At the same time that the students, particularly the women, in this seminar were realizing the long, rich tradition that shaped their place in the field in 1994, they were engaged in an ongoing critique of that tradition and of their current status as women in an academic discipline.

> I'm sorry, but I'm getting sick of these guys, especially that anonymous guy blathering on about all of his terms. These guys had certain people in mind when they thought of souls and audience, and women were certainly not a part of either.
> (Robin's journal, Composition and Rhetoric, 7 Feb. 1994)

> This has felt so disconnected from the rest of my life. Women's literature and feminist theory are my life, what I live by. . . . Quintilian's close relationship with students sounds almost feminist, but it has a bit too much of a power dynamic involved. Every time I started to like him, I was rudely reminded that he was not merely ignoring women, but denying them education and any kind of intellectual, moral capacity.
> (Jennifer's journal, Composition and Rhetoric, 14 Feb. 1994)

After reading *Rhetorica ad Herrenium* and Quintilian's *Institutio Oratoria*, Robin and Jennifer were angry over being excluded from the tradition they were studying. This resistance to the all-male tradition coexisted with students' recovery work as students realized the fact and the weight of rhetorical history in their lives. Robin continually questioned the ethos and context of the male tradition, pointing out offensive lines from the readings and asking, "Does this jar you as much as it did me?" Indeed, the readings as well as the editorial choices in *The Rhetorical Tradition* jarred the seminar each week. The feminist perspectives students brought to the course remained in constant tension with the readings. The students were not cowed by the ancients; they were in dialogue with the power of the canon and actively critiqued and resisted it. Gwen ended her first journal of the course this way: "I'm always suspicious of histories that have a specious lack of women and non-white people, and this includes the history of rhetoric" (4 Feb. 1994). A few weeks later, she described herself as "being gazed at by Cicero" but also as "gazing at Cicero." And, after reading Bizzell's "Opportunities for Feminist Research in the History of Rhetoric," Gwen suggested to the class that Bizzell's collection, our textbook, be retitled *The Male Rhetorical Tradition*. Gwen's ability to gaze back at Cicero and to critique the way the textbook presented the tradition of rhetoric shows how feminist practice in this seminar did re-dress and redefine rhetoric in multiple and radical ways.

Kate's seminar succeeded insofar as it helped students understand the contexts in which they worked and resist the weight of history that had put them in those contexts. But the tensions between recovery and resistance were never completely worked out, even in Kate's mind. One of her journal entries halfway through the course shows her frustration with the rhetorical tradition: her attempts to add women to it but her unwillingness, at the same time, to dismiss its power:

> I've been thinking about Bizzell dropping Christine de Pisan and Cereta in here like this, and I think I'm more than a little annoyed about it. As you know, I've thought, worried, debated, despaired over the lack of women's voices in this course. Despite the recovery of women's voices going on in rhetorical research, I could say that women are shouting loudly to us in their deafening silences. . . . I don't think that dropping these two women into this huge text, giving them 10 pages, is the answer. The "nod" is almost insulting. That's why I included Glenn's article ["Author"] last week too, so that we might have more of a context for thinking about women writing in a man's world. But again, I'll say that I'm convinced this history, all white and male as it is, is necessary knowledge for people who teach, read, write, and especially for people who want to change the world. We are living this heritage in our classes, our careers. It's important to see that there weren't any women's voices operating and to know why.
> (Kate's journal, Composition and Rhetoric, 2 Mar. 1994)

Across the hall, in Joy's Rhetoric of Women Writers class, women's voices *were* being recovered, and the reasons those voices had been silenced were being explored. There, the tensions between resistance and recovery were played out in different, but no less frustrating, surprising, and productive, ways. There were different coattails to ride but the same tradition to subvert.

Recovery and Resistance as Feminist Practice: Reading the Rhetoric of Women Writers

In class last week, someone said, "Traditional rhetoric controls and restricts, so were these women rhetoricians buying into that dominating mentality by using those rhetorical devices?" Jen said that women's rhetoric, even taking into account its traditional forms, opened up the possibility of difference. The binary choices—male, female—were not the only ones. Our own emerging definitions of women's rhetoric(s) emphasize the plural and multiple nature of women's rhetorical practices rather than reduce women's writing to something entirely other, a single mode of discourse that emerges out of some female "essence" or that exists only in opposition to the male tradition. Kris says that women historically did not abandon an adversarial mode for a strictly "connective" mode. Women can't just substitute hierarchies with webs, analytical style for experiential, objectivity for subjectivity, authoritative voice for the voice near at hand, *logos* for *ethos*. Women are continually working among and between these strategies, but always with *awareness* of the choices they're making in a particular location.

(Joy's journal, Rhetoric of Women Writers, 21 Feb. 1994)

Lately classes are offering me a two-fold opportunity for learning: one is the material itself and the other is various pedagogies. I am watching this class with intrigue and watching you as you balance several of the really big issues in academe in this classroom, the tiny microcosm of academe. Issues like male vs. female, feminist vs. humanist, personal experience vs. theory, dominant discourse vs. nondominant are always emerging out of the discussion, and there seems to be a lot of personal investment in a lot of people in the class. I think that creates a great energy and vitality to the class, but it also opens opportunities for people to feel threatened and invalidated. I am watching you attempt to create a safe space for all of us and orchestrate a great balancing act for a sometimes angry group of students. It seems as if you are juggling chain saws or something.

(Heidi's journal, Rhetoric of Women Writers, 8 Feb. 1994)

The course Joy taught further complicated the questions feminists face when teaching rhetoric, theorizing about women's rhetorics, and exploring the sites where traditional rhetoric and women's rhetorics converge and clash. We planned this course to establish a place in the curriculum where we and our students could recover and celebrate women's presence, if not at the center of the rhetorical canon, at least in subverting and remaking traditional rhetorical practices for women's purposes. We wanted students to see that they could draw on a usable and varied tradition of women writers, a tradition that offered rhetorical choices the students might not have seen before. The course gave students the opportunity to read women's writing, to recover coattails that they could ride to invigorate their own writing, and to redress the rhetorical contexts they saw as constraining, hierarchical, and violent. But to use their foremothers as rhetorical models, students needed to understand first the material contexts in which those women wrote, the strategies those women employed to fit or alter their voices in and against their contexts. Students also needed to examine the rhetorical and political contexts of their own lives as writers and readers.

As in Kate's class, resistance and recovery worked together because of the multiple dialogues the course set in motion among women's essays, journals, letters, and speeches from the fourteenth to the twentieth century, some of the writing using all the rhetorical conventions of the time, some of it attempting to alter and subvert those conventions. These women's voices played against the male voices of the western European tradition of rhetoric—a varied tradition, of course, but one with a common foundation in classical rhetoric and common arenas of practice in political and educational institutions that for centuries were reserved for men only. Students' voices, too, complicated and enriched this dialogue. As Heidi's journal suggests, many of the discipline's central questions concerning gender and discourse were enacted in this dialogue: Do women have an authentic rhetoric apart from men? When women speak and write, is there something essentially unique about their rhetoric? Or do women appropriate and use traditional rhetoric, and if so, is their writing therefore less authentic or less feminist? What hierarchies do we confirm or subvert in our thinking about these issues?

One of the first problems feminists face when they begin to explore such questions and to define women's rhetoric is that the paradigms used to define rhetoric (relations among writer, text, reader, context) and the terms used to analyze the rhetorical situation (*ethos, logos, pathos*) derive from a discourse tradition that privileges certain formal stylistic choices. Feminist recovery work, like Cheryl Glenn's essay on Margery Kempe, a profoundly feminist reading, draws on Mikhail Bakhtin, Wayne Booth, and Kenneth Burke for its analysis. But Glenn re-dresses privileged academic rhetoric as feminist analysis. She uses these male rhetoricians to show how Kempe did not accommodate her writing to the idiom of her day but, by engaging with the idiom dialogically, brought into play her multivocal self. And this, of course, is the point we want to make: Glenn uses the tradition itself to break new ground, to reclaim Kempe's writing, and to reread rhetorical theory. Since the language and conceptual constructs most available to women in the discussion of women's rhetoric have been the product of a western European, male tradition, the process of recovery almost immediately demands resistance. It demands at least that women ask, Do these terms that have been accepted as givens work for women in talking about women's writing? Or are other terms needed? If this is the only paradigm available for talking about women's rhetoric, what is left out? What is marginalized?

Such questions arose for Joy even as she was writing the syllabus for her course. How would the class analyze women's rhetoric without the terminology to talk about it, without examining women's rhetoric against the history of rhetoric that had been handed down since Aristotle? Of course the class would read Hélène Cixous, Adrienne Rich, and Virginia Woolf, but how would the students fully understand what these new feminist rhetoricians were arguing for or against if the students did not know something about the rhetorical and intellectual tradition those writers were challenging? Yet Joy was not about to begin a course on the rhetoric of women writers with a minicourse on the rhetorical tradition. The syllabus stated that one of the course goals was to posit new definitions of women's writing, but she knew that to formulate some vision of what women's rhetorics have been and might be, students would need some understanding of the rhetorical context in which women have written so powerfully. To appreciate, for example, how Elizabeth Cady Stanton brilliantly used conventional rhetorical strategies to argue for women's rights and how she turned the established modes of appeal, evidence, and authority to her own uses, students had to understand the rationalist tradition of argument in which the men *and the women* of Stanton's day were steeped.

As students began reading women writers, Joy could see in their journals and discussions that they immediately employed the very binary and exclusionary modes of thinking they were trying to escape. They placed themselves and women writers generally in opposition to what they viewed as the conventional demands of rhetoric. They spoke of women's writing as emotional rather than objective, as personal rather than abstract, as connecting rather than antagonistic. While Joy wanted to affirm the sense of uniqueness and difference and thus the position of recovery in students' assumptions about women's rhetoric, she also wanted the students to see that this essentialist celebration was too simple a stance. Binary definitions risked reinscribing women's writing as outside of, and inferior to, traditional male rhetoric. Readings of women's rhetoric had to be recovered in order to redress their absence, but resisted so that students would not define women's writing as a unified, seamless whole tied to an essential female body. Some feminist theorists see the move through essentialism as a necessary part of the dialogic definition of women's plural, multiple locations. But not all the students were ready to move into this complicated dialogue.

When Joy and the graduate students in the course began discussing some of the conventional paradigms and terms of rhetoric and introducing undergraduate students to rhetorical analysis, some students felt frustrated by the lack of a feminist terminology for speaking about women's writing and resisted attempts to analyze women's rhetoric through what they saw as traditional male methods. One of the undergraduates, Marie, said in her journal, "I am in this class because I want to get away from the traditional analytical style, the male definitions of writing and literature, and the argumentative style that I always feel required to write in. I want to explore my authentic, *female* voice and escape from male rhetoric" (6 Feb. 1994). Marie's comments allude to some of the fundamental epistemological conflicts that arose later in the class, but they point also to a pattern of thinking in recovery work that stops short of analyzing the rhetorical history that has shaped those female voices.

In the tricky business of teaching rhetoric as a feminist, it is important for a teacher to recognize that recovery is often necessarily accompanied by an essentialist celebration of women's rhetoric. This impulse is easy to understand. The recovery of women's writing occurs in the most extreme political reality: it begins in the historical absence of women's writing from the canon of rhetoric, from the culture, and from the classroom. Nothing could be more politically difficult than to break open that absence and assert women's voices. Two early acts of feminist recovery in composition, Joan Bolker's "Teaching Griselda to Write" and Pamela Annas's "Style as Politics," directed attention to women student writers and made the claim of difference an act of resistance to the institutionalized absence of discussion about women's writing. But such studies risked placing women writers in a position of other in relation to the tradition of writing instruction in universities. The discipline's discourse about women's rhetoric has grown much more complex as it has resisted reductionist questions and, Don Kraemer suggests, as it has taken note of the inconsistencies and contradictions in the discussions of gendered writing and the cultural construction of gender.

The Rhetoric of Women Writers course became a site where the disciplinary tensions between essentialism and social construction were played out. Some women, like Marie, wanted a complete escape from traditional male rhetoric and total immersion in and celebration of women's voices. But Marie and the entire class began to see that they could not escape considering the ways in which women's writing, both historically and in the students' immediate contexts, was not separate from that rhetoric. As some students spoke about finding an authentic female voice, the long and varied history of women's writing challenged them to ask also, Who defines that voice? Who claims it? Who benefits from that definition? Does that special status reinscribe some women on the inferior side of another dichotomy?

Rich reminds women to learn their history so that they don't fall into the trap of believing that women's writings are simply upstart instances, abnormal or isolated occasions ("When"). For the students in Joy's class models of diverse women's writing were needed to show that women's rhetorical history is not unified and singular but multivocal and to demonstrate how across the centuries women have used, subverted, accommodated, and resisted the tradition. In composition, only recently have critics begun to use feminist scholarship to examine and reclaim women's writing (see Glenn, "Author" and "Sex"; Swearingen). But rhetorical scholarship on writers like Woolf or Kempe is still often far removed from the examination of students' writing processes and the contexts of women writing in the academy. Joy's course showed that bringing the two strands of research together—on the work of women writers and on the writing of women students— extends and broadens the definitions of women's rhetoric. When Marie and the other women in the class began looking at their writing in relation to the long history of women's writing, they saw that much as they might find argument aggressive and agonistic, they could not cut themselves off from a tradition of argument, because an important part of women's rhetorical history consisted of women arguing: defending their right to an education, asserting proper modes of female conduct, challenging social norms that held them silent and disenfranchised, arguing among themselves and with men about all sorts of public and private issues. Reading women writers allowed students to celebrate and recover women's writing, but it also helped them complicate and resist risky essentialist definitions that ignored how women sometimes argued in forceful, angry, male ways and how women always chose from the rhetorical strategies at hand.

> Women can choose some alternative. They can use traditional rhetoric for their own means, as did Elizabeth Cady Stanton in her speech at Seneca Falls, where she turned men's line of reasoning on its head. They can challenge myths that are patriarchal, as exemplified by Sarah Grimké, who used religious quotation to contradict the myth of women's appropriate and ordained place. They can work to endow women with a sense of worthiness and potential as does Rich in "When We Dead Awaken," or they can "write the body" as Cixous asserts in "The Laugh," meaning they can refuse constructs and social labels. One thing is clear—it is imperative that women write. For as Cixous asserts, "writing is precisely the very possibility of change."
> (Thelma's journal, Rhetoric of Women Writers, 28 Feb. 1994)

Students began to see that women make choices based on personal and public contexts. Looking at the social and rhetorical constraints surrounding women's writing, Thelma saw that women, in using the available rhetoric in their writing, had also subverted it, "had broken its hold over them" (Rich, "When" 35). At the same time, the dynamics of the class, the assumptions about feminism and the authority of theory and practice that students brought to the class and the students' rhetorical (political) positions, made the classroom at times a battleground for many of the conflicts that surround women's rhetoric.

> After class a few of us discussed the direction of class on Thursday—it seemed to some of us to be a kind of "group therapy" as women talked about their experience as writers. But I think, Joy, when you asked, "How can we connect what we are saying about our own rhetoric with ideas of women's rhetoric?" you were bringing the discussion around from the entirely personal to a larger context—a move, by the way, I appreciated and a move that we, as students, need to replicate in our own thinking and discussion. How do we achieve a balance between thinking of our own lives and connecting them with the world at large? In the case of other courses, how do we teach women how to write and think like women yet still teach them the skills they will need to survive in a world where they must now and again write and

think like men to survive certain situations? I think issues of balance are very important here, bringing together the personal and the public. We need the balance between the mother and the father tongues.

(Heidi's journal, Rhetoric of Women Writers, 25 Jan. 1994)

Heidi's journal alludes diplomatically to one of the important conflicts enacted by Joy's class, conflicts that feminists also face in teaching rhetoric. Because the course was for upper-level undergraduate and for graduate students, built into it were tensions that are part of recovery work. A number of undergraduate women hoped to explore their experience in language, their victimization at the hands of patriarchal discourse, and in some cases their belief that writing was, in Toni Cade Bambara's words, a way "to participate in struggle" (154). Like Marie, who wanted to escape traditional argument, some students also resisted theorizing about women's rhetoric in abstract terms, instead talking about their experience to define an authentic female voice. Other women, mostly graduate students, felt they had already done that. As one put it, when she came to Joy's office to complain about the undergraduates: "We're beyond victimization; we want to theorize this; our future jobs demand a theoretical rather than a personal approach" (8 Mar. 1994). These graduate students were critical about what seemed to them a naive need for consciousness-raising. But they were also unsure how to argue their position while maintaining their idea of themselves as feminists, since some had rejected argument as masculine and agonistic.

Examining the ways these women's beliefs in feminist theory and pedagogy conflicted with the absent presence of a male rhetorical tradition helped the class to see at close range the difficulties women encounter in the academy. The students could also see the difficulties of their own positions as women rhetoricians. The conflict provided Joy an opportunity to help students explore the epistemologies underlying their dichotomizing of theory and practice, logic and experience. It also exposed students' assumptions about what constituted a rigorous or theoretical class, about the role of the personal in learning, and about experience as an authoritative basis on which to make claims of knowledge. The dialogue among women writers, the canon of rhetoric, and students' experiences helped the class see that to define certain genres and rhetorical relations as gendered—to see argument as male and narrative as female, for example, or to locate patriarchal discursive authority in the rational mind and feminist authority in subjective experience—not only may be inaccurate but also may limit women's rhetorical options and ignore the rhetorical power of much of women's writing throughout history. The dialogue also highlighted the ways in which even feminist responses are deeply embedded in traditional rhetoric and in the hierarchies the academy perpetuates, as it did here, among undergraduate and graduate curricula, theory, and experience.

Joy discussed these tensions as she talked about her position as a feminist teacher.

> I believe learning is a highly complex social and personal process. Speaking and writing—the use and practice of rhetoric to search for knowledge, to attempt to formulate ideas—are crucial to learning, especially at formative stages when we're just figuring out what we might think. I don't mean that I want us to come to false consensus or to easy answers. But I do believe dialogue is more productive in a class such as this. We know a lot about combat and debate, we know very little about how to sustain an ongoing honest, rigorous dialogue. Especially in this class, we need to have freedom to speculate, to be tentative, to be inarticulate. But we also need to be conscious of our rhetoric—how we speak, how much we speak, who has not spoken, and who is silenced.
>
> (Joy's journal, Rhetoric of Women Writers, 3 Feb. 1994)

We don't want to give the impression that Joy's course simply juxtaposed women's writing against the canon of rhetoric. Alternative rhetorics—written by women like Lorde, Gloria Anzaldúa, Cixous—provided students, as they have provided feminists in composition, with models of rhetoric that resist and disrupt the dominant discourse by violating accepted forms, fracturing stylistic expectations, and writing the taboo content of women's bodies. But like feminists in composition who, Lynn Worsham points out ("Writing" 84), risk appropriating and neutralizing the truly radical possibilities of *écriture féminine* by attempting to reduce it to classroom practices, Joy's students risked trivializing the revolutionary potential of these alternative rhetorics when they assumed them to be simple justifications for unexamined personal writing or prescriptions for how the students should write in all instances. Nevertheless, Cixous's writing in particular allowed students to see an alternative to the tradition against which women's writing has often been judged, and it provided students with opportunities to resee the revolutionary quality they had not clearly understood in Stanton's "Solitude of Self" speech or

Patricia Williams's essays in *The Alchemy of Race and Rights*. Cixous's writing inspired some students to experiment with alternative forms, voices, and subjects that pushed the boundaries of academic writing. But her writing also provoked resistance in some students, because it made them question their rhetorical choices, their feminism, and their accommodation to patriarchal standards.

> I struggled terribly with these readings from *New French Feminisms*. If Cixous is correct in asserting "that writing is precisely the very possibility of change," how can I write in such a way that will challenge governed speech, confirm women in a place other than a place of silence? In my current position as undergraduate, soon to be graduate student, my goals are to write strongly, clearly, and accurately and to write as a woman and a feminist, to blend my academic with my nonacademic voice, to merge theory with praxis, to become my own authority. But as I look at examples of women's writing, the "riskier ones" (like Jane Tompkins) have attained a certain status of establishment, respectability, and safety, the safety to explore various voices, to experiment with style, to write with "nonauthoritative" techniques. It would appear then to me that I must reach this established status first before I can safely experiment. Consequently, I feel I am better off developing my academic voice while I continue to develop my nonacademic voice privately. But how do I write my paper without feeling as though its message is one of acquiescence to the "father tongue"? How do I convey what I perceive to be my reality and its constraints and restrictions? How do I write of my disappointment and rage and fear? Again I feel injustice at my lack of freedom, authority, validity. What words do I use? What voice do I use?
> (Thelma's journal, Rhetoric of Women Writers, 3 Mar. 1994)

Throughout the semester Thelma continued to struggle with her conflicting positions as a feminist and a highly successful student in a male academy still dominated by traditional rhetoric. Thelma's worries about authentic voice, achieving authority, and the necessity of writing to get ahead show that it is not easy to separate women's rhetoric from traditional rhetoric or to identify neatly and conclusively a feminist practice of rhetoric. Sometimes choosing one, sometimes another, Thelma may not know exactly whose coattails she wants to ride—Cixous's, Stanton's, or Aristotle's. But she does now see the complex implications of her choices.

Feminist Pedagogy in Recovery and Resistance

Much of the controversy about women and rhetoric centers on the status of the historical texts and the question of whether any traditional rhetoric is usable for feminists in composition. It sometimes seems that historical texts have such power, weight, and influence that their presence alone compels submission to tradition and patriarchy. We know that texts, canonical and marginal, can operate in powerful, seductive ways, and they did in both these courses. Many of the students in Kate's seminar were changed as teachers, for example, by Plato's insistence that a rhetor must love his audience. Students in Joy's class were inspired and liberated by Cixous's writing. Yet these students also understood that Plato's dialogues exclude women from the realm of true rhetoric; they also realized that Cixous's definitions of women's rhetoric do not automatically help women speak effectively or change their political contexts. In other words, texts alone cannot define a tradition or signal a revolution.

What matters is how historical texts, women's or men's, are read, in what contexts they are read, and how they are received, resisted, and re-dressed by student readers in dialogue with one another and the texts. In a feminist class, where authority is scattered, where students' knowledge and experience become part of the texts in the course, where reflection and self-monitoring bring the rhetoric of the class itself under scrutiny, the influence of texts, however canonical, can be reimagined. When students' voices engage the voices of tradition on an equal footing in discussions and when teachers' voices model their own ongoing struggle with issues, new dialogues disrupt fixed hierarchical categories, roles, and power relations. In a class that attempts a feminist practice, alternative rhetorics can develop and flourish, and students can experience in the academy a site of experimentation and resistance. The complicated dialogues we've described here grow from such a feminist pedagogy and nurture possibilities for agency, resistance, and change—for students but also for us, their teachers, who rode their coattails through these courses.

NOTE

Our essay began as a result of a participant observation study Joy did of Kate's Composition and Rhetoric seminar. Soon after that study, we began writing a new course on the rhetoric of women writers, which we planned to team teach. Although scheduling in the English department made this collaboration impossible, Joy consulted with Kate regularly as she planned and taught the course. Conversations about teaching rhetoric are embedded in and enriched by our ongoing conversations in our collaborative roles as coordinators of composition, as leaders of workshops for new graduate teaching assistants, as teachers in summer writing projects for K-12 teachers, as members of departmental committees, and as women supporting each other and other women in our academic and personal lives.

We would like to thank the students in our courses—Composition and Rhetoric; Rhetoric of Women Writers—for their insights, their willingness to allow us to make their work a part of ours, and their reading of this essay in draft. We are particularly grateful to Kathy Boardman, Gwen Foster, Heidi Jacobs, Gladys Haunton, Kris Mapel-Bloomberg, Robin Miskolcze, Jennifer Putzi, Marie Smith, and Thelma Ross.

Reading and Writing Differences: The Problematic of Experience

Min-Zhan Lu

This essay explores a feminist writing pedagogy that asks teachers and students to examine the political uses and abuses of personal experience when reading and writing differences. As feminist critics have forcefully cautioned us from the perspective of current debate on issues of identity, difference, and representation in literary, cultural, and marginality studies, the right of one class to speak is always based on the oppression and silencing of another (hooks, *Yearning* and *Teaching*; Minh-ha; Probyn; Spivak, "Can"). These critics argue that in validating the authority of the personal, academic feminist readers need to reflect on their privileged social location and be vigilant toward the tendency to invoke experience as an inherent right that erases differences along lines of race, class, gender, or sexual identity. We need to imagine ways of using experience critically: experience should motivate us to care about another's differences and should disrupt the material conditions that have given rise to it.

Using my attempt to teach Sandra Cisneros's short story "Little Miracles, Kept Promises" in a writing-intensive literature class cross-listed with the women's studies program at Drake, a private university in the Midwest, I describe a tendency among us to put our gendered experience forward as a critical criterion for subsuming differences and to separate issues of gender from those of race, class, or sexual identity. I propose teaching practices aimed at combatting this tendency through experimentation with ways of making critical use of our gendered experience. I argue that composition pedagogies based on revision through sequenced reading and writing assignments—revision defined as a means for exploring different ways of seeing—can be used to advance the feminist project of making experience work both experientially and analytically. Such pedagogies are put forward in David

Bartholomae and Anthony Petrosky's *Facts, Artifacts, and Counterfacts* and *Ways of Reading.*

Cisneros's story portrays life near the Texas-Mexico border through a series of short letters left before the statues of saints. When asked to interpret the story, most of my students write about those letters in which issues of gender play a prominent role. My students' papers suggest a shared interest in contesting gender inequality. They also suggest that this interest is enabling, that it helps them connect with lives portrayed in the story that would otherwise appear foreign and strange to them. But their interest in confronting sexism is accompanied by a general indifference to the interlocking of sexism with other forms of oppression. That indifference results in simplistic readings of the letters. To illustrate, I use my students' responses to two letters in the Cisneros story, one signed by Adelfa Vásquez and the other by Barbara Ybañez.

Students often read Adelfa's letter as an example of the older generation's adherence to traditional female roles and Barbara's letter as evidence of the younger generation's struggle against such gender construction. Two sentences toward the end of Adelfa's letter stand out for my students: "Zulema would like to finish school but I says she can just forget about it now. She is our oldest and her place is at home helping us out I told her" (222). One student reads the sentences as pointing to "a culture that intended for the women to stay home and not get an education." Another asks, "If she [Zulema] were male, would an education be granted? . . . The household chores would completely fall into the hands of Adelfa, if Zulema goes to school. Adelfa is confining Zulema to the traditional Mexican role of women." Students do discuss other parts of the letter, such as Adelfa's plea for "clothes, furniture, shoes, dishes, . . . anything that don't eat" (222) and the inadequate disability check the family receives. But such discussion tends to appear in a different section of the students' papers, in the context of the poverty experienced by members of the community. Students approach the Vásquez family's financial plight as separate from rather than intertwined with Adelfa's attempt to convince Zulema that her place is at home. The possibility that Zulema, being the oldest, is needed at home to help relieve the family's economic stress seems overruled by students' conviction that Zulema is needed to help out with house chores, even though there is no reference to that concern in Adelfa's letter. Students' initial interpretation of Adelfa's letter suggests that students are making two assumptions: first, that issues of gender are not interrelated to issues of economic class and, second, that gender divisions are solely a matter of who does the chores around the house.

The same conceptual framework is evident in student approaches to the letter signed by Barbara Ybañez. One student writes, "Ms. Ybañez doesn't want to be subservient to a man. She wants to find someone who will 'cook or clean and look after himself.' Her letter also reveals that she thinks men can become a 'pain in the nelgas.' As another woman, Teresa, says in her letter, men can become 'a heavy cross' that restricts the freedom of the female."

Two other aspects of Barbara's letter stand out for my students: Barbara identifies herself as "Ms. Ybañez," and she is college-educated. As one student puts it, "Ms. Ybañez represents the younger generation who are no longer willing to play the traditional gender roles because they have had the benefit of education." But few students refer to the third paragraph of Barbara's letter: "I would appreciate it very much if you sent me a man who speaks Spanish, who at least can pronounce his name the way it's supposed to be pronounced. Someone please who never calls himself 'Hispanic' unless he is applying for a grant from Washington, D.C."(222).

Their lack of interest in this section again indicates a tendency to separate issues of gender from those of ethnicity. It is also telling that the few students who do refer to this section focus on Barbara's wish to find "a man who speaks Spanish." In their papers they place this fact in a discussion of the younger generation's concern to retain ethnic ties or cultural heritage. My students all ignore the last sentence of the paragraph, where Barbara articulates an interest in a man who shares her contempt for the official label "Hispanic" that Washington, DC, assigns to people like her. Furthermore, while many students notice her description of herself, "Ms.," no one refers to her description of the "educated" man she seeks: Chicano. My students' silence on these aspects of Barbara's letter suggests their identification with the hegemonic indifference to racial and ethnic differences.

In many ways, my students' initial interpretations of Cisneros's story exemplify the kind of essentialism that operates in unreflecting uses of the personal in some versions of feminism and that has been powerfully critiqued by feminists on the margin. The feminist dictum that the personal is political has taught us to recognize the centrality of the gendered experience in the production of knowledge. But as feminists on the margin have repeatedly pointed out, recognition of the primacy of experience, in its most limiting forms, can be an essentializing force and erase differences; such "feminism becomes a password misleading us into a false notion of 'oneness' with all women purely on the grounds of gender" (McRobbie, "Politics" 52). Too often, the gendered experience of the academic researcher or reader (white, straight, middle-class) functions as a universalizing term to overwrite the experiences of others under study. I don't think it is a coincidence that most students enrolled in my course say they are white, of European descent, from middle-class or upper-middle-class families, and committed to feminist issues and that their papers on Cisneros's story demonstrate a yearning for universality. Some of my students later point out, when writing about their self-location as readers, that they are drawn to certain experiences in the story because they have to some degree lived them. As one student puts it, "As much as I try to focus on point of view other than the one I am used to, it may sometimes be that I read a little bit of myself in the text." Many have been told, or know female friends who have been told, to stay home and finish the dishes, and many know parents who don't think education is important for "girls." They have or know of fathers and boyfriends who wouldn't share household chores. And they have been told to take German to keep up their ethnic ties. These experiences have not only figured in and fed into the questions the students bring to Cisneros's text but also have kept the students from attending to the differences between the familiar story of oneself and the story of an other. The task facing a teacher is to help students rethink ways of using personal experience so that readings through the personal will not be at the expense of other stories and selves.

Wrestling with this problem, I have been influenced by the work of feminist critics on the margin, who approach the issue from the perspective of the debate in feminism and cultural studies over issues of identity, difference, and representation. Elspeth Probyn argues for the need to theorize the self as a "double entity," as something that is not "simply put forward" but, rather, "reworked in its enunciation" (1–2). She argues that it is useful to think of experience as working on two levels. Experience can testify to "an immediate experiential self" (16), one revealing the gendered, sexed, classed, and racial facticity of being in the social. But experience can also be used to recognize an epistemological self, a self that politicizes itself by analyzing the material conditions that gave rise to it and that posits ways of changing those conditions while transforming itself in the process. Using Raymond Williams's concept of the structure of feeling and Michel Foucault's notion of the care of the self, Probyn explores how feminists might make experience work on both the experiential and analytic levels. Probyn posits three analytic possibilities for experience. First, experience can be used to analyze the facticity of our material being—the composition of the social formation that creates us (21). Second, it can be used to reveal connections that, in its weakest form, it conceals— conceals, because experience can mask the construction of its own ground. Third, experience can impel an analysis of one's differentiated relations to levels of the social formation (21). The first two kinds of analysis can help us consider not only what our experience allows us to reach toward but also what it might prevent us from reaching. It can prevent us, for example, from reifying itself into the sole criterion for critical analysis, as most of my students seem to have done when interpreting the Cisneros story. Analyzing our experience along these two lines can move us toward the third possibility, where the self is used not as an end in and of itself but as the opening of a perspective that allows us to conceive of transforming ourselves with the aid of others. In this way the self becomes not a mirror of us but, as Stuart Hall puts it, a "representation which is able to constitute us as new kinds of subjects and thereby enable us to discover spaces from which to speak" ("Cultural Identity" 237).

Exploring the analytic possibilities of experience in the three directions mapped by Probyn offers alternative uses of the personal for readers who, like my students, are committed to contesting gender inequality in the United States today. It can help such readers learn ways of reading that use their gendered experience but do not efface difference through omission. This exploring makes them reflect on the connections between various systems of oppression masked by their experience and imagine ways of disrupting their potential implication in other forms of discrimination. A teacher should initiate a series of readings and writings that help students revise their habitual approaches to difference by encouraging them to experiment with alternative ways of using their experiential selves. We need assignments that ask students to explore the analytic possibilities of experience by locating the experience that grounds their habitual approach to differences; by sketching the complex discursive terrain out of and in which the self habitually speaks; by investigating how that terrain delimits our understanding of differences along lines of race, class, sex, and gender; and by exploring personal and social motivations for transforming one's existing self-location in the process of rereading and rewriting.

One composition pedagogy that helps students use their experience critically is to have a sequence of reading and writing that prompts them to investigate and test different ways of seeing and to use that inquiry for revising their familiar ways of seeing (Bartholomae and

Petrosky, *Facts* and *Ways*). I look for texts that call attention to the interlocking of all systems of domination (race, class, sexual identity, religion, ethnicity, age, education, physical norm, gender), that validate the primacy of experience while using it critically, and that offer a vocabulary for theorizing the politics of the personal in feminist projects. Through the years, I have used texts by such feminist critics on the margin as Gloria Anzaldúa, bell hooks, Kobena Mercer, Audre Lorde, Adrienne Rich, Gayatri Spivak, and Trinh T. Minh-ha.

The works of hooks and Minh-ha help my students explore the potential uses and abuses of our gendered experiences when we read and write differences. Hooks's essay "Reflections on Race and Sex" speaks to my students with particular power because it is aimed at feminists and liberation workers who, like them, yearn to eradicate oppression (*Yearning* 13) but tend to take an either-or approach to discrimination along lines of sexual identity, gender, class, and race. Furthermore, the essay appeals to them because hooks's argument for focusing on the interlocking of all systems of oppression is grounded on incidents that are close to home—a crime in the news, a personal account of an attack on a woman by a black man. The students are eager to apply hooks's approach to their daily life—and to their initial readings of Cisneros's story. Another essay that my students feel applies to their situation is Minh-ha's "Difference: A Special Third World Women Issue." They are particularly struck by her argument that the " 'wo-' appended to 'man' in sexist contexts is not unlike 'Third World,' 'third,' 'minority,' or 'color' affixed to woman in pseudo-feminist contexts." Minh-ha convinces them of the need to examine their yearning for universality, that is, the tendency to efface difference through the notion of a generic woman reified from the experiences of white, middle-class heterosexuals (97). The essay also gives them some concrete ideas on how to combat that yearning.

Reading these essays along the line of the potential use and abuse of one's gendered experience in the process of reading-writing differences helps my students and me posit alternative perspectives and thus locate rationales for rereading Cisneros's "Little Miracles" to revise their initial papers. The following is an example of the kind of revision assignment that can come out of such a reading:

Assignment A

"Progressive folks must insist, wherever we engage in discussions of . . . issues of race and gender, on the complexity of our experience in a racist sexist society."

—bell hooks

> *"The understanding of difference is a shared responsibility, which requires a minimum of willingness to reach out to the unknown."*
> —Trinh T. Minh-ha

For this paper, use our class discussions of the essays by hooks and Minh-ha to reread Cisneros's story and critique your initial interpretation of this story in your last paper.

When rereading the Cisneros story, try to approach it from the perspective of the interlocking of issues of race, class, sexual identity, religion, and gender. When critiquing your paper, consider the extent to which you were able to fully acknowledge the complex experiences portrayed in the letters. Locate moments in your paper where you might be said to have taken an either-or approach to the complex interlocking of various systems of domination.

As you can see, the purpose of Assignment A is to ask students to reread Cisneros's story and their initial interpretation from an alternative perspective, one they have formulated from discussing two essays by two feminist critics. This alternative perspective directly challenges the tendency in those who wish to end sexism to subsume differences, a tendency that surfaces in most of my students' papers, but supports those who structure their approaches on the wish to end other forms of domination as well. Rather, it asks students to become more self-conscious about the ways in which their interest in combating one particular form of oppression might delimit—enable as well as prevent them from reading-writing differences. Such a revision assignment is best accompanied by one that helps students use their lived experiences of social domination to locate personal and social reasons for trying out this alternative perspective. My class reads Anzaldúa's essay "La consciencia de la mestiza: Towards a New Consciousness" to explore ways of using the figure of the mestiza to examine the structural underpinning of experience and to talk about its analytic possibilities. Anzaldúa depicts the mestiza as that juncture where beliefs and forces cutting across lines of race, class, gender, sex, ethnicity, and religion collide (387). The image of collision grounds the personal in a complex discursive terrain. Anzaldúa argues that the first step of the mestiza is to take inventory of the baggage inherited from her ancestors—beliefs, values, and viewpoints—so that she "puts history through a sieve, winnows out the lies, looks at the forces that we as a race, as women, have been a part of" (390). My students and I find the image of putting history through a sieve helpful for projecting ways of using our experiential selves to examine the extent to which our view-points illuminate as well as tell lies about our inscription in interlocking systems of oppression. We interpret the sieve as the mestiza's determination to end all forms of oppression. It can help her decide which notions of the familiar to surrender and to which foreign ways of seeing and thinking she should make herself vulnerable. The act of taking inventory and putting history through a sieve offers us a vocabulary for talking about how we as readers can use experience to rework our habitual approaches to differences.

Our reading of the mestiza provides us with another revision assignment:

Assignment B

"As I looked for common passions, sentiments shared by folks across race, class, gender, and sexual practice, I was struck by the depths of longing in many of us. . . . [T]here are many individuals with race, gender, and class privilege who are longing to see the kind of revolutionary change that will end domination and oppression even though their lives would be completely and utterly transformed. The shared space and feeling of 'yearning' opens up the possibility of common ground where all these differences might meet and engage one another."

—bell hooks

"Her [the new mestiza's] first step is . . . a conscious rupture with all oppressive traditions of all cultures and religions. . . . Deconstruct, construct. She becomes a nahual, *able to transform herself into a tree, a coyote, into another person."*

—Gloria Anzaldúa

For this assignment, use the image of the mestiza to locate personal-social motives for revising your initial paper on Cisneros's "Little Miracle" from the perspective put forward by critics such as hooks and Minh-ha.

The following are some questions to get you started:

Take inventory of your personal experiences of oppression along lines of race, gender, class, sex, ethnicity, age, education, physical norm, geographic region, or religion. Which type(s) of discrimination are you most familiar with? In what particular forms? Which have you had least experience with? Why?

Consider the extent to which your personal history might affect how you enact your yearning to eradicate oppression. What particular viewpoints and forces of which you have been a part can be used to advance your interest to combat which type(s) of oppression? Why? What particular "familiar" viewpoints and privileges must be surrendered for you to end which type(s) of oppression? Why? Which foreign ways of seeing and thinking might you need to make yourself vulnerable to? Why?

Examine the ways in which your personal history might have affected your ability to attend to the interlocking of all forms of oppression when you approached differences, such as reading Cisneros's "Little Miracle" in your original paper. For example, how have your experiences in certain forms of oppression enabled you to relate to certain aspects of the text? How has your (lack of) experience in other forms of oppression kept you from engaging with other aspects of the text?

As someone yearning to end discrimination and transform yourself, how might you revise your reading of Cisneros's "Little Miracle" so that your immediate interest in ending particular form(s) of oppression could enhance your interest in rather than keep you from deconstructing other form(s) of oppression operating in society and portrayed in Cisneros's text?

Together, Assignments A and B can motivate students to revise their initial approach to Cisneros's story. Although in our class discussion we focused on the applicability of the image of the mestiza to our approaches to Cisneros's story, we also learned to use the image to analyze the thoughts and actions of several characters portrayed in the story and analyze as well the author's position. Taking inventory, quite a few students observed that their Protestant or nonreligious background made it initially difficult for them not to see as foreign, primitive, or silly the practice of writing letters and leaving charms to "idols." That and their wish to respect cultural differences led them either to avoid discussing the text's references to religion or to approach those references strictly as a unique cultural heritage. Such self-reflection led one student to complicate her gender reading of Barbara's letter by taking into consideration the intersection of gender, race, and religion:

> She doesn't want to be subservient to all "masters": a man, a government, or a god which is keeping her from what she believes she deserves. She is not afraid to say what she wants even if it is

not what the *masters* have chosen for her. She asks for someone "who's not ashamed to be seen cooking or cleaning or looking after himself." She wants someone who never calls himself "Hispanic," when knowing this is the identification expected by those handing out grants in Washington D.C. And she tells the Saint that if the Saint doesn't sent her the "man" she asks, she will "throw him back" and "turn [the] statue upside down." Ms. Barbara Ybañez understands that she has "put up with *too much* too long." She believes she is too intelligent, powerful, and beautiful to put up with *any* of the *masters* running her life.

Attention to her habitual indifference to issues of religion, race, and class led another student to revise her reading of another letter in Cisneros's story signed in code, by a "B2nj1m3n T." In her original paper, this student pointed out that Benjamin probably does not feel safe to write about his "love sadness" for another man in either Spanish or English because homosexual feelings are not acceptable to either community. In her revision, she added, "It is also significant that Benjamin writes to not just Christ but the 'Miraculous Black Christ of Esquipulas.' A black Christ would probably better understand and be able to intercede in Benjamin's behalf because he would understand the prejudice Benjamin faces."

Another student, taking inventory, felt authorized to use her experience as a practicing Catholic and an "older generation" woman, which originally marked her as the other in this classroom, to explore the function of saints for the least powerful of the congregation: women and the poor. She revised her reading of Adelfa's letter by pointing out that "since the male of the house was on disability, the burden of supporting the family falls on other members of the family, including Adelfa and Zulema—the oldest child. St. Martin de Porres was Adelfa's choice of saint because as founder of an orphanage, he knew the problems of feeding hungry children. So he would understand Adelfa and help her make Zulema 'see some sense.'" Writing about her personal history also motivated this student to complicate the notion of ethnic ties that surfaced in the class's interpretation of why characters who think like feminists, such as Ms. Barbara Ybañez and Rosario (Chayo) De Leon, would leave letters and charms to the saints:

> Rosario decides that "all that self-sacrifice, all that silent suffering" of her mother and grandmother is "not me." But she also realizes, because of the taunts she suffered from her relatives when she declared her intention of remaining single and becoming an

artist, that "those who suffer have a special power"—"the power of understanding someone else's pain." This taught her to be proud to be "her mother's daughter and her ancestor's child."

At the same time, reviewing the particularity of her Catholic experience, this student becomes more attentive to the particularity of the Catholic experience portrayed in Rosario's letter:

> To Rosario, the Virgin Mary is not "Mary the mild." For in the Catholicism of her people, [Mary's] name is also the Coalaxopeuh and "our mother Tonantzin," someone with the "power to rally a people when a country was born" and with "Dominion over Serpents." In pleading to the Virgencita, Rosario is saying that she has discovered from her ancestors a powerful weapon for fighting oppressions. And she means to use it to fend off the hurt she feels from the derision she gets from her mother and relatives because she wants to stay single and become an artist.

These revisions, prompted by a sequence of reading and writing assignments that ask students to consider alternative approaches put forward by critics, show that exploring the structural underpinnings of one's experience can motivate students to revise their habitual approaches to differences. That is, writing the personal can motivate students both to use unfamiliar approaches and to use the familiar critically. Writing the personal also authorizes students whose backgrounds are other than those of a majority of the class to use the specificity of their lived experience to open up alternative approaches to the text. For example, writing about his experience as a short person, one of the four male students located a lived reason not only for confirming his intellectual alignment with feminism but also for becoming more aware of his lack of interest in issues of class.

Revision assignments should be followed by an assignment that asks students to theorize the critical use of experience they have enacted so that they can more self-consciously employ this method in the future and outside the classroom:

Assignment C

For this assignment, use the thoughts you have generated doing the last two assignments to write a revision of your original paper on Cisneros's "Little Miracle." When you have finished your revision, comment on a separate sheet of paper about your experience in doing this sequence of assignments. How would you characterize the use of personal experience in this process? How many directions did you take? Which of these directions do you find necessary but difficult? Why? How did you go about overcoming such difficulties?

By such a sequence of reading and writing assignments, composition studies can contribute to students' rethinking the use of self and experience in feminist enunciation. With radical thinkers like Paulo Freire and with the debate on issues of identity, difference, and representation in literary, cultural, and feminist studies, composition has a long tradition of developing critical pedagogies aimed at helping one reflect on one's self-location as a reader-writer and explore ways of changing how one reads, thinks, and lives. The sequencing of reading and writing assignments is not the only method available to compositionists interested in rethinking the use of self and experience in feminist approaches to differences.

The need to explore other ways of utilizing our expertise in critical pedagogy to make experience work both experientially and analytically is urgent for those of us resisting the hegemony of neoconservatism in the United States of the 1990s. As hooks points out in *Teaching to Transgress*, "family values" has become a fix-all magic phrase in discussions of current social problems. Especially alarming is that the family evoked in such discussions is one in which sexist roles are upheld as a stabilizing tradition. Not surprisingly, this vision of family is coupled with "a notion of security that suggests we are most safe with people of our same group, race, class, religion, and so on" (28). The neoconservative rhetoric of "family values" encourages us to subscribe to a social amnesia about the real cause of our problems: the intertwining of racial, sexual, economic, and gender oppressions and the consequent social segregation. The move toward social isolation and amnesia is also prominent in both liberal and conservative models of multiculturalism in college and university classrooms, where cultural diversity is often studied without rigorous reflection on the privileged location that authorizes our right to study and speak about differences. Given such a pervasive conservatism, we should more actively mobilize our expertise in critical pedagogy and feminist thinking to call attention to the interlocking of all systems of oppression in our everyday lives, whether we are debating a solution to social problems like violence and poverty or trying to reach a multicultural interpretation of a text like "Little Miracles."

The feminist project of making experience work on both the experiential and analytic levels is particularly valuable in combatting the hegemony of neoconservative rhetoric, because of feminism's continual emphasis on the primacy of firsthand knowledge. My students' papers on Cisneros's "Little Miracles" show that my students not only have this knowledge but also know how to make it a criterion for critical analysis. I find it heartening that, despite the privileged class and racial background of most students in the private, midwestern campus where I teach, the work of colleagues in the university to establish a women's studies program has produced a sizable number of students versed in the use of the experiential for critical analysis. If we can move them to recognize that gender is not the only determinant of our identity and that to end sexism, we need to use our gendered experiences analytically to fight all forms of oppression, we can broaden our alliances in the struggle against neoconservatism. Furthermore, learning to make experience work both experientially and analytically in our day-to-day teaching and learning can unite teachers and students across the lines of race, class, gender, and sexual identity. We can mobilize our lived experiences of one form of discrimination to end social amnesia about other forms of discrimination. In that critical space, differences can and must engage one another. For it reminds us that, in spite of our best intentions, social isolation and amnesia can result from unreflective use of the experiential and that no one system of discrimination—gender, race, or class—can be eradicated if we do not use our lived experiences analytically to stop other forms of domination.

NOTE

An earlier version of this article was given as a keynote address at the University of Maine Conference on Multiculturalism. My thanks to members of the audience and to Bruce Horner for their comments.

Women and Language in the Collaborative Writing Classroom

Gail Stygall

Many of the problems they experience in the classroom could be alleviated, some of the women said, if talk were more collaborative. Discussing a classroom situation she had enjoyed, one woman said: "It was just wonderful. There were integrated, reciprocal, coexisting dialogues happening most of the time. There were people interrupting people and there were all kinds of things happening. The dialogues, the interaction, was in sync so I was very comfortable."
                    —Cheris Kramarae and Paula A. Treichler

What is happening during a collaborative task is a dialogue between men's and women's language. Although we would expect that male language would dominate, the new social structure of the peer learning group, the lack of a patriarchal presence "teaching," and the presence of strong and vocal women in the group can combine to give women's language the power to surface and to replace men's language.
                    —Carol Stanger

"Discipline" . . . is a type of power, a modality for its exercise, comprising a whole set of instruments, techniques, procedures, levels of application, targets; it is a "physics" or an "anatomy" of power, a technology. . . . [O]ne can speak of the formation of a disciplinary society . . . [n]ot because the disciplinary modality of power has replaced all the others; but because it has infiltrated all the others, sometimes undermining them, but serving as an intermediary between them, linking them together, extending them and above all making it possible to bring the effects of power to the most minute and distant elements.
                    —Michel Foucault

As an educational technology, collaboration has received very little scrutiny at the same time that it has become widely used in both composition and feminist classrooms. Cheris Kramarae and Paula A. Treichler find female students attracted to classrooms in which the process of discussing knowledge is more highly valued than the production of knowledge. Carol Stanger posits a new gender equality in the talk of the collaborative group. Both uses of collaboration, in composition studies and in feminist teaching, were born of the liberal hope in the expansion of educational franchise of the early 1970s, and both set equality of opportunity as the goal of pedagogy. Liberal ideology in both cases assumes that the classroom is a free, open forum, because the instructor can mediate inequalities by articulating, modeling, and enforcing the rules of respectful, relevant exchange and development of positions. But in both the composition and feminist versions of collaboration, when the instructor withdraws, hierarchy and inequality may reappear.

Michel Foucault teaches us that all technologies of talk are part of discursive formations and relations, disciplining at the "most minute" levels (*Discipline* 216), and the collaboration under discussion here is not exempt from the forces of discipline. What scrutiny collaboration has received in the past fifteen years has been primarily from a left-progressive perspective; none at all has come from a feminist position. This essay elaborates, from the perspective of a feminist-critical linguist, the reasons that unstructured collaboration in the writing classroom jeopardizes participatory learning for women students. Given what feminist-critical linguists have known about how women fare generally in conversations outside the classroom, it should come as no surprise that women fail to thrive in classroom working groups, whether the field is composition or women's studies. Does collaboration produce the nonpatriarchal classroom of feminist hope? In the absence of a feminist-critical authority in the writing classroom, the answer must be no.

To examine how collaborative talk works in the writing classroom, I employ a feminist-critical linguistic approach. While I am not suggesting that feminist-critical linguistics yields empirical "truth," I do claim that it provides another position, a platform from which the workings of collaborative talk can be viewed. In this essay I review the perspectives provided by feminist-critical linguistics, then reanalyze three published conversations that are offered as examples of good collaboration. The first conversation, an invented one, is provided by Kenneth Bruffee. In it, we see a female acting as the helpmate for a male struggling to find a topic for his essay. She does all the work; he gains all the benefits. Although the conversation is made-up, it

254 Collaborative Writing Classroom

inscribes deeply held attitudes about conversation in our culture. The second conversation, a recorded and transcribed student working group, is drawn from Martin Nystrand. It demonstrates that students do serious work on their writing in peer groups and also gives evidence of gender roles in talk—and of the discipline that works at the "most minute" level—when one of the female group members, the student-author of the piece under discussion, is nearly silenced while another takes on the voice of the institution for the group. In the third conversation, a transcript drawn from Lester Faigley, we see the forces of gender and language at work in the computer-mediated classroom. Although this transcript demonstrates a radical reallotment of speaking roles, I argue that gender roles are reinscribed here by other means.

Technologies of talk—such as collaboration—are part of discursive relations in educational institutions. In the writing classroom, where collaboration acts to displace teacher authority, we can expect that the intertwined discursive practices of education and patriarchy will reproduce themselves in the absence of authoritative comment from a feminist teacher. From the findings of Elizabeth Sommers and Sandra Lawrence, from bell hooks's discussions of teaching, and from Susan Jarratt's theorizing about feminism and argument, I conclude that women fare better in collaborative talk when the feminist teacher explicitly teaches and models new forms of talk.

Feminist-Critical Linguistics, Conversation, and Education

Feminist linguistics has taken many forms over the past twenty years, from the theoretical projects of the radical feminist linguists such as Dale Spender to the empirical sociolinguistic and discourse-analytic studies by researchers such as Deborah Tannen to the theoretical discussions of the French feminists to the Hallidayan analyses by scholars such as Cate Poynton. I focus here on the empirical analysis of gender and conversation, because much of the work on collaboration in the writing classroom presumes some sort of conversation as its basis. But we must move beyond naive empiricism and also think about the discursive formations of education working in conjunction with those of gender.

As Foucault describes in *Discipline and Punish*, it is not only prisons that act to discipline; it is also schools in which students are made into individual files, ranked, sorted, collected, all under the surveillance of the institution. It is a commonplace that the teacher at the head of the classroom embodies the panopticon. But discipline does not necessarily disappear when the teacher moves away from the head of the classroom. We should expect discipline to continue to operate, if in different forms. With collaboration, we have simply deputized our students to act, in the absence of instruction to the contrary, as those who discipline, that is, using the social roles they bring to the classroom. There are two discourse consequences: first, some student will take up the role and voice of teacher, directing students to the task of collaboration; second, whatever gender roles students bring to class will necessarily be part of the talk of the group. In both cases, institutional discipline is still operating—despite the liberal hope that the need for the teacher, like the state, will eventually wither away.

Unlike feminism or even contemporary composition studies, linguistics has been resistant to poststructural accounts of language, because linguistics is predicated on the assumption of structure in language. All linguists, whether the theoretical descendants of Noam Chomsky's MIT linguistics, of the sociolinguistics of William Labov or Peter Trudgill, or of the combinations of language and the social made by M. A. K. Halliday, believe that language may be analyzed in levels— the divisions into phonetics, phonology, morphology, syntax, semantics, and discourse. Although there is considerable dispute about the relative importance of the different levels and their relation to the social, linguists generally assume that, at least for purposes of analysis, these levels exist. All linguistic analysis begins with the assumption of structure. Analysis of language and gender identifies the structures sensitive to change when gender is a variable.

Both sociolinguists and discourse analysts assign different weight to the reality of their findings. Some report their findings as if they discovered a natural wonder on a colonial expedition: the structure of language emerging from their analysis. Others, such as Deborah Cameron ("Demythologizing"), have attacked the nonpolitical stances of some sociolinguists. Teun van Dijk and other followers of critical linguistics argue that the basic task of that linguistics is to center analysis "on the role of discourse in the (re)production and challenge of dominance. . . . More specifically, critical discourse analysts want to know what structures, strategies or other properties of text, talk, verbal interaction or communicative events play a role in these modes of reproduction" (249–50). Because work in critical linguistics invokes social theorists such as Foucault, Pierre Bourdieu, and Louis Althusser to examine how language, ideology, power, knowledge, and cultural capital interact, I believe Dijk's recent work avoids some of the criticisms developed in Faigley's *Fragments of Rationality*. Faigley's primary criticism of the critical linguistics movement is that it posits a simple one-to-one correspondence between ideology and language. It is a valid criticism of the early forms of critical linguistics but doesn't do justice to the later work of Robert Hodge and Gunther Kress in *Social Semiotics* or Dijk's articulation of a complex critical discourse analysis. Critical discourse analysis informed by social theory is my frame for this essay. As a feminist-critical linguist I expect that, apart from gender, institutional education is generating, maintaining, and situating discursive formations—metarules about speaking rights, genres, erasures.[1]

Issues of language and gender in linguistics have been relatively muted in the United States by the dominant linguistic approach, which posits an autonomous linguistic mental faculty and a universal grammar and has no interest in the social, where gender factors are often most visible. As Cameron observes, "It's hard to imagine a feminist account of Gaelic vowel mutation or a women's phonetic alphabet" (3). That is to say, linguists disagree not about what the forms are but about what the study of those forms means. Thus the feminist linguist doesn't argue that a sound or sentence exists, but that the existence varies with gender. To study forms and not their social uses is to exclude gender (and other hierarchies) from linguistic study. Cameron suggests the possibility of a feminist critique of linguistics. Indeed, in sociolinguistics and in discourse analysis, both subfields of linguistics that are less influenced by the dominant autonomous paradigm, gender has emerged as a relevant category of analysis. While any structuralism-based subfield of linguistics is open to poststructuralist criticism, the observations these two subfields have made about the effect of gender on the language of middle-class, white American adults remain an important means of triangulating accounts of gender and language. Some of these observations are listed in figure 1.

The studies reported in figure 1 are not comprehensive, because they do not integrate the intersections of gender with race, class, and ethnicity, but they do outline some of the most discussed observations in empirical studies of conversational interaction and gender. Robin Lakoff's 1975 work, *Language and Woman's Place*, opens the debate by making observations about stereotypes of language and gender, drawing solely on her own reflections (a typical practice of linguistic theorists in the US) and on the experiences of her close associates. Sociolinguists and later discourse analysts took issue with many of her declarations, but some felt that she had described a powerless form of language—a phenomenon whose existence was confirmed in several

Figure 1
Sample Empirical Observations of Gender
in Conversational Interaction

Sociolinguistic or Discourse Finding	Researcher(s)
Women use more tag questions in cross-sex conversation.	Lakoff
Women use more addressee-oriented, affective tag questions; men use more speaker-oriented, modal tag questions.	Holmes; Cameron, McAlinden, and O'Leary
Women use more hedges.	Lakoff
Men in cross-sex conversations tend to interrupt women more than women interrupt men.	Zimmerman and West
Men and women both interrupt, but they interrupt in different contexts.	James and Clarke
Women in conversation with women overlap cooperatively.	Tannen, *You* and "Relativity"; Coates, "Gossip"
Women frame conversation as a process of rapport building; men frame conversation as independence maintaining.	Tannen, *You* and *Gender*
Men talk more than women in cross-sex conversation.	James and Drakich
Men's turns on the floor are longer.	Edelsky
In cross-sex relationships, women do more of the conversational caretaking.	Fishman; DeFrancisco

later studies.[2] Although all these observations are now quite complicated by context, it would appear that insofar as women are less powerful than men in middle-class American culture, so is their language less powerful, more oriented to relational issues. Many studies of childhood and classroom interaction suggest differentiation along lines of gender. Daniel Maltz and Ruth Borker's discussion of gender and language, for example, suggests that because in the United States boys and girls are socialized into language quite differently, they have grown up in what amount to separate sociolinguistic subcultures. The rules for conversation, Maltz and Borker argue, are learned from ages five to fifteen, when single-sex relationships dominate, and carry over into late adolescence and early adulthood. Thus it would be highly surprising if male and female students came to the collaborative writing group with the same conversational socialization and strategies in hand.

The feminist-critical linguist would want to examine transcripts of classroom conversations in which collaboration was used and ask questions about those conversations before concluding that collaborative peer groups are beneficial to women students. If male students talk more and get their topics onto the conversational floor more readily than female students do, if they ask fewer questions of female students than of male students and interrupt female students more often than they do male students, we might want to give serious thought to the kinds of authority that should operate in the collaborative group in the writing classroom. And if a student takes on the role of the teacher, we would want to interrogate that interpretation of authority and discipline as well.

Bruffee: It Could Be "Any Undergraduate"

Taking a closer look at some published conversations from the perspective of the feminist-critical linguist, I begin with Bruffee's *Collaborative Learning*. While Bruffee's earlier work does not provide transcripts, even invented ones, his 1993 book does. Though Bruffee includes responses to criticisms made in the composition community, especially those made by John Trimbur, the audience for *Collaborative Learning* seems to be college administrators more than other scholars in composition. Bruffee shows a familiarity with postmodern, poststructural thought about knowledge communities; but in the end the book is a curriculum proposal, one that advocates a nonfoundationalist program in which the knowledge students bring to college is affirmed, the social justification of knowledge is examined, the situatedness of knowledge is explored. The "conversation" in figure 2 is invented, and if Bruffee were not so earnest in his presentation of the benefits of collaboration, I might have thought he was parodying a male-female conversation. Bert's assignment is that Bert must "explain to his classmates something he has learned in another course." Conveniently, he runs into Ernestine, who "sees the worried look on his face, and puts two and two together" (58–59). Apparently, Ernestine is supposed to help Bert find a topic for his paper, and she works at this task accordingly. At first glance, the conversation may not seem problematic. Each speaker—one male, one female—has the same number of turns. Though there is some difference in the number of utterances, Bert having 57% of the total, Ernestine 43%, the difference doesn't seem excessive. It is striking, however, when we examine the kinds of utterances. Ernestine asks fifteen questions, whereas Bert asks five, and those five only after she has convinced him that he has a topic. The role Ernestine assumes is very close to the role Pamela

Figure 2
Bruffee's Invented Transcript

Ernestine:	Hey, Bert, what're you going to write your comp essay about?
Bert:	Gee, Ernestine, I don't know.
Ernestine:	What courses are you taking besides comp?
Bert:	Music. Phys Ed. Psych. Physics.
Ernestine:	Which one do you like best?
Bert:	Physics. I'm doing great. I think I'm going to ace it.
Ernestine:	Why not write about that?
Bert:	No.
Ernestine:	Why not?
Bert:	No, Ernestine. No. Absolutely not. It's too hard. Nobody'd understand what I'm saying. Anyway, nobody cares about physics. They think it's boring. Everybody'd be bored.
Ernestine:	I wouldn't be. I liked physics in high school. I'm taking it next term. What're you doing in physics right now?
Bert:	Well, we just finished atomic structure and radiation.
Ernestine:	What about them?
Bert:	Well, uh . . . oh, Ernestine, no. I tell you I can't write about physics and that's that.
Ernestine:	Aw, come on, Bert. What's radiation?
Bert:	It's energy. Different kinds of matter give off different kinds of energy.
Ernestine:	What kinds?
Bert:	Light. Light is radiation. There are different kinds.
Ernestine:	Bert, come on. What other kinds?
Bert:	Oh, X-rays, cosmic rays, particle radiation, that sort of thing.
Ernestine:	So, there you are. Write about them.
Bert:	Mm, . . . no. Too complicated. But you know what? I could write about what radiation does to you if you get too much of it.
Ernestine:	Do you have enough to say about that for a paper?
Bert:	Sure. The teacher lectured about it. Showed pictures too. Ugh. And you know, I remember seeing a TV show about it last spring. There's a section in the textbook about it, too. That may help.
Ernestine:	What could you say about it? What kind of position would you take?
Bert:	Well, maybe something like, Radiation changes cell structure. How about that?

Figure 2
Bruffee's Invented Transcript (cont.)

Ernestine:	What does changing cell structure do to you?
Bert:	Mainly it gives you cancer and gives your children birth defects.
Ernestine:	There you are, Bert. You've got a position—radiation changes cell structure—and two paragraphs to support it, one on radiation-induced cancer and one on radiation-induced birth defects. You're home free.
Bert:	Gee, Ernestine, do you think so? Do you think people would be interested? Radiation sickness is really awful, Ernestine. Why, do you know what happens first if you get too much radiation? Your . . .
Ernestine:	Wait. Wait. Stop, Bert. Don't tell me any more about it. Make the comp teacher sick, not me. Serve him right. But you know what?
Bert:	What?
Ernestine:	I'm not bored.
Bert:	Gee, Ernestine, thanks.

Source: Bruffee, *Learning* 58–59

Fishman describes in her analysis of transcripts of three couples' ordinary, daily conversation. Fishman finds that women work to keep conversation going, by asking questions, by having their topics deferred in favor of those offered by their male partners, and by engaging in a subordinate role that is supportive and encouraging. Women, she says, are the "'shitworkers' of routine interaction" (405).

Bruffee remarks at the close of his invented conversation that Ernestine has done a considerable amount of work in this conversation but that, of course, "any undergraduate" could have fulfilled the same role (60). But it wasn't any undergraduate, it was a female undergraduate, and she was acting in accordance with her allotted conversational role: to maintain the conversational floor for the benefit of the male speaker.

Nystrand: Talking about Writing

Much of the research done on peer writing groups has been descriptive, focused on what the group members say to one another. Even with a social constructivist model of language and learning, it has been difficult to theorize about collaborative writing groups. There should be a good match between a theory that says that we learn language socially and a practice that says that writing is best taught in collaborative groups. Yet although a gesture has been made toward studying how collaboration suppresses dissent (see Trimbur, "Consensus") and enforces class lines (see Myers), we have looked very little at how gendered social roles operate in collaborative writing groups. Specifically, we have not considered how collaboration produces and instills discipline at the microlevel.

Foucault contends that seriation and hierarchization produce discipline in schools:

> From the seventeenth century to the introduction, at the beginning of the nineteenth, of the Lancaster method, the complex clockwork of the mutual improvement school was built up cog by cog: first the oldest pupils were entrusted with tasks involving simple supervision, then of checking work, then of teaching; in the end, all the time of all the pupils was occupied either with teaching or with being taught. The school became a machine for learning, in which each pupil, each level and each moment, if correctly combined, were permanently utilized in the process of teaching. (165)

Though collaboration rarely works as efficiently as Foucault describes it (nor did the Lancaster method work that well), thinking about collaboration as discipline is useful. Because the teacher is not in direct control, some student must move into that vacated supervisory position. It should be no surprise that in Martin Nystrand's transcript of a collaborative session in a writing classroom the student is a woman. Most of the teachers college students have had in language arts and English courses in their precollege education were women. Sociolinguistic research indicates, also, that women are more likely to act as language conservators than as language innovators. Though this finding has been disputed by feminist linguists, it remains a widely held view of the relation between women and language.[3] Whom do we imagine correcting our grammar? The image is almost always female.

Nystrand provides striking examples of how social roles affect a peer group's discussion. We see a woman writer remain silent while three others discuss her text (fig. 3); we see a woman function as the group's voice of discipline (fig. 4). In neither case does the woman student materially benefit from being a part of the collaborative group. Both the silent author and the voice of discipline only reproduce the available gendered roles.

Figure 3 is taken from Nystrand's extensive transcript of a writing group's discussion of a paper. Before this segment begins, a female group member's paper has been read to the group. Only three of the four members speak; the writer of the paper is silent. She is not required to remain silent, as some forms of peer writing groups prescribe. The assignment was to write a critical essay, and her topic was how the media slant representations of events. Defining features of the genre of critical essay was, in Nystrand's view, a significant part of the discussion. And, indeed, a reading of the transcript shows that the students are talking about genre in relation to personal experience and about the writer's relation to experience and evidence.

Tom opens the discussion in turn 1 by stating that he enjoyed the

Figure 3
Nystrand Peer Writing Group Transcript, First Segment

Turn	Speaker	Text of Turn
1	Tom:	That was really—I—I enjoyed the first paragraph really good. I thought—um—"slant"—"slant" was a good word—"slant their stories"—um—stuff like that—um—
2	Jean:	Um—this one right here on the second page it says "one day on the way to school"—I think that's too related to you—It's—you gotta detach it more.
3	Tom:	Yeah—Make it—make it general.
4	Jean:	Should I do that on my paper too?
5	Rick:	You can't do that on your paper.
6	Jean:	Maybe my whole paper just stinks.
7	Rick:	No, just 'cause you have personal experiences in it doesn't mean it stinks. I don'—*your* paper was about band. When you document—you know—you can't use documented proof on something like that.
8	Jean:	So I have to use my own—right.
9	Rick:	Well, unless you know of something—
10	Jean:	'Cause when she was reading that through I noticed it on hers and then I thought it's the same on—as mi—mine—like—
11	Rick:	But hers—hers is a paper where she could get—you know?—examples and stories that didn't *have* to deal with her.
12	Tom:	Yeah, I think that would end up—you have to—

Source: Nystrand 191

paper, but his statement is marked by several false starts and hesitations. Perhaps his training in group work—"Always start with something positive"—is in conflict with his difficulty with the language of feeling, a difficulty typical of young adult males. With an initial false start and a switch in focus from the paper ("That was really") to his feeling ("I—I enjoyed the first paragraph"), combined with three place-holding *um*s, Tom conveys that he is afraid that he can't hold the conversational floor. Because this group is working well into the semester, Tom's fear may be based on an expectation of losing the floor to Jean or to Rick. Indeed, at Tom's second hesitation, Jean echoes his *um* and initiates her first bid for the floor. Without waiting for the writer to ask for specific commentary, Jean selects herself as the next speaker. She changes the direction of the discussion by her topicalization "this one right here" and in effect tells the author not to use "I" or be too personal in a critical essay. Tom confirms Jean's criticism in turn 3 by interpreting not being personal as being general.

Jean introduces a new topic with her question in turn 4 about her own paper, and this second topic remains on the floor until she connects it back to the writer's paper in turn 10. Rick enters the conversation at turn 5 and assists Jean in maintaining her topic. Jean's declaration in turn 6 is an indicator of her intention to continue control of the conversation. The type of statement in turn 6 is sometimes called response-controlling, because normal conversational politeness demands that any respondent deny the truth of the statement. Predictably, Rick says no at the beginning of his turn, releasing Jean from the obligation of providing evidence in her paper because of its grounding in personal experience. Jean confirms Rick's response in turn 8, with a topic-closing "right." Rick actually offers to continue Jean's second topic in turn 9, with a slight shift in orientation indicated by his "well." Jean's topics and interests hold throughout this twelve-turn segment, with the writer completely outside the conversation.

Figure 4 is a continuation of the discussion in figure 3. Though the writer does speak in this and subsequent segments, it is always in response to Jean's queries and directives. The author is like students in student-teacher conferences who cannot direct attention to their concerns. We are never really sure that she wished to discuss the issue of her personal knowledge of her essay topic. Because Jean blocks her access to the floor by speaking in the disciplinary voice, the author never initiates discussion. Even more important, Jean's control of the floor is in the service of filling the teacher's vacated role. Jean focuses on nuance of phrase (turns 2 and 4), narrowness of topic (turns 7 and 10), unity of story line (turn 10). And she makes suggestions. We could

Figure 4
Nystrand Peer Writing Group Transcript, Second Segment

Turn	Speaker	Text of Turn
1	Rick:	That's why I think that you—it—it—
2	Jean:	You just have to change the phrasing a little bit.
3	Author:	How about if I just started out "I heard a conversation that gave a perfect example of the media slanting a story"?
4	Jean:	That's still—I think it's still too close.
5	Tom:	Yeah.
6	Rick:	But if she doesn't do that she's gonna have to like say where—where she's got this information from—That's what I—I kinda want to know about this.
7	Jean:	What is the bus? What does the bus have to do with it maybe? Take the bus out too—
8	Rick:	That's where—where she heard it.
9	Author:	Yeah.
10	Jean:	Right. But that doesn't have anything to do with the story.
11	Tom:	No. It doesn't.
12	Author:	Okay.
13	Jean:	And that's kind of—
14	Author:	How could I—how could I introduce the story into the paper so that it didn't sound like something—that—something that I'm just making up?
15	Jean:	Okay.
16	Tom:	Does anybody have that one paper on—um—
17	Jean:	How 'bout for—for instance—um—
18	Rick:	Mention the conversation a little bit.

Source: Nystrand 192–93

imagine a teacher in a student-teacher conference making these same points. And it fits educational and patriarchal discursive practices that Jean is a woman. With discipline's requirement that some students take on the teaching role so intertwined with the patriarchal educational system that distributes the precollege and first-year college composition slots to women and the serious scholarly roles to men, it may be easy to miss that the disciplinary discourse is itself gendered. Neither Jean nor the writer can advance an independent agenda. While Nystrand appropriately characterizes his students' conversation about

the text at hand as a discussion of genre, he avoids the issue of the relations among discipline, education, and gender.

Faigley: Gender Iterations in the Computer-Mediated Classroom

Although Lester Faigley was initially entranced by the multiplicity of
voices and displacement of the teacher in the computer-networked
classroom, his subsequent experience made him less sanguine. The
final transcript he offers shows a devolution into gender warfare and
name-calling that would dismay any teacher, a kind of behavior made
possible probably only by the use of pseudonyms and the iterations
and echoes of computer-mediated communication.

It is to the original, more hopeful first transcript that I turn here.
In a class in which the female-to-male ratio is 17:4, Faigley presents
and discusses 87 messages of a 191-message session from a computer-
mediated writing course titled Writing and Thinking. He initiates the
discussion by offering two paragraphs from an assigned reading from
James Spradley and Brenda Mann's *The Cocktail Waitress*, an ethnog-
raphy of the working life of bar waitresses. The paragraphs deal with
the gender-role confusion of a waitress named Holly.[4] Holly's confusion is generated by a job in which her sexuality plays so prominently;
she works in a male world, serving primarily male customers, so her
livelihood is dependent on her ability to stay in a traditional woman's
role. Faigley's asking the class who wrote the passage, Spradley or
Mann, prompts a discussion of gender, authorship, and text. Faigley
tells of the exceptionally high student participation rate and the occur-
rence of "hot messages"—messages to which there are many responses (180). On gender issues arising from the transcript, he says,
"Even if patriarchal social structures do not vanish when students use
Interchange (note that several of the women chose male pseudonyms),
some of the socially defined limits are mitigated" (181).

I challenge this observation. If some socially defined limits based on
gender are mitigated, others arise to take their place, leaving us with
little in the way of net improvement for women students conversing by
computer in the writing classroom. The ideologies of gender, instead
of being identified in the usual back-and-forth classroom exchange
among a handful of high-participation students, are more thoroughly,
more completely dispersed throughout the classroom, powerful iterations on the theme of gender determinism. And although computer-
mediated discussion does allow an opening for everyone's response,

the number and rapidity of message exchanges are too great for the instructor to monitor them all.

In the ordinary classroom, talk is controlled by the teacher. The teacher decides who talks and when, decides when a student must stop talking, decides which topics are appropriate, what connections from one's reading or personal experience may be publicly linked to the topic, and what digressions are acceptable. Although the degree of control over classroom talk in fact varies, classrooms in which teachers talk and students listen or students talk one at a time are the most common. Discourse analysts working in classrooms have observed what has been called the IRE (initiation, response, evaluation) pattern, in which the teacher opens with an inquiry, the student makes a response, and then the teacher evaluates that response.[5] As Courtney Cazden observes, the teacher is thereby guaranteed two-thirds of the classroom floor time (160). It has also been observed in United States classrooms at all age levels that a small group of high-participation students usually controls the classroom floor, the rest of the class remaining silent listeners. Thus the broad participation that Faigley describes in his study is unusual. Figure 5 shows a radical redistribution of classroom speaking roles.

Twenty out of twenty-one students attending that day participated. A graduate student teacher, JoAnn Campbell, also participated (the class she was teaching used the same reading materials as Writing and Thinking but did not meet in the computer-mediated classroom). She wrote more than Faigley did; her words, in eight turns, accounted for about 10% of the transcript. In six turns, President Reagen (the student's spelling) accounted for 8.4%, and Faigley accounted for 7.7%. Thus the two teacher figures accounted for 18.4% of the messages. The next ten students in the table produced remarkably similar passages of the transcript.

The issue of pseudonyms does not straightforwardly mitigate social limits, as it might first appear. Two of the males are identified by Faigley—President Reagen and Greg Harvey. Faigley indicates that there are four males in the class altogether. But only six names are female—jane doe, Karen, angel, Rae, Megan, and Dolly Wolly—though of course we have no reason to assume that the students behind these names are all female. There are three ambiguous names (t.c., Mickey, and LSP) and nine male names (Art, A. Hitler, jimmy, Kenny g, xerxes, Gordon Sumner, fred, George Strait, and Mickey Mouse). Clearly, the anonymity of typically male names is preferred by many, perhaps even by a majority, of the female students. Rhetorical cross-dressing contributes to our understanding of gender displayed in the classroom

Figure 5
Distribution of Talk in Faigley Transcript

Name	Words	Turns	Percent of Floor	Words per Turn
JoAnn	374	8	10.7	47
President Reagen*	294	6	8.4	49
Lester Faigley	270	9	7.7	29
LSP	259	5	7.4	52
Kenny g	229	5	6.6	46
Mickey	218	5	6.2	44
Art	212	5	6.1	42
t.c.	190	5	5.5	38
Karen	176	6	5.1	29
Rae	162	2	4.5	81
xerxes	148	4	4.3	37
jimmy	132	3	3.8	44
Gordon Sumner	128	5	3.8	26
jane doe	120	3	3.4	40
angel	102	3	2.9	34
Mickey Mouse	98	2	2.8	49
A. Hitler	96	4	2.8	24
fred	77	2	2.2	38
Megan	59	1	1.7	59
Dolly Wolly	58	1	1.7	58
Greg Harvey*	43	1	1.2	43
George Strait	40	1	1.1	40
Total	3,485	87	100.0	40

*Asterisk indicates a known male student.

Source: Faigley

discussion. As I have argued in "Gendered Textuality: Assigning Gender to Portfolios," one result of rhetorical cross-dressing may be that students take on gender roles that create opportunities for repetition of restrictive understandings of sex and gender (see Stygall et al.). Students who choose a gender role different from their sexed body are likely to select the most stereotypical version of that role—the hard-edged, argumentative male; the soft, self-disclosing female—rather than an androgynous or less conventional mixture of traits.

The overall redistribution of speaking roles in this computer-mediated classroom led Faigley to conclude that he had "become a student in his own class" (181). Yet the discursive formations of education are powerful, and looking at the data in another way yields a different impression. The two teachers perform their roles through the use of interrogatives. Faigley asks six questions in his nine turns; Campbell asks twelve questions in her eight turns. No student uses his or her turn to pose questions to the entire group. Also, although the attention paid to the teachers does indeed diminish by the end of this eighty-seven-message transcript, participants' responding to them accounts for half the messages. Control of the talk, then, is still very much in the hands of the teacher figures.

But it is in the discussion about the gender of the writer of the paragraphs that the ideological functions of gender in this culture become apparent. Most of the initial messages are in response to the two teacher messages posed at the beginning of the session, first Faigley's asking which coauthor of *Cocktail Waitress* wrote the paragraphs, then Campbell's query about the possibilities of women working together for change. Messages 4 through 21, and several more after Campbell's hot message (22), respond directly to Faigley's question. Twelve respondents think Brenda Mann wrote the passage, six think James Spradley did, and three feel either could have been the writer. But then the participants begin to respond to message 22, in which Campbell asks why waitresses accepted such behavior from their male coworkers and customers.

Two positions that emerge in the transcript could be expected to appear in a regular classroom when women's issues are raised: the feminist position and the "men have rights too" position. In figure 6, xerxes exemplifies the first and LSP the second. In message 14, xerxes tentatively moves into the discussion by agreeing with Karen. Karen said she thought Spradley wrote the paragraph, because it ended with "Mark or another bartender would give you a loving pat—and tell you how much you were appreciated. It was a good feeling to be needed" (qtd. in Faigley 169). Karen commented that she couldn't see a woman discussing the feeling of being needed in that way. Xerxes, taking a step further, connects feeling needed with feeling used. After the discussion turns to Campbell's question, xerxes sketches a scenario in which waitresses are powerless to change how they dress and how they are treated. By message 61, xerxes is agreeing enthusiastically with what xerxes perceives Campbell's position to be, that

Figure 6
Messages of Xerxes and LSP

Turn	Text of Turn
	xerxes
14	I agree Karen. The statement about "feeling needed" bothered me, too. I mean feeling needed is one thing, but feeling used is quite another.
46	I think the waitresses dress the way they do because the person in charge gives them certain dress codes. Also, if they complain too much to the men they serve they are in danger of losing their tips and possibly their jobs.
61	JoAnn, yes! The role of women in this society is laid out on t.v. in magazines—everywhere and the role that is prescribed is not a good one. But, if enough women realize that to look like a fashion model and to please men is not where it's at eventually some radical changes will happen.
74	LSP, there will always be small instances where reverse discrimination occurs, but really can we justify everything by saying it happens to a few men as well?
	LSP
16	I think Brenda Mann wrote it, or at least said it in an interview.
31	Maybe these women like the way the men treat them. There are people out there who have to find other ways of being needed. It does sound as if women are putting themselves in demeaning positions, but maybe it's true. I don't know.
45	I agree with Old Pres. I think the waitresses probably make themselves to look good to get better tips. That's different from dressing up to impress your boyfriend or girlfriend.
66	I think that if the women don't want to put up with the men they should find another line of work or wait tables in a different setting. I know a lot of women don't like the way men treat them, but what about the men who get tormented by a bunch of drunk women and strip joints. They could be dancing and taking their clothes off too, yet you never hear much about them complaining about the harassment because they are getting tips put into their G-strings.
80	There are more than a few places. Pres. Reagan said that he gets remarks from women who have had a few drinks and he's a waiter that works banquets and stuff like that. I'm not saying that male discrimination is more prevalent than female discrimination, but it does exist and you don't hear about it as much. What about the things male nurses go through, or male secretaries. It's out there.

Source: Faigley

contemporary popular culture offers women few good roles and that radical change must ensue. Finally, in message 74, xerxes undercuts the validity of the argument that discrimination happens to men as well; in one of the few interrogatives from a student in this transcript, xerxes points to the "small instances" where such discrimination occurs.

If xerxes marks out some textual, feminist space, LSP seems to mark space for the more traditional male, in ways quite different from the conservative economic arguments advanced by President Reagen. In LSP's first turn, LSP seems to suggest that Mann is just another waitress for Spradley to interview and not the coauthor of *The Cocktail Waitress*. In LSP's next turn, LSP suggests that perhaps waitresses like being treated as they are, even though what they live with on the job might be "demeaning." In turn 45, LSP agrees with President Reagen that waitresses try to look better to get better tips, a hint at prostitution, when that behavior is contrasted with making oneself look better for a romantic partner. By turn 66, LSP expresses sympathy for "the men who get tormented by a bunch of drunk women and strip joints" and says strippers shouldn't complain about sexual harassment because they're getting good money. In turn 80, LSP retreats somewhat, replying to xerxes by acknowledging that the occurrences are higher for women and that although discrimination against men isn't as widely discussed as discrimination against women, it does exist. LSP accounts for 7.4% of the talk, behind only the two teachers and President Reagen.

The other responses that emerge in the transcript we might not expect in a regular classroom: the ongoing iterations of gender ideology. In figure 7, three repeating messages are grouped:

1. Traditional sexual orientation is binary.
2. Women must observe restricted sexual roles.
3. The world is naturally controlled by financial Darwinism.

Although the first message is repeated only once, it sets an important and early frame in the discussion for the other repeating messages. No one in this classroom suggests that sexual orientation is anything but traditional and heterosexual, yet of course there are other options. After the discussion centers on gender roles as stereotypically binary, the message posters who want to articulate a feminist position have difficulty. Both turns 5 and 21 imply that to step outside traditional gender roles is to risk homosexuality. Thus, in this classroom, if you are a feminist—that is, if you do not act in a traditionally feminine

Figure 7
Gender Iterations

Turn	Speaker	Text of Turn
Sexual Orientation as Binary		
5	A. Hitler	Brenda Mann must have said this, unless James Spradley likes getting called sweetie and honey by men.
21	George Strait	I think Brenda wrote the paragraph because it describes what men do to waitresses in bars. I doubt these men were doing this to other men.
Women's Sex Roles and Sexual Aggression		
41	fred	I think the waitress is partially to blame in her situation. She could protest this environment if the waitresses banded together. It seems that the waitresses acted this way to define their femininity, just as the men wanted to show their masculinity. The women work at the bar because they cannot express their femininity in their situations such as school and other jobs.
83	Art	The point being that when men make comments about women, and grab at them, it is almost accepted by most people as normal, but when a woman makes comments to a man she is considered loose.
84	A. Hitler	Correct, Lester. It is socially accepted for a man to grab a woman's butt or make a remark towards her, but if the roles are reversed people think the woman is drunk or crazy or a whore.
Financial Darwinism		
40	A. Hitler	I think the women, divided for some reason, were afraid to protest their conditions individually for fear of being fired.
52	Gordon Sumner	You have to remember that it is a job requirement to dress in a certain fashion, and an occupational hazard to be bothered by drunken men. They can always quit if they don't want to put up with it.
54	Kenny g	Xerxes has a good point. IF the waitress says anything to her customer or her boss she/he runs the risk of losing money. The reason most people are in this line of work is for the money.

Figure 7
Gender Iterations (cont.)

Turn	Speaker	Text of Turn

Financial Darwinism (cont.)

| 57 | Mickey Mouse | Waitresses are not the only ones who have to put up with being called things such as "sweetie" and "honey." I work in an office where the women secretaries are called these sorts of names by the older (and higher status) men. They have to put up with it also, because if they don't they will get on these people's bad side real fast. |
| 69 | Mickey | Basically, I think it is just whoever is at the bottom end of the totem pole has to put up with everyone else. It just so happens that the waitresses are below the customers and the waitresses are female while the customers are male. Can anyone give me an example of where women are above men on the totem pole? |

Source: Faigley

way—you risk being called deviant, even if you are decidedly hetero-sexual. Feminism is a position outside the binary gender roles available. This attitude is expressed throughout the discussion but is perhaps most focused in fred's midpoint comment about women wanting to work in a job like waitressing so that they can "express their femininity." Toward the close of the transcript, Art and A. Hitler speak about the sexual double standard, once again affirming that only a binary choice is available.

Even more pervasive than the double standard in this discussion is the ideology of financial Darwinism and the role gender plays in economic realities. A. Hitler, Gordon Sumner, Kenny g, and Mickey Mouse all recognize the problem of being a female employee in a patriarchal economy. The lack of agency in the waitress's working conditions is apparent in all four messages. A. Hitler mentions the fear of protesting working conditions but does not say to whom such a protest might be addressed. Gordon Sumner speaks of job requirements and occupational hazards—unpleasant, to be sure, but the result of natural forces at work. In Kenny g's message, the waitress is responsible for the situation, the male customer is not: if she "says anything," she will not make money. Mickey Mouse says that in white-collar offices as well the female workers must get along, go along.

Mickey broadens the scope by offering the observation that waitresses are below customers in the world's hierarchy, which problem is not based on gender inequality but "just so happens."

Faigley tells us that all eighty-seven messages were written in a twenty-minute period. Though there were two teachers responding, the rapidity and wide dispersion of student response served to undercut the feminist-critical authority Faigley and Campbell represented in the classroom, the most collaborative classroom discussed in this essay. Faigley reports that some researchers, Cynthia Selfe and Jerome Bump among them, have praised the computer-mediated writing classroom for increasing women's participation in classroom discussion. But women's increased participation only produces textual echoes of the gender ideologies that progressive teachers hope to overcome.

Missing in these three conversations is a feminist-critical authority who can act as a counterweight to the disciplining of students by gender and education. Elizabeth Sommers and Sandra Lawrence have examined classroom conversation in peer writing groups under two different frameworks. The first, originally the position of Sommers, was that for women students peer groups would work best with little or no teacher intervention. She reports, "Believing that schools give too little control to students, she wanted students to retain ownership of their drafts, their groups and their talk, and to understand that meaning is not handed from teachers to students but developed in collaboration." Lawrence, her collaborator in this project, provided the second framework; she "felt that students had little experience responding to one another's written texts or working in groups, [so] she gave them specific guidelines and procedures for conducting peer group sessions" (9). Lawrence's rules included a fairly prescribed speaking protocol, in which each student was required to speak in turn while the others listened. Sommers and Lawrence selected eight peer-group sessions out of approximately a hundred (for both teachers in an academic term) and analyzed the tapes of those sessions for women's participation compared with men's. They found that in the teacher-directed peer groups, women's participation rates matched men's but that in the student-directed groups, women's participation was markedly lower. Sommers and Lawrence conclude, "Female participants in student-directed groups learned yet another lesson about gender and power, providing female students with one more 'chilling' school experience" (29).

Bruffee, Nystrand, and Faigley certainly didn't abandon their classrooms to student chaos, a fear of many newcomers to collaborative pedagogy, but all three advocated the teacher's withdrawal from the

activities of the collaborative group. Bruffee advocates a particular activity for collaborative groups in the form of descriptive outlining but
clearly recommends that teachers "remain uninvolved in any direct
way" (45). For Nystrand, the teacher's withdrawal from the peer group
serves a Vygotskyan rearticulation of the social aspects of learning to
write. He says:

> We may regard intensive peer review as a formative social
> arrangement in which writers become consciously aware of the
> functional significance of composing behaviors, discourse strate-
> gies, and elements of text by managing them all in anticipation of
> continuous reader feedback . . . [and what] writers take from
> their groups largely emerge in ways that are often evident first in
> the social interaction of peer review.   (211)

If that social interaction turns out to reinscribe gender inequalities,
and this feminist-critical linguistic analysis shows it does, then teacher
withdrawal from the group and teacher trust in the social interaction
are unwarranted. For Faigley, even though gender ideologies were not
scrutinized as in a feminist-critical linguistic analysis, the agonistic
quality of the classroom discourse becomes apparent, as does the need
to theorize postmodern discourse more deeply.

Advocating a general, academic knowledge community, as Bruffee
does, and a feminist, cooperative, collaborative utopia, as Stanger
does, oversimplifies and flattens the complexities and conflicts of students struggling to position themselves in relation to the academy and
in complex social forces. Susan Jarratt makes a case for the feminist
teacher who, like bell hooks, creates the classroom in which rigorous,
critical argument takes place and for the teacher who helps students
confront truths "in the heat of argument" ("Feminism" 121). The feminist teacher of composition who uses collaboration must also be willing to use her authority in the classroom to model a different kind of
discourse for women students. The model proposed by Sommers and
Lawrence is a beginning but remains insufficient in the face of more
complex intersections of the forces of discipline in education and gender, such as those found in the Nystrand conversation. Moreover, if we
know now that unstructured collaboration holds hazards for women
students, we can assume that the same is true for students of color. A
constant analysis of the technologies of talk used in writing classrooms
can address the problem. Chandra Mohanty argues:

> Resistance that is random and isolated is clearly not as effective
> as that which is mobilized through systemic politicized practices

of teaching and learning. Uncovering and reclaiming subjugated knowledge is one way to lay claim to alternative histories. But these knowledges need to be understood and defined pedagogically, as questions of strategy and practice as well as of scholarship, in order to transform educational institutions radically.

(qtd. in hooks, *Teaching* 22)

Using feminist-critical linguistics to foreground the discourse features and interactions sensitive to gender differentiation and inequality, we can be more active in collaborative writing classrooms, in confronting, analyzing, and teaching alternatives in the feminist writing classroom.

NOTES

[1]For a discussion about the relation between critical discourse analysis and Foucauldian social theory, see Stygall, *Trial Language*, chapter 1.

[2]See especially O'Barr for a discussion of powerless language in the courtroom.

[3]See Spender's *Man Made Language* for a discussion of the paradox of women being both language conservators and language innovators.

[4]The two paragraphs read:

> At times, some of the girls sensed it vaguely. But for Holly, the mixture of feelings was always there, sometimes clear and intense, other times beneath the surface. Working at Brady's made her feel more like a woman and less like a woman than anything she had ever experienced. And these conflicting emotions were often simultaneous, causing her to both question and accept the identity of "Brady Girl."
>
> Brady's Bar was a man's world and being part of it brought an excitement all its own. You dressed for the men, served drinks to the men, laughed at jokes told by the men, got tips and compliments from men, ran errands for men. Men called you sweetie and honey and sexy. Men asked you out and men made passes. . . . And as you left after work, Mark or another bartender would give you a loving pat—and tell you how much you were appreciated. It was a good feeling to be needed.
>
> (qtd. in Faigley 169)

[5]For a more complete discussion of classroom discourse patterns, see Barnes; Stubbs; Cazden.

Feminist Writing Program Administration: Resisting the Bureaucrat Within

Amy Goodburn and Carrie Shively Leverenz

> *For me and others accountable for writing instruction, the political is immediate and personal. We live each day with the messy, mixed meanings and consequences of conjoining political action and political discourse with teaching and learning in writing classrooms.*
> —Louise Wetherbee Phelps

In the last decade, compositionists who also identify themselves as feminists have begun to consider how a commitment to feminism does and should inform research and teaching about writing. Although composition has been slow to recognize the power of feminist thought to inform and transform the profession, feminism's influence is finally being felt, in increased attention to gender as a category of difference in composition research (Flynn, "Composing"; Kirsch; Ray; Sullivan), in explicit attempts to connect feminist theory and composition theory (Holbrook; S. Miller, *Carnivals*; Ritchie; Worsham, "Writing"), and in efforts to construct feminist writing pedagogies (Annas; Caywood and Overing, *Teaching*; Hollis, "Feminism"; Jarratt, "Feminism"; Lamb). What does it means for feminism to inform a site of composition studies that remains surprisingly undertheorized: that of writing program administration? As Michael Pemberton has pointed out, many jobs for composition specialists involve administrative responsibilities that include budget management, public relations, and the hiring, training, and evaluation of staff. In carrying out these responsibilities, writing program administrators operate in a complex web of power relations dictated to a great extent by institutional and cultural norms. It is crucial that feminist administrators who wish to challenge existing power relations understand the norms that nurture and support those relations.

In this essay, drawing on our experiences with a writing program in the throes of reform, we identify constraints that can impede the restructuring of power relations according to what compositionists like Marcia Dickson, educational theorists like Shirley Grundy, and sociologists like Kathy Ferguson have called feminist principles of management. These principles include nonhierarchical collaboration, shared leadership, and the recognition of multiple sources of authority. Perhaps the most difficult constraint for us to work against (because it was the most invisible) was our compliance with bureaucracy, which, according to Max Weber, is characterized by concrete divisions of labor, a hierarchical organization of personnel in which managers supervise subordinates, and rigid rules of operation that ensure bureaucratic control over production. In *The Feminist Case against Bureaucracy*, Ferguson argues that the power structures in bureaucracies are oppressive and need to be challenged, not merely by our hiring more women but also by our introducing feminist discourse into the discourse of bureaucracy. We agree with Ferguson that is it not enough simply to substitute women for male managers or even to change administrative structures. Ultimately, for feminist models of writing program administration to succeed, administrators must ground any and all changes in an ongoing practice of critical self-reflection. Only by recognizing and reflecting on our inscription in dominant and dominating ideologies of labor and management can we develop the critical consciousness necessary to resist them.

Although much of the scholarship on writing program administration has focused on practical rather than theoretical issues, a few compositionists have been concerned with the issue of power relations among administrators and their various constituents. As historians of composition like Susan Miller have noted, writing programs and the people who run them are often positioned as subordinates in the English departments where they are typically housed (*Carnivals*). Perhaps as a result, compositionists like Gary Olson and Joseph Moxley, and more recently Edward White, have argued that writing program administrators need to seize and wield the kind of power traditionally accorded to other academic administrators, a bureaucratic power manifested in control over budgets, staff, and program policy. Recently, these calls for bureaucratic power have been critiqued by compositionists, some overtly feminist, who wish to refigure power relations among those working in writing programs. For example,

Louise Wetherbee Phelps suggests that Nel Noddings's "ethics of care" can provide a starting point for administrators who must decide how to handle the power they inevitably have over others. In this model, the writing program administrator has power, but it is the benevolent power to care for and nurture others.

Dickson offers another critique of bureaucratic power, even of the benevolent sort, arguing that feminist administration must involve collaboration among the staff rather than management by a single person. In her words, "the only productive way to direct a writing program is to acknowledge that no one person can or should have ultimate control; faculties should collaboratively direct the writing program themselves" (140). The form of collaboration Dickson recommends is one that Lisa Ede and Andrea Lunsford have termed "dialogic"; it is characterized by shared leadership among group members, group goal setting, and a recursive rather than linear process of collaboration as the group continually works to consider each member's perspective. Although Ede and Lunsford do not expressly label dialogic collaboration feminist, in their study of workplace collaboration they find that dialogic collaboration is practiced more often by women, hierarchical collaboration practiced more often by men. For Dickson, an administrative model based on dialogic collaboration is "more concerned with doing away with hierarchies than with perpetuating them" and allows for the "blurring of lines of authority and control." The administrator shares leadership with others in the program, trusting them enough to "turn the asylum over to the inmates" (148). Jeanne Gunner argues similarly for the benefits of a decentered writing program administrative structure, one in which the program is collectively administered by staff members who elect representatives and serve on committees. From Gunner's perspective, a decentered administrative model is more democratic, granting power to those writing program staff members, such as non-tenure-track instructors, who are often disenfranchised in the university ("Decentering").

In the year that we worked as graduate administrative assistants in a large first-year writing program, we had the opportunity to participate in a restructuring of administrative power informed by feminist critiques of bureaucracy like those offered by Ferguson and Dickson. As graduate students who were invited to share with the director responsibility for revising curriculum, revamping TA training, and reconceiving program policies and procedures, we felt indeed like inmates suddenly given some control over their fate and the fate of other inmates. Although we were initially excited by the chance to play important roles in what promised to be a dramatic reform of the writing program, our feminist dream of doing so through nonhierarchical collaboration and shared leadership was often lost sight of in the ensuing struggles for power, authority, ownership, and control. In retrospect, we believe that our frustration with the new models of administration we were trying to enact reveals the degree to which we had been influenced by bureaucratic models of administration—those that Dickson, Ferguson, and Grundy term patriarchal. That is, we expected and even desired the very kind of administrative structure we were seeking to transform.

Institutional Context

The large state-funded research university in which we worked has an extensive writing program that requires three writing courses of all students. The first is a first-year composition course housed in the English department. Taught mainly by a cadre of graduate students and lecturers, it enrolls approximately fourteen hundred students per quarter. During the year in which we participated as administrative assistants to the program, the department was in the midst of curricular and policy reform at the undergraduate and graduate levels. On the basis of the recommendations of a departmental self-study, an external review, and a year-long evaluation of the various writing courses by faculty members and graduate students, a committee of fifteen wrote a seventy-seven-page report that described and evaluated the first-year writing program and made several recommendations for change. In particular, the committee recommended that the first-year writing program involve more graduate students and faculty members in policy making and curriculum development, that the director encourage "coherent" yet "diverse pedagogical approaches" and "acknowledge more directly the political and social issues underlying the teaching of composition," and that new TAs be provided with a "theory-intensive yet practice-oriented" introduction to teaching.[1]

To carry out these recommendations, the English department appointed an interim director of first-year writing (after the current director resigned), a woman who had been an administrator in another part of the writing program, housed across campus, for over fifteen years. Elaine's first administrative act was to hire six graduate students—five women and one man, with diverse backgrounds in literature, creative writing, and composition studies—to assist her. All the graduate assistants were hired because of their interest in revising the first-year writing curriculum and working with new teachers of writing. But we two, writing our doctoral dissertations in composition and applying for academic jobs that entailed administrative responsibility, saw this opportunity as a fitting culmination to our graduate careers. We felt that merging our scholarly interests with our pedagogical and administrative experiences could result in meaningful change. We agreed with Elaine that the culture of the English department was individualistic, noncollaborative, and hierarchically organized around divisions of labor that worked against the recommendations of the committee and our goals for the writing program. But we resolved to realize those recommendations and transform the culture of the writing program by encouraging dialogic collaboration, shared leadership, and diverse sources of authority in policy making, curriculum development, and teacher training.

As the months of hard work wore on, however, we found that despite our initial enthusiasm, we were increasingly resistant to the nonhierarchical collaboration and shared leadership that we had so strongly advocated. Our resistance to these feminist goals is described and analyzed here in three areas of administrative work: collaboratively writing a syllabus for First-Year College Composition, leading a prequarter professional development workshop for incoming TAs, and acting as facilitators of weekly peer-group teaching meetings.

Resisting Dialogic Collaboration

When Elaine spoke of the need for collaboration among the writing program staff, we were excited about what we imagined this work would involve: the equal participation of all staff members and a valuing of multiple perspectives. Unfortunately, this ideal existed only in our heads. Although both of us had previous administrative experience in the English department, most of that experience involved traditional or bureaucratic configurations of labor: supervisors set policy and made plans; we carried out those plans. Consequently, despite our ideals, we found ourselves influenced by our experiences with hierarchical models of collaboration; that is, we expected a leader to initiate group work, control group processes, set deadlines, assign tasks, and evaluate our progress. We also expected our primary accountability to be to the leader rather than to other members of the group. These expectations were frustrated when we attempted as a group to determine goals, set agendas, monitor group processes, and take responsibility for accomplishing tasks.

One of the most important—and difficult—collaborative tasks the staff engaged in was the reconceptualization of the first-year writing course that incoming TAs would be required to teach. The process began with our writing separately a series of memos describing our vision of first-year writing. We then worked as a group to review textbooks and articulate criteria for judging their appropriateness. To our frustration we had to remake decisions constantly in response to group members' differing opinions about what kind of writing course they wanted teachers to teach. Eventually we reached some agreement about the focus and goals of the course and went on to select reading assignments, construct essay prompts, and produce a fifty-page, day-by-day, annotated syllabus for new TAs. Elaine served primarily as an adviser during this process. Thus, in Dickson's terms, she had turned the asylum over to the inmates. Our being given the responsibility for designing the core first-year writing course that all new TAs would teach should have felt liberating, but it was more frustrating than liberating. Wasn't the director more qualified than we to make the big decisions? Wouldn't it have been easier—and more efficient—if she just told us what kind of course to design? She was the one with the PhD; we were only graduate students and administrative underlings.

Carrie's resistance to egalitarian collaboration came to the fore one day after a long and exhausting staff meeting, during which it seemed we had gone in endless circles discussing our goals for first-year college composition, no one idea taking precedence and no one person asserting clear control over the meeting.[2] Carrie was walking across campus to get some dinner before teaching her evening class. Elaine walked with her, anxious to hear how she thought things were going. Frustrated by what Carrie felt was a lack of leadership on Elaine's part, Carrie said she wished Elaine had been more explicit about what she thought a first-year writing course should be. Elaine looked at Carrie quizzically and said, "But I thought I had. You know, when all of us wrote memos describing our goals for the course." Because Carrie had been led by bureaucratic models of administration to expect a leader's voice to carry more weight and to be directive, she was confused by what seemed a lack of direction from Elaine. Studies have shown that women's leadership is often not acknowledged even when women perform tasks identified as leadership tasks when men perform them. But Carrie's disappointment with Elaine as a leader was not due simply to Elaine's being a woman. Carrie had extensive experience working for women administrators, but the leadership style of other administrators—and Carrie's own—seemed based on the belief that a leader has ultimate responsibility for and control over the group.

Our goal of nonhierarchical collaboration was complicated not just by assumptions that a single person should be in control of a group but also by our tendency to value some group members' contributions more than others'. As feminists committed to breaking down traditional hierarchies and valuing differences among people, we wanted our writing program to be inclusive, to allow for and encourage multiple perspectives, including those of staff members without academic specialties in rhetoric and composition. Our decision to design the first-year writing curriculum collaboratively, we believed, was a step in this direction. Unfortunately, the very differences in our experiences and backgrounds that we believed would make the writing program stronger resulted in conflicts that we found troubling and sought to erase. (Carrie remembers being particularly concerned that the annotated syllabus be consistent in language and tone, that we work to erase differences and create univocality, even though there were seven people writing and revising it.)

Allowing everyone's voice to be heard on every aspect of the core curriculum was time-consuming and, at times, exasperating. Some of that exasperation is revealed in a memo Carrie sent to the group regarding an essay assignment she had written:

> Here's a draft of what I imagine Unit Four might look like. I say "I" instead of "we," because although [Elaine] and I thought we might be able to write this unit together fairly quickly, we found that before we could do so, we still had to spend a long time describing our visions of the course, which, not surprisingly, proved to be not exactly alike (but not irreconcilable either). I agreed to go home and write up what I thought Unit Four was supposed to do, so that we would at least have a draft of this section for Wednesday's meeting.
>
> After I did so, [Elaine] called to let me know that what I imagined for this section was not fitting very well with what other syllabus writers were imagining (again, not surprising). Since I had already done the work, [Elaine] told me to bring what I'd written, and we could talk about our differences (for the millionth time— sigh) at the meeting.
>
> I'm saying all this only to say, don't freak when you read this if it strikes you as not at all what you imagined. We can talk about it (again).

This memo describes a scene that recurred throughout the writing of the syllabus: the work done by one group member was inevitably undone by others whose perspectives differed. Carrie's frustration seemed directed at the inefficiency of the collaborative process. But Carrie remembers feeling equally frustrated that her individual contribution was not being valued by the others and that her expertise as a composition specialist was not being acknowledged. Although recent discussions of collaboration suggest that group work can give people an opportunity to recognize and value differences (Trimbur, "Consensus"), these discussions do not take into account the ways in which bureaucratic models of work breed competitiveness, making people ill-prepared to participate in a cooperative effort.

Our resistance to dialogic collaboration in writing program administration was also related to a desire for ownership of our work, a desire exacerbated by the need to translate that work into lines on our vitae. Again, this motivation to own the products of one's labor is attributable to the influence of dominant work models, especially in the academy, where people show their worth by pointing to what they as individuals have accomplished. The fact that expertise is identified with individuals rather than with groups became especially apparent when we were interviewing for jobs. (It didn't help that the two of us were competing for many of the same jobs.) For example, without being aware of it, Carrie always used the pronoun *we* to discuss the writing program—the course we designed, the teaching workshop we organized, and so on. One curmudgeonly (it seemed to her) interviewer remarked, "Who is this 'we' you keep referring to—can't you say what it is that *you* did?" Caught off guard, Carrie began to describe her individual contributions to the program, but even as she did so, she was forced to admit—to her interviewers and to herself—that most of the credit for the program had to go to the staff as a whole. After all those endless discussions, it was impossible to tell whose ideas were whose. It was a moment of triumph for nonhierarchical collaboration, but a moment that also gave a job seeker pause.

Resisting Multiple Sources of Authority

We have been focusing on the forces that constrain feminist writing program administration from within the program staff—and, indeed, from within each of us. It is not surprising that resistance increased when the new writing program moved from the private space of our staff meetings into the public space of the prequarter teaching workshop required of all graduate teaching assistants entering the program. In the early summer, we sent TAs a packet of materials that introduced them to the goals of the course, of the writing program, and of the profession, along with a letter written by Elaine that introduced herself and us. Other than this packet, the prequarter workshop was the first public representation of the writing program and thus the first opportunity for new TAs to respond to what we thought was a progressive first-year writing course and progressive administrative structure.

In keeping with our goal to work collaboratively with TAs rather than to direct them, at the staff development workshop we gave the new TAs a detailed syllabus that was theoretically coherent and yet "in process" so that they would feel comfortable critiquing it and making it their own. We also sought to provide them with opportunities for reflection and dialogue about the goals of the writing program. In doing so, we believed we were valuing multiple sources of authority by emphasizing the knowledge and experience that the new TAs already had and by presenting ourselves as coparticipants with them in the process of constructing knowledge about teaching. On the first day of the workshop, to emphasize our common experience with the TAs rather than privilege our institutional authority, we asked them to share a learning experience—as teachers or students—outside a classroom setting.

We fought the urge to provide teaching tips in this workshop, wanting to model for TAs the kind of reflection we hoped they would enact with their students—a model of teacher-student relations based on the "dialogue, connectedness, and contextual rules" that Peter Mortensen and Gesa Kirsch describe as feminist (557). We provided TAs with opportunities to critique traditional assumptions about what constitutes teacher authority in the classroom. What we did not expect was that the critique of institutional authority would be directed at us, the writing program staff. Our attempts to reject traditional notions of authority and leadership were soon complicated by the TAs' responses (and our own) to those attempts.

On the third day of the workshop, one of the new TAs, a woman in her late thirties, privately told Elaine that some of the "young women" on the staff did not speak with authority. At a meeting later that day, Elaine repeated the TA's statement without elaborating on it, and when Amy asked if Elaine agreed with that statement, Elaine said, "Yes." When Amy pressed to know why Elaine agreed, an uneasy silence filled the room. For Amy, this moment highlighted the contradictory feelings that she had about nonhierarchical authority in the training workshop and in the writing program in general. Initially, she was angered by the TA's comment and wanted to know which TA had said it and why. Assuming that she was one of the young women on the staff being criticized for lacking authority, Amy wanted Elaine to explain why the TA was reading Amy's actions in this way. Although we had deliberately designed the workshop to give authority to the TA's prior experience, Amy also wanted her individual authority about the teaching of writing valued, and she was angry not to be given the opportunity to respond to the TA's criticism. Amy was frustrated that Elaine had not defended her or the other women on the staff as being authoritative. Given that one of our program goals was to reject the patriarchal notions of administration that governed English department culture, Amy was puzzled that Elaine had not asked the TA to explain why the TA thought the young women on the staff lacked authority or to reflect on how the TA's definition of authority might be problematic.

In retrospect, we can see this episode as an example of the complexities involved when writing program administrators try to enact an ethic of care for multiple and competing constituencies. Elaine may have felt that affirming the new TA's power to critique the staff was more important than protecting our egos. Moreover, defending our institutional authority as writing program assistants might have worked against the dialogic model of collaboration that we hoped to achieve among the new TAs, the graduate student assistants, and the director. Since dialogic collaboration depends on an equalization of power among groups, Elaine may have been reluctant to discuss the issue of authority so early in the term. As mentioned above, we staff members were still struggling with the power relations that continued to constrain our work together. Adding forty new TAs to the configuration brought new pressures—especially the pressure to meet traditional expectations about leadership and management—that we were unprepared to address.

The experience of being criticized by a new TA was particularly painful for Amy. Elaine's refusal to name the TA or to provide details about the TA's comment left Amy unable to prove her competence in composition theory and practice. It was this desire to prove herself, to rebut the TA's comment rather than to reflect on its implications, that revealed her investment in the bureaucratic system, where leaders have greater authority and power than followers. That the comment seemed to be based also on gendered assumptions of what constitutes authority made the criticism even harder to take. As Mortensen and Kirsch suggest, men and women often fail to recognize "authoritative gestures that arise particularly from women's experience" (561). Amy wanted to prove that she was a competent leader in the masculinist terms that the TA valued. At that moment, all Amy's philosophical beliefs about connected knowing, dialogic collaboration, and shared authority went out the window. If the TA wanted authority, Amy would give her authority. Only later did she realize the degree to which she had internalized patriarchal notions about what it means to be a leader—to direct rather than share, to prove rather than question, to assert rather than listen. And because her response reified masculinist notions of authority, it foreclosed the possibility of using the TA's critique as a springboard for raising issues about gendered notions of authority with other TAs in the workshop.

Resisting Shared Leadership

Another example of our attempts to deconstruct hierarchies in writing program administration was our reliance on peer groups as a site of teacher training. At the beginning of the term, each writing program assistant was made a facilitator of a group of five or six new TAs. These groups, which met two hours a week and counted as independent study credit, were designed as a place where new TAs could discuss issues that arose in their teaching. Although the peer-group meetings were intended to be loosely connected to the course the TAs were taking in the theory and practice of teaching composition, co-taught by Elaine and another faculty member, the groups also worked autonomously, each assistant being responsible for answering the needs of that assistant's group. This configuration reflected our hope that we would serve with Elaine as coleaders of the new TAs and, more generally, of the writing program. But this feminist ideal of shared leadership was contested when issues of confidentiality and authority exposed the power relations inherent in even the most egalitarian groups.

As peer-group leaders, we were constantly aware of competing loyalties and responsibilities, and in this respect our position was similar to Elaine's. We felt simultaneously a responsibility to the first-year writing program, to the director, to the TAs we were leading, to their students, to our philosophies about writing instruction and writing programs, and to the composition profession. When these various responsibilities conflicted, as they inevitably do in any writing program, it was difficult for us to decide whose interests should prevail. Problems that arose in individual peer groups were a matter to be discussed by the administrative staff as a whole, since all the staff shared responsibility for supporting new TAs in their professional development. But nothing had prepared us for this shared leadership. Instead, we wanted the autonomy that we experienced as classroom teachers—and that is prized in the name of academic freedom in most colleges and universities. Success in the classroom is a matter of individual success, of a teacher's individual talent. Whatever we might have believed philosophically about shared leadership, this emphasis on individual responsibility and individual success carried over into our work as peer-group leaders and led to anxiety over matters of confidentiality and authority, especially in regard to the issue of sharing with the staff events that occurred in peer-group meetings or privately between individual staff members and individual TAs.

For instance, a TA in Amy's peer group described in her teaching journal a written response that she had made to a student. Amy considered the response inappropriate. To address this TA's journal, Amy copied a short article about teacher response as a rhetorical act and used this article and the TA's journal as the basis for her weekly peer-group meeting. After exchanging journals, the peer group discussed ways that the TA's comments might have been read by her student and offered alternative responses. The TA who had written the journal thanked her peer group for helping her to see how she could respond more productively, and the group decided to continue discussing teacher response in upcoming meetings.

During that week's writing program staff meeting, when Elaine asked us to share issues arising in peer groups, Amy summarized what had happened but didn't give names. At the end of the account, Elaine asked Amy for the name of the TA who had written the journal, because Elaine wanted to schedule a conference with the TA. Amy resisted naming the TA, and a long and intensely painful discussion about conflicting loyalties followed. The director's need to know what was going on in the program was pitted against our need as writing program assistants not to have to tell.

When Amy was asked to name the TA in her group, she felt a tension between doing what her employer asked—revealing in more detail what had happened—and protecting the anonymity of her group members. If the TA thought she was being punished for being honest in her journal, she would not bring similar issues to the group. As a peer-group leader, Amy felt a responsibility for protecting her TAs, for giving them spaces to share their concerns without fear of penalty. But this urge to protect TAs from the director's gaze highlighted the degree to which Amy did not consider herself to be a coleader with Elaine in the administration of the writing program. Like Carrie, who felt uneasy when given the task of writing the syllabus with rather than for Elaine, Amy felt uneasy sharing responsibility with Elaine for the administration of the peer groups. In part, Amy's uneasiness stemmed from the institutional fact that Elaine had hired her and therefore could fire her, a power that Amy did not share. In Amy's previous experiences assisting writing program administrators, her opinion was valued but certainly not given equal weight to the directors'. Because Amy did not feel like a coleader with Elaine, she viewed the peer group as a site where she could assert what individual authority she thought she had. Her interest in confidentiality thus reflected a wish to protect her authority as a peer-group leader as well as the desire to protect the TAs from criticism or punitive action. Although Amy understood that Elaine was responsible to the students in the TAs' classes and so needed to know what was happening in them, she felt that Elaine's insistence on her naming the TA who had responded inappropriately to a student reflected a lack of respect for Amy's personal judgment. Paradoxically, sharing leadership meant the dilution of what little authority Amy felt she had as a peer-group leader—an individual authority as distinguished from the collective authority of the writing program staff and one she was not going to surrender easily.

A further constraint on our efforts to share leadership was that the TAs also assumed that there could be only one leader. One writing program assistant reported overhearing a group of new TAs describe us as moles whose job it was to report disloyal teaching practices to Elaine. This statement reveals the degree to which they saw the director as the creator of the syllabus and us as her assistants who carried out her policies. Our unconscious alliance with traditional models of administration thus intensified when the TAs we worked with and for expected us to act according to such models.

The Need for Critical Reflection

We have presented these episodes from our experiences both to illustrate the difficulties we faced in enacting feminist principles of writing program administration and to suggest ways that that goal might be problematized and reframed. As Grundy suggests, administrators constantly need to ask themselves, "How can I engage in forms of critical, self-reflective, and collaborative work which will create conditions so that the people with whom I work can come to control their knowledge and practice [as educators]?" (174). The writing of this essay has been one outlet for us to reflect, critically and collaboratively, on practices, a starting place for understanding the myriad factors that shaped and constrained our work. There are no easy answers to be drawn from this analysis. Indeed, as we shared and analyzed our experiences, we realized the degree to which our initial assumptions about feminist practice limited how we could enact it.

In many ways, our attempts to subvert traditional models of administration were undermined (by ourselves and others) because we relied primarily on structural change—collaboration instead of single authorship in the production of the syllabus, creation of peer-led teaching groups, and so on—without engaging in the critical self-reflection that must accompany such change. In Grundy's terms, we rejected a bureaucratic model of leadership in favor of what Grundy calls, after Jürgen Habermas, a "practical" one (Grundy 169–70), a model that Phelps might say represents an ethics of care, a model to create productive relationships among workers and make work processes meaningful. Though such change is beneficial, it does not require workers and managers to engage in the critical self-reflection that is crucial to a feminist model of administration that would be, in Grundy's words, "emancipatory" for all those working in the program (171–73).

Examining how our bureaucratic notions of leadership undermined our feminist principles brought to mind bell hooks's statement: "It is necessary for us to remember, as we think critically about domination, that we all have the capacity to act in ways that oppress, dominate, wound (whether or not that power is institutionalized). It is necessary to remember that it is first the potential oppressor *within* that we must resist" (*Talking* 394; emphasis added). One of the most valuable insights we gained from reflecting on our experience is that the implementation of structural change in institutions is not likely to be conflict-free. In fact, it may never result in the permanent, meaningful transformation many feminists hope for. Struggles over power, authority, and leadership are not barriers to enacting feminist principles; they are the embodiment of them. The challenge of feminist writing program administration, then, is not just to change administrative structures but also to foreground the inevitable resistance and conflict that result and to make critical reflection about that resistance and conflict as much a part of the program as a new syllabus or new teacher training workshops.

Indeed, a benefit of our taking up the challenge to change administrative practices is that, after a year of struggle and endless talk, we were able to reflect on our experiences in a transformative way—particularly through the numerous e-mail exchanges and long-distance phone calls involved in the collaborative writing of this essay. Without those experiences, we would not have been able to take with us to our new jobs (both of which involve program administration and teacher training) an appreciation of the internal and external constraints that make the enacting of feminist principles (nonhierarchical collaboration, shared leadership, multiple sources of authority) a difficult, at times painful, yet ultimately rewarding process.

At our new institutions, we hope to continue foregrounding with colleagues, staff, and students our feminist goals of nonhierarchical collaboration and shared leadership while acknowledging the resistance and conflict that those goals create. We hope to create a language that the writing program staff can share for talking about resistance and conflict, not in personal but in institutional terms. Moreover, we hope to continue the process of interrogating our own internalized assumptions about what it means to be a teacher, an administrator, and a leader. Although the ideology of work that pervades our culture may remain stubbornly the same, we will continue to reflect on and contend with the forces that constrain our efforts to transform that ideology, including the force exerted by the bureaucrat within.

NOTES

[1]Although we quote from this committee's report, we have not cited it since to do so would compromise the anonymity of the institution and the people we describe. Readers who wish to know more about the report may contact either of the authors of this essay.

[2]We use the pronoun *we* when describing our more or less common experiences in the program but refer to ourselves in the third person when describing events that involved only one of us. This distinction is to some extent artificial, since we each had a different common experience and since our individual experiences overlapped in ways difficult to sort out. But such are the limits of language.

A Feminist Critique of Writing in the Disciplines

Harriet Malinowitz

In his preface to *The Order of Things*, Michel Foucault cites a passage from Jorge Luis Borges that

> quotes a "certain Chinese encyclopedia" in which it is written that "animals are divided into: (a) belonging to the Emperor, (b) embalmed, (c) tame, (d) sucking pigs, (e) sirens, (f) fabulous, (g) stray dogs, (h) included in the present classification, (i) frenzied, (j) innumerable, (k) drawn with a very fine camelhair hairbrush, (l) *et cetera*, (m) having just broken the water pitcher, (n) that from a long way off look like flies." (xv)

Foucault's instant response to this surprising list—so radically divergent from the Humane Society's taxonomy of dogs, cats, turtles, birds, and gerbils or the zoo's of monkeys, lions, bears, giraffes, and seals—is to laugh. His laughter, he says, "shattered . . . all the familiar landmarks of my thought—*our* thought, the thought that bears the stamp of our age and our geography—breaking up all the ordered surfaces and all the planes with which we are accustomed to tame the wild profusion of existing things" (xv).

In the academy, the wild profusion of existing knowledge is tamed by the disciplines, conventionally grouped in the knowledge domains of the social, natural, and human sciences. Characterized by fealty to both subject and method, the disciplines don't simply describe knowledge, they legitimate it by creating zones and codes of acceptable scholarship that effectively bracket out all that is not always already the progeny of those zones and codes. For example, as the queer writer Jeffrey Escoffier has pointed out, the disciplinary knowledge of fields such as medicine, psychiatry, religion, law, literature, and film would have rendered patently impossible the thought that undergirded the formation of a lesbian and gay rights movement had there not been an

291

extracurricular domain of vernacular knowledge in which to critique the norms, stereotypes, and misinformation purveyed by the disciplines. Even now, the bid of lesbian and gay studies for academic legitimacy may be compromised because the field hovers at the border between an identity based on disciplinary knowledge and the political identity that spawned the field. Similarly—and preceding the emergence of queer studies by a decade or so—women's studies, along with ethnic studies and labor studies, swam against the current, going from the extracurriculum of movement politics toward an academic structure that lacked (or refused to provide) an appropriate space to contain it. Yet the project of women's studies in the past quarter century has not been an assimilationist one; on the contrary, women's studies has been rooted in a radical critique of disciplinary knowledge and of the constraints on logic and belief that that knowledge enforces.

It is in this context that I situate my discussion of writing across the curriculum (WAC)—or, more specifically, of one of its two principal strands, known as writing in the disciplines (WID). As Judy Kirscht, Rhonda Levine, and John Reiff have observed, a philosophical and tactical divide seems to exist in the world of WAC theorists and writing program faculty members between proponents of writing to learn (WTL) and those of WID. This conflict is "variously expressed as voice versus discourse, learning versus performance, process versus form" (369). WTL practitioners ask themselves, "What can composition contribute to teaching in other disciplines?" They attempt to "offer the disciplines a sense of writing as an integral part of the learning process" (370). WTL has been described as a form of "experiential learning" that fosters dialogue and personal expression (Fulwiler) and as "a personally engaging transaction through which the learner makes her own connection and builds her own meaning" (Mayher, Lester, and Pradl 1). WID practitioners, in contrast, ask, "What kind of writing do you do in your discipline?" (Kirscht, Levine, and Reiff 370), to help students negotiate with discipline-specific knowledge and learn the discourses, practices, and conventions employed when writing and thinking in particular disciplines. Often, however, these two different approaches are conflated in the literature and in professional discussions—particularly when claims are being made for WAC's radicalizing effect on the academy. For instance, at a 1995 CCCC convention panel called Writing across the Curriculum as Subversive Activity, Carl Lovitt deemed WAC capable of "subverting faculty and institutional cultures" and of "building communities through communication" because its "emphasis on teaching, learning, and the pursuit of literacy affirms common denominators in the educational experience." On the same panel, Elaine Maimon asserted that WAC is trans-formative because it undermines unexamined institutional assumptions (such as the idea that a curriculum is composed of discrete units of content or that an instructor must be a quiz show emcee rather than a mentor). In an article on the politics of WAC, Toby Fulwiler ventured the notion that WAC is not only political but "maybe even quietly revolutionary," because it "ask[s] institutions to make choices about goals, governance, methods, and the allocations of resources" (179) and because it "creates change" by "address[ing] simultaneously the inertia of student, faculty, and institution alike" (187).

I share the values of these scholar-practitioners in the sense that I, too, appreciate egalitarian structures, noncompartmentalized learning, and an accountable, noninert academy. I also think that WTL has made progress in changing certain stultifying notions about how students learn and has introduced productive alternative teaching strategies. Yet while I am convinced that WTL has the potential to be politically subversive in entrenched regimes of knowledge, I'm disturbed by the aura of vagueness that surrounds most accounts of exactly what structures are being subverted, who benefits from these structures (and how), and, in short, just what sort of politics we're talking about. What makes a revolution of method indeed a revolution? What specific power arrangements and belief systems are bolstered by the methods WTL is advocating and challenging? Why hasn't WAC allied itself with other force fields in the academy that have set out to dismantle existing systems of knowledge production— such as women's studies? Are we afraid of getting *too* political? of having an agenda? Do we want to have our revolution and eat our neutrality, too?

My skepticism grows when I consider the claims made for WAC's ability to effect institutional change through WID, whose political stance strikes me as, if anything, counterrevolutionary. I don't doubt that writing in the disciplines may be helpful to students as they seek entrance to particular intellectual or professional communities and learn to write and speak in ways that will identify them as credible members of those communities. Yet as WID now exists, it doesn't help students critically assess how forms of knowledge and method are hierarchically structured in disciplines so that some achieve canonical or hegemonic status whereas others are effectively fenced out. In the absence of such a critical framework, students are easily beguiled by the mystique of dominant knowledge systems, which are bolstered by and in turn legitimate asymmetrical social, material, and ideological arrangements.

In this essay I argue that supporting students in their quest for disciplinary legitimacy represents an implicit endorsement of existing disciplinary structures—a conservative move, and a particularly surprising one, given the professed aim of WAC faculty members to disrupt those structures. I also present women's studies as an example of a field that is housed in the academy but that nevertheless operates in a resistant mode, attempting to disrupt learning as usual in ways that are somewhat similar to WTL and quite contrary to WID, since women's studies seeks to challenge rather than accommodate the prevailing logic and politics of disciplinary order. I believe that women's studies may furnish an alternative model on which WAC can define and construct itself, though the choice to do so would entail a radical philosophical repositioning of WAC that would certainly affect adversely its already vulnerable position in the academy. Ultimately, the model of women's studies raises questions that have long permeated composition studies—about the relation between practical instruction and ideology and between our roles as enablers of successful student absorption into existing systems and our roles as facilitators of critical reflection about those systems. Critical reflection has, of course, its own attendant danger—namely, that it will lead one to an oppositional stance, and brand one an outlaw vis-à-vis the very institution with which one sought a productive relationship. Thus the questions raised for WAC are politically charged.

It was four years ago, when I sat on two committees at my university, that I first began to think about WAC's role in sustaining the logic of the disciplines. Being in a frenzied period of activity after some decades of dormancy, the university was just then developing a campuswide WAC program and a women's studies program for the first time. As chair of the women's studies planning group, I was concerned that aside from our school's honors program, which served only a small number of students, there was no vehicle for proposing truly interdisciplinary courses on our campus. Thus there could be no women's studies in itself; all our courses, even the introductory course and the feminist theory course, would have to coincide with—in fact, emerge from—courses offered in the disciplines.

At the same time, I served on the WAC committee, and the discussions there about WID deepened my worries about women's studies, since the WAC committee's well-intentioned aim seemed destined to bolster the very structures that locked out feminist education. I saw this destiny embedded in the language of WID literature. Kirscht, Levine, and Reiff recount Art Young's explanation of WID at a WAC video conference: WID "aims to make majors 'proficient' in their fields—so that an engineering student, for example, will 'read, write, and solve problems like an engineer'" (qtd. in Kirscht, Levine, and Reiff 371). Similarly, a biology student will be encouraged to think like a biologist, a philosophy student to think like a philosopher. Many involved with WID acknowledge that there is no one way that biologists or philosophers think; that, in fact, each discipline is composed of multiple (and competing) discourses; and that students' engagement with these discourses will help them understand that spheres of knowledge are themselves contested and constructed domains (Russell, "Origins" and "Perspective"; Bazerman, "Criticism" and "Stage"; Odell; Jones and Comprone; Kirscht, Levine, and Reiff). Yet there is little discussion of how the territorial mapping of knowledge in the existing disciplines still serves to organize and constrain the ways we conceive of knowledge, or of how dominant ideologies in the disciplines determine which forms of knowledge will even be allowed into the fray. WID does not generally present itself as a force that would help a student think like a feminist (or like a Marxist or a black nationalist).

Some WID theorists claim that bringing rhetorical inquiry to bear on disciplinary knowledge will illuminate the seams and ruptures in established disciplines. Kirscht, Levine, and Reiff make this case, arguing that the WTL-WID schism is a false one and that a number of WID theorists with social constructionist leanings have shown how process-oriented WTL methods can in fact be put to effective use in WID: "The disciplines are introduced as centers of inquiry rather than as banks of knowledge, and disciplinary conventions are presented as emerging from communally negotiated assumptions about what knowledge is and about the methods for shaping it" (374). Kirscht, Levine, and Reiff do not elaborate, though, on how a student can come to apprehend the process of negotiation whereby the center of a field's inquiry is established; on the latitude actually permitted in any field to deviate from rigid "banks of knowledge"; on which voices are engaged in (or excluded from) "communal" negotiations about the acceptance of ideas; or, in fact, on what makes any domain a community. Do the parties whose interests are ultimately overridden in the negotiation remain part of the community? If so, what role do they play? If not, what happens to them—and how, if at all, does their absence inflect the discourse that triumphs? Also—an important question—how might a triumphant *way* of looking at particular subject matter end up itself shaping and controlling *what* will count as knowledge in the field? Anne Herrington found, through her work with WID in a psychology course called Methods of Inquiry in Psychology, that a particular writing style (no use of first-person pronouns, no references to personal experience, preference for passive voice) was enforced by the instructors, because, they claimed, all members of the field should conform to the guidelines set forth in the third edition of the *Publication Manual of the American Psychological Association.* Yet, Herrington suggests, the "objectivist epistemology taught in the course," which "divorces the researcher from the research study," remained conceptually unavailable and mysterious to students; its weight as a disciplinary value was concealed behind the smoke screen of a set of linguistic conventions taught "as if [the epistemology] were only style—only strict, restrictive formalities." " 'It's just not done' was . . . the explanation for not using first-person pronouns."

Feminist researchers have long argued that the supposedly communal assumption of neutrality in objectivist data interpretation (which ignores the subjective experience of the investigator) permits sexist attitudes to infiltrate studies undetected and seriously affect results. For instance, heavily funded medical studies over the course of many years provided information about heart disease that experts in the field presented as significant to all, though the data was gleaned only from male research subjects. At the same time, the lack or underrepresentation of studies on issues that solely or primarily concern women—such as breast cancer—has been criticized by feminists. It often falls to advocacy groups composed of "victims" of various diseases of the nonelite to draw attention to phenomena overlooked in the laboratories of objective science. In a *New York Times* op-ed piece, the feminist biologist Anne Fausto-Sterling demonstrated that despite the "consensus" in scientific (and popular) domains that the human species is divided into two genders, hermaphrodites provide clear evidence of at least five gender configurations—though hermaphrodites are most often surgically and socially altered from birth to fit into the "objectively" constituted categories waiting to receive them. The feminist psychologists Toby Epstein Jayaratne and Abigail J. Stewart write that Stanley Milgram's "famous studies of 'obedience,' in which participants were led to believe they were administering painful shocks to another person (actually a 'stooge' of the experimenter) in the name of 'teaching,' may be considered in light of [feminist methodological] issues." Among the numerous gender-based criticisms that Jayaratne and Stewart apply to Milgram's studies, one is that all the studies involve a male victim and a male experimenter. In addition, Milgram's analysis of his research subjects' reckless abdication of moral responsibility when deferring to authority "ignored both economic and personal safety factors which may in fact motivate 'obedience' among those without power" (87).

WID theory tends to ignore the voices that have been relegated to the radical fringes of disciplines. In truth, a powerful cycle is at work: if those who break with disciplinary convention remain unpublished and untenured, they become offstage voices, noncontenders in the central arena, where the action is. Those theorists in the central arena who do recognize that disciplinary knowledge is contestable recognize only a limited (and relatively compatible) array of players—much as pundits of electoral politics factor only Democrats and Republicans (and an occasional billionaire) into their appraisal of the future of the country. Such players, though jockeying for power, agree like good sports on the rules of the game, which makes for a pretty amicable atmosphere. Thus it is possible for Charles Bazerman, a spokesperson for the competing-voices branch of WID, to write:

> Discourse studies of the disciplines, which aim to understand the dynamics of each field and the state of play into which each new participant enters, can help build the intellectual foundations for courses that enable students to enter into disciplines as empowered speakers rather than as conventional followers of accepted practice. . . . With a sense of individual power, students can press at the bit of the disciplinary practices they are trained into or run up against. Seeing through the appearances of the discourse allows them to keep the fundamental goals of the field in front of them. They can ask what kind of communication structures, patterns, and rhetorics will enable the fields to achieve these goals, how [students] can contribute to those ends as individuals, and in what way the goals achieved through a single disciplinary discourse coordinate (if at all) with social goals from other forms of social discourse. By understanding how knowledge is constructed, they can judge what knowledge it is they wish to construct. ("Criticism" 67–68)

I very much share Bazerman's view that examining the discursive practices of disciplines and fostering students' abilities to "press at the bit" of inherited disciplinary rituals are good things. I worry, however, that he and others depict the enactment of these goals in ways that obfuscate or trivialize the real struggles that must be involved. In Bazerman's description of how one might negotiate among the multiple discourses in a discipline, difference doesn't seem to entail conflict;

instead, it is assumed that knowledge is constructed by a friendly aggregate of voices and that when one challenges predominant voices, it is not at one's peril. The ways that discourses maintain regimes of power and suppress alternative forms and sources of power are not addressed. Ultimately, "seeing through the appearances of the discourse"—as if any discourse is but one transparent scrim among others—reveals the "fundamental goals of the field," which are a unified, collective entity, after all. Bazerman leaves me wondering: What resources are available for challenging goals that are so fundamental? How effective will those resources be? Most of all, how risky will it be for anyone, particularly a novice in the field, to take issue with ideas of such formidable status?

In Bazerman's textbook *The Informed Writer: Using Sources in the Disciplines*, the message to students is similar: Disciplines are not unitary, but this is not problematic, because "members of a discipline agree" that certain types of arguments and evidence "are convincing and reliable," and thus "disciplines develop specific ways of thinking" (379, 386). Implicit here is the belief that all rational minds can ultimately be persuaded to reach procedural consensus—or perhaps that certain voices are marginal enough not to count. Bazerman's references to "the distinctive writing styles of specific disciplines" and to the criteria for "what constitutes disciplinary knowledge in the field" (381, 380) suggest, if not absolute agreement among members of a discipline, then at least a controlling interest on the part of particular styles, methods, and perspectives, which subsumes the claims of alternative approaches. Consider the following passage from *The Informed Writer:*

> Using whatever argumentative format and evidence are currently considered *most authoritative*, researchers write to convince colleagues to accept their findings as *reliable knowledge*. When members of a discipline accept new arguments as *valid claims*, researchers come to rely on those claims to carry on their own research. New research is almost always based on previous, now *established* claims.   (380; emphasis added)

Though serious controversies do exist in disciplines over what is authoritative, reliable, valid, or even established—to the point where faculty members risk loss of tenure, students risk loss of support from mentors, and scholarship may go unpublished—Bazerman does not address those tensions. Students entering a discipline are therefore likely to remain unaware of suppressed perspectives as well as of the dangers of becoming attached to those perspectives, if students finally do become aware of them. Bazerman doesn't suggest that disciplines are static, and he does convey the idea that lively debates in disciplines lead to new ways of thinking. But much is omitted, because he takes the common approach of analyzing the differences diachronically:

> As disciplines evolve, modes of argument change in corresponding ways. The invention of the scientific journal in the seventeenth century, for example, necessitated the invention of a form for scientific journals. The form evolved over the years, so that an experimental report published in 1665 bears little resemblance to one published today. (385)

Most students would be dismayed if an article in the current issue of the *Journal of Neurophysiology* resembled one of its forebears from 1665; they are amply familiar with the notion of historic change in the production of cultural artifacts, from many years of schooling and parental reminiscence. However, a synchronic analysis of intradisciplinary disagreement would reveal a more unsettling picture, one in which truth doesn't simply triumph but is the pawn of political maneuvering and human prejudice. The early years of AIDS research are a prime example. Consider also the immense difficulty, until the 1990s, of sustaining an academic career if one produced queer scholarship or insisted that nutrition was a vital component of allopathic medical training or suggested, as the legal scholar and would-be presidential appointee Lani Guinier has, that voting majorities be entitled to rights less sweeping than those to which they are accustomed.

Bazerman does write, "Separate research groups may have various underlying assumptions about their subject, may be interested in separate problems and questions, and may look at different aspects of the same general subject that defines the discipline" (387), but his treatment of the issue is disappointingly superficial. Using the hypothetical case of a college political science or government department, he explains that political philosophers and historical scholars may take different approaches. Yet these faculty members, instead of representing a cacophonous assemblage of ideologies and methodologies, belong to one field's accepted and mutually recognizable subdisciplines, which, as Bazerman illustrates, logically and neatly complement each other by working toward a common goal; it is considered the role of each to contribute a piece of the larger picture (a picture that all agree is sane). No one involved in the field is in danger of being associated with a lunatic fringe because of ideas expressed or of the production of work that is beyond accepted notions of decency, democracy, or civilization as we know it. Interestingly, Bazerman's one allusion to actual political tension concerns writing from Eastern Europe that deals with "the difficulties of life within the former Soviet satellites" (388), whereas he presents the United States uncontestably as a modern democracy. Critiques launched by the interdisciplinary studies programs that have most significantly punctured the warm and fuzzy ideal of United States democracy—women's, ethnic, labor, lesbian and gay, and cultural studies—remain unarticulated and invisible here, though scholars in those programs are also (and usually more officially) affiliated with traditional departments. Thus Bazerman presents the disciplines as they have traditionally presented themselves—untroubled by serious ideological acrimony and by the marginalization of those groups and perspectives that threaten to disturb the illusion of cordial collegial interchange.

That Bazerman's account of reading and writing in the disciplines omits any mention of the enormous impact of feminist scholarship in the academy suggests that the very notion of the disciplines constricts our vision of what kind of knowledge is possible. Though writing in the disciplines may help students look at disciplinary categories in new and illuminating ways, the intransigence of the disciplines' position in the academy *as* the reigning categories of knowledge leaves students confined to writing only *across* the curriculum and *in* the disciplines, and it precludes their writing *out* of the inherited order of things and *into* new forms of curriculum.

Some argue that higher education and intellectual production are far more elastic than they used to be. Clifford Geertz's perception is that genres have blurred, interpretive strategies have crossed disciplinary borders, disparate fields are looking to one another for fresh symbols and metaphors for concept building, and hermeneutic and subjective forms of inquiry are increasingly employed by scholars and researchers to refigure social thought. According to Geertz, the new "interpretive turn" has even reached "positivist strongholds" in the academy (233). He worries, however, that various forms of local knowledge may become uncritically absorbed into one another as part of a euphoric impulse to forge commonalities without recognition of the specificity of conditions that have given rise to knowledge in particular locales. Knowledge that is useful in the "grand actuality" of the global village is neither that which remains remote and insular nor that which is forced into false congruence with other systems. Instead, Geertz says, there should be a mutual recognition, a "way of turning

[the] varieties [of local knowledge] into commentaries one upon another, the one lighting what the other darkens" (233).

Geertz's belief that "blurred genres" have occasioned the "refiguration of social thought" (20) is a widely accepted position on the state of late-twentieth-century education. But some researchers are less convinced than others that the vanguard of theory has actually made its way into the trenches of learning. When Judith Langer investigated the relation between how various fields have come to discuss knowing and how knowing is transacted in classrooms, she found telling discrepancies. The three disciplines she examined—biology, American history, and American literature—would seem to have arrived at certain shared transdisciplinary values, particularly "an increasing focus on the tentative nature of 'truth,' leading to an emphasis on the need for active *questioning* and *interpreting* rather than on simple accumulation of facts" and a "shift[ing] away from a belief in a verifiable, constant, and stable body of knowledge" (72–73). But she found that, though these values were celebrated in journal articles and in the commentary of teachers she interviewed, in the actual courses mastery of content and discipline-specific forms of interpretation (which remained implicit instead of being articulated in class discussions) were paramount. In each discipline, Langer discovered that "the literature on practice reflects little of the underlying principles that are guiding the related discipline-based scholarship," so that "when they were asked about the value of a specific course, the teachers stressed major issues and themes. References to ways of thinking were infrequent" (75, 76). Moreover, "Asked about the kinds of reasoning and interpreting they expected from their students, and about the kinds of justification or evidence their students should offer when writing, the teachers spoke from the vantage point of their own field" (78).

Bonnie B. Spanier, who describes herself as "a scientist and a feminist" (193), addresses more specifically the erasure of ideology in scientific discourse and practice. Like Langer, she is unconvinced that transdisciplinary, postmodern ways of knowing have infiltrated scientific research; she contends that "most scientists disallow the view of the new social studies of science (including feminist critiques) that all aspects of science, like any other human endeavor, embody and reflect power relations—the usual inequitable ones" (195). Women and people of color, vastly underrepresented in the sciences, are socialized in scientific communities to internalize the white, Western, male value system, which, in Spanier's account, retains its indelible imprint on research practices: "Indeed, there is no equivalent in science education of the reader-response movement in the teaching of literature" (195). It is the refusal of the genres, of the disciplines, to blur that Spanier laments. She blurs them herself by invoking the literary theorist and critic Judith Fetterley to argue that it should be a goal of science education to make "resisting readers" of its students. But the dominant, current-traditional practice of science education fails to do this. Moreover, in Spanier's experience, feminist students who bring resisting approaches to their science classes are discouraged and "ultimately find it difficult to reconcile their feminist values with their interest in science" (204). Spanier believes that WAC is a potential importer of extradisciplinary perspectives that can make scientists more aware of the multiple approaches it is possible to draw on in their domains.

Spanier is proposing something fundamentally different from what is usually suggested by writing in the disciplines. WID theory generally assumes either that students will learn the discourse of a discipline (as if the dominant discourse is the only one possible) or that students will come to see how multiple and competing discourses constitute a discipline (as if the discourses exist in a state of democratic colloquy). Spanier's essay breaks with both these views by contesting the idea that disciplines or genres are formed by local knowledge in Geertz's sense. Whereas for Geertz local knowledge is comparatively discrete and homogeneous, though open to exchange with and influence by the knowledge of other locales, for Spanier what counts as local knowledge is only the tip of the iceberg: the reigning ideology in a system that has effectively submerged competing claims and denied the truth of its heterogeneity.

Other feminist scholars have raised questions about the suppression of particular ideologies—including ideologies that shape method—in the existing disciplines. The feminist psychologist Barbara Du Bois contends that we "literally *cannot see women* through traditional science and theory" (110) and says of methodology:

> The science-making that is in fact based on different values than those prevailing in the culture at a given time, and thus attempts to discover, explore and explain different realities, tends to be ignored—or attacked as "unscientific." This judgment can frequently be understood for what it really is: not in fact a judgment about science, but a charge of heresy.   (106)

The sociologist and African American studies scholar Patricia Hill Collins writes that black feminist thought "can best be viewed as subjugated knowledge" that has been "suppress[ed] . . . in traditional sites of knowledge" (202). She explains:

> Given that the general culture shaping the taken-for-granted knowledge of the community of experts is permeated by widespread notions of Black and female inferiority, new knowledge claims that seem to violate these fundamental assumptions are likely to be viewed as anomalies. Moreover, specialized thought challenging notions of Black and female inferiority is unlikely to be generated from within a white-male-controlled academic community because both the kinds of questions that could be asked and the explanations that would be found satisfying would necessarily reflect a basic lack of familiarity with Black women's reality. (203)

And the economist Barbara R. Bergmann writes:

> Most economists have an ideological commitment to the free enterprise system and spend their professional lives trying to disprove assertions that it does not function well. . . . Mainline economists conduct their analyses under the assumption that economic activity is the free interaction of rational beings, whose only concern in buying and selling goods, services, and labor is to advance their material advantage. Economists make a professional practice of ignoring the fact that people, even those with above-average rational abilities, may have stereotyped attitudes about women, may have false beliefs about women's abilities, may be influenced by tradition or religion, or may be proud of having been born with the superior status of a male, a status they may desire to protect. ("Task" 132)

Much of the literature of composition studies focuses on the resistance of students; on their difficulty in decentering the assumptions they have acquired from family, religion, and mass media; and on their struggles to become fluent in academic discourse. David Bartholomae writes: "Our students . . . have to appropriate (or be appropriated by) a specialized discourse, and they have to do this as though they were easily or comfortably one with their audience" (139). Yet are our students any more resistant than many of our colleagues to ideas with which they are uncomfortable or unfamiliar, ideas that do not reassure them that their world is safe, not provisional, not an invention? And is it only our students who discover themselves to be actors in the drama of appropriation that Bartholomae describes—or are we, too, often painfully reminded that faking it is the prerequisite for our work's legitimization, as we see alternative discursive, episte-mological, and methodological frameworks discredited, alternative knowledge claims scorned or ignored?

To return, then, to Bazerman: Has he imagined the costs to the ca-reers of "empowered speakers," the institutional rewards that accrue to "conventional followers of accepted practice" ("Criticism" 67)? If a mentor's work stands to lose prestige and credibility when an appren-tice brings alien critical discourses—feminism, for instance—to bear deconstructively on entrenched notions of validity, what happens? I contend that despite the discussions among the intellectual elite about tensions that drive canon debates, about the evolution of the disci-plines in a postmodern world, and about paradigm shifts in the way we make and view knowledge, the reactionary element in each of these struggles generally sustains itself by positing an essentialized notion of the discipline. The discipline possesses authority and tenacity because it is so familiar; its power is the power of the incumbent.

Writing-in-the-disciplines consultants lack the disciplinary knowl-edge necessary to equip students in the enterprise of questioning conventional renditions of the disciplines. Such an initiative, to be effective, would have to come from the disciplines themselves, which is why WID's role has principally been one of persuasion. And here I think we have come full circle: if, as some critics of writing in the disciplines—Kurt Spellmeyer ("Ground," "Comment") and Daniel Mahala—suggest, the nature of the disciplines qua disciplines sup-presses the heteroglossia that informs and inherently destabilizes systems of knowledge, doesn't that suppression signal the great un-likelihood that writing in the disciplines will work within disciplinary structures *and* fulfill its utopian intentions?

Hybrid Knowledge

Janet Giltrow and Michele Valiquette write that genre is "a system for administering communities' knowledge of the world—a system for housing knowledge, producing it, practicing it"—and that "users of a genre share not only knowledge of the genre but also a particular con-figuration of knowledge-of-the-world, this common ground forming a community of interest" (47, 48). Herrington and Charles Moran de-scribe Geertz's view of local knowledge as "one that sees the disci-

plines as discourse communities, each with its own preferred epistemological stance, preferred topoi, preferred modes of proof—local
conventions that form locally accepted modes of thought and of discourse" (234).

I find these views of disciplines as discourse communities compelling. But the composition of discourse communities itself needs examining. As Joseph Harris, Linda Brodkey ("Subjects"), and others
have pointed out, discourse communities contain dissonant voices
and competing interests, and their members identify at greatly varying
levels with the goals and beliefs ascribed to the community as a whole.
Geertz's notion of discrete, localized (though mutually respectful and
illuminating) knowledge domains seems to suppose that what is local
is unitary. The early second wave of feminism based much of its thinking on this supposition, and feminism has been reeling and learning
from that mistake ever since. Much early 1970s feminist writing held
that the category of women signaled not only a collective of bodies
bound together by the fact of their common oppression but also an
epistemological location—that is, it constituted a site of local knowledge (in the spiritual or experiential, not geographical, sense). Sexism
was viewed as a universal form of oppression, so that—to blur genres
by taking an analogy from transformational grammar—the *deep structure* of patriarchy was believed to extend throughout the world, though
its *surface structure* touched women in different cultures in different
ways. This belief made possible certain generalizations about gender:
one could read or know or behave morally *as a woman*.

In the late 1970s, a body of work began to be produced by feminists
of color that challenged the universalizing theories of white middle-
class feminists; this work was collected in anthologies and came to
be widely read in the early 1980s (e.g., Lorde, *Sister*; hooks, *Ain't I a
Woman, Feminist Theory*; Hull, Scott, and Smith; Moraga, *Loving*;
B. Smith, *Girls*; Moraga and Anzaldúa; Gómez, Moraga, and Romo-
Carmona). Feminists of color pointed out that white middle-class
feminism had subsumed the diverse realities of women in its localized knowledge, thus distorting or erasing the experience of more-
subjugated women, much as men had historically done to women.
Identity was not singular, they said, but composed of multiple, interlocking strands. The Combahee River Collective, a black feminist
group in Boston that included a number of lesbians, wrote, "We believe that sexual politics under patriarchy is as pervasive in black
women's lives as are the politics of class and race. We also often find it
difficult to separate race from class from sex oppression because in
our lives they are most often experienced simultaneously" (365). The

collective, in other words, stressed that its thinking refuted the knowledge of any one particular locale. It was the hybridity of its members' identities that gave it a point of view. They were able, for example, to criticize lesbian separatism for reasons that many white feminists arrived at only much later when terms like *essentialism* came into vogue: "We do not have the misguided notion that it is [men's] maleness, per se—i.e., their biological maleness—that makes them what they are. As black women we find any type of biological determinism a particularly dangerous and reactionary basis upon which to build a politic" (367).

Feminist discourse has grappled since that time with the question of how to responsibly theorize about women as a class when we each inhabit numerous terrains/identities/knowledges simultaneously. But it has also used its theorizing of gender as a starting point from which to track the effects or suppression of hybrid identity in all forms of knowledge making. Women's studies syllabi often reveal both the importance and difficulties of accounting for the myriad ways any topic can be explored when a range of identity positions is imagined and addressed. For instance, when teaching a course on women's history, how does one manage to include different women's experience as it occurred in a variety of time periods, movements (suffrage, education, abolition, temperance, labor, settlement-house, birth-control, antiwar), ethnic contexts (slavery, immigration, the holocaust, the reservation, the convent, mestiza culture), class contexts (mill towns, spheres of leisured affluence, domestic employment, the military, prostitution, suburbia), and sexuality contexts (heterosexuality, lesbianism, bisexuality, marriage, Boston marriage, celibacy, and such "outlaw" experience as S and M)? And each of these can be broken down further. If you wanted to study white lesbians in the 1950s, you'd need to investigate the butch-femme bar scene for the working-class experience, the organization Daughters of Bilitis for the middle-class experience, and the expatriate scene in Paris for the aristocrat experience (Faderman). Furthermore, how can we make useful generalizations about women in particular geographic locations when we take into account the fact—pointed out by the editors of the United States women's history anthology *Unequal Sisters*—that "the Anglo 'West' is also the Mexican 'North,' the Native American 'homeland' and the Asian 'East'" (DuBois and Ruiz xii)?

This degree of complication can and has become the stuff of jokes. Feminists are believed by many to fetishize fairness, holding others as well as themselves to standards of accountability that have been labeled "politically correct." But this sort of dismissal suggests a discomfort not only with particular political ideas but also with the notion that the knowledge domains that are visible and accessible to us (and are thus manipulable by us) are composed of an interfusion of less visible knowledge domains, which in turn are composed of domains even less visible. Such fragmentation resists analysis by all the methods we know. As the feminist theorist Gloria Anzaldúa might put it, local knowledge is really mestiza knowledge—though, to maintain its coherency and its highly localized identity, its dominant faction may suppress some of its variegated parts. If genres have only just begun to seem blurred, it may be because a host of social forces have finally revealed that forms of knowledge always gnaw at other forms of knowledge, that competing beliefs, interests, and interpretive systems always threaten to blur the clarity of disciplines. In the traditional academy, the forces behind this threat have been subdued to a remarkable extent. Though disciplines may indeed be discourse communities, we can't begin to identify the competing voices in them until we analyze the hegemonic arrangements that sustain their structure.

Hyphenated Knowledge

Ironically—or perhaps not—nowhere does women's studies seek to disrupt systems of dominance and rigidly partitioned knowledge more than in its own ranks. Particularly distinguishing women's studies from its disciplinary neighbors is the centrality of its concern with subjectivity. This concern forms the basis for women's studies' repudiation of canonical knowledge, including its own; and this concern has plunged women's studies into an ongoing interrogation of what it means to be a community of knowers and thinkers.

The term *feminism* has been dismantled and provisionally reassembled innumerable times, with the plural form, *feminisms*, now predominately in use and the term *hyphenated feminisms* frequently invoked to signal some of the best-known strains of feminist thought. A feminist theory course may sequentially or interactively explore Enlightenment/liberal feminism, Marxist/socialist feminism, existentialist feminism, radical feminism, women-of-color feminism, lesbian feminism, psychoanalytic feminism, and postmodern feminism as variant approaches to describing women's oppression and composing strategies for overcoming it (see Tong; Jaggar and Rothenberg; Donovan; Clough). Although the hyphenated feminisms do constitute a new taxonomy of knowledge, this taxonomy is a descriptive and provisional one rather than one that purports to solidify the landscape of feminist knowledge.[1] It is, of course, relatively easy for feminism to conceive of its organization as constructed, since it is a young field and a great many of its practitioners have participated in its construction. What is important, though, about the hyphenation paradigm is that it decentralizes feminism and asserts the medium of competing discourses as its message.

The feminisms, lacking in coherence even individually, may be variously seen as complementary or incommensurable. Traditions as diverse as liberalism, Marxism, and psychoanalysis have been faulted by feminist writers for failing to consider women as a class; but the appropriated notion of class differs dramatically according to the feminist scenario. For radical feminists, gender becomes the fundamental category of oppression; for Marxist feminists, women's economic subordination in capitalist modes of production is the key item to be addressed; for lesbian feminists, the patriarchal institution of compulsory heterosexuality persuades women to forgo the potential of their collective power and settle instead for the immediate rewards of what Adrienne Rich calls the "lie" of male identification ("Heterosexuality"). Whatever the relations and conflicts among these feminisms, women's studies' foregrounding of process makes manifest rather than effaces feminism's discontinuities and internal disruptions.

On Subversion

Women's studies as a knowledge field is the result of systematic exclusion; the first decade of feminist scholarship was an era of diving into the voids androcentric research had carved, of reimagining the world with women in it. Confronting knowledge conceived according to the epistemological standpoint of one powerful group left feminist scholars understandably suspicious of discrete and autonomous spheres of knowledge production. Women's studies pedagogy also repudiated inherited disciplinary frameworks and their requirements for specialization. It did this to disrupt familiar fiefdoms of hegemonic knowledge and to make possible the kinds of political and intellectual alliances necessary for generating an effectively counterhegemonic body, and a radically new form, of work.

Furthermore, because women, both as scholars and as the objects of scholarly inquiry, have endured nonnormative status in all forms of the academy's work, women's studies is positioned to regard academic enterprises from a perspective different from those of the traditional disciplines. The outsider in the academy, women's studies is by now a familiar resident but one nonetheless habituated to fighting fiscally, theoretically, and programmatically for its life and to creating its own, alternative legitimacy as it functions in counterpoint to mainstream intellectual and professional thought. One might say that women's studies operates as a fifth column, working to subvert from within the institutionalization of the very hierarchies that sustain social inequality. Women's studies subverts by refusing to be admitted to the inside on the insider's terms, by choosing not to renounce its marginality, by exploiting its heuristically unique angle of vision. Maintaining its identification and alliance with marginal identities and perspectives, rejecting the conflation of insider status and what "counts" with theoretical validity, women's studies beams its gaze at knowledge domains written off the map, those poised on the exterior of the loose consensus of meaning that binds the privileged enclaves of culturally dominant thought. Rather than advocate the mimicry and ultimate mastery of privileged discourses, women's studies encourages the articulation of counterdiscourses that undermine the consolidation of privilege.

What sort of model is women's studies for WAC? That depends on what WAC's proponents want to subvert and on how radical a stance they are prepared to take. If writing in the disciplines is a movement sincerely committed to Bazerman's vision, a movement in which "students can press at the bit of disciplinary practices they are trained into or run up against" by "seeing through the appearances of the discourse," then students should be helped to examine the extensive, though largely hidden, hybridity of disciplines. WID faculty members should encourage faculty members in the disciplines to be direct with students about how disciplinary conventions and belief systems are structured, to introduce students to the work of noncanonical as well as established members of the field, and to provide various frameworks for evaluating the reasons existing disciplinary margins and centers contain the particular inhabitants they do. Faculty members in the disciplines should be honest with students about the politics of outside funding and the control of disciplinary resources, helping students see that knowledge has market value and that this value is in large part determined by ideologies (such as nationalism and patriarchy) that are far larger than the university. Students should know that they have strategic choices—to play by the established rules or to challenge them—and should be helped to find appropriate support for either choice. WID faculty members might also converse with faculty members in the disciplines about presenting disciplinary offerings in more explicit, hyphenated ways (e.g., "capitalist-economics," "socialist-economics," "feminist-economics," "racial-economics," "imperialist-economics," etc.).

Of course, such suggestions will necessitate vast curricular change and will not endear WID faculty members to their departmental hosts. Students, moreover, should be prepared for the possibility that their challenging the rules will incur the wrath of those powerful forces in the discipline on which their future success most depends. When is that risk justified? In my view, only when students have a tremendous personal or ideological investment in a piece of reality that a department has squeezed out of existence.

In its most radical form, writing, by facilitating a return of the academically repressed, can repudiate the legacy by which privileged discourses and epistemological categories are institutionally recertified. It seems that such a task would fall, if anywhere, to writing to learn, given WTL's emphasis on jazzlike improvisational dialogue with course material and WTL's encouragement of maverick approaches to ideas. Perhaps WTL and WID could merge to act on Spanier's suggestion that we encourage students to become "resisting readers" of their disciplines; or they could merge to act on Herrington's proposal that we urge students to reflect on the rhetorical practices that foreclose entire realms of thought. But if WTL really wanted to upend the disciplines, it would have to grapple with difficult ideological content; and WID, as it now stands, would be hard pressed to promote such a project, since there is a fundamental conflict between its goal of helping students achieve successful disciplinary performances and any subversion of the hegemonic arrangement of the existing disciplines. Students who attempt to subvert the disciplines put themselves in a vulnerable position; by challenging reality as set forth by the landlords of knowledge domains, they align themselves with the disenfranchised. Women's studies does this, but in a particularly deliberate, considered, and collective way. The goal of feminist education has never been to prepare students to participate in the world as it exists; the goal, rather, has been to help them develop the skills to deconstruct and transform that world. Lack of identification with the highest privileges of the academy and old boys' networks has been central in cultivating a feminist methodological, epistemological, and rhetorical stance. To identify more with the object than with the subject of research, more with the viewed than with the viewer, to be one whose subjective interests are not represented in research design, is to feel inevitably distanced from and uninvested in the pursuit of knowledge in its conventional forms. As Sandra Harding, a feminist philosopher of science, has put it:

> While employers have often commissioned studies of how to make workers happy with less power and pay, workers have rarely been in a position to undertake or commission studies of anything at all, let alone how to make employers happy with less power and profit. Similarly, psychiatrists have endlessly studied what they regard as women's peculiar mental and behavioral characteristics, but women have only recently begun to study the bizarre mental and behavioral characteristics of psychiatrists.
> ("Is There" 8–9)

To ask in whose interests research is performed and what values it supports is ultimately to expose the fallacy of the adage that knowledge is valuable for its own sake. A feminist analysis of the established disciplines reveals that their boundaries and the knowledge they contain are not designs of some inevitable logic but metaphysical creations posing as the Real. One aim of women's studies is to expose that illusion; if WAC shares that aim, an alliance between the two might yield interesting results. But the alliance must acknowledge that faculty members and students in women's studies take risks because of deeply held beliefs and feelings—not about how knowledge ought to be approached in the abstract but about how those choices shape people's entire lives. Those working in each strand of WAC need to ask themselves in what interests their work is performed and what values that work supports. The answers may reveal whether they want to find new ways of encountering, or only new ways of taming, in Foucault's words, the wild profusion of existing things.

NOTES

Many thanks to Anne Herrington—a feminist committed to writing across the curriculum—for responding to this essay in progress and for steering me toward some very useful sources.

[1]There is disagreement even about this. Judith Grant contends that the notion of hyphenated feminisms is a "feminist orthodoxy" that masks certain core concepts in feminist theory. Daphne Patai and Noretta Koertge criticize women's studies for being ideologically rigid and intolerant of internal dissent. Indeed, women's studies, like WAC, offers a highly idealized self-

description, and there are certainly feminist academics who are locked firmly in their partisan positions, eschewing interdisciplinary frameworks and using traditional discourses and positivist research approaches. This essay represents the goals and scope of women's studies as they have been articulated broadly by and in the women's studies discourse community, with the caveat that this community is not more cohesive and homogeneous than any other and needs to be interpreted with the same healthy skepticism as that with which I am suggesting other disciplines be approached.

RESPONSE TO PART III

Writing Back

Lisa Ede and Andrea Lunsford

14 June 1995

Dear Joy, Kate, Min-Zhan, Gail, Amy, Carrie, and Harriet:

It's a typical June day here in Oregon—cool, cloudy, and drizzly. Summer will indeed come to the Northwest eventually, but probably not in time for Andrea's three-day visit to Corvallis. So here we are, sitting contentedly in Lisa's study, grateful for the electric heater that intermittently warms this chilly room. Over the twenty-something years of our friendship and coauthorship, we've been in this room or rooms like it many times, mixing talk of family, friends, and colleagues with periods of intense reading and writing and equally intense bouts of cooking and baking, with long walks and shopping excursions and conversations that seem to go on now even when we are not physically together—and with the odd argument, misunderstanding, or tension. Your essays, the essays that we've spent the last week reading and last night and this morning discussing, cover the floor. They make us wish you were here with us now.

The pages you sent us speak in important and complex ways to us about feminism, about composition, about feminisms and composition. But, as sometimes happens when texts are most fertile, most productive, the more we discussed your essays, the more we found ourselves wishing for face-to-face conversation, for the kind of situated dialogue that only real-time, real-place interactions enable.

What questions would we ask you if we were all lounging together on Lisa's study floor, sipping wine and nibbling on the raspberries and strawberries that are just coming on in the garden? For starters, we'd probably ask you to talk about how you wrote your essays—how you came to your topics, the paths you took in developing them, the risks you saw yourselves taking (and not taking). We'd want to know if you

313

struggle as writers, as we do, particularly now that the question of the forms in which we write is one we no longer take for granted. We'd want to ask you where you find yourselves professionally these days, how you are positioned by and in your departments and universities and what those positionings have to do with your essays. And we'd want to know about the persons you are when you're not in your classrooms or your studies—about the passions for cooking, movies, rock climbing, or the theater that energize you and about the relationships that sustain you as you move through your lives.

Out of this sense of missing you, of all the talk we wish we could have right now, comes this letter to you. We want to write to thank you for the pages you've sent, to appreciate in print the contributions you have made to our thinking, to point to a number of intriguing themes we see running through your texts, and to raise even more questions for and with you. We write this letter in the hope that you'll write back, that you'll keep those essays coming. Perhaps most of all, we write this letter in the hope that the dialogue that you have begun and that we take up here can extend beyond our particular conversation, that others will talk back to and with all of us.

> In the world of the southern black community I grew up in, "back talk" and "talking back" meant speaking as an equal to an authority figure. It meant daring to disagree and sometimes it just meant having an opinion.   (hooks, *Talking* 5)

Did you know (could you have known?) that, among well over a hundred writers cited in your essays, the only one you all have in common is bell hooks? We noted this common source accidentally and on reflection enjoyed the ways in which hooks's voice reverberates in your conversation, highlighting a point here, introducing an example there, challenging received wisdoms almost everywhere. Why does your mutual (though varying) use of hooks seem to us particularly fitting? Is it because she inhabits so clearly and forcefully the intersections between theory and practice, between feminism, pedagogy, literacy, and social action? Is it because she confronts these intersections directly in the concrete contexts of her own life—and seems never content to ask easy questions about them?

> How can a feminist pedagogy help avoid essentializing women or reproducing existing power relations . . . [and] put in motion intersecting dialogues that involve students in what Lynn Worsham calls "the ongoing criticism of everyday life" . . . ? These are

> not easy questions, especially as they play out in the pragmatic
> contexts of classrooms.   (Ritchie and Ronald, this volume)

Ah, the pragmatic—and, we would add, maddening, exhilarating, always changing—contexts of our pedagogical scenes. We've thought and talked a lot about those pragmatic contexts and about the "not easy questions" Joy and Kate raise at the opening of their essay, especially as we've tried to engage your essays in conversation. Pressing each other for overall impressions of your work, for big-picture issues that stood out for us in part 3, we agreed almost immediately that the emphasis on pedagogy was refreshing and reaffirming, even as it raised very hard questions (like the one we've just noted in the quotation from Joy and Kate's essay). After all, ever since the earliest critique in composition studies of what has come to be called the current-traditional paradigm, many teachers of writing have recognized the inadequacy of a pedagogy based on the transmission model of learning—what Paulo Freire dubs the banking system of education (*Pedagogy*). And many teachers of writing, particularly feminist teachers of writing, have argued strenuously for alternatives to this pedagogy. But your essays take an important step beyond advocating alternatives; they explicitly describe and sometimes enact both the opportunities and the problems inevitably presented by attempts to move from pedagogies that reproduce "existing power relations" to those that nurture "intersecting dialogues." Joy and Kate show us in concrete detail just how complex (and exciting) teaching the rhetorical canon became for them once they moved from a transmission pedagogy into the exploratory, resisting, and multivoiced contexts entailed by their use of feminist pedagogy. Each of your essays in this section thinks through, with, and against traditional conceptions of pedagogy in the context of writing program administration, of writing across the curriculum, of writing-intensive literature courses, and of courses that employ collaborative learning and writing practices.

In using "pedagogy" to name an overarching concern in all your essays, we are (as we're sure you have already noted) extending and reshaping the generally understood signification of this term. We do so intentionally, believing with Jennifer Gore that questions of pedagogy are inevitably questions about "how and in whose interests knowledge is produced and reproduced" (5). Had we stuck with traditional understandings of pedagogy, we would have had to bracket questions of program administration—of the relationship of teaching assistants with peer mentors and of peer mentors with the director of the program, for instance—as distinct and separable from questions of classroom pedagogy. Yet as both Harriet's and Amy and Carrie's essays indicate, such bracketing forecloses essential questions, questions that encourage those engaged in WAC activities to inquire "in what interests their work is performed and what values that work supports" (Malinowitz) or those engaged in writing program administration to recognize and reflect "on our inscription in dominant and dominating ideologies of labor and management" (Goodburn and Leverenz).

Thus your essays have reaffirmed for us the importance of recognizing that pedagogies are deeply inscribed in particular social and institutional contexts that are themselves always raced, gendered, classed, and otherwise delimited. And you've also reminded us that pedagogies are always relational, always realized through the tenuous links between and among teachers, students, knowledge structures, and multiple (often competing) contexts. Perhaps most important, your essays have evoked the dynamic, organic nature of pedagogy, the sense in which *pedagogy* is not a noun but a verb, an acting out of a complex and deeply interactive struggle for understanding, growth, and change.

> [Without a] critical framework, students are easily beguiled by the mystique of dominant knowledge systems, which are bolstered by and in turn legitimate asymmetrical social, material, and ideological arrangements.   (Malinowitz, this volume)

> Struggles over power, authority, and leadership are not barriers to enacting feminist principles; they are the embodiment of them.   (Goodburn and Leverenz, this volume)

Your essays also remind us that the struggle for and over pedagogies always involves issues of agency and authority—of teachers, administrators, and students; of communities; and of structures of knowledge. In varying ways, all your essays circle around the creation, status, and efficacy of authority. Where does it lie? Harriet asks. In the discipline and its methodology? In discursive power itself? In learners and teachers willing to push at the boundaries of a discipline? How can we teach in and about a tradition that authorizes only masculine texts and values? ask Kate and Joy. How might the experiential be embodied most effectively in poststructuralist understandings of authority? adds Min-Zhan. For Amy and Carrie, a central question is whether we can find ways of sharing authority that are not appropriated by discursive, institutional, and social hierarchies. And Gail further complicates this question by arguing that in some pedagogical circumstances such hierarchies can have a salutary, heuristic value.

We've thought a lot ourselves about issues of authoring, authorizing, and authority, and we very much liked hearing the stories you tell here, particularly insofar as those stories are specified and grounded in the concrete particulars of your classrooms. As feminists and as compositionists, we've long felt the need to move through and beyond the contemporary crisis of agency and authority, a crisis that in some circles has led either to a sense of deep cynicism and despair or to a paralysis of responsibility. Your essays offer varying ways to avoid that slippery slope. Not that we don't see implicit conflicts, even overt disagreements, among your representations of authority, but that's part of what we are responding to positively here. As Carrie and Amy suggest, only by living in and through such conflicts—and by engaging in extensive and deep reflection on them—can we hope to enact an authority informed by feminist principles. And only in this way can we enable students (and ourselves) to build the kind of critical framework Harriet calls for, one that lets us resist "the mystique of dominant knowledge systems."

> We need to imagine ways of using experience critically: experience should motivate us to care about another's differences and should disrupt the material conditions that have given rise to it.
>
> (Lu, this volume)

What happens when you engage in the kind of deep and extensive critical reflection Amy and Carrie call for or confront the need, articulated by Harriet, for building critical frameworks? These questions lead to yet another theme that weaves itself through your essays, one bringing a set of key terms—*experience, difference,* and *resistance*—into varying ratios with one another. Out of this terministic dance come several important insights. Gail argues that what a teacher intends as shared, nonhierarchical collaboration may actually reinforce our culture's silencing of women students, that teachers' desires to resist traditional academic hierarchies and structures may displace or prevent more significant challenges to conventional cultural norms. Harriet addresses the triad of terms in another way, arguing that disciplinary (and hence disciplining) experiences may be resisted, at least to some degree, through a recognition of difference—and she challenges those working in writing-across-the-curriculum programs to ask themselves whether they are willing to live out the consequences of such resistance. But Kate and Joy argue that principles of resistance and difference can enable teachers and students, working together, to experience the traditional rhetorical canon in ways that challenge "the mystique of dominant knowledge systems" (Malinowitz), disrupting the "material conditions that have given rise to [teachers' and students' experiences]" (Lu). Taking yet another tack, Carrie and Amy argue for writing program administration as a fertile site of investigation into how experience gets written into the practices of writing programs as well as for the role that difference and resistance play in negotiating that experience. And Min-Zhan, in an intriguing spin on the relation between expressivist and social constructionist–critical pedagogies, argues that "making experience work both experientially and analytically" can help students and teachers value difference as well as resist contemporary neoconservative hegemonies.

It's no accident that we use the term *argue* to describe the gist of your essays. Your essays do argue—but they do not prescribe. In reading your essays, we were both struck by the extent to which they work to resist what Lynn Worsham refers to as composition study's pedagogical imperative, that disciplinary desire that impels those engaging in inquiry to translate their results "into a pedagogical practice or at least some specific advice for teachers" ("Writing" 96). Rather than offer such generalized advice to others, we notice, you tend to engage in intensive self-scrutiny and self-reflection. And as we've already noted, you also anchor your analyses in particular settings, bringing in the voices of your students and colleagues and reporting on localized conversations and debates. These specifics, it seems to us, allow you to explore an exceedingly complex calculus of relations without losing sight of the need, in Gail's words, to "examine the consequences." They also show that many of the curricular and administrative judgments compositionists are called on to make are deeply situated. They emphasize how difficult it can be to determine whether this or that action in this or that context represents a productive embodiment of resistance, a reification of the status quo, or something else entirely.

What is true of teaching and administration is equally true of writing. And so we conclude this letter by raising a question we kept returning to during the days we talked and wrote together about your work. What significance, if any, should we (or other readers) attach to the fact that your essays tend to accept and embody, rather than to transgress, the conventions of traditional academic prose? Does this acceptance and embodiment mark a place of paradox and difficulty or does it represent a judicious response to your specific rhetorical situations—an appropriate claiming and naming of your authority as writers (or does it represent something else entirely)? The essays in part 3 demonstrate the impossibility of coming to general, fixed, or monolithic conclusions about questions like these; they emphasize instead the necessity of engaging in highly situated critical reflection.

In so doing, your essays reflect changes that have taken place in both composition studies and feminism during the past twenty years. As women and as scholars who have lived through these changes, we have our own specifications of this experience. When we think back to our early engagements with feminism and composition studies in the early 1970s, we are particularly struck by the extent to which our sense of mission in both arenas led us to pursue a dream of progress that encouraged us to yearn for global, monolithic solutions. It has taken us a long time to see the limitations of this yearning and to recognize just how important it is to acknowledge and interrogate the complexity of our experiences. Our earliest interest in collaborative practices, for instance, was marked by a deep longing to change understandings of discursive practice and to change the academic institutions in which those discursive practices held such powerful sway. We thought that if we could simply demonstrate the facticity of collaboration, point up its many strengths, such change might take place. We were thinking, we now realize, in generalized, often essentialist, and binary ways. Our ongoing research into local and highly contextualized collaborative practices, however, called this thinking into question and challenged us to acknowledge that collaborative practices are as varied as individual practices, that the mode of collaboration that we originally identified as dialogical—and that we longed to value as potentially liberatory and feminist—could in particular locations and situations actually resist liberatory and feminist goals.

In their own ways, feminism and composition studies have made much the same journey, coming by differing paths to the need for a highly specified and contextualized understanding of social action, learning, and writing.[1] Some critics, alarmed at this shift, fear that it will lead to a vulgar relativism or to the cynicism, despair, and paralysis we mentioned earlier. Your work does not, however, lead in this direction. For while you recognize and honor the complex and situated nature of knowledge making, you do not flinch from making choices, from taking stands. At their very best, your essays transcend the binary choice between a dream of progress and a deadening relativism, enacting instead not a situational but a carefully situated ethics. While feminism and composition studies may—and probably will—pursue different, sometimes even contradictory, goals, the need for full exploration of the choices and possibilities involved in such an

ethics should inform work in both areas. We think the investigations
you have undertaken provide suggestive avenues that both feminists
and compositionists may profitably travel.

So, dear Joy, Kate, Min-Zhan, Gail, Amy, Carrie, and Harriet (and
Susan, Lynn, and readers as yet unknown to us), here are our
thoughts. Hoping that they find you in good health and good times
and, always, that fruitful work lies ahead.

Yours in feminism and in composition—
Lisa and Andrea

NOTE

[1]What we're evoking here might well be termed sensitivity to the rhetorical
situation. In fact, as we've been writing this letter, we've often thought of and
discussed an essay that, if we ever write it, will respond to a growing collection
we've made of calls by feminists for nonpositivist, contingent, ethically sensitive theories of knowledge and communication. For instance, Leslie Wahl Rabine concludes her critique of deconstruction with this statement: "If the
metaphysical oppositions and the imposing of a single phallocentric truth can
be oppressive, the bringing into play of bottomless deconstructive strategies
can in certain situations be equally so. The deconstruction of metaphysical oppositions always takes place in a context of social hierarchy where speaker
and listener, writer and reader, are placed in power relations with each other,
no matter what the content of the text. Whether this play is progressive depends on who does it to whom, what is its historic or institutional context, and
who makes the rules" (28). What is rhetoric but this?

From Principles to Particulars (and Back)

Margaret Lindgren

As a feminist composition teacher, I spend a good deal of time think-ing about when and how my pedagogical choices reflect my values. Lately, I've found myself asking questions. On what assumptions about knowledge does this writing assignment rely? Can I disagree with this student without stifling the student's authority with my own? Have these students been empowered? How do I know? How do they know? These hard questions originate in my desire to make the language that expresses my beliefs accountable to my circumstances, and they illustrate the complications I face as I work to instantiate my principles. It seems to me that the essays in part 3 can be read as ef-forts to reflect on that same project—the project of taking our words seriously and examining how, in particular situations, we do (or don't) actualize them.[1]

These essays, though highlighting different discontinuities that arise for those with allegiances to both feminism and composition studies, contribute to a project valued by both: the ongoing process of interro-gating our ideas and experiences so that we can more closely align our spoken with our practiced values. Harriet Malinowitz asks those of us who argue for the importance of writing in the disciplines to enact in more concrete ways our belief that the hierarchical structuring of knowledge into disciplines can and should be questioned. Gail Stygall warns those of us who rely on collaborative learning in writing groups that another reality, the always active and socially accepted conversa-tional practices that reinforce individualism and male domination, can pollute our efforts and leave us theoretically comfortable but ped-agogically ineffective. Amy Goodburn and Carrie Leverenz suggest that by refusing to look closely at the specific, multiple, and conflicting interests in play when groups of professionals work together for institutional change, we risk reinscribing the very egoistic and hierarchical practices we seek to transform. Joy Ritchie and Kate Ronald remind us that being content with a focus on what we teach can lead us as practitioners to ignore how our teaching processes reveal what we value as much as if not more than the texts we choose do. Finally, Min-Zhan Lu points out an important conflict that can arise when we attempt to instantiate multiple values simultaneously.

These discontinuities are, I think, inevitable. Tensions arise whenever we attempt to actualize our values, in part because language ultimately requires that an abbreviated expression or term (e.g., "shared authority," "experience," "collaboration"), however well defined, be chosen to represent complex, interactive, and changing realities. So when those expressions are applied to our professional activities, the ambiguities and situational complications that they don't (and can't) represent demand attention. But the interaction of feminism and composition requires that we examine our circumstances, bring the various factions invoked in them into dialogue with one another, and consider new and more egalitarian ways to respond to the conflicts that emerge.

I suggest neither that we stop speaking (because words can't express the complexities of our lived experience) nor that we stop acting (because circumstances prevent us from enacting our words with any consistency). Instead, I propose, as do the other authors in part 3, that we consider how intertwined the processes of articulating and actualizing our values are, so that we can study the discontinuities that arise when we attempt to make our words and actions accountable to one another. By studying the situational complications of our lived realities, we will be able to construct new ways of responding, with more-complex theories and more-consistent practices, as feminist writing scholars and practitioners. In response, then, I focus on two concepts—experience and collaboration—that are valuable to both feminist and composition studies and that figure in the situations explored by the authors included in part 3.

Experience

Personal experience, in both feminist and composition studies, is often interpreted as the particulars of one's life circumstances, and valuing it means including those particulars when engaging in intellectual reflection. Ritchie and Ronald illustrate that tradition when they stress the importance of teaching rhetorical texts in the contexts of students' experiences and suggest journal writing, with the teacher as an active participant and the experience of study as an acceptable topic, as a pedagogical tool to evoke dialogue. We see the potential of such activity in the student Gladys's journal of 17 January, where she identifies her context—a movement from working with women "in church basements and dark, unheated community centers" to taking part in "the professional theoretical conversation"—and describes her reading of the canonical rhetorical texts as necessary if she is to "maintain a credible identity in *both* groups" (emphasis added). Even though Gladys's standards for credibility are drawn from her scholarly activities, she resists the separation of the two domains. She believes rhetorical theory to be relevant to the circumstances of "women, who, for countless reasons, had been 'under served' by the educational system earlier in their lives" and looks to articulate that connection more fully. Making and exploring such connections, however, is a more complicated process than it might at first seem, for it requires that Gladys consider difficult questions. To whose advantage is it that certain portions of the population remain underserved educationally? How has rhetorical theory been complicit in creating a culture in which questions of advantage are ignored? Can a process that advantages some over others be resisted? And if so, how?

The dialogue is hard to sustain. On 31 January, when Gladys writes of her experience of the course and of how a reminder from Ronald helps her realize how inclined she is to sit awestruck at the feet of the authorities whose texts she reads, we see that what she calls her cultural conditioning has to some degree already interrupted her ability to think critically about the texts in question. We don't know if Gladys ever revisited her desire to make space in this new environment for her previous professional experience. One would hope that the kind of journal writing she engaged in would encourage such revisiting, but it would not be surprising if her seeking credibility in the academy overshadowed her concern that her experience outside the academy be validated as well. However obvious the gaps are between our circumstances and our intellectual processes for naming and understanding, no single graduate course is likely to bridge those gaps sufficiently. Perhaps students could keep another kind of journal, one not tied to a particular course but, rather, charting the discontinuities recognized throughout a course of study. Perhaps such a journal would encourage

324 Response to Part III

the kind of recursiveness necessary if students are to address such questions in depth.

But there's another perspective on experience alluded to in these essays, a perspective that has received less scholarly attention: personal experience can and does impose limitations. Ritchie illustrates how reliance on experience can lead students to naive and essentialist reading postures. The impulse to rely on simplistic readings is born, in part, of students' desires to "explore their experience in language, their victimization at the hands of patriarchal discourse." Ritchie describes the tensions faced when a teacher wants both to take the students' goals and experiences into consideration and to problematize and contextualize texts, including renditions of experience.

Lu draws our attention to how students' personal experiences can subtly narrow students' interpretive choices as readers. She proposes that being told to stay home and do the dishes and encountering adults who don't believe education is important for women lead students in their reading to focus on gender issues as separate from economic issues and to ignore passages that indicate the importance of ethnic differences. If economic need or ethnic difference lies outside students' experience, students responding only to the aspects of the text with which they can identify will miss important interpretive possibilities.

Naming her problem as "to help students rethink ways of using personal experience so that readings through the personal will not be at the expense of other stories and selves," Lu responds first by expanding her (and our) understanding of experience and then by translating that reconceptualization into pedagogical practice. The assignment sequence she creates asks her students to interpret texts that include several forms of difference and then to interpret their interpretations on the basis of new information about interpretation drawn from arguments that emphasize differences other than gender. Students, that is, are asked to articulate, critique, and thus revise their activities as readers.

In a conceptually similar way, Ritchie utilizes a journal strategy to bring into dialogue the different perceptions of how experience is understood by different class members. She emphasizes as well how the particular texts chosen, because of their diversity and multiplicity despite their common authorship by women, force her students to complicate their reading postures.

Collaboration

Goodburn and Leverenz offer an impressively detailed picture of how, despite their goals of enacting dialogic collaboration and shared leadership, their attempt to work with others to improve a writing program was hampered by conflicts between their explicit identifications as feminists and their implicit identifications with bureaucracy. Goodburn and Leverenz were often frustrated by a lack of leadership, anxious that their expertise was not sufficiently appreciated, fearful that a program that had no individual ownership would not enhance their credibility on the job market, and betrayed by and disloyal to various members of the competing constituencies involved in the project. Though they valued collaboration, working with others resulted in more complications and fewer rewards than they anticipated.

I am struck by the acuity with which the authors identify their conflicting motivations. To be good feminists, they choose and participate in processes that provide for inclusion and shared authority, but these feminist values do not erase other needs. Goodburn and Leverenz need recognition for a successful project. They also want to be respected by and respectful of the multiple and competing constituencies involved, even as their power to express and gain that respect is sometimes limited by the very institutional structures that create the competition. Such conflict is often disallowed by the unspoken assumption that individual circumstances and interests play no role in collaborative efforts.

Stygall takes collaboration as her topic when she focuses on conversations among students in writing groups. She argues that conversational moves such as false starts, turn taking, and topic changing are efforts by speakers to assert individual domination and that when male students exercise this domination, the likelihood that women students (and perhaps other marginalized groups) will engage in participative learning is diminished. Stygall warns us as teachers of the danger of assuming that conversation is always evidence of collaborative learning and asks us to rethink our assumptions about what does and does not constitute a truly collaborative exchange.

Since Stygall, Goodburn, and Leverenz are asking for more from the concept of collaboration, it may be possible to use Elspeth Probyn's analytic structure (as described by Lu) to revise our understanding of it. Probyn's contribution begins with her admonition that we think of experience as working on two levels—material and epistemological.

Materially experience is the "felt facticity" of being in the social, but epistemologically experience is a tool that "overtly politicizes its own being by analyzing the material conditions . . . and positing ways of changing those conditions" (21). Materially collaboration looks like any act that involves more than one person in the creation of a text, but epistemologically we might also imagine collaboration as a tool with which groups can reflect on their processes, on the situational factors that affect both what they decide and how they decide it, and on how they might engage differently with those circumstances to minimize the limitations imposed by them.

Goodburn and Leverenz, though they don't cite Probyn, summarize their experience as illustrating that "struggles over power, authority, and leadership are not barriers to enacting feminist principles; they are the embodiment of them." They advise us to confront the resistance that inevitably results when institutional change is attempted in any collaborative way, to think critically about the act of resisting bureaucracy, and to "create a language" by which groups can talk about "resistance and conflict." They suggest that others do as they have done: interrogate internalized assumptions about bureaucratic life so as to overcome the forces that oppose efforts to change the ideology of bureaucracy. We might imagine meetings (or sets of memos) in which participants articulate their individual stakes in a project and then respond to one another's perceptions or a public statement that expresses both the intention and the means to equalize the power relations made unequal by institutional positionings.

Stygall doesn't invoke Probyn either, but she too is concerned with how collaboration might be utilized to change the conditions that limit its definition. She calls for a "feminist-critical authority," a teacherly presence who might mediate the inequities implanted in students by the cultural conditions of hierarchy and domination. Stygall offers only one suggestion of how such an authority might proceed: a prescriptive approach to turn taking in a peer-group situation. Even that, she concludes, would be only a beginning and an insufficient one because of the complexity of the problem. If we take our cue, however, from Lu, Ritchie, and Ronald, we can begin to formulate other possibilities. Suppose, for example, that Kenneth Bruffee's students or Lester Faigley's students were asked to read essays about the role of gender in conversational practice and then to read and interpret, with those perspectives in mind, the transcripts of their conversations. And if Jean, Rick, Tom, and the anonymous author of the piece referred to in the segments quoted from Martin Nystrand were asked to keep journals about their discussions, perhaps, after some reading about how false starts, turn taking, and topic changing can be interpreted, they might be enabled to compare the individual circumstances that engendered their conversational behavior and to construct, together with the teacher, knowledge about how power and control can be resisted and collaborative efforts enhanced.

Back to Principles

Efforts at collaboration, whether in writing groups or in writing program administration, are efforts to resist the romantic notion of the solitary author removed from reality. In this sense, addressing the problems raised by Goodburn, Leverenz, and Stygall is deeply relevant to the ongoing work of both feminists and compositionists. In the same way, respect for experience grows from a desire to keep daily life relevant even as we expand our intellectual activities, and both feminists and compositionists will be served as well by the effort to value personal experience. Malinowitz identifies what seems to me a uniquely feminist attitude when she reminds us that the "goal of feminist education has never been to prepare students to participate in the world as it exists; the goal, rather, has been to help them develop the skills to deconstruct and transform that world." She ties this principle to her critique by suggesting that students be taught the processes by which disciplinary conventions are structured, provided with various frameworks for evaluating who becomes canonical and who does not (and why), and given real choices about whether to follow or resist dominant conventions. But Malinowitz's suggestion can also provide a structure in which the topics of experience and collaboration fit.

While feminist pedagogy is based on the principle that education should foster social change, composition pedagogy is not (necessarily). Indeed, writing is still assumed by many to be one of the skills needed for students to gain social and economic standing. And while literary theory, cultural studies, and critical pedagogy have greatly influenced teaching practice, professional conversations, and research in composition, Malinowitz, Goodburn and Leverenz, Stygall, Lu, and Ritchie and Ronald all point to ways in which we (both as a field and as individuals) remain entrenched in familiar and nonegalitarian conditions. These conditions prevent us from recognizing how frequently we encourage the reproduction rather than the deconstruction of the world. Addressing the issues considered by the authors in part 3 requires time, energy, meetings, memos, conflicts, and risk with regard to classroom and administrative practices—not the stuff traditionally valued in academic environments. If the issue of change is important enough, though, we will find ways to identify our complicities and then to narrow the gaps between our principles and the particulars of our lives.

NOTE

[1]My use of pronouns of the first person plural is meant to suggest not the existence of a coherent and conflict-free discourse community of readers but, rather, the possibility (hope) that the concerns and situations this volume addresses are shared in some collective fashion.

After Words: A Choice of Words Remains

Lynn Worsham

> *We die. That may be the meaning of life. But we do language.*
> *That may be the measure of our lives.*
> —Toni Morrison

> *and I ask myself and you, which of our visions will claim us*
> *which will we claim*
> *how will we go on living*
> *how will we touch, what will we know*
> *what will we say to each other.*
> —Adrienne Rich

Working through the essays collected in this volume, I want to piece together a way of doing feminism at the end of a century that has seen two waves of feminist movement and now anticipates a third.[1] What I hear in the words collected here, what I have learned from a century (and more) of struggle, is this: The immediate and most pressing task for feminism's third wave is to forge a collective subject capable of making mass movement—if not a sisterhood, exactly, then surely an alliance that does not protect us from our differences but finds in difference, disagreement, and even despair occasions to hear one another's words; an alliance that recognizes that our histories and experiences are not only diverse in all the ways we have learned to name them, they are also intertwined in complex and mutually determining ways. The lesson to be remembered at the end of this century of struggle is that there is no need to eradicate difference to find solidarity, no need to share common oppression to fight oppression, even those forms that may not affect us directly or individually. The collective subject these essays seek to forge finds its identity in collective struggle—at the crossing of "subject" and "process," as Susan Jarratt suggests.

It is at this crossing that I locate what Ellen Gil-Gomez calls the feminist practice of piece-making. A practice that sustains the fragments of individual identity and allows the conflicts they raise to exist, piece-making, undertaken at a different level, also provides a way to forge feminism's collective subject—a way to construct and reconstruct the "we" that tries its political luck and wagers itself at a particular time and place (see Desmet's essay in this volume). Working heuristically with the figural possibilities of piece-making, I want to link this feminist practice to peacemaking, understood here as process rather than goal. Peacemaking, in other words, is not oriented toward the resolution of conflict (whether final or provisional) and toward the formation of a spurious unity or a sentimentalized harmony; rather, it moves, without compromise, toward a positive recognition and acceptance of difference as the basis for solidarity and collective struggle. To do this piecework, this work of peacemaking, feminist writing that will take us into the next historical period must make difference its byword; an open hand, not a clenched fist, its sign.[2]

Indeed, feminist hands are made of words—the words we have chosen to work through as well as the words that work through us, on us, and beyond us to shape still other subjects in other times and places—and the essays in this volume offer, in this time and place, the open hand of a feminist writing that invites the generation of more words, other words in the ongoing process of piece/peacemaking. Each essay represents one piece, one choice of words, and thereby offers through its own work of piece-making a rhetoric for feminism. Taken together, the essays suggest that in any given enunciative moment a choice of words always remains for each of us to make individually, a choice that will place us, or fail to place us, alongside one another in a side-by-side relation of association and alliance. Faced with this implied challenge, I want to piece together some of the choices figured in these essays and thereby extend an open hand in a metonymic gesture of alliance. My own work of piece-making here represents one choice among many possibilities and is intended to lead to the generation of more and other words, to circle back into this volume to locate other pieces that may be stitched by feminist hands into a process of peacemaking. Let *generation* be my choice of words, then, offered here as a productive topos, a gathering place for chosen words and a crossing place where, as Min-Zhan Lu suggests, "differences can and must engage one another."

While this choice of words arises, most immediately, from the way these essays work on me, Toni Morrison's 1993 Nobel Prize lecture compels its formulation. Morrison shapes her lecture as a story, because narrative, she says, is one of the principal ways we absorb knowledge (8). Her "once upon a time" gives life and new meaning to a familiar proverb whose wisdom would guide the choices we make: A bird in the hand is worth two in the bush. Morrison gives this proverb a plot, characters, and a sense of conflict by placing the bird in the hands of young people who approach an old black woman, the blind but wise daughter of slaves, to test her vision and her wisdom with a question that will expose her as the fraud they think she is. Their question turns on her difference from them—her blindness—which they construe as a disability. They ask, "Is the bird . . . living or dead?" The old woman hears their mocking words and reproves them with this reply: "I don't know whether the bird you are holding is dead or alive, but what I do know is that it is in your hands. It is in your hands" (11). Thus begins a confrontation between generations, a confrontation shaped by the gulf of experience dividing young and old, by the impasse of perspectives, by the blind hostilities and bitter grievances over failures each places in the hands of the other. In Morrison's hands, the bird becomes language, and the answer to the question, Is it living or dead?, ultimately will be placed in the hands of both young and old.

Both must see that there is a clear choice to make and that all are accountable for the fate of language and, through language, for the survival of each and every one. Yet the choice, as Morrison figures it, is as difficult as it is simple: On the one hand, there is dead language, which is more than a language no longer spoken or written, more than an inscrutable proverb. Death-dealing language "actively thwarts the intellect, stalls conscience, suppresses human potential. Unreceptive to interrogation, it cannot form or tolerate new ideas, shape other thoughts, tell another story, fill baffling silences" (14). Dead language "does more than represent violence; it is violence; does more than represent the limits of knowledge; it limits knowledge" (16). It is "official language smitheried to sanction ignorance and preserve privilege." Sexist, racist, theistic, and statist, it is the policing language of mastery, exclusion, and domination that blocks "access to cognition for both the excluder and the excluded" (19). On the other hand, there is living language, conceived as a living thing, as agency, as "an act with consequences." Living language is a "poem full of vitamins," a "history connected to experience," passed from generation to generation "to help us start strong" (27). It breaks through the barrier, erected by dead language, between wisdom and generosity. "[W]hether it laughs out loud or is a cry without an alphabet, the choice word or the chosen silence," living language surges unmolested "toward knowledge not its destruction" (21). "Refusing to monumentalize, disdaining the 'final

word,' the precise 'summing up,' " living language is interrogative, critical, and visionary in "its ability to limn the actual, imagined and possible lives of its speakers, readers, writers" (20). This "word-work" is
"generative," Morrison writes, for "it makes meaning that secures our
difference, our human difference" (22).

Through a narrative that moves from blindness and confrontation
to recognition and dialogue between old and young, Morrison secures
the difference that language makes and demonstrates the necessity
and the difficulty of working through generational differences to discover that living is the work we, young and old, can only do together,
with hands made from words that reach in both directions across generations, across the many differences that divide us. The word-work of
generation draws us into the heart of living language and its power
both to secure difference and to make a shareable world, and thus it
leads us, if we follow its line of flight, to the possibility of collective
identity and collective struggle.

Here the idea of a political generation suggests itself. Unlike a biological age-group (or what sociologists call an age cohort), political
generation refers to the collective subject created at the crossing of social forces and historical events. Constituents of a political generation
are linked by shared social conditions and formative experiences, including experiences organizing for social change, that generate in
them enduring political commitments.[3] The concept of a political generation, then, is a temporal and spatial concept—a "signifying space,"
in Julia Kristeva's view—that allows for both temporal succession and
the parallel existence of different generations in one historical moment (209).[4] Like any concept—for example, and the one most troubling to feminists, "woman"—the concept of a political generation can
only be judged inadequate, that is, if we expect our concepts to provide
the precise summing up, the final word. An alternative view and a
more modest expectation is to see that a given concept places in our
hands particular possibilities and thereby suggests a direction for
thought and action. In this view, the work attempted by the concept of
political generation is to hold together the pieces of collective identity,
to secure difference and yet account for what is shared and shareable.

While my choice of words arises from the way the essays in this volume work on me and from the call issued in Morrison's meditation on
language, it is also compelled by the measure taken of the present moment—an unusual, even an unprecedented, moment—in the history
of feminist movement in the United States. Feminism has existed long
enough, in both popular culture and higher education, to find itself divided not only along the lines policed by commitments to theory and

practice but also along generational lines. Movements for social change, especially those involving a fundamental restructuring of gender, race, or class relations, survive over decades and centuries, and in that time they undergo waxing and waning levels of mobilization characterized by different styles of activism.[5] During the inevitable down times, movement sustains itself through what Verta Taylor calls "abeyance structures"—those organizational forms that provide sites of activism and movement survival when mass protest is not feasible because of a hostile economic and political climate. Academic feminism, which is already a multigenerational endeavor, arguably can be seen as an abeyance structure. It has achieved unprecedented institutional presence and epistemic authority in higher education in a hostile economic climate and a social context shaped by almost thirty years of antifeminist backlash and more than fifteen years of postfeminist complacency. In this context of hostility and apathy, academic feminism has proved to be an important site (but not the only one) for developing the knowledge, resources, and new constituents perhaps for another phase of movement—a multiracial, multiclass, truly heterosexed (including many sexualities) third wave mobilized to end the economic and cultural exploitation of women throughout the world.

The complacency that often attends success does not describe the tenor of relations within feminism today. The present moment is an especially tense one that has generated biting words exchanged among feminists in conflict over the feminisms that will take us into the next historical period.[6] In response to the many feminists who claim, in this volume and elsewhere, that feminism is already in its third wave, I would offer this reminder: the concept of wave refers to a period of mass mobilization that occurs in the midst of ongoing struggle. In the absence of any evidence of the mass mobilization of women on either the national or global scene, it cannot be said with any certainty that a third wave is now taking shape. What can be said with certainty is that in its current usage the concept of wave is in danger of losing an important dimension of meaning, a loss that will effectively mystify the nature of the challenges we face. What can also be said with certainty is that the successful formation of a collective subject largely depends on how we understand and handle conflict. When the conflicts among feminists are reduced simply to matters of theory or method, when they set white feminists against feminists of color, straight feminists against lesbian feminists or queers, something goes unheard. The conflicts in feminism today occur among feminists who came to feminism at different times and in different places and consequently see themselves and feminist struggle quite differently.

It does seem to be much easier (and more expedient) to get our differences in hand, and manage conflict, by mapping the field spatially, naming different structures of oppression, locating points of intersection, and differentiating between different kinds of feminism.[7] This spatializing approach tends to freeze difference in static categories and obscures the fact that our differences are constituted "in time," that how we listen and what we hear—which words we choose, which words choose us—have a lot to do with when and where we come of political age, when and where we enter feminist movement (Logan, this volume). Intersecting histories of gender, race, and class relations provide us with different doors through which we enter feminist movement, and while the formation of political identity depends on "what the doors are, how they are ordered, and how people are supposed to proceed through them" (Desmet, this volume, quoting Elizabeth Spelman), collective struggle does not require that we enter through the same door, at the same time, or in the same way. The task of forging a collective subject capable of making and sustaining mass movement requires a recognition that we also live in "the specific gravity of hours,"[8] an understanding of the historically specific convergences of gender, race, class, and sexuality that give experience its distinct weight and density. In this hour of struggle, the process of peacemaking requires that we find ways of speaking and listening to feminists who have come of political age at different times—at different moments in the history of gender, race, and class relations, at different moments in the history of United States and global feminisms. What will we say to each other? How will I listen? What words will I choose? How will we go on living?

Learning to Measure the Specific Gravity of Difference

Her name was Betty, but she was known as "Blue Betty"—both in the white part of town, where she first acquired this mordant adjective, and across the railroad tracks, in the black neighborhood, where *blue* surely would have signified differently. There is more of this story than I will tell here, but I want to work through one piece of it for reasons that are both pedagogical and political: the story offers material for exploring how the essays in this volume educate my hands to do the word-work of living language. More specifically, it offers a concrete way of "thinking dialectically," as Suzanne Clark terms it in this volume—in this case, reading generational differences and connections dialectically as they take place specifically across the stress points of gender, race, and class. The account of how Betty came to be known as Blue Betty was placed in my hands again and again by my mother and, along with it, an emergent feminist sensibility, for this story was one of the means by which my mother made race and gender the terms of everyday struggle. Yet there is nothing simple about my decision to work with this story here. On the one hand, there is something in the story of Blue Betty that feels like a question, something that will not let me pass, something that calls on me to keep working through rather than taking up the subject position it produced for me and thereby to put into play the complex convergence of differences that have shaped my choices (in this volume, see Caughie; Logan). If, as Pamela Caughie suggests, my pedagogical obligation is to provide students with occasions and strategies for working through certain subject positions, and if my ethical obligation is to put into play the risks that are felt and lived, then I must educate myself first by working theory close to the bone, by asking the question close to home.[9] On the other hand, there is something in this story that feels like a dead thing, "the real thing" I would change a whole history (or update the story to the disco beat of postmodern theory) in order to disavow. Perhaps this is not a story to pass on. Perhaps I should just "let it pass," leave this piece in the dark privacy of personal memory—"baggage," as Lu might say, that could so effortlessly, through a chosen silence, go unclaimed. Caught in the hands of this story, I think I hear the question confronting each generation: How do I know what to pass on, what to let pass, and how to take responsibility for the legacy of the past? How, or to what extent, do I (can I) choose?

In other words: Working through this story here—wording it as my mother did and rewording it with terms offered in this volume—represents a provisional response to feminists of color who have challenged me (and, indeed, all white feminists) to tell the truth and be accountable, to name the enemy within, and to examine the specificities of the role race has played in this white life. Barbara Smith puts the challenge thus: "You can't run the tape backward and start from scratch, so the question is, what are you going to do with what you've got? How are you going to deal responsibly with the unalterable facts of who and what you are, of having or not having privilege and power?" (qtd. in Russo 309). The process of peacemaking requires a thoughtful response to this challenge; it requires responsive listening, or what Leslie Roman calls "a relational politics of dialogue," a politics of "speaking with," which is the necessary antecedent to "speaking for"

(82).[10] It requires that white feminists forgo the privilege of changing the subject once again so that they can "get it right, say the right things, make the right moves" without revealing too much of themselves (see Caughie, this volume). In any response to Smith's challenge, however thoughtful and well-educated, there can be no safety in the words chosen, no refuge—no sheltering harbor and no hiding place—in abstract, dematerialized categories of difference. Indeed, in the very effort to get it right the subject reveals its true colors (Gwaltney 21, 59). For me there is, then, only the intimate and inescapable knowledge that the choice of words—my own, my mother's—is washed in a history of whiteness. This knowledge must recognize and respect what Jarratt calls the difference between the collective "we" and the "I" demanded by personal narrative and must remember that since the personal is first and always political (and therefore transsubjective), personal pronouns may sometimes serve a collective function.

When I was two or three years old, my mother returned to what passes in this society as real work—full-time paid employment outside the home. (She had been doing both paid and unpaid work at home.) My parents were desperate to propel themselves squarely into the middle class, and post–World War II affluence seemed to place that goal within reach. A few weeks before she started her entry-level clerical job, she began to talk to me, to prepare me for the ways my life was going to change. Because I was, in her words, an oversensitive child, she anticipated that I might not handle these changes well. She explained that someone would be coming to our house each day to take care of me. She said the woman's name was Betty, and, she added, Betty was "colored." At the time—the mid-1950s—we lived in a small town in the piney woods of east Texas, which was about as deep into the deeply segregated South as one could go. My mother felt it necessary to remark Betty's difference because, she explained, if I had ever actually seen a colored person, I surely would have forgotten. She was trying to avoid any surprises that might cause a difficult child to become impossible. Today she might say, if she had the language, that she was trying to push back a fear of difference she assumed I would almost naturally possess in a world strictly segregated by the binary of white and other.

In the days before her return to work, my mother asked me periodically who was going to take care of me during the day, which was her way of reminding me of the upcoming change in my routine. From the first time I heard this question I replied, without hesitation, "Blue Betty." Nonplussed by this response, my mother always suggested, by way of explanation, that perhaps blue was the only color I knew at the time, and so I must have figured that "colored" meant blue; or perhaps, she continued, the child's error was just another way of seeing. At this point in her recitation of the story, my mother always paused as if to take the measure of her audience and to flash a knowing smile in my direction. In her account, I was happy and content as I awaited Blue Betty's arrival, and my mother made no effort to educate me, although this was not because she thought it best to leave well enough alone. (It would be years before I held enough pieces of my mother's history to begin to understand her chosen silence.) In my mother's account, Betty was amused when she first heard her name transformed—so much so that from that day on she also called herself Blue Betty.

I have no independent recollection of these events, except a vague memory of Betty and that everyone I knew in that small east Texas town called her Blue Betty, even long after my father moved us north in pursuit of the great American dream of dignity through upward mobility. In the image I hold in memory, Betty has always been a remarkably black woman, a tall and imposing figure whose blackness over the years has become suffused with a deep blue-violet, an indigo mood. As for the origins of her name, I have only the story as my mother told it, and she recited it often, whenever family and friends gathered—for Sunday afternoons, holidays, family reunions, weddings, and funerals—whenever the adults sat around the supper table telling tales that all began "Remember when . . ."[11] When I was a child, I always hung around on the edges of adult talk until this story was told, because it worked the way my mother intended it to work: it nourished the starving girl-child of a father who aggressively denied his daughters the power of naming and the right to choose a vision.[12]

"Narrative is radical," Morrison writes, "creating us at the very moment it is being created" (*Lecture* 27). Uneducated and without the material and symbolic resources that her choices provided me with, my mother possessed what I would now call a tacit understanding of the cultural work that narrative performs. Storytelling, I would come to understand, was her way of mitigating the violence of the Father's (my father's) law, of connecting personal experience to public history, of giving context to my life. It was her way of enacting mercy and creating a measure of justice, because her repeated telling of this story resisted the essentialist forms of sexism and racism she saw around her, in her immediate surroundings, in the faces of friends and family. In the story of Betty's renaming, my mother found an opening in the way gender and race had been narrated in her life, and she used it to make an opening in the way they would be narrated in mine, an opening that suggested the possibility of resignification. In the events recounted in the story, my mother found evidence, and she worked the story as evidence, that racial terms and gender constructions are entirely artificial and arbitrary, that there is nothing natural or obvious about what color means or what it means to be female. That I never seemed to notice, and left unremarked, the fact that Betty was not blue moved her to think of the story as an instrument for disarticulating meaning from pigmentation, anatomy from destiny. She found evidence that race and gender are given meaning through the agency of human beings in concrete social and historical contexts. It was my mother's (certainly all too white and feminine) way of talking back, of interrupting the dominant story, of opening a different door—of creating, as Nedra Reynolds might say, a sense of agency. Through this story, as well as through many others, my mother worked—in barely perceptible and often inarticulate ways—to politicize the context in which I grew up. A bird in the hand, this story was perhaps the first piece in a process she initiated, a process of making white and color, male and female, visible in dynamic relation to each other and in terms of collision and collusion.

Narrative may be radical, interrogative, and visionary, but the story of Blue Betty is so commonplace that perhaps it absorbs all light without refracting it, without producing prismatic knowledge. Perhaps it is truly blue in only one sense—vulgar in its fanciful and sentimental coloring of a cliché, indecent and base in its self-congratulation. How many countless women of color have been reduced, through white rhetorics, to a pair of hands nurturing and sustaining the lives of white others?[13] How do I alibi a name that participates so transparently in a long history linking the power of naming to the unlawful prerogative of the dominant to seize bodies and lives and force displacement to other lands, other locations of meaning and value (see Spillers, "Mamma's Baby"; Huggins 25–56)? Certainly, *blue* may have accurately named the color of an African American woman's pain, the pain of a woman forced by economic necessity to cross into hostile territory to take care of some white woman's pampered child for a meager wage.[14] *Blue* may have accurately named Betty's lived relation to the brutalizing realities of a racist, patriarchal society where postwar affluence made possible the rise of the black bourgeoisie while also successfully maintaining the unequal distribution of economic opportunities along lines of race and gender. *Blue* may even have accurately named my own relation to this story for many years. But there is a world of difference between the blind accuracy of a choice of words and knowing the truths that generate a sense of choice as a cover for racist, sexist, and classist social practices.

This story and the nimbus of emotion surrounding it have changed color many times, beginning in the 1960s with its collision with the social movements of the time. At times, I could not bear to hear the story spoken, would not hear the recitation of what it carried in its words. At times, the story has been a dead thing in my hands, and I wanted no part of it to touch me, wanted to take no responsibility for my ancestry. Yet the story has always had a hold on me, worrying a piece of my mind, and my peace of mind, the way a hunting dog worries the throat of its prey. Sometimes it has been Betty, alias Blue Betty, who has ignited critical moments of (self)discovery (see Morrison, *Playing* viii). But it is neither Blue Betty nor Betty who generates this particular meditation on accountability; it is the white woman who occupies the center of an alible narrative, the white women whose presence blot out the historical and material specificity of women of color. Lately, I have come to see the story in terms suggested by Christy Desmet—as a "judicial moment," one that typically occurs in intergenerational relationships. The easiest exit from this moment is through the finality of an unnuanced judgment of guilt or innocence, condemnation or reprieve—then slam the door and never open it again. Taking this easy exit is, in my view, the prerogative of a whiteness that historically has been a racial category into which people actively place themselves, through choice and struggle, and by dissociating themselves from their ancestors.[15] The more difficult task is to find the doors that shape events, experiences, and the stories we tell and to imagine passage back through them. The obligation is to make judgment an equitable act—an act of mercy that results from an effort to take a measure of the pieces and weigh mitigating circumstances by historicizing them—as well as an act that works through the principle of equivalence to restructure relations of difference by revising existing categories (in this volume, see Desmet; Jarratt).

Yet this application of general principles to specific situations in understanding agency—in other words, the effort to preserve one's goodness and innocence by acting according to principles instead of feeling—has also been read as a performance of whiteness.[16] Thus equity and the mercy it produces must be grounded, not just philosophically but also politically, in the practice of sympathy or, more accurately, empathy, as the first step in a process Desmet calls friendship and I call peacemaking, a process that requires one to see feelingly from another's point of view. If the principle of equivalence is to complete the work of equity by altering the system of doors that defines identity, then it too must find a ground in emotion and tap the revolutionary potential of emotion for disrupting and revising relations of difference, for breaking with the material and cultural practices that historically have given whiteness its supreme and colorless value. The obligation, then, is to see that the doors have an emotional coloration, that they are patterns of feeling—orchestrated in historically specific ways by the categories of gender, race, class, and sexuality—that give an affective shape to experience and the stories we tell. The obligation is not only to understand the role that emotion plays in the formation of identity and the perpetuation of oppression but also to seize emotion's potential for making collective struggle. To break with white supremacy as an epistemological standpoint requires an affective standpoint that transmutes feminist guilt, shame, defensiveness, and anger into the kind of outrage that makes change.[17] It requires that I move from seeing blue to seeing red.

If I return to the story of Blue Betty with this obligation in hand, I have to return to the 1950s and 1960s and the polite but aggressively racist and patriarchal context in which my mother told the story. I have to go South, to that region where, as James Baldwin observes, "segregation has worked brilliantly. . . . [It] has allowed white people, with scarcely any pangs of conscience whatever to create, in every generation, only the Negro they wished to see" (qtd. in Goldfield 13).[18] I have to return to the familiar and estranging rules and customs of a racialized southern etiquette that has rendered whites certain of their superior knowledge and yet willfully unknowing, a code of gesture and conduct that has rendered blacks invisible but for a staged identity and whites ignorant of how blacks see them (see Goldfield 1–23; hooks, *Black Looks* 165–78). I have to situate myself somewhere within that system of control that has placed in white hands the power to choose the nature of the contact to be established between white and black—regardless of whether those hands were calloused by hard labor or spongy soft from living entirely at the expense of others. I have to pass through the prevailing white (and southern) belief in benign race relations, which has veiled blackness in happy faces and washed whiteness with innocence and benevolence. I have to move into the orbit of experience in which whiteness is and has been, as bell hooks says, the terrible, the terrifying, and the terrorizing—or, if not terrorizing in every case, then certainly the cause of a pervasive uneasiness, a tense awareness that a wrong word or gesture could have serious consequences (hooks 165–78; Goldfield 7). I have to see myself—white person, white woman, white feminist—as the legitimate heir to generations of mordacious rage, righteous bitterness, and weary hatred produced by generations that have refused to recognize and respect difference and thereby denied the existence of others. I have to see that white is the primary color, the source, of human misery in the world (see hooks 11; Morrison, *Beloved* 89).

I also have to relinquish a hard-won measure of economic possibility and find myself backed into a corner by a convergence of terror, shame, and self-loathing wrought by sexism and poverty, a corner (and also a door) that made marriage not only an economic necessity for many women, including many white women, but also a specific way (especially when joined to motherhood) white women have enacted racial solidarity with white men.[19] I have to know what I was never supposed to know: Being born female—in any time and place—means being born into a status created by white men's hatred of and contempt for women. Knowing this, Marilyn Frye warns, is not enough. Although history produces many different ways of articulating race and gender, learning whiteness (regardless of one's skin color) has functioned as a way for a girl-woman "to lever herself up out of a kind of nonbeing (the status of woman in a male supremacist social order) over into a kind of Being (the status of white in a white supremacist social order)" ("Woman" 160). As Frye points out, racism translates the desire for Being—that is, full status as an economic and political agent—into the aspiration to whiteness. Thus whiteness, which does not save white women from the condition of women in a patriarchal social order, presents the key obstacle to their forming necessary connections with women of color. I have to see whiteness as a history and politics of loneliness—not a loneliness that knows the absence of other people but a loneliness so profound that, in refusing to recognize and respect difference, it has never truly admitted the possibility of other people, of people whose difference is not construed as a threat or as an excuse for exploitation.[20]

A history and politics of loneliness: for my mother, the story of Blue Betty was finally a story for and about her daughter, and this fact alone makes it a blue-eyed story for a blue-eyed world, a world in which white people learn to expect that they (their issues, perspectives, problems) take center stage.[21] It is a story that cast me in the role of an innocent in a corrupt world, the color-blind child whose ignorance is recast as superior knowledge, the daughter of an unruly woman who never was quite so unknowingly white that she could not question the system of privilege set up by racial and gendered structures but who nevertheless remained blind to the material differences that make color the suffering of white.[22] Because whiteness remains, in my mother's telling of the story and thus in its early, formative effect on me, a figure of wisdom, innocence, and goodness, the story must be heard in a way my mother did not consciously intend—as a racist story, one that perpetuates as surely as it resists white supremacy. Although she tried to work race and gender together in this story to render both open to resignification, there is an important sense in which it also put race at the service of gender and color at the service of whiteness. Working through this piece of meaning makes both of us, my mother and me, the exploitative white mistresses using a black woman to do our work for us (Caughie, this volume). Blue Betty may have made Betty visible as more than a pair of hands doing the physical labor my mother could choose not to do (see hooks, *Black Looks* 168). But the figure that does not exist in my mother's telling is Betty herself, or, rather, Betty exists only as an exoticized figure, a trope that dematerializes the black female body and affirms the power and presence of "female" and the wisdom of "white." Doing the cultural work my mother could not do without Blue Betty's helping hand, the story (along with others like it) has worked to place me in the category of white and helped confer on my white life a sense of identity, agency, and privilege, and thus it begs to be read in the strongest terms Morrison offers—as yet another instance of the "unabated power of a white woman gathering identity unto herself from the wholly available and serviceable lives of Africanist others" (*Playing* 25). Beyond the blue-eyed narrative and its unlawful prerogative, there is Betty: the unconsulted, appropriated ground that secures, materially and emotionally, this white woman's life.

The violence enacted through this blue-eyed story is beyond measure, for it gives no access to Betty's very different, very particularized reality. The violence continues to be enacted, in other words, as long as Betty remains a silent, speechless figure in a white fantasy. If I am to keep working through what has been placed in my hands, then I have to find Betty in the story and revise it by listening for a silence that also speaks. I have to recenter the story on the one who secures my existence, on the generations that have sustained white lives (Frankenberg 1–22). The only significant details for me to work with are Betty's apparent amusement and her adoption of the qualifier added to her name. What generated her choice of word and feeling? Did her amusement cover a tense awareness of the weight of every word and gesture? Can terror also smile? Were these the gestures of a staged identity required by southern racial etiquette, the signs of apparent deference, compliance, and conformity to the official story of benign race relations—that is to say, evidence of the black woman's shrewd self-interest, in which she only appears to reinforce the hegemonic story while working it to her advantage, making the white woman her unknowing instrument? The creation of a disguise depends, after all, on a firm grasp of the codes of meaning that are being manipulated and resisted. Did not Betty's choice of word and feeling also control the meaning and function of the story, the nature of the contact established between black woman and white? Could her posture of deference have been less apparent than real? Was it the mark of good will and noble character; was her choice of word and feeling an affirmation—not of whiteness but of Betty's own African and African American roots? Africans forced into slavery in America were people of manners, and the white southern way of life—its language, code of conduct, manners, religion, food, music, and patterns of work—is, according to William Piersen, much more a product of Africans (some of whom were the only true nobility in antebellum America) and African Americans than European Americans and the social stratification imposed by racism. The hands that were so cruelly exploited to tend generations of white children, as W. J. Cash comments, also educated and influenced "every gesture, every word, every emotion and idea, every attitude" of those generations (qtd. in Fishkin 439). Is there a way to revise the story of Blue Betty to make it less a white fantasy of female bonding across racial (and generational) lines and more nearly a long overdue acknowledgment of Betty's influence, a recognition that the South (indeed American culture as a whole) has always been multicultural—or, in Albert Murray's words, "incontestably mulatto" (qtd. in Fishkin 454)?

What finally complicates the story of Blue Betty is that my maternal heritage is mixed—Scots-Irish and Native American. The latter my mother did not disclose to me until I was an adolescent, and then only after I found, secreted among her belongings, a tobacco-colored photograph (circa 1890). This photograph was disappeared after my mother's death—no doubt to justify the margins of an unlawful history and assuage the anxiety created by evidence of a woman passing. Still, I recall in vivid detail the dark-skinned, dark-haired woman, a maternal grandmother, sitting on the front porch of a ramshackle house. She was wearing work clothes and a man's black fedora. A shotgun lay across her lap. Her jaw was set in a fierce certainty that was already familiar to me even then; she was not smiling. Nor was my mother smiling when I presented the photograph and asked for the true story that would fill a baffling silence. But she had only a couple of lines of information, which never generated a narrative, no matter how often I pressed for more. She simply did not know. In the image of this grandmother, in an image I can only hold in memory now, I see the nameless woman whose lineage was first whited out by the father's hand and whose unsmiling presence haunted my mother's life (and questions my own), a mute reminder of the collision within—between the raced other and the racist other. What made my mother keep the photograph, if not a fugitive desire to articulate, to pronounce and link, her life to this ancestor? What made her choose silence, even in the face of a fierce certainty that knows when you kill the ancestor, you kill yourself?[23] I want to know this grandmother's story and place it alongside mine. I want to see my mother and myself in the picture, sitting beside her, forming what Jarratt might call an embodied metonymy, a side-by-side relation of association and alliance. I want to see the life of this "no name woman" branching into mine.[24] Is my desire merely to reclaim the (racialized) maternal body that, Caughie warns, is not a feminist project? Or is it a belated effort to reclaim the many pieces of a complex history and a hybrid identity and revise the story once again, but this time seeing that white is a color and that racism is every white person's ancestry?

I know I cannot choose one ancestor without claiming all. There is certainly no justice in such a choice, and very little mercy. I must choose to see my mother's life, in all its narrative particularity, branching into mine. What I have most immediately is her chosen silence and her choice words, and also the sense that in her experience, much differently than in mine, "white" was always an unstable term and a precarious occupation, never simply an unmarked ground. Never so middle-class or color-blind as to think the problem had no name, she passed—both with and without the "as"—living the collision of discrepancies that occur at the crossing place of being female in a male-supremacist regime of value, being not-quite-white in a white-supremacist social order, and being always unutterably poor regardless of her thoroughly practiced middle-class pretensions. Never coming to terms with the fragility of her identity, never resolving into a coherent whole the pieces of her self, she lived the double bind, lived the collision and the collusion of subject positions without trying to reclaim the humanist subject she never possessed as her first place, as her home. Class and race were the doors through which she passed on her way to a political understanding of gender, with the bone-crushing experience of poverty shaping every fiber of her life and in ways that directly, but more inaccessibly, branch into my middle-class security.[25] Because poverty so framed her existence—conspiring with sexism and racism to filter every nuance of experience through feelings of inadequacy, worthlessness, shame, and terror (not of being exposed as a fraud but of being put out of doors)—her lived experience of class position, which for her was "the real thing," served also as a set of blinders that did not allow her to see more clearly the dynamic interdependence of gender, class, and race that her choices ultimately have made possible for me. She claimed, because she could claim, the privilege of linking her life—her material survival and her symbolic value—to the race privilege of her poor white father and the race and class privilege of her husband, both of whom made their unlawful claim to bodies and lives by seizing the power to define who is white and woman and who is not and who may claim legitimate, beloved standing in the world (see Jordan). My mother knew that race is a social and political classification, that white is a category into which people place themselves. Knowing what she knew, she never rejected the privilege of white skin, knowing only too well, and trading on the fact, that one is not born but, rather, becomes a white woman. This was never a simple or unself-conscious choice. I believe the specter of poverty that always haunted her life made her choose, again and again, to cast her lot with white men.

Narrative is radical, especially when commonplace, for it is in the interstices of the everyday that identity and experience are produced. Because the story of Blue Betty figured so early and for many years in the construction of identity and experience, working through this narrative has seemed to be one small way of dealing responsibly with the inalterable facts of what has made me who and what I am: a white woman feminist whose political consciousness has been shaped at a particular moment in the history of capitalism, patriarchy, and white supremacy. Given the history of race relations in the United States, perhaps Marilyn Frye is right in her conclusion that there is only one correct line at this time on the matter of racism, that a white person "must never claim not to be a racist, but only to be an anti-racist" ("Being" 126).[26] If the lesson to be learned from my mother's life, from a history of choices and their consequences, is that one is not born but becomes a white woman, then my choice is clear but in no way easy: to unbecome white—to work to end white supremacy through an interrogation of whiteness and an articulation of antiracist forms of whiteness.

Moving beyond the Politics of Loneliness

A political understanding of the world, or of any part of it, does not happen all at once. The light comes on by degrees, intensified by moments when the turning is more fundamentally transformative than at other moments. The process that tries to piece these moments together is not smooth, linear, or evolutionary; it is uneven, dialectical, and riddled. The process is hardly guaranteed by having the "best" (political) intentions or the "correct" theory (or body) in hand. Myriad factors (personal and impersonal, theoretical and practical) influence and determine what, when, and how we know. We do not see things that are right before our eyes; we know things before we know them; we forget, if only momentarily, other things as we try to hold together all the pieces of a hard-won knowledge. And typically the blood simmers or boils at various times and with varying degrees of insight and apprehension. My point here is simply this: The development of political consciousness—in an individual, a discipline, or a social movement—is always a process, an ongoing, painstaking, transgenerational process of two steps forward, one step back, three stumbling steps sideways into the nearest ditch. Even when there are no barriers erected between generosity and wisdom, many hands are needed to pull any one of us from the mire and to support the development of political consciousness and commitment to social change over time. If collective identity is about seeing oneself as part of a group and if the task at hand is to forge a collective subject capable of making and sustaining a third wave—a multiracial, multiclass, multigenerational, heterosexed mass movement to end the economic and cultural exploitation of all women—then how will we negotiate the many conflicts that inevitably emerge at the crossing of subjects and processes?

In an essay that touches on generational politics in academic feminism, Alice Jardine identifies three generations of women professors in the United States academy, only two of which are explicitly political feminist generations: those who received their degrees before 1968, between 1968 and 1978, and after 1978. Because it was difficult if not impossible for women professors to undertake explicitly political feminist research and scholarship before 1968, the first academic generation is not a political generation. Each of the two post-1968 generations has developed its own style of explicitly feminist research and scholarship. In Jardine's view, what is more important than the concept of generation for understanding the political problems facing feminists is "the question of one's discursive, political positioning vis-à-vis the women's liberation movement" (76–77). In an endnote, she writes, "There are today, for example, women across all the generations in the academy who do 'feminist this and that' but maintain no historical or current political relationship to the women's [liberation] movement" (84). The problems (and conflicts) facing academic feminists, in other words, occur at the crossing (and, I would add, the often crossed purposes, investments, and interests) of the professional, the political, and the personal.

However we may number the generations of explicitly political academic feminists, those of us who come to feminism through the door of the academy will understand ourselves as feminists, and understand feminism, differently from those who enter through other doors. For this reason, I depart from Jardine's otherwise insightful commentary to suggest that one's relation to the women's liberation movement or to mass-based feminist movement in general (in the US and globally) is an important element shaping the identity of a political generation and its articulation and negotiation of conflicts. On the one hand, I want to say that academic feminists who have no historical or current relation to feminist movement are not less political, in any necessary or absolute sense, than those feminists who maintain that connection. At the very least, those of us who come to political age in the academy and make classroom practice and academic publication the exclusive sites of activism understand the political differently from nonacademics—in terms complicated and fully contained by what passes in the academy as professional achievement and service.[27] On the other hand, I have to say that there are political consequences for those of us who "do" feminism in ways that form no explicit relation to feminist movement, consequences for women in whose name feminism moves.

For instance, we may not grasp how limited is the role academic feminism plays as an abeyance structure that in twenty years has become a relatively safe harbor, insulated in many ways from a persistently hostile social and economic climate. With our energies consumed in the day-to-day demands of teaching and service, with our attention focused on the pitched battles in feminist theory, we may misrecognize the true sources of hostility and mistake the institutional changes we have made in higher education, most of which have been only cosmetic, for the revolution itself. Undertaking explicitly political teaching and research but doing so in ways that are strangely cut off from the long history of movements for fundamental social change, we may lose a sense of the primary context of relevance for oppositional knowledge. Many of us may believe, for example, that we are actively resisting the gender genocide taking place around the world through our latest research article presented at an annual professional conference (see Jordan). We who try our luck here—in the college classroom or the academic publication—work a particular corner of the world, a corner that is not especially important to the overwhelming majority of women throughout the world. This does not mean that an academic feminism or a feminist composition studies that maintains no relation to an international feminist movement is entirely irrelevant, simply recuperative, or utterly domesticated. On the contrary. But a sober recognition of our exclusive address should add a few qualifications to the claims we make about what we do, qualifications that apply equally to any feminist color one may choose to fly— from red feminism (Marxist) and pink feminisms (socialist and postmodern), which claim one end of the political spectrum, to blue-eyed cultural femininisms, which typically get placed at the other end (in this volume, see Hesford; Kelsh; Schell). Most important, when we are cut off from feminism's social and historical context and caught in the crossing of the professional, the political, and the personal, we may unwittingly work against (or simply fail to work toward) the formation of a collective subject capable of making and sustaining a third wave of feminist movement.

This last concern is of particular interest, because it leads to what I think is perhaps the central problem in academic feminism—its politics of loneliness—and this problem returns us to peacemaking as that process of recognizing and accepting difference that is so necessary for collective struggle.[28] In the last years of the last decade of the twentieth century, feminism for many feminists names first an academic subject matter to be mastered, a course or curriculum of study (something to know)—in other words, a badge that certifies specialized knowledge and abilities, including a sense of critical agency and textual activism (something to do). The point to emphasize here is that once feminism becomes a means by which the scholar and teacher achieves individual recognition and distinction, the political has crossed into the professional, and the professional is always in danger of double-crossing the political. This crossing of the political and professional is rendered by the hands of society, which sets up a scheme of racialized and gendered values, sorts us into classes, and doles out recognition, respect, and reward to individuals according to the acquisition of knowledge and abilities that demonstrate personal worth. The political-professional thus becomes fully personalized. Higher education fits into this social order as a hand into a perfectly sized glove; it engineers a form of consciousness in which the individual standing out from the masses is the exemplar of human worth and dignity, and thereby it pits one individual against another in a dynamic of competition calibrated ultimately to secure hegemony for white and male. In the present economy of scarcity, scarcity both material and symbolic, there is little support for one to see oneself as part of a group, especially a politicized group that not only questions the legitimacy of this structure of value but also plots its end.[29]

Academic feminism inevitably finds itself in a relation of collusion with the very system it opposes when its primary function is to confer distinction on individual scholars and teachers and on disciplines like composition studies. It is significant that composition studies began to develop a feminist analysis of language and writing belatedly—only after feminism had produced an extensive body of knowledge and acquired unprecedented prestige in the academy. In composition, explicitly feminist political research and scholarship became possible in the late 1980s and on the heels of the more generalized turn to politics and history in literary and cultural studies. The timing of composition's turn to feminism should give us pause rather than offer an occasion for self-congratulation. Because the field of composition studies is already deeply marked by (and invested in) issues of recognition and legitimacy, conflicts between feminists there are likely to be especially vehement or else show a vacant tolerance, neither of which alternatives will invite the kind of engagement with difference necessary to forge a collective subject. In any case, nailing one's feminist colors to the mast at this point may work more effectively to claim distinction for the individual and for the individual discipline than to move struggle outside the academy and into the streets.

The successes of academic feminism, in short, render visible the way in which it is inevitably caught in the machinery of the racialized and gendered class politics that structure social relations in the academy as well as in United States society at large. Reclaiming the maternal body and the maternal plot line may not be feminist projects, but at the crossing of the professional, the political, and the personal, academic feminists nonetheless labor to reproduce the social relations of what is at base a class society (in this volume, see Caughie; Schell; Kelsh). This contradiction is particularly apparent in the way generational conflicts typically take shape. As Jardine writes from her feminist psychoanalytic perspective, "Accusations fly about on both sides as to who is really feminist or not; who has been recuperated or not; who is just miming the masters (is it the often more history-minded mothers or the more theory-minded daughters?); whose fault it is that there is a general perception that feminism has become facile, tamed while, precisely, the humanities are being feminized" (77). In Jardine's view, this familial psychodrama—specifically, the oedipalization of the mother-daughter relationship—is unavoidable, given the material and symbolic power that feminists (both "mothers" and "daughters") wield over one another, given the structures of debt and gift and the demand for recognition that organizes intergenerational relationships in a predominantly white, patriarchal academy. The question here is not whether "good" feminists should compete with one another or differ, aggressively or politely, over substantive issues (see Jarratt, "Feminism"; Miner and Longino). The question is whose interests are served by the way we choose to handle our conflicts.

Reframed in the terms of class analysis, this psychodrama represents an instance of the way class conflict is internalized and played out as a conflict between individuals who locate themselves in different generations as different signifying spaces. In an effort to validate ourselves as individuals by demonstrating our distinctive knowledge and abilities, we engage in an aggressive competition for recognition and deploy a narrative of supersession in which one generation (often understood as one wave) constructs its identity through biting words that excoriate another. For example, claims about a third wave are typically grounded in the following assessment of feminism's recent history: Second-wave feminism, which ended more than twenty years ago, was overwhelmingly middle-class and therefore elitist, white and therefore racist, heterosexual and therefore homophobic. It was too focused on gender and consequently excluded women for whom gender was not the primary category of difference that structured their oppression. Its analysis of sexual politics was misguided and alienating because it too vehemently named men (of every race and class) the enemy. Its politics were never radical enough, which made the slide into reformism all too predictable. This narrative carries a measure of truth, to be sure, but it also offers an overly narrow view of the second wave and the nature of the challenges feminists have faced. At the very least, it forgets the many second-wave feminists who have been explicitly, albeit imperfectly, antiracist, antiheterosexist, antielitist, and anti-imperialist.

Supersession is only one way to articulate a relation to one's ancestors. And it may well be a way that is washed in whiteness and gendered masculine, a way that is arrogantly classist in its intellectual elitism.[30] Supersession may be a choice driven by the interests of the ruling scheme of racialized and gendered values, which pits each of us against the other for tokens of recognition. That scheme distracts us from the true sources of injury to human dignity and worth and enlists us to work against the formation of a collective subject. Supersession is a choice driven by the tropologic of metaphor and synecdoche, in that one part, one moment in the history of feminist movement seeks to represent the whole.[31] In its effort to set aside feminist texts, theories, or practices as useless, obsolete, misguided, or pernicious—to expose the blindness of one feminism and the fraudulence of another—supersession follows the logic of substitution and fails to accept that differences in political perspective are constituted in time. If the desire of supersession is to break absolutely with feminism's past, then it is proudly ignorant of the fact that we always live, actively, in configurations of the past. Seduced by the rhetorical power of supersession, we mistake the goal of feminism—to be itself superseded in the eclipse of white-supremacist, patriarchal social relations—for the means to achieve that goal. In short, when conflict and the way we handle it erect impassable barriers between feminists, barriers between generosity and wisdom, *generation* (or *wave*) becomes an efficient instrument for achieving what Laura Brady calls "the reproduction of othering," and feminism becomes a politics of loneliness.

The challenge for feminists is to realize that connections and conflicts across generational lines are, as Nancy Whittier observes, one of the most important forces directing feminism's course. The challenge for each new generation of feminists is to keep working feminist terms, texts, theories, and figures, to keep working through the stories we tell about who we are and who we were. Because modes of intergenerational relationship vary from time to time and across race, class, and gender lines, perhaps one way to work across the many lines that divide us is to listen to how those who are other than ourselves articulate their relationships to their ancestors. Perhaps in this way we can learn to link the survival of each to the living memory of all.

This, then, is what the essays collected here suggest: a way of doing feminism that seeks to hold in living memory the specific historical forces that have shaped feminist statements, making certain words necessary for one generation and other words possible for another; a way of doing feminist work that is tough-minded because self-critical, politically courageous because engaged with multiple differences, and generous to prior selves, to different generations of feminists.[32] Without whom, nothing. To move forward for the sake of all women, especially for those women at whose expense any one of us lives, we need the help of all "the raging stoic grandmothers,"[33] living and dead, black and white and brown and blue and red, whose words may not be the words I would choose or the words I want to hear, but they steady the course and help us bear the weight of too much history. If there are words we cannot choose again (and these words will vary from time to time), then there are still other words to choose that speak their truth with a sense of history, with gratitude for what the raging, stoic grandmothers made possible in their time and place, and without bitterness for what they could not, would not see—merciful words that take no shortcuts through anyone's storied experience.

NOTES

[1]Throughout this essay, I have not used the definite article *the* when referring to feminist movement, except when the reference is to the women's liberation movement of the late 1960s and early 1970s. This omission, a common practice in feminist scholarship, is meant to emphasize the fact that feminist movement is a process—global, multifaceted, and multigenerational—and that this ongoing process has endured over centuries. In my view, the definite article should be used to refer to a specific time, place, and practice of feminism.

[2]Along with the obvious reference to the closed fist of logic and the open hand of rhetoric, the reference here is to the symbol for the women's liberation movement and second-wave feminism, featured on the cover of Robin Morgan's *Sisterhood Is Powerful*: a closed fist inside the symbol for woman. In suggesting the symbol of an open hand for the third wave, I do not want to deny the lasting vitality of the metaphor of sisterhood, which feminists in the women's liberation movement understood as a symbol of unity that encompassed all women and still acknowledged their diversity (see Vogel 2).

[3]Although the idea of generational difference dates back to Homer, Plato, and Aristotle, Karl Mannheim was the first to formulate the concept of a political generation. The literature on political generations is extensive. Nancy Whittier offers an excellent bibliography in her study of generational differences in feminism at the local level of Columbus, Ohio. See also Zook on generational differences in black feminist movement.

[4]As Whittier explains, women's experiences in the New Left and civil rights movements generated several microcohorts in the late 1960s that worked together to form the women's liberation movement. Some of these microcohorts coalesced into one political generation; others formed another. Contemporaneous divisions among microcohorts or between political generations led to conflicts in the movement.

[5]The literature on social movements is vast but quite useful in understanding the social context of academic feminism. For more discussion of the women's movement from various theoretical perspectives on social movements, see Ryan; Taylor; Whittier. For discussion of social movement theory, see S. Lyman; Cohen; Offe.

[6]Not that conflict is something new for feminists. Even in the early years of the second wave, the women's liberation movement, which distinguished itself from the liberal feminists of NOW, was a highly divided, deeply factionalized movement. For accounts of the many conflicts in the early second wave, see Echols; Ryan. The literature on the conflicts in academic feminism is extensive. See Hirsch and Keller; Landry and MacLean; Weisser and Fleischner. For

explorations of the conflicts between white and black feminists, see Joseph and Lewis; Caraway; Golden and Shreve; Moraga and Anzaldúa.

[7]Flynn's review essay on feminism and composition is one such effort. She gives us "working definitions of selected feminisms"—liberal feminism, radical feminism, cultural feminism, and postmodern feminism—that form what she calls a "common vocabulary" for evaluating feminist work in composition studies ("Review" 202). But the problem of course is that this admittedly selective vocabulary leaves too much out—for example, materialist feminisms that would include Marxist feminism (represented in this volume by Kelsh) and socialist feminism (represented by Schell) in its genealogy.

[8]"Between the tension of these actual walls / We live, and the specific gravity of hours." These words are from May Sarton's poem "Intimation" in *Letters from Maine*. Although the poem does not explicitly deal with the politics of race, class, gender, and sexuality, these lines suggest to me the complex relationality that shapes our social and political lives, a relationality that is both spatial (organized by the "walls" of gender, race, class, and sexuality) and temporal or historical (suggested in the figure of "specific gravity of hours").

[9]In taking the position of a student in relation to the essays in this volume, I hope to emphasize two related efforts: One, I want to break with what I understand is the obligation of the genre of the afterword—to provide an authoritative summing up and concluding judgment of what precedes it. I want to emphasize, in other words, the sense of process to which this volume is committed. Two, I want to self-consciously work against the racialized context in which I also write and break with a white rhetoric that arrogantly assumes the right to speak and teach rather than listen and learn.

[10]See Caughie in this volume for more on the politics of speaking for. Compare with Ebert, who makes a strong case against the kind of dialogue and conversation espoused in various poststructuralist (feminist) discourses. She suggests that pluralism, multiculturalism, and multiplicity have been deployed to silence and suppress a "radical diversity," by which she means class antagonism and class conflict. In *Ludic Feminism and After*, she writes: "The dialogical, in short, masquerades as openness, but it is, in fact, a restricted, closed space in which the dominant frames of intelligibility . . . violently exclude not only oppositional knowledges but also suppress the 'real' material relations of exploitation" (44). Although I agree with her assessment of the dangers of dialogue, I also think feminists abandon the ideal of dialogue at their peril.

[11]Over the years, I asked my mother about this story, among others, and what she intended in its repeated telling. I wanted to check my understanding of her intention against hers. Although the terms in which I have represented her meaning are my own—she did not know the scholarship that would help her choose her words—I have tried to stay within the circle of her thought and its limitations.

[12]The research, writing, and revising of this essay took place during my father's final suffering of terminal cancer. It is deeply marked by the experience of this loss but, regrettably, it cannot convey any nuanced sense of the complexity of his story or of my relation to him.

[13]For discussion of the representation of black women as mother and mammy, see Caughie in this volume; Collins; Christian; hooks, "Black Women Intellectuals"; C. Johnson; T. Harris; Piersen.

[14]In 1950, 42% of black women were employed in domestic service, a decline of 18% since 1940 (Giddings 240–41). This decline is largely attributable to black men and women entering professional and semiprofessional jobs. To my knowledge, Betty always worked as a domestic.

[15]Roediger provides an illuminating discussion of the dramatic and complex process of becoming white. Irish immigrants, for example, made the transition from Irish in America to Irish Americans to white Americans. In this process, white ethnics become less specifically ethnic, not only by seeking assimilation into the category of American but also by choosing to disaffiliate with nonwhite or not-yet-white traditions and heritage. See especially 182–98.

[16]Among the many studies that detail the elements of what I call white rhetorics are Frye, "Being" and "Woman"; Frankenberg; Roediger; Gwaltney; Dyer; Ross; Keating; Fishkin.

[17]Here I am articulating two lines of thought: One, I am following hooks's suggestion that antiracist whites break with white supremacy as an epistemological standpoint by which we come to know the world and that they love blackness without assuming the role of cultural tourist (*Black Looks* 9–20). Two, I am suggesting a way to reinvigorate and extend the life of the concept of a feminist standpoint by developing the notion of an affective standpoint. In these efforts, feminist theory on the political uses of emotion has been enormously helpful to me. See Russo; Spelman, "Anger"; P. Lyman; Fisher; Bartky.

[18]Here I do not mean to suggest this process of misrecognition and projection is a phenomenon of the past. Given the fact that, as Frankenberg suggests, a color-and-power-evasive discourse of race prevails in white society, whites still create only the black faces they wish to see. My use of the past tense here is intended to try to historicize this process of misrecognition and projection.

[19]In the 1950s, half the adult poor were women, with women of color constituting a disproportionate percentage of this population. By the late 1970s—at the time that my mother decided (for the last time) she would not divorce my father but would rather die (literally) than follow large numbers of (white, middle-class, divorced) women into poverty—women constituted two-thirds of the adult poor. See F. Davis 332–36. My mother died in 1979.

[20]My thinking on whiteness as a politics of loneliness has been shaped specifically by Benjamin's psychopolitical theory of recognition, which argues that a sense of self is socially and intersubjectively produced (*Bonds*); by Sennett and Cobb's exposition of the way the internalization of class conflict pits one individual against another; and by Morrison's fiction, which can be read as a sustained meditation on the politics (i.e., the racialization) of loneliness. *Sula*, for example, differentiates between two kinds of loneliness: a loneliness that knows the absence of other people and a loneliness so profound, the word has no meaning—a solitude that does not admit the possibility of other people (123).

[21]"The ever-loving blue-eyed world," Christine Ammer explains, is the cartoonist Walt Kelly's way of saying, through his opossum, Pogo, that the world is basically a good place (56). Noted for the habit of feigning death when in danger, opossums also have poor eyesight. Because of these attributes (the ability to go blind, deaf, and dumb when cornered), I would suggest the opossum as an emblem of whiteness—that is, if it did not do this benign creature an injustice.

[22]See Omi and Winant's excellent study of racial formation in the United States. Their research provides the critical race theory from which I am working. See also Frankenberg's study of the social construction of whiteness, which is based on Omi and Winant's work and has been enormously helpful to me in thinking through race. Frankenberg identifies three moments in the history of discourses on race difference: (1) before the 1920s, a discourse of essentialist racism, which speaks of biological inequality; (2) from the 1920s to the 1960s, a discourse of essential sameness, which is both color-evasive (color-blind) and power-evasive; (3) since the 1960s, a race-cognizant discourse articulated by people of color. As Frankenberg observes, color- and power-evasive discourse replaced essentialist racism and remains dominant today, although it has incorporated some elements of race-cognizant discourse. Echoing Logan's sobering observation in this volume that multiculturalism is not as revolutionary as it may appear, Frankenberg suggests that too many versions of multiculturalism remain power-evasive. She concludes: "One can, in fact, argue that struggles between power evasion and race cognizance are being fought on the terrain of multiculturalism" (15).

[23]The way women of color have treated the importance of the ancestor greatly influenced my thinking about the way white people (white feminists) articulate a relationship to their ancestors. See especially Morrison's "Rootedness," where she states that when African Americans do not keep in touch with the ancestor, they are lost (344).

[24]"Unless I see her life branching into mine, she gives me no ancestral help," writes Kingston in the first story of *The Woman Warrior*, which is entitled "No Name Woman" (8).

[25]An example of the kind of poverty that cuts deeply into a life: My mother managed to graduate from what we would now call high school, but throughout her primary and secondary education she attended school only on every third day. There were three girls in her family who shared one pair of shoes. Her brother went to school every day.

[26]Although any analogy between sexism and racism is dangerous, I would extend Frye's conclusion to men, especially left-leaning white men who, unlike too many movement men of the 1960s, identify as feminists and see themselves as key architects of feminist theory. In other words, perhaps men should not claim to be feminists and thereby claim, implicitly or explicitly, that they are not sexist. Perhaps they should claim only to be antisexist. Recent efforts in feminist theory, which focus on the structural and institutional forms of sexism and abandon the kind of analysis of sexual politics undertaken by early second-wave feminists (Millett; Firestone; Morgan), have made

it easy for many men to think sexism is some other man's problem or a problem with institutions rather than every man's problem. Just as race does not apply only to people of color, just as racism is a white issue and white people's problem, men still have the obligation to address sexism in their own lives in an ongoing process of self-critique that names the enemy within.

[27]The use of the plural pronoun in this paragraph is troublesome to me, for the I who chooses to use it here does not see herself in the we to which it refers. In other words, my political consciousness was not shaped exclusively or firstly in the academy. In an effort to avoid the supercilious rhetoric of "us" and "them," I use "we" here to insist on the possibility of a collective subject that recognizes and accepts the differences included in "we."

[28]For many years, feminists of color have remarked on what I call a politics of loneliness in white (academic) feminism, saying that white feminists simply do not know what they are missing in having no knowledge of or association with women of color. See, for example, B. Smith, "Criticism" and "Racism."

[29]In an especially useful analysis of the emotional meaning of "class"—in other words, of the ways in which class conflict is internalized (and personalized)—Richard Sennett and Jonathan Cobb argue that the pervasive discontent created in a capitalist social order maintains inequality. More specifically, they argue that the ideology of competitive individualism, fired by pervasive discontent, leads us to turn on one another rather than on the system; hence it is difficult for the left to organize and mobilize the discontented for fundamental social change.

[30]Research on gender differences in intergenerational relationships (see Schneider; Steinem) suggests that women and men experience (biological) generational succession differently. Through their children women experience succession as an extension of themselves, whereas men tend to understand succession in terms of displacement. The model of biological generational succession has dominated research on political generations and the role of intergenerational conflict in the formation of revolutionary agents. See Mullaney's discussion of the inappropriateness of the male model for revolutionary women (243–65).

[31]See Worsham, "Appendicitis," which develops a feminist reading practice from the tropologic use of metonymy. See also Worsham, "Reading Wild," which examines synecdoche and the violence of interpretation.

[32]Rich's essay "Notes toward a Politics of Location" shows how one feminist, a veteran of the second wave, undertakes this work. In her effort to work from one concept of experience (experience as the ground and foundation of knowledge) to a different concept (experience as something that must be interpreted), I see the difference that generation makes. The first concept's constant reassertion suggests to me how difficult it is for one to escape one's historical formation.

[33]The "raging stoic grandmothers" is from Rich's poem entitled "Natural Resources" in *The Dream of a Common Language* (66).

Contributors

Laura Brady, associate professor at West Virginia University, teaches composition and women's studies. Her publications include articles in *Writing on the Edge*, *Computers and Composition*, and *Journal of Business and Technical Communication*. She is an associate editor for *Women and Language*.

Pamela L. Caughie, associate professor of English, teaches twentieth-century literature and theory, feminist theory, and cultural studies at Loyola University, Chicago. She is currently completing *Passing and Pedagogy: The Dynamics of Responsibility*, to be published by University of Illinois Press. Essays from this work appear in *College English*, *PMLA*, and *English Studies / Culture Studies*, ed. Isaiah Smithson and Nancy Ruff (Urbana: U of Illinois P, 1994). She is author of *Virginia Woolf and Postmodernism* (Urbana: U of Illinois P, 1991).

Suzanne Clark, associate professor of English at the University of Oregon, has written about women, rhetoric, teaching, and modernism. She is author of *Sentimental Modernism: Women Writers and the Revolution of the Word* (Bloomington: Indiana UP, 1991). Her current project is a book on the cold war, gender, and the rhetoric of stories.

Christy Desmet, associate professor of English at the University of Georgia, teaches rhetorical theory, writing, literary theory, and Renaissance literature. She is author of *Reading Shakespeare's Characters: Rhetoric, Ethics, and Identity* (Amherst: U of Massachusetts P, 1992) and has written essays about gender and rhetoric in Renaissance drama and in later appropriations of Shakespeare. She is currently working on the relation between rhetoric and feminist jurisprudence.

Lisa Ede is professor of English and director of the Center for Writing and Learning at Oregon State University. Her publications include *Work in Progress: A Guide to Writing and Revising* (New York: St. Martin's, 1994) and, with Andrea A. Lunsford, *Singular Texts / Plural Authors: Perspectives on Collaborative Writing* (Carbondale: Southern Illinois UP, 1990).

Ellen M. Gil-Gomez, assistant professor of English at Russell Sage College, teaches ethnic American literatures, feminist theory, women's literature, and honors composition. Her current research interests include contemporary women of color, lesbian studies, and identity and performance theories.

Amy Goodburn, assistant professor of English at the University of Nebraska, Lincoln, teaches composition and rhetoric, literacy studies, and educational theory and research. Her current research focuses on critical and feminist pedagogies, teacher identity and institutional communities, and discourses of race and religion in student texts.

Gail E. Hawisher, professor of English and director of the Center for Writing Studies at the University of Illinois, Urbana, is widely published in composition studies. With Cynthia Selfe she has edited the *CCCC Bibliography of Composition and Rhetoric* (Carbondale: Southern Illinois UP, 1991–94) and currently edits *Computers and Composition: An International Journal for Teachers of Writing*. Her articles have appeared in *College Composition and Communication*, *College English*, *Research in the Teaching of English*, *Works and Days*, and *Written Communication*. Her recent projects include *Computers and the Teaching of Writing in Higher Education, 1979–1994: A History* and an ongoing study of the online lives of academic women in composition studies.

Wendy S. Hesford, assistant professor of English at Indiana University, Bloomington, teaches courses in composition, autobiography, and literacy studies. She has articles in two other anthologies: *Writing in Multicultural Settings*, ed. Carol Severino, Juan C. Guerra, and Johnnella E. Butler (New York: MLA, 1997) and *Genres of Writing: Mapping the Territories of Discourse*, ed. Wendy Bishop and Hans Ostrom (Boynton, forthcoming). Her book tentatively titled "Reframing Autobiography: Pedagogy and the Culture of the Academy" is forthcoming (U of Minnesota P).

Susan Jarratt, professor of English and director of Women's Studies at Miami University, Oxford, is author of *Rereading the Sophists: Classical Rhetoric Refigured* (Carbondale: Southern Illinois UP, 1991), which received honorable mention in the MLA's Mina P. Shaughnessy Prize competition for best book in rhetoric and composition in 1991. She has published articles on feminist pedagogy and histories of rhetoric in *ADE Bulletin*, *College Composition and Communication*, *College English*, *Hypatia*, *Pre/Text*, *Rhetoric Review*, and *Rhetoric Society Quarterly*. She is currently at work on a book titled "Dispositions: Rhetoric, Difference, and Public Space," which deals with the ways visual and verbal rhetorics articulate social difference.

Deborah Kelsh, a PhD candidate in the State University of New York, Albany, program Writing, Teaching, and Criticism, is working on a dissertation in Marxist theory, "Desire and the Matter of Class: Cultural Studies and the Knowledge Industry in the Wake of (Post)Structuralism." Her publications include an essay, "Team Teaching Conflicts," in *The Writing Instructor* (14.3 [1995]).

Carrie Shively Leverenz, assistant professor of English at Florida State University, directs the Reading/Writing Center and supervises the computer-supported writing classrooms. Her research interests are collaboration, reader-response theory, teacher training, and multicultural literacy. She and Amy Goodburn are currently at work on a book about graduate students' initiation into the academy.

Margaret Lindgren codirects the Freshman Writing Program at the University of Cincinnati. A graduate of Georgetown University and Miami University, Oxford, her dissertation is an interview-based study of adult women students in first-year composition classes. Her scholarly interests are teacher education, feminism and composition studies, and the effects of teachers' comments on students and their writing.

Shirley Wilson Logan, assistant professor of English and director of the Professional Writing Program at the University of Maryland, College Park, teaches writing, the history of rhetoric, and African American literature. She has written articles on computers and writing. Her essays on nineteenth-century black women have appeared in *Sage: A Scholarly Journal on Black Women* and *Nineteenth-Century Women Learn to Write*, ed. Catherine Hobbs (Charlottesville: UP of Virginia, 1995). She edited *With Pen and Voice: A Critical Anthology of Nineteenth-Century African-American Women* (Carbondale: Southern Illinois UP, 1995) and is currently writing a book on nineteenth-century black women's persuasive discourse.

Min-Zhan Lu, associate professor of English at Drake University, teaches composition, literary and cultural criticism, and autobiography. Her essays on the use of cultural dissonance in teaching have appeared in *College Composition and Communication*, *College English*, the *Journal of Basic Writing*, the *Journal of Education*, and the *Journal of Teaching Writing*.

Andrea Lunsford, distinguished professor of English and vice chair of rhetoric and composition at Ohio State University, Columbus, coauthored with Robert Connors *St. Martin's Handbook* (New York: St. Martin's, 1992). She edited *Reclaiming Rhetorica: Women in the Rhetorical Tradition* (Pittsburgh: U of Pittsburgh P, 1995).

Harriet Malinowitz, associate professor of English and director of Women's Studies at Long Island University, Brooklyn, is author of *Textual Orientations: Lesbian and Gay Students and the Making of Discourse Communities* (Portsmouth: Boynton, 1995). Her essays and reviews have appeared in *Conditions*, *Frontiers*, *Journal of Advanced Composition*, *The New Lesbian Studies* (New York: Feminist, 1996), *New Directions for Women*, *NWSA Journal*, *Pre/Text*, *The Women's Review of Books*, and *The Right to Literacy* (New York: MLA, 1991). She also writes lesbian and feminist stand-up comedy.

Margaret Morrison, professor of language and literature and director of the Writing Center at Maryland Institute College of Art, is the editor of *LGSN: Lesbian and Gay Studies Newsletter*, the official publication of the Gay and Lesbian Caucus of the MLA. She is working on a fictional hypertext called "Currents" and a book on the feminist-queer rhetorics of laughter.

Nedra Reynolds, associate professor of English at the University of Rhode Island, teaches writing and rhetorical theory. Her articles and book reviews have appeared in *College Composition and Communication, Journal of Advanced Composition, Journal of Teaching Writing,* and *Rhetoric Review.* She has contributed chapters to *Ethos: New Essays in Rhetorical and Critical Theory,* ed. James S. Baumlin and Tita French Baumlin (Dallas: Southern Methodist UP, 1994) and to *New Directions in Portfolio Assessment: Reflective Practice, Critical Theory, and Large-Scale Scoring,* ed. Laurel Black, Donald A. Daiker, Jeff Sommers, and Gail Stygall (Portsmouth: Boynton, 1994).

Joy Ritchie, a women studies faculty member and cocoordinator of composition courses at the University of Nebraska, Lincoln, is currently writing about feminist theory and pedagogy in composition's history. Ritchie and Ronald are involved in continuing collaborative research on literacy and on women's rhetoric.

Kate Ronald is the Roger and Joyce L. Howe Professor at Miami University, Oxford. She teaches in the English department and works with the School of Business to integrate writing across the curriculum. Her latest project, "Reason to Believe: Romanticism, Pragmatism, and the Possibility of Teaching," coauthored with Hephzibah Roskelly, is forthcoming (SUNY).

Eileen E. Schell, assistant professor of writing and English at Syracuse University, teaches first-year composition, advanced composition, composition theory, and rhetorical theory. She was formerly codirector of the writing program at Virginia Tech. Her writing has appeared in *College Composition and Communication, Composition Studies / Freshman English News,* and *Discourse: Theoretical Studies in Media and Culture.* She also has articles in two anthologies: *Keywords in Composition Studies,* ed. Paul Heilker and Peter Vandenberg (Portsmouth: Boynton, 1996), and "Genres of Writing: Mapping the Territories of Discourse," ed. Wendy Bishop and Hans Ostrom (forthcoming, Boynton). She is author of *Gypsy Academics and Motherteachers: Gender, Contingent Labor, and Writing Instruction* (Portsmouth: Boynton, 1997).

Gail Stygall, associate professor of English language and literature at the University of Washington, teaches writing, rhetoric, discourse analysis, and the theory and practice of teaching writing. She is director of the Expository Writing Program. She has written on portfolios, basic writers, and legal discourse and is author of *Trial Language: Differential Discourse Processing and Discursive Formation* (Amsterdam: Benjamins, 1994). She is now at work on "The Discourse of Divorce" and she is the current editor of the *CCCC Bibliography of Composition and Rhetoric.*

Patricia Sullivan, professor of English at Purdue University, teaches in the graduate rhetoric program. Her research intersects rhetoric, technology, methodology, and professional writing. In *Electronic Literacies in the Workplace: Technologies of Writing* (Urbana: NCTE, 1996), she and coeditor Jennie Dautermann participate in discussions of how literacy issues in the workplace are complicated by the widespread use of technology. In *Opening Spaces: Writing Technologies and Critical Research Practices*, she and James E. Porter advance a postmodern rhetoric of methodology for computers and composition (Ablex, 1997).

Lynn Worsham, associate professor of English at the University of Wisconsin, Milwaukee, teaches rhetorical theory, cultural studies, and multicultural women's literature. She has chapters in *Contending with Words: Composition and Rhetoric in a Postmodern Age*, ed. Patricia Harkin and John Schilb (New York: MLA, 1991), and *Writing Histories of Rhetoric*, ed. Victor J. Vitanza (Carbondale: Southern Illinois UP, 1994). Her articles and reviews have appeared in *Composition Studies / Freshman English News, Discourse, Journal of Advanced Composition, Journal of the American Forensic Association, Pre/Text,* and *Rhetoric Society Quarterly.*

Works Cited

AAUP Committee G on Part-Time and Non-Tenure-Track Appointments. "Report: The Status of Non-Tenure-Track Faculty." *Academe* July-Aug. 1993: 39–48.

AAUP Subcommittee on Part-Time Faculty. "The Status of Part-Time Faculty." *Academe* Mar.-Apr. 1981: 29–39.

Abel, Elizabeth. "Black Writing, White Reading: Race and the Politics of Feminist Interpretation." *Critical Inquiry* 19 (1993): 470–98.

Abel, Emily K. *Terminal Degrees: The Job Crisis in Higher Education.* New York: Praeger, 1984.

Aisenberg, Nadya, and Mona Harrington. *Women of Academe: Outsiders in the Sacred Grove.* Amherst: U of Massachusetts P, 1988.

Alarcón, Norma. "The Theoretical Subject(s) of *This Bridge Called My Back* and Anglo-American Feminism." *Making Face, Making Soul / Haciendo Caras: Creative and Critical Perspectives by Women of Color.* Ed. Gloria Anzaldúa. San Francisco: Aunt Lute, 1990. 356–69.

Alcoff, Linda. "Cultural Feminism versus Post-structuralism: The Identity Crisis in Feminist Theory." *Signs: Journal of Women in Culture and Society* 13 (1988): 405–36.

———. "The Problem of Speaking for Others." *Cultural Critique* 20 (1991–92): 5–32.

Alexander, Adele Logan. *Ambiguous Lives: Free Women of Color in Rural Georgia, 1789–1879.* Fayetteville: U of Arkansas P, 1991.

Althusser, Louis. "Ideology and Ideological State Apparatuses." *Contemporary Critical Theory.* Ed. Dan Latimer. San Diego: Harcourt, 1989. 61–102.

Ammer, Christine. *Seeing Red or Tickled Pink: Color Terms in Everyday Language.* New York: Penguin, 1992.

Anderson, Worth, et al. "Cross-Curricular Underlife: A Collaborative Report on Ways with Academic Words." *College Composition and Communication* 41 (1990): 11–36.

Annas, Pamela. "Style as Politics: A Feminist Approach to the Teaching of Writing." *College English* 47 (1985): 360–71.

Anzaldúa, Gloria. *Borderlands / La Frontera: The New Mestiza.* San Francisco: Aunt Lute, 1987.

——. "La consciencia de la mestiza: Towards a New Consciousness." Colombo, Cullen, and Lisle 386–95.

Armstrong, Nancy. *Desire and Domestic Fiction: A Political History of the Novel.* New York: Oxford UP, 1986.

Aronowitz, Stanley, and Henry Giroux. *Education under Siege.* South Hadley: Bergin, 1985.

Ashton-Jones, Evelyn, and Dene Kay Thomas. "Composition, Collaboration, and *Women's Ways of Knowing*: A Conversation with Mary Belenky." *Journal of Advanced Composition* 10 (1990): 275–92.

Bailey, Mary. "The Proper Study of Womankind . . ." Rev. of *The Reproduction of Mothering*, by Nancy Chodorow. *Ms. Magazine* Oct. 1978: 89.

Ballif, Michelle. "Re/Dressing Histories; or, On Re/Covering Figures Who Have Been Laid Bare by Our Gaze." *Rhetoric Society Quarterly* 22 (1992): 91–98.

Balsamo, Anne. "Cultural Studies and the Undergraduate Literature Curriculum." Berlin and Vivion 145–64.

Balsamo, Anne, and Michael Greer. "Cultural Studies, Literary Studies, and Pedagogy: The Undergraduate Literature Course." Downing 275–307.

Bambara, Toni Cade. "What It Is I Think I'm Doing Anyhow." *The Writer on Her Work.* Ed. Janet Sternburg. New York: Norton, 1980. 153–68.

Bannerji, Himani, et al. *Unsettling Relations: The University as a Site of Feminist Struggles.* Boston: South End, 1991.

Barker, Thomas T., and Fred O. Kemp. "Network Theory: A Postmodern Theory for the Writing Classroom." Handa 1–27.

Barnes, Douglas. *From Communication to Curriculum.* London: Penguin, 1976.

Barrett, Michele. *The Politics of Truth: From Marx to Foucault.* Stanford: Stanford UP, 1991.

——. "Some Different Meanings of the Concept of 'Difference': Feminist Theory and the Concept of Ideology." *The Difference Within.* Ed. Elizabeth Meese and Alice Parker. Philadelphia: Benjamins, 1989. 37–47.

Bartholomae, David. "Inventing the University." *When a Writer Can't Write.* Ed. Mike Rose. New York: Guilford, 1985. 134–65.

Bartholomae, David, and Anthony Petrosky. *Facts, Artifacts, and Counterfacts: Theory and Method for a Reading and Writing Course.* Upper Montclair: Boynton, 1986.

——, eds. *Ways of Reading: An Anthology for Writers.* 2nd ed. Boston: Bedford, 1990.

Bartky, Sandra Lee. *Femininity and Domination: Studies in the Phenomenology of Oppression.* New York: Routledge, 1990.

Bathrick, David. "Cultural Studies." *Introduction to Scholarship in Modern Languages and Literatures.* Ed. Joseph Gibaldi. New York: MLA, 1992. 320–40.

Batson, Lorie Goodman. "Defining Ourselves as Women (in the Profession)." *Pre/Text: A Journal of Rhetorical Theory* (1988): 207–09.

Bauer, Dale M., and Susan C. Jarratt. "Feminist Sophistics: Teaching with an Attitude." Downing 149–65.

Bazerman, Charles. "From Cultural Criticism to Disciplinary Participation: Living with Powerful Words." Herrington and Moran 61–68.

———. *The Informed Writer: Using Sources in the Disciplines.* 5th ed. Boston: Houghton, 1995.

———. "The Second Stage in Writing across the Curriculum." *College English* 53 (1991): 209–12.

Beauvoir, Simone de. *The Second Sex.* Trans. H. M. Parshley. New York: Vintage, 1989.

Bechtel, Judith. "Why Teaching Writing Always Brings Up Questions of Equity." Caywood and Overing, *Teaching* 179–83.

Belenky, Mary Field, Blythe McVicker Clinchy, Nancy Rule Goldberger, and Jill Mattuck Tarule. *Women's Ways of Knowing: The Development of Self, Voice, and Mind.* New York: Basic, 1986.

Benhabib, Seyla. *Situating the Self: Gender, Community, and Postmodernism in Contemporary Ethics.* New York: Routledge, 1992.

Benjamin, Jessica. *The Bonds of Love: Psychoanalysis, Feminism, and the Problem of Domination.* New York: Pantheon, 1988.

———. Rev. of *In a Different Voice,* by Carol Gilligan. *Signs: Journal of Women in Culture and Society* 9 (1983): 297–98.

Bennahum, David. "Fly Me to the MOO: Adventures in Textual Reality." *Lingua Franca* June 1994: cover, 22–36.

Bergmann, Barbara R. "Feminism and Economics." *Academe* Sept.-Oct. 1983: 22–25.

———. "The Task of a Feminist Economics: A More Equitable Future." *The Impact of Feminist Research in the Academy.* Ed. Christie Farnham. Bloomington: Indiana UP, 1987: 131–47.

Berlant, Lauren. "National Brands / National Body: *Imitation of Life.*" *Comparative American Identities: Race, Sex, and Nationality in the Modern Text.* Ed. Hortense J. Spillers. New York: Routledge, 1991. *Identities* 110–40.

Berlin, James A. "Composition Studies and Cultural Studies: Collapsing Boundaries." Gere, *Field* 99–116.

———. "Poststructuralism, Cultural Studies, and the Composition Classroom: Postmodern Theory in Practice." *Rhetoric Review* 11 (1992): 16–33.

———. "Poststructuralism, Semiotics, and Social-Epistemic Rhetoric: Converging Agendas." *Defining the New Rhetorics.* Ed. Theresa Enos and Stuart C. Brown. Newbury Park: Sage, 1993. 137–53.

———. "Rhetoric and Ideology in the Writing Class." *College English* 50 (1988): 477–94.

Berlin, James A., and Michael J. Vivion, eds. *Cultural Studies in the English Classroom.* Portsmouth: Boynton, 1992.

Bigglestone, William E. *They Stopped in Oberlin: Black Residents and Visitors of the Nineteenth Century.* Arizona: Innovation Group, 1981.

Bizzell, Patricia. *Academic Discourse and Critical Consciousness.* Pittsburgh: U of Pittsburgh P, 1992.

———. "Cognition, Convention, and Certainty: What We Need to Know about Writing." *Pre/Text: A Journal of Rhetorical Theory* 3 (1982): 213–44.

———. "The Ethos of Academic Discourse." Bizzell, *Discourse* 31–38.

———. "Opportunities for Feminist Research in the History of Rhetoric." *Rhetoric Review* 11 (1992): 50–58.

Bizzell, Patricia, and Bruce Herzberg, eds. *The Rhetorical Tradition.* New York: St. Martin's, 1990.

Bloom, Allan. *The Closing of the American Mind: How Higher Education Has Failed Democracy and Impoverished the Souls of Today's Students.* New York: Simon, 1987.

Bloom, Harold. *The Western Canon.* New York: Harcourt, 1994.

Bloom, Lynn Z. "Hearing Our Own Voices: Life-Saving Stories." Fontaine and Hunter 89–102.

Bolker, Joan. "Teaching Griselda to Write." *College English* 40 (1979): 906–08.

"The Boxer Uprising Symposium." *Oberlin Shansi Memorial Association Newsletter* 91 (1995): 1.

Brannon, Lil. "M[other]: Lives on the Outside." *Written Communication* 10.3 (1993): 457–65.

Brodkey, Linda. "Modernism and the Scene(s) of Writing." *College English* 49 (1987): 396–418.

———. "On the Subjects of Class and Gender in 'The Literacy Letters.'" *College English* 51 (1989): 125–41.

———. "Postmodern Pedagogy for Progressive Educators." *Journal of Education* 169 (1987): 138–43.

———. "Writing on the Bias." *College English* 56 (1994): 527–47.

Brodkey, Linda, and Michelle Fine. "Presence of Mind in the Absence of Body." *Disruptive Voices: The Possibilities of Feminist Research.* By Michelle Fine. Ann Arbor: U of Michigan P, 1992. 77–96.

Brody, Miriam. *Manly Writing: Gender, Rhetoric, and the Rise of Composition.* Carbondale: Southern Illinois UP, 1993.

Brooks-Higginbotham, Evelyn. "African-American Women's History and the Metalanguage of Race" *Signs: Journal of Women in Culture and Society* 17 (1992): 251–74.

Brown, Sterling A. "*Imitation of Life*: Once a Pancake." *Opportunity: A Journal of Negro Life* Mar. 1935: 87–88.

Bruffee, Kenneth A. *Collaborative Learning: Higher Education, Interdependence, and the Authority of Knowledge.* Baltimore: Johns Hopkins UP, 1993.

Bullock, Richard H., and John Trimbur, eds. *The Politics of Writing Instruction: Postsecondary.* Portsmouth: Boynton, 1991.

Burke, Kenneth. "The Philosophy of Literary Form." *The Philosophy of Literary Form: Studies in Symbolic Action.* 1941. 3rd ed. Berkeley: U of California P, 1973. 1–137.

Burns, Margie. "Service Courses: Doing Women a Disservice." *Academe* May-June 1993: 18–21.

Butler, Judith. *Bodies That Matter: On the Discursive Limits of "Sex."* New York: Routledge, 1993.

———. "Contingent Foundations: Feminism and the Question of 'Postmodernism.'" Butler and Scott 3–21.

———. *Gender Trouble: Feminism and the Subversion of Identity.* New York: Routledge, 1990.

———. "Poststructuralism and Postmarxism." *Diacritics: A Review of Contemporary Criticism* 23.4 (1993): 3–11.

Butler, Judith, and Joan W. Scott, eds. *Feminists Theorize the Political.* New York: Routledge, 1992.

Cameron, Deborah. "Demythologizing Sociolinguistics: Why Language Does Not Reflect Society." *Ideologies of Language.* Ed. John E. Joseph and Talbot J. Taylor. London: Routledge, 1990. 79–93.

———. *Feminism and Linguistic Theory.* 2nd ed. New York: St. Martin's, 1990.

Cameron, Deborah, Fiona McAlinden, and Kathy O'Leary. "Lakoff in Context: The Social and Linguistic Functions of Tag Questions." Coates and Cameron 74–93.

Canaan, Joyce E. "Is 'Doing Nothing' Just Boys' Play? Integrating Feminist and Cultural Studies Perspectives on Working-Class Young Men's Masculinity." Franklin, Lury, and Stacey 109–25.

Caraway, Nancie. *Segregated Sisterhood: Racism and the Politics of American Feminism.* Knoxville: U of Tennessee P, 1991.

Carby, Hazel V. *Reconstructing Womanhood: The Emergence of the Afro-American Woman Novelist.* New York: Oxford UP, 1987.

Carlson, Ellsworth C. *Oberlin in Asia: The First Hundred Years, 1882–1982.* Oberlin: Oberlin Shansi Memorial Assn., 1982.

Cayton, Mary Kupiec. "Writing as Outsiders: Academic Discourse and Marginalized Faculty." *College English* 53 (1991): 647–60.

Caywood, Cynthia L., and Gillian R. Overing, Introduction. Caywood and Overing, *Teaching* xi–xvi.

———, eds. *Teaching Writing: Pedagogy, Gender, and Equity.* Albany: State U of New York P, 1987.

368   *Works Cited*

Cazden, Courtney B. *Classroom Discourse: The Language of Teaching and Learning.* Portsmouth: Heinemann, 1988.

CCCC Committee on Professional Standards. "A Progress Report from the CCCC Committee on Professional Standards." *College Composition and Communication* 42 (1991): 330–44.

CCCC Executive Committee. "Statement of Principles and Standards for the Postsecondary Teaching of Writing." *College Composition and Communication* 40 (1989): 329–36.

Certeau, Michel de. *The Practice of Everyday Life.* Trans. Stephen Rendall. Berkeley: U of California P, 1988.

Childers, Karen, et al. "A Network of One's Own." DeSole and Hoffmann 117–227.

Chiseri-Strater, Elizabeth. *Academic Literacies: The Public and Private Discourse of University Students.* Portsmouth: Boynton, 1991.

Chodorow, Nancy. *The Reproduction of Mothering: Psychoanalysis and the Sociology of Gender.* Berkeley: U of California P, 1978.

Chordas, Nina. "Classrooms, Pedagogies, and the Rhetoric of Equality." *College Composition and Communication* 43 (1992): 214–24.

Christian, Barbara. *Black Feminist Criticism: Perspectives on Black Women Writers.* New York: Pergamon, 1985.

Cisneros, Sandra. "Little Miracles, Kept Promises." Colombo, Cullen, and Lisle 221–32.

Cixous, Hélène. "The Laugh of the Medusa." *New French Feminisms.* Ed. Elaine Marks and Isabelle de Courtivron. New York: Schocken, 1981. 334–49.

Clark, Suzanne. "Rhetoric, Social Construction, and Gender: Is It Bad to Be Sentimental?" Clifford and Schilb 96–108.

"Class of '94 Plaque." *Oberlin Shansi Memorial Association Newsletter* 91 (1995): 2.

Clifford, John. "The Subject in Discourse." Harkin and Schilb 38–51.

Clifford, John, and John Schilb, eds. *Writing Theory and Critical Theory.* New York: MLA, 1994.

Clough, Patricia Ticineto. *Feminist Thought: Desire, Power, and Academic Discourse.* Cambridge: Blackwell, 1994.

Coates, Jennifer. "Gossip Revisited: Language in All-Female Groups." Coates and Cameron 94–122.

———. *Women, Men, and Language: A Sociolinguistic Account of Sex Differences in Language.* New York: Longman, 1986.

Coates, Jennifer, and Deborah Cameron, eds. *Women in Their Speech Communities.* New York, Longman, 1988.

Code, Lorraine. *What Can She Know? Feminist Theory and the Construction of Knowledge.* Ithaca: Cornell UP, 1991.

Cohen, Jean L. "Strategy or Identity: New Theoretical Paradigms and Contemporary Social Movements." *Social Research* 52 (1985): 663–716.

Collins, Patricia Hill. *Black Feminist Thought: Knowledge, Consciousness, and the Politics of Empowerment.* New York: Routledge, 1990.

Colombo, Gary, Robert Cullen, and Bonnie Lisle, eds. *Rereading America: Cultural Contexts for Critical Thinking and Writing.* 2nd ed. Boston: Bedford, 1992.

Combahee River Collective. "A Black Feminist Statement." *Capitalist Patriarchy and the Case for Socialist Feminism.* Ed. Zillah R. Eisenstein. New York: Monthly Review, 1979. 362–72.

Cooper, Anna Julia. "The Higher Education of Women." *A Voice from the South.* 1892. New York: Oxford, 1988. 48–79.

———. "Womanhood a Vital Element in the Regeneration and Progress of a Race." Logan 53–74.

Cooper, Bruce S., and Denis P. Doyle. "Education Supply: Will It Create Demand?" *Education Week* 20 Mar. 1996: 48+.

Cornell, Drucilla. *Beyond Accommodation: Ethical Feminism, Deconstruction, and the Law.* New York: Routledge, 1991.

———. "Gender Hierarchy, Equality, and the Possibility of Democracy." *American Imago* 48 (1991): 247–63.

———. "Sex-Discrimination Law and Equivalent Rights." *Dissent* 38 (1991): 400–405. Rpt. in Cornell, *Transformations* 147–55.

———. "Sexual Difference, the Feminine, and Equivalency." *Yale Law Journal* 100 (1991): 2247–75. Rpt. in Cornell, *Transformations* 112–45.

———. *Transformations: Recollective Imagination and Sexual Difference.* London: Routledge, 1993.

———. "The Violence of the Masquerade: Law Dressed Up as Justice." *Cardozo Law Review* 11 (1990): 1047–64.

Cotter, Jennifer. "An Open Letter on Feminist Pedagogy." *Alternative Orange* 3.2 (1993): 6–10.

Cover, Robert. *Narrative, Violence, and the Law: The Essays of Robert Cover.* Ed. Martha Minow, Michael Ryan, and Austin Sarat. Ann Arbor: U of Michigan P, 1992.

Crosby, Christina. "Dealing with Differences." Butler and Scott 130–43.

Crowley, Sharon. "A Letter to the Editors." Clifford and Schilb 319–26.

———. *A Teacher's Guide to Deconstruction.* Urbana: NCTE, 1989.

———. "Three Heroines: An Oral History." *Pre/Text: A Journal of Rhetorical Theory* (1988): 202–06.

Daumer, Elisabeth, and Sandra Runzo. "Transforming the Composition Classroom." Caywood and Overing, *Teaching* 45–62.

Davis, Angela Y. *Women, Race, and Class.* New York: Vintage, 1983.

Davis, Diane. "Breaking Up [at] Totality: A Rhetoric of Laughter for Politics and Pedagogy." Diss. U of Texas, Arlington, 1995.

Davis, Flora. *Moving the Mountain: The Women's Movement in America since 1960.* New York: Simon, 1991.

Dean, Terry. "Multicultural Classrooms, Monocultural Teachers." *College Composition and Communication* 40 (1989): 223–37.

DeFrancisco, Victoria Leto. "The Sounds of Silence: How Men Silence Women in Marital Relations." *Discourse and Society* 2 (1991): 413–23.

DeJoy, Nancy. "Critical Discursive Practices and Literate Subjectivities: Redefining the Terms of Composition Studies through the Work of James A. Berlin." *Mediations* 18 (1994): 37–52.

de Lauretis, Teresa. "Eccentric Subjects: Feminist Theory and Historical Consciousness." *Feminist Studies* 16 (1990): 115–50.

Deletiner, Carole. "Crossing Lines." *College English* 54 (1992): 809–17.

Delpit, Lisa D. "Skills and Other Dilemmas of a Progressive Black Educator." *Harvard Educational Review* 56 (1986): 379–85.

DeMott, Benjamin. *The Imperial Middle.* New Haven: Yale UP, 1990.

Derrida, Jacques. "Force of Law: The 'Mystical Foundation of Authority.'" *Deconstruction and the Possibility of Justice.* Ed. Drucilla Cornell, Michel Rosenfeld, and David Gray Carlson. New York: Routledge, 1992. 3–67.

———. "The Politics of Friendship." *Journal of Philosophy* 85 (1988): 632–44.

———. "Signature, Event, Context." *Margins of Philosophy.* Trans. Alan Bass. Chicago: U of Chicago P, 1982. 307–30.

DeSole, Gloria, and Leonore Hoffmann, eds. *Rocking the Boat: Academic Women and Academic Processes.* New York: MLA, 1981.

Dibbell, Julian. "A Rape in Cyberspace; or, How an Evil Clown, a Haitian Trickster Spirit, Two Wizards, and a Cast of Dozens Turned a Database into a Society." *Village Voice* Dec. 1993: 36–42.

Dickson, Marcia. "Directing without Power: Adventures in Constructing a Model of Feminist Writing Programs Administration." Fontaine and Hunter 140–53.

Dijk, Teun A. van. "Principles of Critical Discourse Analysis." *Discourse and Society* 4 (1993): 249–83.

Doane, Janice, and Devon Hodges. *From Klein to Kristeva: Psychoanalytic Feminism and the Search for the "Good Enough" Mother.* Ann Arbor: U of Michigan P, 1992.

Donovan, Josephine. *Feminist Theory: The Intellectual Traditions of American Feminism.* New York: Continuum, 1991.

Downing, David B., ed. *Changing Classroom Practices: Resources for Literary and Cultural Studies*. Urbana: NCTE, 1994.

Du Bois, Barbara. "Passionate Scholarship: Notes on Values, Knowing, and Method in Feminist Social Science." *Theories of Women's Studies*. Ed. Gloria Bowles and Renate Duelli Klein. Boston: Routledge, 1983. 105–16.

DuBois, Ellen Carol, and Vicki L. Ruiz. *Unequal Sisters: A Multicultural Reader in U. S. Women's History*. New York: Routledge, 1990.

Dyer, Richard. "White." *Screen* 29.4 (1988): 44–64.

Ebben, Maureen. "Women on the Net: An Exploration of Gender Dynamics on the Soc.Women Computer Network." Diss. U of Illinois, Urbana, 1993.

Ebben, Maureen, and Cheris Kramarae. "Women and Information Technologies: Creating a Cyberspace of Our Own." Taylor, Kramarae, and Ebben 15–27.

Ebert, Teresa L. "The 'Difference' of Postmodern Feminism." *College English* 53 (1991): 886–904.

———. *Ludic Feminism and After: Postmodernism, Desire, and Labor in Late Capitalism*. Ann Arbor: U of Michigan P, 1996.

———. "Ludic Feminism, the Body, Performance, and Labor: Bringing Materialism Back into Feminist Cultural Studies." *Cultural Critique* (Winter 1992–93): 297–324.

———. "(Untimely) Critiques for a *Red Feminism*." *Transformation* 1 (1995): 113–49.

Echols, Alice. *Daring to Be Bad: Radical Feminism in America, 1967–1975*. Minneapolis: U of Minnesota P, 1989.

Ede, Lisa, and Andrea A. Lunsford, *Singular Texts / Plural Authors: Perspectives on Collaborative Writing*. Carbondale: Southern Illinois UP, 1990.

Edelsky, Carole. "Who's Got the Floor?" Tannen, *Gender* 189–227.

Edgell, Stephen. *Class*. New York: Routledge, 1993.

Eichhorn, Jill, et al. "A Symposium on Feminist Experience in the Composition Classroom." *College Composition and Communication* 43 (1992): 297–322.

Elbow, Peter. "Closing My Eyes As I Speak: An Argument for Ignoring Audience." *College English* 49 (1987): 50–69.

———. "Reflections on Academic Discourse: How It Relates to Freshmen and Colleagues." *College English* 53 (1991): 135–55.

———. *Writing without Teachers*. New York: Oxford UP, 1973.

Eldred, Janet Carey, and Gail E. Hawisher. "Researching Electronic Networks." *Written Communication* 12. 3 (1995): 330–59.

Ellsworth, Elizabeth. "Why Doesn't This Feel Empowering? Working through the Repressive Myths of Critical Pedagogy." *Harvard Educational Review* 59 (1989): 297–324.

Escoffier, Jeffrey. "Intellectuals, Identity Politics, and the Contest for Cultural Authority." *Found Object* 2 (1993): 31–44.

Europa, Europa. Dir. Agnieszka Holland. CCC Filmkunst; Les Films de Losange, 1991.

Ewald, Helen Rothschild, and David E. Wallace. "Exploring Agency in Classroom Discourse; or, Should David Have Told His Story?" *College Composition and Communication* 45 (1994): 342–68.

Faderman, Lillian. *Odd Girls and Twilight Lovers: A History of Lesbian Life in Twentieth-Century America.* New York: Columbia UP, 1991.

Faigley, Lester. *Fragments of Rationality: Postmodernity and the Subject of Composition.* Pittsburgh: U of Pittsburgh P, 1992.

Faludi, Susan. *Backlash: The Undeclared War against American Women.* New York: Crown, 1991.

Fausto-Sterling, Anne. "How Many Sexes Are There?" *New York Times* 12 Mar. 1993: A29+.

Ferguson, Ann. *Blood at the Root: Motherhood, Sexuality, and Male Dominance.* London: Pandora, 1989.

Ferguson, Kathy. *The Feminist Case against Bureaucracy.* Philadelphia: Temple UP, 1984.

Firestone, Shulamith. *The Dialectics of Sex: The Case for Feminist Revolution.* New York: Morrow, 1970.

Fisher, Berenice. "Guilt and Shame in the Women's Movement: The Radical Ideal of Action and Its Meaning for Feminist Intellectuals." *Feminist Studies* 10 (1984): 185–212.

Fishkin, Shelley Fisher. "Interrogating 'Whiteness,' Complicating 'Blackness': Remapping American Culture." *American Quarterly* 47 (1995): 428–66.

Fishman, Pamela. "Interaction: The Work Women Do." *Social Problems* 25 (1977): 397–406.

Flannery, Kathryn T. "Composing and the Question of Agency." *College English* 53 (1991): 701–13.

Fletcher, Robert Samuel. *A History of Oberlin College.* 2 vols. Chicago: Donnellay, 1943.

Flower, Linda, and John R. Hayes. "A Cognitive Process Theory of Writing." *College Composition and Communication* 32 (1981): 365–87.

Flynn, Elizabeth A. "Composing as a Woman." *College Composition and Communication* 39 (1988): 423–35.

———. "Composition Studies from a Feminist Perspective." Bullock and Trimbur 137–54.

———. "Review: Feminist Theories / Feminist Composition." *College English* 57 (1995): 201–12.

Fontaine, Sheryl L., and Susan Hunter, eds. *Writing Ourselves into the Story:*

Unheard Voices from Composition Studies. Carbondale: Southern Illinois UP, 1993.

Foucault, Michel. *Discipline and Punish: The Birth of the Prison*. Trans. Alan Sheridan. New York: Pantheon, 1977.

———, ed. *I, Pierre Rivière, Having Slaughtered My Mother, My Sister, and My Brother . . . A Case of Parricide in the Nineteenth Century*. Trans. Frank Jellinek. Lincoln: U of Nebraska P, 1975.

———. "Of Other Spaces." *Diacritics: A Review of Contemporary Criticism* 16.1 (1986): 22–27.

———. *The Order of Things: An Archaeology of the Human Sciences*. New York: Vintage, 1973.

Fox, Tom. "Literacy and Activism: A Response to bell hooks." *Journal of Advanced Composition* 14 (1994): 564–70.

Frankenberg, Ruth. *White Women, Race Matters: The Social Construction of Whiteness*. Minneapolis: U of Minnesota P, 1993.

Franklin, Sarah, Celia Lury, and Jackie Stacey, eds. *Off-Centre: Feminism and Cultural Studies*. New York: Harper, 1991.

Fraser, Nancy. "Sex, Lies, and the Public Sphere: Some Reflections on the Confirmation of Clarence Thomas." *Critical Inquiry* 18 (1992): 595–612.

Freire, Paulo. *Pedagogy of the Oppressed*. New York: Continuum, 1970.

———. *The Politics of Education*. South Hadley: Bergin, 1985.

Frey, Olivia. "Beyond Literary Darwinism: Women's Voices and Critical Discourse." *College English* 52 (1990): 507–26.

———. "Equity and Peace in the New Writing Class." Caywood and Overing, *Teaching* 93–105.

Friedman, Susan Stanford. "Authority in the Feminist Classroom: A Contradiction in Terms." *Gendered Subjects: The Dynamics of Feminist Teaching*. Ed. Margo Culley and Catherine Portugues. New York: Routledge, 1985. 203–08.

———. "Making History: Reflections on Feminism, Narrative, and Desire." *Feminism beside Itself*. Ed. Diane Elam and Robyn Wiegman. New York: Routledge, 1995. 11–53.

Friend, Christy. "Ethics in the Writing Classroom: A Nondistributive Approach." *College English* 56 (1994): 548–67.

Frost, Clare. "Looking for a Gate in the Fence." Fontaine and Hunter 59–69.

Frye, Marilyn. "On Being White: Thinking toward a Feminist Understanding of Race and Race Supremacy." *The Politics of Reality*. Freedom: Crossing, 1983. 110–27.

———. "White Woman Feminist." *Willful Virgin: Essays in Feminism*. Freedom: Crossing, 1992. 147–69.

Fulwiler, Toby. "The Quiet and Insistent Revolution: Writing across the Curriculum." Bullock and Trimbur 179–87.

Fuss, Diana. *Essentially Speaking: Feminism, Nature, and Difference.* New York: Routledge, 1989.

Gale, Frederic G., ed. *Multiculturalism in the Writing Classroom.* Spec. issue of *Teaching English in the Two-Year College* 21 (1994): 91–160.

Gappa, Judith. "Employing Part-Time Faculty: Thoughtful Approaches to Continuing Problems." *AAHE Bulletin* 37.2 (1984): 3–7.

Gappa, Judith, and David Leslie. *The Invisible Faculty: Improving the Status of Part-Timers in Higher Education.* San Francisco: Jossey-Bass, 1993.

Gasché, Rodolphe. *The Tain of the Mirror: Derrida and the Philosophy of Reflection.* Cambridge: Harvard UP, 1986.

Geertz, Clifford. *Local Knowledge: Further Essays in Interpretive Anthropology.* New York: Basic, 1983.

George, Diana, and Diana Shoos. "Issues of Subjectivity and Resistance: Cultural Studies in the Composition Classroom." Berlin and Vivion 200–10.

Gere, Anne Ruggles, ed. *Into the Field: Sites of Composition Studies.* New York: MLA, 1993.

———. "Kitchen Tables and Rented Rooms: The Extracurriculum of Composition." *College Composition and Communication* 45 (1994): 75–92.

Giddings, Paula. *When and Where I Enter: The Impact of Black Women on Race and Sex in America.* New York: Bantam, 1984.

Gill, Mark Stuart. "Terror On-Line." *Vogue* Jan. 1994: 163+.

Gillam, Alice M. "Feminism and Composition Research: Researching as a Woman." *Composition Studies / Freshman English News* 20.1 (1992): 47–54.

Gilligan, Carol. *In a Different Voice: Psychological Theory and Women's Development* Cambridge: Harvard UP, 1982.

Giltrow, Janet, and Michele Valiquette. "Genres and Knowledge: Students Writing in the Disciplines." *Learning and Teaching Genre.* Ed. Aviva Freedman and Peter Medway. Portsmouth: Heinemann-Boynton, 1994. 47–62.

Giroux, Henry A. *Disturbing Pleasures: Learning Popular Culture.* New York: Routledge, 1994.

———. "Insurgent Multiculturalism and the Promise of Pedagogy." *Multiculturalism: A Critical Reader.* Ed. David Theo Goldberg. Oxford: Blackwell, 1994. 325–43.

———. "Modernism, Postmodernism, and Feminism: Rethinking the Boundaries of Educational Discourse." *Postmodernism, Feminism, and Cultural Politics: Redrawing Educational Boundaries.* Ed. Giroux. Albany: State U of New York P, 1991. 1–59.

Giroux, Henry, and Peter McLaren, eds. *Between Borders: Pedagogy and the Politics of Cultural Studies.* New York: Routledge, 1994.

Glasser, Ira. Preface. *Speaking of Race, Speaking of Sex: Hate Speech, Civil*

Rights, and Civil Liberties. By Henry L. Gates, Jr., et al. New York: New York UP, 1994. 1–16.

Glenn, Cheryl. "Author, Audience, and Autobiography: Rhetorical Technique in *The Book of Margery Kempe.*" *College English* 54 (1992): 540–53.

———. "Sex, Lies, and Manuscript: Refiguring Aspasia in the History of Rhetoric." *College Composition and Communication* 45 (1994): 180–99.

Golden, Marita, and Susan Richards Shreve, eds. *Skin Deep: Black and White Women Write about Race.* New York: Doubleday, 1995.

Goldfield, David R. *Black, White, and Southern: Race Relations and Southern Culture, 1940 to the Present.* Baton Rouge: Louisiana State UP, 1990.

Gómez, Alma, Cherríe Moraga, and Mariana Romo-Carmona, eds. *Cuentos: Stories by Latinas.* New York: Kitchen Table, 1983.

Gore, Jennifer M. *The Struggle for Pedagogies: Critical and Feminist Discourses as Regimes of Truth.* New York: Routledge, 1993.

Goulston, Wendy. "Women Writing." Caywood and Overing, *Teaching* 19–30.

Graff, Gerald, and Bruce Robbins. "Cultural Criticism." *Redrawing the Boundaries: The Transformation of English and American Literary Studies.* Ed. Stephen Greenblatt and Giles Gunn. New York: MLA, 1992. 419–36.

Gramsci, Antonio. *An Antonio Gramsci Reader: Selected Writings, 1916–1935.* Ed. David Forgacs. New York: Schocken, 1988.

Grant, Judith. *Fundamental Feminism: Contesting the Core Concepts of Feminist Theory.* New York: Routledge, 1993.

Graphics, Visualization, and Usability Center. "GVU's Sixth WWW User Survey Home Page." Online. Internet. 22 Feb. 1997. Available http://www.cc.gatech.edu/gvu/user_surveys/survey-10-1996.

Grimm, Nancy. Account. "The Part-Time Problem: Four Voices." By Elizabeth A. Flynn, John F. Flynn, Nancy Grimm, and Ted Lockhart. *Academe* Jan.-Feb. 1986: 14–15.

Grossberg, Lawrence, Cary Nelson, and Paula Treichler, eds. *Cultural Studies.* Proc. of University of Illinois Conference on Cultural Studies, 4–9 Apr. 1990, Urbana. New York: Routledge, 1992.

Grundy, Shirley. "Educational Leadership as Emancipatory Praxis." *Gender Matters in Educational Administration and Policy.* Ed. Jill Blackmore and Jane Kenway. London: Falmer, 1993. 165–77.

Guinier, Lani. *The Tyranny of the Majority: Fundamental Fairness in Representative Democracy.* New York: Free, 1994.

Gump, Janice Porter. "Gender Differences: Their Genesis and Regeneration." *Contemporary Psychology* 24 (1979): 657–58.

Gunner, Jeanne. "Decentering the WPA." *Writing Program Administration* 18 (1994): 8–15.

———. "The Fate of the Wyoming Resolution: A Professional Seduction." Fontaine and Hunter 107–22.

Gwaltney, John Langston. *Drylongso: A Self-Portrait of Black America*. New York: New, 1993.

Habermas, Jürgen. *The Structural Transformation of the Public Sphere*. Trans. Thomas Burger and F. Lawrence. Cambridge: MIT P, 1989.

Hall, Stuart. "Cultural Identity and Diaspora." *Identity, Community, Culture, Difference*. Ed. Jonathan Rutherford. London: Lawrence, 1990. 222–37.

———. "Cultural Studies and Its Theoretical Legacies." Grossberg, Nelson, and Treichler 277–94.

———. "Cultural Studies and the Centre: Some Problematics and Problems." *Culture, Media and Language: Working Papers in Cultural Studies, 1977–79*. London: Hutchinson, 1980. 15–47.

———. "Cultural Studies: Two Paradigms." *Media, Culture, and Society* 2 (1980): 57–72.

Handa, Carolyn, ed. *Computers and Community: Teaching Composition in the Twenty-First Century*. Portsmouth: Boynton, 1990.

Haraway, Donna. "A Cyborg Manifesto: Science, Technology, and Socialist-Feminism in the Late Twentieth Century." *Contemporary Literary Criticism: Literary and Cultural Studies*. 3rd ed. Ed. Robert Con Davis and Ronald Schleifer. New York: Longman, 1994. 567–95.

Harding, Sandra. "Is There a Feminist Method?" *Feminism and Methodology*. Ed. Harding. Bloomington: Indiana UP, 1987. 1–14.

———. "Who Knows? Identities and Feminist Epistemology." *(En)Gendering Knowledge*. Ed. Joan E. Hartman and Ellen Messer-Davidow. Knoxville: U of Tennessee P, 1991. 100–20.

———. *Whose Science? Whose Knowledge? Thinking from Women's Lives*. Ithaca: Cornell UP, 1991.

Harkin, Patricia. "The Postdisciplinary Politics of Lore." Harkin and Schilb 124–38.

Harkin, Patricia, and John Schilb, eds. *Contending with Words: Composition and Rhetoric in a Postmodern Age*. New York: MLA, 1991.

Harper, Phillip Brian. *Framing the Margins: The Social Logic of Postmodern Culture*. New York: Oxford UP, 1994.

Harris, Joseph. "The Idea of Community in the Study of Writing." *College Composition and Communication* 40 (1989): 11–22.

Harris, Trudier. *From Mammies to Militants: Domestics in Black American Literature*. Philadelphia: Temple UP, 1982.

Haug, Frigga. "The Quota Demand and Feminist Politics." *New Left Review* Jan.-Feb. 1995: 136–45.

Heidegger, Martin. *Being and Time*. Trans. John Macquarrie and Edward Robinson. New York: Harper, 1962.

Hennessy, Rosemary. *Materialist Feminism and the Politics of Discourse*. New York: Routledge, 1993.

Herring, Susan C. "Gender and Democracy in Computer-Mediated Communication." *Nordlyd: Tromso University Working Papers on Language and Linguistics* 23 (1995): 1–20.

Herring, Susan C., Deborah Johnson, and Tamra DiBenedetto. "Participation in Electronic Discourse in a 'Feminist' Field." Address. Berkeley Women and Language Conf. U of California, Berkeley. Apr. 1992.

Herrington, Anne. "Writing Their Way / Writing Mine: Writing for a Psychology Methods Course." Conf. on Coll. Composition and Communication Convention. Cincinnati. 1992.

Herrington, Anne, and Charles Moran. *Writing, Teaching, and Learning in the Disciplines*. New York: MLA, 1992.

Hesford, Wendy. "Autobiography and Feminist Writing Pedagogy." *Genres: Mapping the Territories of Discourse*. Ed. Wendy Bishop and Hans Ostrom. Upper Montclair: Boynton, forthcoming.

———. "Writing Identities: The Essence of Difference in Multicultural Classrooms." *Writing in Multicultural Settings*. Ed. Carol Severino, Juan C. Guerra, and Johnnella E. Butler. New York: MLA, 1997. 133–49.

Hevia, James. "Leaving a Brand on China: Missionary Discourse in the Wake of the Boxer Movement." *Modern China* 18 (1992): 304–32.

Hill, Mike. Reviewer's report. "Symposium: The Subject of Pedagogical Politics / The Politics of Publication." *College Literature* 21.3 (1994): 16.

Hirsch, E. D., Jr. *Cultural Literacy: What Every American Needs to Know*. Boston: Houghton, 1987.

Hirsch, Marianne, and Evelyn Fox Keller, eds. *Conflicts in Feminism*. New York: Routledge, 1990.

Hodge, Robert, and Gunther Kress. *Social Semiotics*. Ithaca: Cornell UP, 1988.

Hoffer, Peter Charles. *The Law's Conscience: Equitable Constitutionalism in America*. Chapel Hill: U of North Carolina P, 1990.

Holbrook, Sue Ellen. "Women's Work: The Feminizing of Composition Studies." *Rhetoric Review* 9 (1991): 201–29.

Hollis, Karyn. "Feminism in Writing Workshops: A New Pedagogy." *College Composition and Communication* 43 (1992): 340–48.

———. "Liberating Voices: Autobiographical Writing at the Bryn Mawr Summer School for Women Workers, 1921–1938." *College Composition and Communication* 45 (1994): 31–60.

Holmes, Janet. "Women's Language: A Functional Approach." *General Linguistics* 24 (1984): 149–78.

Holt, Mara. "Knowledge, Social Relations, and Authority in Collaborative Practices of the 1930s and the 1950s." *College Composition and Communication* 44 (1993): 538–55.

Homans, Margaret. "'Women of Color' Writers and Feminist Theory." *New Literary History: A Journal of Theory and Interpretation* 25 (1994): 73–94.

hooks, bell. *Ain't I a Woman: Black Women and Feminism.* Boston: South End, 1981.

———. *Black Looks: Race and Representation.* Boston: South End, 1992.

———. "Black Women Intellectuals." *Breaking Bread: Insurgent Black Intellectual Life.* By hooks and Cornel West. Boston: South End, 1991. 145–64.

———. *Feminist Theory: From Margin to Center.* Boston: South End, 1984.

———. *Outlaw Culture: Resisting Representations.* New York: Routledge, 1994.

———. "Reflections on Race and Sex." Hooks, *Yearning* 57–64.

———. "Representing Whiteness in the Black Imagination." Grossberg, Nelson, and Treichler 338–46.

———. *Talking Back: Thinking Feminist, Thinking Black.* Boston: South End, 1989.

———. *Teaching to Transgress: Education as the Practice of Freedom.* New York: Routledge, 1994.

———. *Yearning: Race, Gender, and Cultural Politics.* Boston: South End, 1990.

Houston, Marsha. "The Politics of Difference: Race, Class, and Women's Communication." *Women Making Meaning: New Feminist Directions in Communication.* Ed. Lana F. Rakow. New York: Routledge, 1992. 45–59.

Howard, Rebecca Moore. "Reflexivity and Agency in Rhetoric and Pedagogy." *College English* 56 (1994): 348–55.

Howe, Florence. "Identity and Expression: A Writing Course for Women." *College English* 32 (1971): 863–71.

Huber, Bettina. "Women in the Modern Languages, 1970–90." *Profession 90.* New York: MLA, 1990. 58–73.

Huggins, Nathan Irvin. *Black Odyssey: The African-American Ordeal in Slavery.* New York: Random, 1977.

Hull, Gloria T., Patricia Bell Scott, and Barbara Smith, eds. *All the Women Are White. All the Blacks Are Men, but Some of Us Are Brave: Black Women's Studies.* New York: Feminist, 1982.

Hurst, Fannie. *Imitation of Life.* New York: Collier, 1933.

———. Letter. *Opportunity: A Journal of Negro Life* 13 Apr. 1935: 121.

———. "The Sure Way to Equality." *Negro Digest* June 1946: 27–28.

Imitation of Life. Dir. John Stahl. Universal, 1934.

Irigaray, Luce. *This Sex Which Is Not One.* Trans. Catherine Porter. Ithaca: Cornell UP, 1985.

Jacobson, Carl. "The Memorial Arch Is a Unique Monument." *Observer* 25 Nov. 1993: 6.

Jaggar, Alison M., and Paula S. Rothenberg, eds. *Feminist Frameworks: Alternative Theoretical Accounts of the Relations between Women and Men.* 3rd ed. New York: McGraw, 1993.

James, Deborah, and Sandra Clarke. "Women, Men, and Interruptions: A Critical Review." Tannen, *Gender* 231–80.

James, Deborah, and Janice Drakich. "Understanding Gender Differences in Amount of Talk: A Critical Review of the Research." Tannen, *Gender* 281–312.

Jameson, Frederic. *The Political Unconscious: Narrative as a Socially Symbolic Act.* Ithaca: Cornell UP, 1981.

Jardine, Alice. "Notes for an Analysis." *Between Feminism and Psychoanalysis.* Ed. Teresa Brennan. New York: Routledge, 1989. 73–85.

Jarratt, Susan C. "Feminism and Composition: The Case for Conflict." Harkin and Schilb 105–23.

———. "Performing Feminisms, Histories, Rhetorics." *Rhetoric Society Quarterly* 22 (1992): 1–6.

———. *Rereading the Sophists: Classical Rhetoric Refigured.* Carbondale: Southern Illinois UP, 1991.

Jarratt, Susan C., and Nedra Reynolds. "The Splitting Image: Contemporary Feminisms and the Ethics of *Ethos.*" *Ethos: New Essays in Rhetorical and Critical Theory.* Ed. James S. Baumlin and Tita French Baumlin. Dallas: Southern Methodist UP, 1992. 37–63.

Jayaratne, Toby Epstein, and Abigail J. Stewart. "Quantitative and Qualitative Methods in the Social Sciences: Current Feminist Issues and Practical Strategies." *Beyond Methodology: Feminist Scholarship as Lived Research.* Ed. Mary Margaret Fonow and Judith A. Cook. Bloomington: Indiana UP, 1991. 85–106.

Jikui, Li. "How to View the Boxers' Religious Superstitions." *Chinese Studies and History* 29.3–4 (1987): 98–112.

Johnson, Barbara. "Thresholds of Difference: Structures of Address in Zora Neale Hurston." *A World of Difference.* Baltimore: Johns Hopkins UP, 1987. 172–83.

Johnson, Cheryl. "Participatory Rhetoric and the Teacher as Racial/Gendered Subject." *College English* 56 (1994): 409–19.

Johnson, Richard. "What Is Cultural Studies Anyway?" *Social Text* 16 (1986–87): 38–80.

Jones, Adrienne. Speech. Open Forum on Racism, Intimidation, Freedom of Speech: Rebuilding the Oberlin Community. Finney Chapel, Oberlin Coll. 12 Nov. 1993.

Jones, Robert, and Joseph J. Comprone. "Where Do We Go Next in Writing across the Curriculum?" *College Composition and Communication* 44 (1993): 59–68.

Jordan, June. "Where Is the Sisterhood?" *Progressive* 60.6 (1996): 20–21.

Joseph, Gloria, and Jill Lewis. *Common Differences: Conflicts in Black and White Feminist Perspectives.* Boston: South End, 1981.

Junker, Clara. "Writing (with) Cixous." *College English* 50 (1988): 424–36.

Kaplan, Nancy, and Eva Farrell. "Weavers of Webs: A Portrait of Young Women on the Net." Online. Internet. 22 Feb. 1997. Available http: raven.ubalt.edu/staff/kaplan/weavers/weavers.html.

Karabel, Jerome. "Fighting Words." Rev. of *Teaching to Transgress* and *Outlaw Culture*, by bell hooks. *New York Times* 18 Dec. 1994, sec. 7: 27.

Keating, AnnLouise. "Interrogating 'Whiteness,' (De)Constructing 'Race.'" *College English* 57 (1995): 901–18.

Keller, Evelyn Fox, and Helene Moglen. "Competition: A Problem for Academic Women." Miner and Longino 21–37.

Kerber, Linda K., Catherine G. Greeno, Eleanor Maccoby, Zella Luria, Carol B. Stack, and Carol Gilligan. "On *In a Different Voice*: An Interdisciplinary Forum." *Signs: Journal of Women in Culture and Society* 11 (1986): 304–33.

Kingston, Maxine Hong. *The Woman Warrior: Memoirs of a Girlhood among Ghosts*. New York: Vintage, 1989.

Kipnis, Laura. "(Male) Desire and (Female) Disgust: Reading *Hustler*." Grossberg, Nelson, and Treichler 373–91.

Kirsch, Gesa E. *Women Writing the Academy: Audience, Authority, and Transformation*. Carbondale: Southern Illinois UP, 1993.

Kirsch, Gesa E., and Patricia A. Sullivan, eds. *Methods and Methodologies in Composition Research*. Carbondale: Southern Illinois UP, 1992.

Kirscht, Judy, Rhonda Levine, and John Reiff. "Evolving Paradigms: WAC and the Rhetoric of Inquiry." *College Composition and Communication* 45 (1994): 369–80.

Koblitz, Neal. "Bias and Other Factors in Student Ratings." *Chronicle of Higher Education* 1 Sept. 1993: B3.

Koch, Wendy. "Quality of Life for Women Assessed." *Times Union* [Albany] 18 Aug. 1995: A1+

Koppes, Clayton. Speech. Open Forum on Racism, Intimidation, Freedom of Speech: Rebuilding the Oberlin Community. Finney Chapel, Oberlin Coll. 12 Nov. 1993.

Kraditor, Aileen. *The Ideas of the Woman Suffrage Movement, 1899–1929*. Garden City: Doubleday, 1971.

Kraemer, Don J., Jr. "Gender and the Autobiographical Essay: A Critical Extension of the Research." *College Composition and Communication* 43 (1992): 323–39.

Kramarae, Cheris, and H. Jeanie Taylor. "Women and Men on Electronic Networks: A Conversation or a Monologue?" Taylor, Kramarae, and Ebben 52–61.

Kramarae, Cheris, and Paula A. Treichler. "Power Relationships in the Classroom." *Gender in the Classroom: Power and Pedagogy*. Ed. Susan L. Gabriel and Isaiah Smithson. Urbana: U of Illinois P, 1990. 41–59.

Kristeva, Julia. "Women's Time." *The Kristeva Reader*. Ed. Toril Moi. New York: Columbia UP, 1986. 187–213.

Laclau, Ernesto, and Chantal Mouffe. *Hegemony and Socialist Strategy*. London: Verso, 1985.

Lakoff, George, and Mark Johnson. *Metaphors We Live By*. Chicago: U of Chicago P, 1980.

Lakoff, Robin. *Language and Woman's Place*. New York: Harper, 1975.

Lamb, Catherine E. "Beyond Argument in Feminist Composition." *College Composition and Communication* 42 (1991): 11–24.

Landry, Donna, and Gerald MacLean. *Materialist Feminisms*. Cambridge: Blackwell, 1993.

Langer, Judith A. "Speaking of Knowing: Conceptions of Understanding in Academic Disciplines." Herrington and Moran 69–85.

Langston, Diane, and Trent Batson. "The Social Shifts Invited by Working Collaboratively on Computer Networks: The ENFI Project." Handa 140–59.

Larrabee, Mary Jeanne, ed. *An Ethic of Care: Feminist and Interdisciplinary Perspectives*. New York: Routledge, 1993.

Lather, Patti. *Getting Smart: Feminist Research and Pedagogy with/in the Postmodern*. New York: Routledge, 1991.

Lawrence, Charles, III. "If He Hollers Let Him Go: Regulating Racist Speech on Campus." Matsuda et al. 53–88.

Lay, Mary M. "Feminist Theory and the Redefinition of Technical Communication." *Journal of Business and Technical Communication* 5 (1991): 348–70.

Leacock, Eleanor Burke. Introduction. *The Origin of the Family, Private Property, and the State*. By Frederick Engels. New York: International, 1972. 7–68.

Leslie, David W., Samuel E. Kellams, and G. Manny Gunne. *Part-Time Faculty in American Higher Education*. New York: Praeger, 1982.

Letter. *Oberlin Review* 12 Nov. 1993: 10.

Lewis, Magda. "Interrupting Patriarchy: Politics, Resistance, and Transformation in the Feminist Classroom." Luke and Gore, *Feminisms* 167–91.

Logan, Shirley Wilson, ed. *With Pen and Voice: A Critical Anthology of Nineteenth-Century African-American Women*. Carbondale: Southern Illinois UP, 1995.

Looser, Devoney. "Composing as an 'Essentialist'? New Directions for Feminist Composition Theories." *Rhetoric Review* 12 (1993): 54–69.

Lorde, Audre. "Age, Race, Class, and Sex: Women Redefining Difference." *Race, Class, and Gender in the United States: An Integrated Study*. Ed. Paula S. Rothenberg. New York: St. Martin's, 1995. 445–51.

———. "The Master's Tools Will Never Dismantle the Master's House." Moraga and Anzaldúa 98–101.

———. *Sister Outsider: Essays and Speeches by Audre Lorde.* Freedom: Crossing, 1984.

Lovitt, Carl. "Subverting Faculty and Institutional Cultures." Conf. on Coll. Composition and Communication Convention. Washington, DC. 24 Mar. 1995.

Lu, Min-Zhan. "Conflict and Struggle: The Enemies or Preconditions of Basic Writing?" *College English* 54 (1992): 887–913.

Luke, Carmen, and Jennifer Gore, eds. *Feminisms and Critical Pedagogy.* New York: Routledge, 1992.

———. "Women in the Academy: Strategy, Struggle, Survival." Luke and Gore, *Feminisms* 192–210.

Luxemburg, Rosa. *Rosa Luxemburg Speaks.* 1970. Ed. Mary-Alice Waters. New York: Pathfinder, 1994.

Lydon, Mary. *Skirting the Issue: Essays in Literary Theory.* Madison: U of Wisconsin P, 1995.

Lyman, Peter. "The Politics of Anger: On Silence, Ressentiment, and Political Speech." *Socialist Review* May-June (1981): 55–74.

Lyman, Stanford M. *Social Movements: Critiques, Concepts, Case-Studies.* New York: New York UP, 1995.

Lyon, Arabella. "Antipluralist Stances in the Academy." Conflicts with/in Academic Feminisms: Negotiating Diversity, Negotiating Hierarchy. Conf. on Coll. Composition and Communication Convention. Convention Center, Nashville. 16 Mar. 1994.

Lyotard, Jean-François. *The Postmodern Condition: A Report on Knowledge.* Trans. Geoff Bennington and Brian Massumi. Minneapolis: U of Minnesota P, 1984.

Mahala, Daniel. "Writing Utopias: Writing across the Curriculum and the Promise of Reform." *College English* 53 (1991): 773–89.

Maimon, Elaine. "Growing Up Subversive." Conf. on Coll. Composition and Communication Convention. Washington, DC. 24 Mar. 1995.

Maltby, Paul. Reviewer's report. "Symposium: The Subject of Pedagogical Politics / The Politics of Publication." *College Literature* 21.3 (1994): 15.

Maltz, Daniel M., and Ruth A. Borker. "A Cultural Approach to Male-Female Miscommunication." *Language and Society Identity.* Ed. John J. Gumperz. Cambridge: Cambridge UP, 1982. 192–216.

Mannheim, Karl. "The Problem of Generations." *Essays in the Sociology of Knowledge.* Ed. Paul Kecskemeti. London: Routledge, 1952. 276–332.

Markus, Maria. "Women, Success, and Civil Society: Submission to, or Subversion of, the Achievement Principle." *Feminism as Critique: Essays on the*

Politics of Gender in Late-Capitalist Societies. Ed. Seyla Benhabib and Drucilla Cornell. Cambridge: Blackwell, 1987. 96–109.

Marx, Karl. *A Contribution to the Critique of Political Economy*. Trans. N. I. Stone. Chicago: Kerr, 1904.

———. *The Process of Capitalist Production*. Trans. Samuel Moore and Edward Aveling. Ed. Friedrich Engels. 1867. Rev. Ernest Untermann. 1906. Chicago: Kerr, 1912. Vol. 1 of *Capital: A Critique of Political Economy*.

———. *The Process of Capitalist Production as a Whole*. Trans. Ernest Untermann. Ed. Friedrich Engels. 1894. Chicago: Kerr, 1909. Vol. 3 of *Capital: A Critique of Political Economy*.

Marx, Karl, and Friedrich Engels. *The Communist Manifesto*. Trans. Samuel Moore. 1888. Introd. and notes A. J. P. Taylor. 1967. New York: Penguin, 1986.

———. *The German Ideology*. Trans. Intl. Publishing. 1947. Rev. Lawrence and Wishart. 1970. Ed. C. J. Arthur. New York: Intl., 1989.

Matheson, Kimberly. "Women and Computer Technology." *Contexts of Computer-Mediated Communication*. Ed. Martin Lea. New York: Harvester, 1993. 66–88.

Matsuda, Mari. "Public Response to Racist Speech: Considering the Victim's Story." Matsuda et al. 17–52.

Matsuda, Mari, et al., eds. *Words That Wound: Critical Race Theory, Assaultive Speech, and the First Amendment*. Boulder: Westview, 1993.

Mayher, John S., Nancy Lester, and Gordon M. Pradl. *Learning to Write / Writing to Learn*. Upper Montclair: Boynton, 1983.

McCarthy, Cameron. "Multicultural Discourses and Curriculum Reform: A Critical Perspective." *Educational Theory* 44.1 (1994): 81–98.

McRobbie, Angela. *Feminism and Youth Culture: From Jackie to Just Seventeen*. Boston: Unwin, 1991.

———. "The Politics of Feminist Research: Between Talk, Text, and Action." *Feminist Review* 12 (1982): 46–57.

———. "Settling Accounts with Subcultures: A Feminist Critique." McRobbie, *Feminism* 16–34.

Mercer, Kobena. "'1968': Periodizing Postmodern Politics and Identity." Grossberg, Nelson, and Treichler 424–49.

Middleton, Joyce Irene. "Back to Basics; or, The Three R's: Race, Rhythm, and Rhetoric." *Teaching English in the Two-Year College* 21 (1994): 104–13.

Mies, Maria. *Patriarchy and Accumulation on a World Scale: Women in the International Division of Labour*. London: Zed, 1986.

Miller, Nancy K. "Criticizing Feminist Criticism." Hirsch and Keller 349–69.

———. *Subject to Change: Reading Feminist Writing*. New York: Columbia UP, 1988.

Miller, Susan. "The Feminization of Composition." Bullock and Trimbur 39–53.

———. *Rescuing the Subject.* Carbondale: Southern Illinois UP, 1989.

———. *Textual Carnivals: The Politics of Composition.* Carbondale: Southern Illinois UP, 1991.

———. "Tracing Cultural Studies: Marxism, Feminism, Structuralism." Conf. on Coll. Composition and Communication Convention. San Diego. 2 Apr. 1993.

———. "Writing Theory::Theory Writing." Kirsch and Sullivan 62–83.

Millett, Kate. *Sexual Politics.* Garden City: Doubleday, 1970.

Millward, Jody, and Susan K. Hahn. "Other Choices, Other Voices: Solutions to Gender Issues." Women in the Academy: Can a Feminist Agenda Transform the Illusion of Equity into Reality? Conf. on Coll. Composition and Communication Convention. Grand Hyatt Hotel, Washington. 22 Mar. 1995.

Minghan, Ding. "Some Questions Concerning the Appraisal of the Boxer Movement." *Chinese Studies and History* 29.3–4 (1987): 24–41.

Minh-ha, Trinh T. "Difference: A Special Third World Women Issue." *Women, Native, Other: Writing Postcoloniality and Feminism.* Bloomington: Indiana UP, 1989. 79–116.

Miner, Valerie, and Helen E. Longino, eds. *Competition: A Feminist Taboo?* New York: Feminist, 1987.

Minow, Martha. *Making All the Difference: Inclusion, Exclusion, and American Law.* Ithaca: Cornell UP, 1990.

Mitchell, Juliet. "Psychoanalysis, Feminism, and Politics: A Conversation with Juliet Mitchell." With Toril Moi. *South Atlantic Quarterly* 93 (1994): 925–49.

Modern Language Association. "Statement on the Use of Part-Time Faculty." *A Career Guide for PhDs and PhD Candidates in English and Foreign Languages.* Rev. English Showalter. New York: MLA, 1985. 58–59.

Mohanty, Chandra Talpade. "On Race and Voice: Challenges for Liberal Education in the 1990s." Giroux and McLaren 145–66.

Moraga, Cherríe. *Loving in the War Years.* Boston: South End, 1983.

———. Preface. Moraga and Anzaldúa xiii-xix.

Moraga, Cherríe, and Gloria Anzaldúa, eds. *This Bridge Called My Back: Writings by Radical Women of Color.* Watertown: Persephone, 1981; New York: Kitchen Table, 1983.

Morgan, Robin, ed. *Sisterhood Is Powerful.* New York: Random, 1970.

Morris, Meaghan. *The Pirate's Fiancé: Feminism, Reading, Postmodernism.* New York: Verso, 1988.

Morrison, Toni. *Beloved.* New York: Penguin, 1988.

———. *Nobel Prize for Literature Lecture.* New York: Knopf, 1994.

———. *Playing in the Dark: Whiteness and the Literary Imagination.* Cambridge: Harvard, 1992.

———. "Rootedness: The Ancestor as Foundation." *Black Women Writers (1950–1980).* Ed. Mari Evans. New York: Anchor, 1984. 339–45.

———. *Sula.* New York: Penguin, 1973.

Mortensen, Peter, and Gesa E. Kirsch. "On Authority and the Study of Writing." *College Composition and Communication* 44 (1993): 556–72.

Mullaney, Marie Marmo. *Revolutionary Women: Gender and the Socialist Revolutionary Role.* New York: Praeger, 1983.

Murray, Donald. *Write to Learn.* 2nd ed. New York: Holt, Rinehart, 1987.

Myers, Greg. "Reality, Consensus, and Reform in the Rhetoric of Composition Teaching." *College English* 48 (1986): 154–73.

Nelson, Cary, Paula A. Treichler, and Lawrence Grossberg. "Cultural Studies: An Introduction." Grossberg, Nelson, and Treichler 1–16.

Neustadtl, Sara. Rev. of *Women's Ways of Knowing,* by Mary Field Belenky, Blythe McVicker Clinchy, Nancy Rule Goldberger, and Jill Mattuck Tarule. *New York Times Book Review* 5 Oct. 1986: 38.

Newton, Judith. *Starting Over: Feminism and the Politics of Cultural Critique.* Ann Arbor: U of Michigan P, 1994.

Nichols, Bill. "Getting to Know You . . . Knowledge, Power, and the Body." *Theorizing Documentary.* Ed. Michael Renov. New York: Routledge, 1993. 174–92.

Nietzsche, Friedrich. *Beyond Good and Evil.* Trans. Walter Kaufmann. New York: Vintage, 1966.

———. On the Genealogy of Morals *and* Ecce Homo. Trans. Walter Kaufmann. New York: Vintage, 1969.

Noddings, Nel. *Caring: A Feminine Approach to Ethics and Moral Education.* Berkeley: U of California P, 1984.

Nussbaum, Martha C. "Equity and Mercy." *Philosophy and Public Affairs* 22 (1993): 83–125.

———. *Love's Knowledge: Essays on Philosophy and Literature.* Oxford: Oxford UP, 1990.

Nystrand, Martin. *The Structure of Written Communication: Studies in Reciprocity between Writers and Readers.* Orlando: Academic, 1986.

O'Barr, William F. *Linguistic Evidence.* Chicago: U of Chicago P, 1983.

Odell, Lee. "Context-Specific Ways of Knowing and the Evaluation of Writing." Herrington and Moran 86–98.

Offe, Claus. "New Social Movements: Challenging the Boundaries of Institutional Politics." *Social Research* 52 (1985): 817–68.

Ohmann, Richard. *Politics of Letters.* Middletown: Wesleyan UP, 1987.

Olson, Gary A. "Bell hooks and the Politics of Literacy: A Conversation." *Journal of Advanced Composition* 14 (1994): 1–19.

Olson, Gary A., and Joseph M. Moxley. "Directing Freshman Composition: The Limits of Authority." *College Composition and Communication* 40 (1989): 51–59.

Omi, Michael, and Howard Winant. *Racial Formation in the United States: From the 1960s to the 1990s.* 2nd ed. New York: Routledge, 1994.

Patai, Daphne, and Noretta Koertge. *Professing Feminism.* New York: Basic, 1994.

Pemberton, Michael A. "Tales Too Terrible to Tell: Unstated Truths and Underpreparation in Graduate Composition Programs." Fontaine and Hunter 154–73.

Penticoff, Richard, and Linda Brodkey. "'Writing about Difference': Hard Cases for Cultural Studies." Berlin and Vivion 123–44.

Perry, William G. *Forms of Intellectual and Ethical Development in the College Years.* New York: Holt, Rinehart, 1970.

Peterson, Linda H. "Gender and the Autobiographical Essay: Research Perspectives, Pedagogical Practices." *College Composition and Communication* 42 (1991): 70–83.

Phelps, Louise Wetherbee. "A Constrained Vision of the Writing Classroom." *Profession 93.* New York: MLA, 1993. 46–54.

Phelps, Louise Wetherbee, and Janet Emig, eds. *Feminine Principles and Women's Experience.* Pittsburgh: U of Pittsburgh P, 1995.

Piersen, William D. *Black Legacy: America's Hidden Heritage.* Amherst: U of Massachusetts P, 1993.

Pollitt, Katha. "Are Women Morally Superior to Men?" *Nation* 28 Dec. 1992: 799–807.

Poovey, Mary. "The Abortion Question and the Death of Man." Butler and Scott 239–56.

———. "Cultural Criticism: Past and Present." *College English* 52 (1990): 615–25.

———. "Feminism and Postmodernism: Another View." *Boundary 2: An International Journal of Literature and Culture* 19.2 (1992): 34–52.

Porter, James E., and Patricia Sullivan. "Working across Methodological Interfaces: A Postmodern Rhetoric for the Study of Computers and Writing in the Workplace." *Electronic Literacies in the Workplace: Technologies of Writing.* Ed. Patricia Sullivan and Jennie Dautermann. Urbana: NCTE, 1996. 294–322.

Poynton, Cate. *Language and Gender: Making the Difference.* Oxford: Oxford UP, 1989.

Pratt, Mary Louise. "Arts of the Contact Zone." Bartholomae and Petrosky, *Ways* 440–56.

Probyn, Elspeth. *Sexing the Self: Gendered Positions in Cultural Studies.* London: Routledge, 1993.

Rabine, Leslie Wahl. "A Feminist Politics of Non-identity." *Feminist Studies* 14 (1988): 11–31.

Rafter, John. "Asian Student Takes Credit for Graffiti." *Oberlin Review* 12 Nov. 1993: 1.

Ray, Ruth. *The Practice of Theory.* Urbana: NCTE, 1993.

Reagon, Bernice Johnson. "Coalition Politics: Turning the Century." B. Smith, *Girls* 356–68.

Reinharz, Shulamit. *Feminist Methods in Social Research.* New York: Oxford UP, 1992.

"Remembering Mama Too Much." *Time* 26 Feb. 1979: 52.

"Retention Rates of African-American College Students." *Journal of Blacks in Higher Education* 6 (1994–95): 56.

Riccardi, Nicholas. "Student Faces Fire after Meeting." *Oberlin Review* 12 Nov. 1993: 1+.

Rich, Adrienne. "Compulsory Heterosexuality and Lesbian Existence." *Powers of Desire: The Politics of Sexuality.* Ed. Ann Snitow, Christine Stansell, and Sharon Thompson. New York: Monthly Review, 1983. 177–205.

———. "Natural Resources." *The Dream of Common Language.* New York: Norton, 1978. 60–67.

———. "Notes toward a Politics of Location." *Blood, Bread, and Poetry: Selected Prose, 1979–1985.* New York: Norton, 1986. 210–31.

———. "When We Dead Awaken: Writing as Revision." *On Lies, Secrets, and Silence: Selected Prose, 1966–1978.* New York: Norton, 1978. 33–49.

Richlin, Amy. "The Ethnographer's Dilemma and the Dream of a Lost Golden Age." *Feminist Theory and the Classics.* Ed. Nancy Sorkin Rabinowitz and Richlin. New York: Routledge, 1993. 272–302.

Ritchie, Joy. "Confronting the 'Essential' Problem: Reconnecting Feminist Theory and Pedagogy." *Journal of Advanced Composition* 10 (1990): 249–71.

Robertson, Linda R., Sharon Crowley, and Frank Lentricchia. "Opinion: The Wyoming Conference Resolution Opposing Unfair Salaries and Working Conditions for Post-secondary Teachers of Writing." *College English* 49 (1987): 274–80.

Robinson, Amy. "It Takes One to Know One: Passing and Communities of Common Interest." *Critical Inquiry* 20 (1994): 715–36.

Roediger, David. *Towards the Abolition of Whiteness: Essays on Race, Politics, and Working Class History.* London: Verso, 1994.

Roman, Leslie. "White Is a Color! White Defensiveness, Postmodernism, and Anti-racist Pedagogy." *Race, Identity, and Representation in Education.* Ed. Cameron McCarthy and Warren Crichlow. New York: Routledge, 1993. 71–88.

Rose, Mike. *Lives on the Boundary.* New York: Penguin, 1989.

Rose, Robert L. "Is Saving Legal?" *The Informed Argument: A Multidisciplinary Reader and Guide*. Ed. Robert K. Miller. 3rd ed. New York: Harcourt, 1992. 95–98.

Rosenau, Pauline Marie. *Postmodernism and the Social Sciences: Insights, Inroads, and Intrusions*. Princeton: Princeton UP, 1992.

Ross, Thomas. "Innocence and Affirmative Action." *Critical Race Theory: The Cutting Edge*. Ed. Richard Delgado. Philadelphia: Temple UP, 1995. 551–63.

Rouse, P. Joy. "Margaret Fuller." *Oratorical Culture in Nineteenth-Century America: Transformations in the Theory and Practice of Rhetoric*. Ed. Gregory Clark and S. Michael Halloran. Carbondale: Southern Illinois UP, 1993. 110–36.

Rubin, Donnalee. *Gender Influences: Reading Student Texts*. Carbondale: Southern Illinois UP, 1993.

Ruddick, Sara. "Maternal Thinking." *Feminist Studies* 6 (1980): 342–67.

———. *Maternal Thinking: Toward a Politics of Peace*. Boston: Beacon, 1989.

Russell, David R. "American Origins of the Writing-across-the-Curriculum Movement." Herrington and Moran 22–42.

———. "Writing across the Curriculum in Historical Perspective: Toward a Social Interpretation." *College English* 52 (1990): 52–73.

Russo, Ann. " 'We Cannot Live without Our Lives': White Women, Antiracism, and Feminism." *Third World Women and the Politics of Feminism*. Ed. Chandra Talpade Mohanty, Ann Russo, and Lourdes Torres. Bloomington: Indiana UP, 1991. 297–313.

Ryan, Barbara. *Feminism and the Women's Movement: Dynamics of Change in Social Movement Ideology and Activism*. New York: Routledge, 1992.

Safa, Helen I. "Women and Industrialisation in the Caribbean." *Women, Employment, and the Family in the International Division of Labour*. Ed. Sharon Stichter and Jane L. Parpart. Philadelphia: Temple UP, 1990. 72–97.

Sarton, May. *Letters from Maine*. New York: Norton, 1984.

Schilb, John. "Cultural Studies, Postmodernism, and Composition." Harkin and Schilb 173–88.

Schneider, Beth. "Political Generations in the Contemporary Women's Movement." *Sociological Inquiry* 58 (1988): 4–21.

Schriner, Delores, and William Rice. "Computer Conferencing and Collaborative Learning: A Discourse Community at Work." *College Composition and Communication* 40 (1989): 472–78.

Scott, James. *Domination and the Arts of Resistance*. New Haven: Yale UP, 1980.

Scott, Joan. "The Evidence of Experience." *Critical Inquiry* 17 (1991): 773–97.

Sedgwick, Eve Kosofsky. *Epistemology of the Closet*. Berkeley: U of California P, 1990.

Selfe, Cynthia L., and Paul Meyer. "Testing Claims for Online Conferences." *Written Communication* 8.2 (1991): 163–92.

Sennett, Richard, and Jonathan Cobb. *The Hidden Injuries of Class*. New York: Vintage, 1972.

Shaughnessy, Mina P. *Errors and Expectations: A Guide for the Teacher of Basic Writing*. New York: Oxford UP, 1977.

Shirk, Margaret. "Eclecticism and Competing Logics in Composition." Unpublished paper.

Showalter, Elaine. *A Literature of Their Own: British Women Novelists from Brontë to Lessing*. Princeton: Princeton UP, 1977.

Simeone, Angela. *Academic Women: Working towards Equality*. Boston: Bergin, 1987.

Slack, Jennifer Daryl, and Laurie Anne Whitt. "Ethics and Cultural Studies." Grossberg, Nelson, and Treichler 571–92.

Slevin, James. "Depoliticizing and Politicizing Composition Studies." Bullock and Trimbur 1–21.

Smart, Carol. "Problem of Rights." *Feminism and the Power of the Law*. London: Routledge, 1989. 138–65.

Smith, Barbara, ed. *Home Girls: A Black Feminist Anthology*. New York: Kitchen Table, 1983.

———. "Racism and Women's Studies." Hull, Scott, and Smith 48–51.

———. "Toward a Black Feminist Criticism." Hull, Scott, and Smith 157–75.

Smith, Paul. *Discerning the Subject*. Minneapolis: U of Minnesota P, 1988.

Smith, Sidonie. *Subjectivity, Identity, and the Body: Women's Autobiographical Practices in the Twentieth Century*. Bloomington: Indiana UP, 1993.

Smith, Valerie. "Reading the Intersection of Race and Gender in Narratives of Passing." *Diacritics: A Review of Contemporary Criticism* 24.2–3 (1994): 43–57.

Smithson, Isaiah, and Nancy Ruff, eds. *English Studies / Culture Studies*. Urbana: U of Illinois P, 1994.

Smolla, Rodney A. *Free Speech in an Open Society*. New York: Random, 1993.

Soja, Edward. *Postmodern Geographies*. London: Routledge, 1989.

Soliday, May. "Literacy Narratives." *College English* 56 (1994): 511–26.

Solomon, Barbara Miller. *In the Company of Educated Women*. New Haven: Yale UP, 1985.

Sommers, Elizabeth, and Sandra Lawrence. "Women's Ways of Talking in Teacher-Directed and Student-Directed Peer Response Groups." *Linguistics and Education* 4 (1992): 1–36.

Spacks, Patricia Meyer. *The Female Imagination*. New York: Knopf, 1975.

Spain, Daphne. *Gendered Spaces*. Chapel Hill: U of North Carolina P, 1992.

Spanier, Bonnie B. "Encountering the Biological Sciences: Ideology, Language, and Learning." Herrington and Moran 193–212.

Spellmeyer, Kurt. "Comment and Response." *College English* 52 (1990): 334–38.

———. "A Common Ground: The Essay in the Academy." *College English* 51 (1989): 262–76.

Spelman, Elizabeth V. "Anger and Insubordination." *Women, Knowledge, and Reality: Explorations in Feminist Philosophy*. Ed. Ann Garry and Marilyn Pearsall. Boston: Unwin, 1989. 263–73.

———. *Inessential Woman: Problems of Exclusion in Feminist Thought*. Boston: Beacon, 1988.

Spender, Dale. *Man Made Language*. 2nd ed. London: Pandora, 1990.

———. *Nattering on the Net: Women, Power and Cyberspace*. North Melbourne, Austral.: Spinifex, 1995.

Spillers, Hortense. "Mamma's Baby, Papa's Maybe: An American Grammar Book." *Diacritics: A Review of Contemporary Criticism* 17.2 (1987): 65–81.

Spivak, Gayatri Chakravorty. "Can the Subaltern Speak?" *Marxism and the Interpretation of Culture*. Ed. Cary Nelson and Lawrence Grossberg. Urbana: U of Illinois P, 1988. 271–311.

———. *The Post-colonial Critic*. Ed. Sarah Harasym. New York: Routledge, 1990.

Spradley, James, and Brenda Mann. *The Cocktail Waitress*. New York: Wiley, 1975.

Sproull, Lee, and Sara Kiesler. *Connections: New Ways of Working in the Networked Organization*. Cambridge: MIT P, 1991.

Stabile, Carol A. *Feminism and the Technological Fix*. New York: Manchester UP, 1994.

Stanger, Carol. "The Sexual Politics of the One-to-One Tutorial Approach and Collaborative Learning." Caywood and Overing, *Teaching* 31–44.

Stanley, Liz, and Sue Wise. *Breaking Out, Again: Feminist Ontology and Epistemology*. London: Routledge, 1991.

Stanton, Elizabeth Cady. "The Solitude of Self." *Man Cannot Speak for Her: A Critical Study of Early Feminist Rhetoric*. Vol. 2. Ed. Karlyn K. Campbell. New York: Praeger, 1989. 120–45.

Stanton, Elizabeth Cady, Susan B. Anthony, and Matilda Joslyn Gage. *History of Woman Suffrage*. Vol. 2. 1881. New York: Sourcebook, 1970.

Starr, Frederick S. Letter to Oberlin College community. 9 Nov. 1993.

Starr, Frederick S., Alfred MacKay, and Patrick Penn. Letter to Oberlin College community. 19 Nov. 1993.

Stearns, Carol Zisowitz, and Peter N. Stearns. Introduction. *Emotion and Social Change: Toward a New Psychohistory*. Ed. Stearns and Stearns. New York: Homes, 1988. 1–21.

Stearns, Peter N. "Anger at Work: A Contemporary Approach." *Anger: The Struggle for Emotional Control in America's History*. Ed. Carol Zisowitz Stearns and Stearns. Chicago: U of Chicago P, 1986. 110–56.

Steinem, Gloria. "Why Young Women Are More Conservative." *Outrageous Acts and Everyday Rebellions*. New York: Penguin, 1983. 238–46.

Sterling, Dorothy. *We Are Your Sisters: Black Women in the Nineteenth Century*. New York: Norton, 1984.

Stewart, Donald. "Some History Lessons for Composition Teachers." *Rhetoric Review* 3 (1985): 134–43.

Stotsky, Sandra. "Conceptualizing Writing as Moral and Civic Thinking." *College English* 54 (1992): 794–808.

Stubbs, Michael. *Discourse Analysis: The Sociolinguistic Analysis of Natural Language*. Chicago: U of Chicago P, 1983.

Stygall, Gail. *Trial Language: Differential Discourse Processing and Discursive Formation*. Amsterdam: Benjamins, 1994.

Stygall, Gail, et al. "Gendered Textuality: Assigning Gender to Portfolios." *New Directions in Portfolio Assessment: Reflective Practice, Critical Theory, and Large-Scale Scoring*. Ed. Laurel Black et al. Portsmouth: Boynton-Heinemann, 1994. 248–62.

Suleiman, Susan Rubin. *Risking Who One Is: Encounters with Contemporary Art and Literature*. Cambridge: Harvard UP, 1994.

Sullivan, Patricia A. "Feminism and Methodology in Composition Studies." Kirsch and Sullivan 37–61.

Swearingen, C. Jan. "Plato's Feminine: Appropriation, Impersonation, and Metaphorical Polemic." *Rhetoric Society Quarterly* 22 (1992): 109–24.

Tannen, Deborah, ed. *Gender and Conversational Interaction*. New York: Oxford UP, 1993.

———. "The Relativity of Linguistic Strategies: Rethinking Power and Solidarity in Gender and Dominance." Tannen, *Gender* 165–88.

———. *You Just Don't Understand: Women and Men in Conversation*. New York: Ballantine, 1990.

Taylor, H. Jeanie, Cheris Kramarae, and Maureen Ebben, eds. *Women, Information Technology, and Scholarship*. Urbana: Center for Advanced Studies, 1993.

Taylor, Verta. "Social Movement Continuity: The Women's Movement in Abeyance." *American Sociological Review* 54 (1989): 761–75.

Thompson, Becky, and Sangeeta Tyagi, eds. *Beyond a Dream Deferred: Multicultural Education and the Politics of Excellence*. Minneapolis: U of Minnesota P, 1993.

Tompkins, Jane. "Me and My Shadow." *New Literary History: A Journal of Theory and Interpretation* 19 (1987): 169–78.

———. "A Short Course in Post-structuralism." *College English* 50 (1988): 733–47.

Tong, Rosemarie. *Feminist Thought: A Comprehensive Introduction.* Boulder: Westview, 1989.

Transcript of speak-out held in Oberlin Coll. South Hall. 11 Nov. 1993.

Trimbur, John. "Composition Studies: Postmodern or Popular." Gere, *Field* 117–32.

———. "Consensus and Difference in Collaborative Learning." *College English* 51 (1989): 601–16.

———. "Cultural Studies and Teaching Writing." *Focuses: A Journal Linking Composition Programs and Writing Center Practice* 1.2 (1988): 5–18.

Tronto, Joan C. *Moral Boundaries: A Political Argument for an Ethic of Care.* New York: Routledge, 1993.

———. "Women and Caring: What Can Feminists Learn about Morality from Caring." *Gender/Body/Knowledge: Feminist Reconstructions of Being and Knowing.* Ed. Alison M. Jaggar and Susan Bordo. New Brunswick: Rutgers, 1989. 172–87.

Tryselaar, Anneke, John Kearney, and David Schneider. "Students Storm Cox, Protesting Racism." *Oberlin Review* 12 Nov. 1993: 7+.

Tuckman, Barbara H., and Howard P. Tuckman. "Part-Timers, Sex Discrimination, and Career Choice at Two-Year Institutions: Further Findings from the AAUP Survey." *Academe* Mar.-Apr. 1980: 71–76.

Tuckman, Howard P., and George Biles. *Part-Time Faculty Personnel Management Policies.* New York: Macmillan, 1986.

Tuckman, Howard P., William D. Vogler, and Jaime Caldwell. *Part-Time Faculty Series.* Washington: AAUP, 1978.

Tuell, Cynthia. "Composition Teaching as 'Women's Work': Daughters, Handmaids, Whores, and Mothers." Fontaine and Hunter 123–39.

United States. Dept. of Education. *Faculty and Instructional Staff: Who Are They and What Do They Do?* Washington: Natl. Center for Educ. Statistics, 1994.

Van Gelder, Lindsy. "Carol Gilligan: Leader for a Different Kind of Future." *Ms. Magazine* Jan. 1984: 37+.

———. "The Strange Case of the Electronic Lover." *Computerization and Controversy: Value Conflicts and Social Choices.* Ed. Charles Dunlap and Rob Kling. New York: Academic, 1991. 364–75.

Vitanza, Victor. "An Experience on the Net." Electronic mailing list message. Online. Internet. 11 July 1997. Available FTP: jefferson.village.Virginia.edu:80/˜spoons/pretext/eberly3.html.

Vogel, Lise. *Woman Questions: Essays for a Materialist Feminism.* New York: Routledge, 1995.

Wallace, M. Elizabeth. "Who Are These Part-Time Faculty Anyway?" *Part-Time Academic Employment in the Humanities.* Ed. Wallace. New York: MLA, 1984. 3–29.

Warner, Michael. "The Mass Public and the Mass Subject." *Habermas and the Public Sphere.* Ed. Craig Calhoun. Massachusetts: MIT P, 1992. 377–401.

Watkins, Evan. *Work Time: English Departments and the Circulation of Cultural Value.* Stanford: Stanford UP, 1989.

Weber, Max. *The Theory of Social and Economic Organizations.* Trans. A. M. Henderson and Talcott Parsons. New York: Free, 1964.

Weisser, Susan Ostrov, and Jennifer Fleischner, eds. *Feminist Nightmares. Women at Odds: Feminism and the Problem of Sisterhood.* New York: New York UP, 1994.

West, Robin. *Narrative, Authority, and Law.* Ann Arbor: U of Michigan P, 1993.

White, Edward M. "Use It or Lose It: Power and the WPA." *Writing Program Administration* 15.1–2 (1991): 3–12.

Whitford, Margaret. *Luce Irigaray: Philosophy in the Feminine.* New York: Routledge, 1991.

Whittier, Nancy. *Feminist Generations: The Persistence of the Radical Women's Movement.* Philadelphia: Temple UP, 1995.

Wicke, Jennifer. "Postmodern Identities and the Politics of the (Legal) Subject." *Boundary 2: An International Journal of Literature and Culture* 19.2 (1992): 10–33.

Wicke, Jennifer, and Margaret Ferguson. "Introduction: Feminism and Postmodernism; or, The Way We Live Now." *Feminism and Postmodernism.* Ed. Wicke and Ferguson. Durham: Duke UP, 1994. 10–33.

Wiegman, Robyn. "Black Bodies / American Commodities: Gender, Race, and the Bourgeois Ideal in Contemporary Film." *Unspeakable Images: Ethnicity and the American Cinema.* Ed. Lester D. Friedman. Urbana: U of Illinois P, 1991. 308–28.

Williams, Fannie Barrier. "The Intellectual Progress of the Colored Women of the United States since the Emancipation Proclamation." Logan 106–19.

Williams, Patricia J. *The Alchemy of Race and Rights.* Cambridge: Harvard UP, 1991.

Wittig, Monique. *Les guérillères.* Trans. David Le Vay. Boston: Beacon, 1985.

———. "The Straight Mind." *Feminist Issues* (1980): 103–11.

Wolgast, Elizabeth H. *Equality and the Rights of Women.* Ithaca: Cornell UP, 1980.

Women's Studies Group. "Women's Studies Group: Trying to Do Feminist Intellectual Work." *Women Take Issue.* London: Hutchinson, 1978. 7–17.

Woolf, Virginia. *Three Guineas*. San Diego: Harcourt, 1938.

Worsham, Lynn. "Emotion and Pedagogic Violence." *Discourse: Journal for Theoretical Studies in Media and Culture* 15.2 (1992–93): 119–48.

———. "Kenneth Burke's Appendicitis: A Feminist's Case for Complaint." *Pre/Text: A Journal of Rhetorical Theory* 12 (1991): 67–95.

———. "Reading Wild, Seriously: Confessions of an Epistemophiliac." *Rhetoric Society Quarterly* 22 (1992): 39–62.

———. "Writing against Writing: The Predicament of *Ecriture Feminine* in Composition Studies." Harkin and Schilb 82–104.

Wright, Elizabeth, ed. *Feminism and Psychoanalysis: A Critical Dictionary*. Oxford: Blackwell, 1992.

Wyche-Smith, Susan, and Shirley K. Rose. "One Hundred Ways to Make the Wyoming Resolution a Reality: A Guide to Personal and Political Action." *College Composition and Communication* 41 (1990): 318–24.

Young, James. *The Texture of Memory: Holocaust Memorials and Meaning*. New Haven: Yale UP, 1993.

———. *Writing and Rewriting the Holocaust: Narrative and the Consequences of Interpretation*. Bloomington: Indiana UP, 1988.

Zavarzadeh, Mas'ud, and Donald Morton. "Theory Pedagogy Politics: The Crisis of 'the Subject' in the Humanities." *Theory/Pedagogy/Politics: Texts for Change*. Ed. Morton and Zavarzadeh. Urbana: U of Illinois P, 1991. 1–32.

Zimmerman, Don H., and Candace West. "Sex Roles, Interruptions, and Silences in Conversation." *Language and Sex: Difference and Dominance*. Ed. Barrie Thorne and Nancy Henley. Rowley: Newbury, 1975. 105–29.

Zook, Kristal Brent. "A Manifesto of Sorts for a Black Feminist Movement." *New York Times Magazine* 12 Nov. 1995: 86–89.

Index